CENTER FOR CREATIVE LEADERSHIP

THE CENTER FOR CREATIVE LEADERSHIP HANDBOOK OF LEADERSHIP DEVELOPMENT

THE BOOK TEAM
(From left to right): Marian N. Ruderman, Wilfred H. Drath, Victoria A. Guthrie, Maxine A. Dalton, Cynthia D. McCauley, Russ S. Moxley, Ellen Van Velsor, Patricia J. Ohlott, Martha W. Hughes-James, Christina A. Douglas, Lily Kelly-Radford, Patricia O'Connor Wilson, Craig T. Chappelow. Not shown: Dana G. McDonald-Mann, Michael H. Hoppe.

THE CENTER FOR CREATIVE LEADERSHIP HANDBOOK OF LEADERSHIP DEVELOPMENT

Cynthia D. McCauley, Russ S. Moxley,
Ellen Van Velsor, Editors

Jossey-Bass Publishers
San Francisco

CENTER FOR CREATIVE LEADERSHIP
Greensboro Brussells
Colorado Springs San Diego

Copyright © 1998 by Jossey-Bass Inc., Publishers, 350 Sansome Street, San Francisco, California 94104.

Jossey-Bass books and products are available through most bookstores. To contact Jossey-Bass directly, call (888) 378–2537, fax to (800) 605–2665, or visit our website at www.josseybass.com.

Substantial discounts on bulk quantities of Jossey-Bass books are available to corporations, professional associations, and other organizations. For details and discount information, contact the special sales department at Jossey-Bass.

www.josseybass.com

 Manufactured in the United States of America on Lyons Falls Turin Book. This paper is acid-free and 100 percent totally chlorine-free.

Credits are on p. 482.

Library of Congress Cataloging-in-Publication Data

The Center for Creative Leadership handbook of leadership
  development / Cynthia D. McCauley, Russ S. Moxley, Ellen Van
Velsor, editors. — 1st ed.
        p. cm. — (A joint publication of the Jossey-Bass business & management series and the
        Center for Creative Leadership)
    Includes bibliographical references and index.
    ISBN 0-7879-0950-5 (acid-free paper)
    1. Leadership. 2. Creative ability in business. I. McCauley,
Cynthia D. (Cynthia Denise), date. II. Moxley, Russ S., date. III.
Van Velsor, Ellen. IV. Center for Creative Leadership. V. Series.
HD57 .C38 1998
658.4'092—ddc21   98-19684

FIRST EDITION
HB Printing 10 9 8 7 6 5 4

A JOINT PUBLICATION OF THE JOSSEY-BASS
BUSINESS & MANAGEMENT SERIES AND
THE CENTER FOR CREATIVE LEADERSHIP

CONTENTS

Preface xi

Acknowledgments xvii

The Authors xix

Introduction: Our View of Leadership Development 1

Ellen Van Velsor, Cynthia D. McCauley, Russ S. Moxley

PART ONE: LEADERSHIP DEVELOPMENT: EXPERIENCES 27

1 360-Degree Feedback 29

Craig T. Chappelow

2 Feedback-Intensive Programs 66

Victoria A. Guthrie, Lily Kelly-Radford

3 Skill-Based Training 106

Dana G. McDonald-Mann

4 Job Assignments 127

Patricia J. Ohlott

5 Developmental Relationships   160

Cynthia D. McCauley, Christina A. Douglas

6 Hardships   194

Russ S. Moxley

PART TWO: LEADERSHIP DEVELOPMENT: PROCESS   215

7 A Systems Approach to Leadership Development   217

Russ S. Moxley, Patricia O'Connor Wilson

8 Enhancing the Ability to Learn from Experience   242

Ellen Van Velsor, Victoria A. Guthrie

9 Assessing the Impact of Development Experiences   262

Ellen Van Velsor

PART THREE: LEADERSHIP DEVELOPMENT: ISSUES   289

10 Leadership Development Across Race and Gender   291

Marian N. Ruderman, Martha W. Hughes-James

11 Cross-Cultural Issues in Leadership Development   336

Michael H. Hoppe

12 Developing Leaders for Global Roles   379

Maxine A. Dalton

13 Approaching the Future of Leadership Development   403

Wilfred H. Drath

Afterword   433

Russ S. Moxley, Ellen Van Velsor, Cynthia D. McCauley

About the Center for Creative Leadership   441

References   447

Name Index   465

Subject Index   469

PREFACE

As an institution, the Center for Creative Leadership (CCL) has devoted much of its energy and resources to understanding how to help people in their quest to become better leaders. We at the Center have approached this task from both research and practice perspectives; that is, we have tried to both study the process of leadership development systematically and intervene in that process. In nearly thirty years of work, we have gained a wealth of insights; created leadership development models, tools, and programs; and, we believe, had a positive impact on the learning and growth of leaders worldwide.

This handbook serves to summarize and integrate much of what we have come to understand about leadership development. Its goal is to provide you with both a conceptual understanding of the elements of leadership development and practical ideas about how people can enhance their leadership capacity and how organizations can contribute to that process.

We have written this book for people in organizations who design and implement development processes. In many organizations, this responsibility belongs primarily to human resource and training professionals. But, more and more, line managers are playing an increasingly active role in the development of their staffs. Although we had HR professionals in mind as our primary audience, we hope that line managers who want to be more sophisticated in their practice of leadership development find useful ideas in the handbook.

Roots of the Book

First, a word about the sources of the ideas in this handbook. Although all the authors brought their own experience and expertise to bear on their chapters, each was also influenced by and drew from numerous streams of research and practice at the Center. We would like to point out some of these streams.

One of our core activities at CCL is running weeklong feedback-intensive leadership development programs for midlevel or senior managers. This activity began in the early 1970s with what has become our flagship program, the Leadership Development Program. More than four thousand managers complete this program each year. In addition, our work has broadened to include other programs, including one designed specifically for top executives (Leadership at the Peak), another built around a behavioral simulation that challenges participants to run a company (the Looking Glass Experience), one that extends over time and thus allows participants a chance to practice and integrate their learnings with back-home experiences (LeaderLab), and numerous others customized for specific organizations.

Because we wanted to evaluate and improve our feedback-intensive programs, we began studying their impact. What we learned not only helped us refine our programs but also gave us a window on how leadership development unfolds over time and how to best assess learning and change. Evaluation studies continue to be a central part of the Center's research activities.

As part of our assessment activities, we were one of the first organizations to routinely use 360-degree feedback instruments in our leadership development work. Providing organizations with these tools and training people in how to use them have become a core activity at CCL. Not only did we put a great deal of research into developing these instruments but we have continued to investigate the dynamics of the 360-degree feedback process.

Another stream of research that has greatly influenced this handbook started with a project that ultimately produced the book *Lessons of Experience.* Through interviews and open-ended questionnaires, executives told the stories of their developmental experiences—the events and people that shaped them as managers and leaders. From this initial research flowed further study of developmental assignments and relationships, as well as research into the ability to learn from experience. We learned to integrate the tools and ideas from this stream by designing and delivering a program for human resource professionals, Tools for Developing Successful Executives. The participants in this program are a continuous source of learning for us as they work to apply the program's concepts to the executive development processes in their own organizations.

Although the *Lessons of Experience* research looked at the experiences that developed young managers into senior leaders, another important stream of research and application focused on how senior managers can continue to learn and grow once they have reached the top. Much of this research was conducted in an action research mode: systematically studying efforts to help senior managers get feedback and change fairly ingrained behaviors. These processes are used today in our Awareness Program for Executives (APEX).

A final important research thrust looked at issues in developing women and people of color for higher-level management positions in corporations. CCL's history in this area (often referred to as "glass ceiling" research) is summarized in Chapter Ten. Again, on this topic we have connected our research to practice through our programs, such as The African-American Leadership Development Program and The Women's Leadership Program.

What the Handbook Doesn't Cover

Although *Handbook* in the title may suggest exhaustive and comprehensive coverage of a particular field, this book does not cover everything that could conceivably be examined in the domain of leadership development. Leadership and development are broad concepts that can be approached from many different perspectives. Because of our particular history of research and practice, we have developed a certain perspective on leadership development. It is the various aspects of leadership development *within this perspective* that we cover in this handbook. Thus the handbook

- *Does not provide a comprehensive review of leadership theories.* There are a number of excellent reviews of the various ways scholars have approached and understood leadership (see Clark and Clark, 1994; Rost, 1991; Yukl, 1989). In the Introduction, we the editors of this handbook share a view of leadership development that has evolved within CCL. This view does not neatly fit into any of the classic categories of leadership theories (such as trait theories, situational theories, or transformational theories). Rather, we have tended to borrow ideas from various theories and integrate them.

- *Does not present an overarching model of leadership.* Unlike a number of our colleagues in the leadership development field (Bass, 1985; Covey, 1991; Kouzes and Posner, 1987), we do not present a single, detailed model of leadership that frames and delineates the practices, principles, or behaviors of effective leaders. One reason for this is that we are trying to represent a collective perspective. In our work at CCL, we use numerous specific models to describe how effective leaders think and act. What unites these models is an underlying assumption that improvement of leadership skills, behaviors, competencies, or practices (however you categorize and label them) requires personal development. In the Introduction, we articulate several broad capacities that people develop over time and that enable them to more effectively take on leadership roles.

- *Does not cover all methods of leadership development.* In this handbook, we focus on those methods in which CCL as an organization has considerable experience and expertise. Therefore, you do not find much specific mention of knowledge-building educational experiences (used commonly in university settings with a heavy emphasis on case studies), sensitivity group experiences (developed and used extensively by National Training Laboratories), outdoor-adventure experiences (popularized by Outward Bound), action learning programs (articulated by Reg Revans, variations of which are being used ever more frequently in organizations), and team learning approaches (popularized by Peter Senge and his colleagues at MIT). However, in our work we do borrow from all these approaches, and there are individual CCL staff members who have considerable expertise with them.

Organization of the Book

We have organized the handbook into four major sections. The first is the introductory chapter, in which the editors summarize our view of leadership development. As we know, there are various perspectives on leadership and on development, and it is important for you to know the perspective this book takes. Thus the Introduction is an important framing chapter for the book, providing our basic assumptions and a model of the key elements in leadership development. Because the remaining chapters all refer back to this model, we strongly urge that you review this Introduction before moving on to other chapters in the handbook.

Part One focuses on separate, specific developmental experiences. This, the longest part of the handbook, conveys the core of our knowledge about methods of leadership development. Each chapter in Part One describes a particular type of developmental experience. The first three are about comparatively structured, formal experiences: 360-degree feedback (Chapter One), feedback-intensive leadership development programs (Chapter Two), and skill-based training programs (Chapter Three). The next three describe more "naturally occurring" experiences: job assignments (Chapter Four), developmental relationships (Chapter Five), and hardships (Chapter Six).

Part Two looks more closely at the leadership development process. Chapter Seven discusses how organizations can take a systemic approach to leadership development. Chapter Eight looks at what the individual brings to the development process: the ability to learn. Chapter Nine provides insights on how to evaluate the impact of leadership development initiatives in organizations.

The final part contains four chapters that explore issues in leadership development. In the first parts of the handbook, we draw on the broad array of our research and application experience. But in Part Three we remind ourselves that although our experience in leadership development has been in some ways broad, in other ways it has been narrow. Although we have operations and alliances outside the United States, the Center staff is primarily from this country. Participants in our programs and in our research projects have been predominantly from middle or senior levels of management in for-profit, U.S.-based companies; accordingly, the majority are white males.

As we move from working mainly with white males to working more with women and people of color (Chapter Ten), as we work with people from other cultures (Chapter Eleven), and as we work with leaders in global organizations (Chapter Twelve), we are learning more about leadership development. These chapters present what we have learned thus far and surface questions that we have yet to answer. Finally, as we work with these increasingly diverse groups of leaders and with intact teams (rather than with individual leaders), we are developing new ways of understanding leadership. The final chapter (Chapter Thirteen) offers one such new lens on leadership and its implications for leadership development.

Putting this handbook together has helped us clarify and integrate our knowledge and perspectives on leadership development. Our primary goal is to present that knowledge in a way that others can make use of in their efforts to create developmental experiences and design leadership development processes. At the same time, the process of codifying our knowledge has raised new questions and possibilities. Thus, we see this handbook as capturing one primary view at a particular point, a view that we hope will broaden and deepen in future editions.

ACKNOWLEDGMENTS

I t is impossible to name all of our colleagues and clients who have contributed to developing the knowledge contained in this book. The knowledge has developed over time through numerous projects and programs. As authors, we feel privileged to be part of the CCL community; we want to acknowledge the entire community as the source of our knowledge and thank them for their support in putting the handbook together.

There are particular colleagues to whom we do need to draw special attention: individuals who took the time to read, reflect on, and provide invaluable feedback on various chapters. Our special thanks for this work go to John Alexander, Stéphane Brutus, Leo Burke, Billy Campisciano, Martin Davidson, Robert C. Dorn, Irwin L. Goldstein, Geert Hofstede, Bill Howland, Betsy Jacobson, Karen Kirkland, Ellen Ernst Kossek, Ancella Livers, Sam Manoogian, Jennifer Martineau, Chuck Palus, Sharon Rogolsky, Harold Scharlatt, Gretchen Spreitzer, Jodi Taylor, Jill Wachholz, Martin Wilcox, and Meena Wilson. We are also grateful to the five anonymous reviewers of the book manuscript, who made their way through an unpolished draft and provided us with an external perspective and insightful critique.

We could not have put this handbook together without the help of two talented individuals: Maggie Stuckey and Edna Parrott. Maggie was the "editors' editor." Her knowledge of the craft of writing, the questions she raised about the content and structure of the evolving manuscript, and her ability to make our ideas more accessible to the reader has contributed in a fundamental way to this book. Edna was instrumental in coordinating much of our work. Her ability to manage our computer files, pull information together from all the authors, get everything in the right format, and stay on top of the work flow was a major asset to us in putting the manuscript together. Thanks, Maggie and Edna, for the tremendous job you both did.

THE AUTHORS

Craig T. Chappelow is the product director for individual development products at the Center for Creative Leadership. In this role he is responsible for the Center's family of psychometric instruments and business simulations, which help executives shape their development and enhance their effectiveness. Originally trained as a chemist, he developed a wide range of business experience at National Starch and Chemical Corporation, Glidden Corporation, and the University of Virginia, before joining the Center in 1988. He has used 360-degree feedback instruments with hundreds of senior executives domestically as well as in England, Ireland, Australia, New Zealand, and Belgium. He received his B.S. from MacMurray College and his M.Ed. from the University of Vermont.

Maxine A. Dalton is a research scientist and program manager at the Center for Creative Leadership. She received her B.S. in nursing from Vanderbilt University, an M.A. in rehabilitation counseling from the University of South Florida, and an M.A. and Ph.D. in industrial and organizational psychology from the University of South Florida. She was a consultant with Drake Beam Morin for five years before coming to the Center in 1990. She is the author of several articles on the 360-degree-feedback process, has trained hundreds of feedback specialists, and has given feedback to many individuals and groups. She has also worked with human resource development professionals in a program designed to teach them how to implement developmental processes using CCL concepts and tools. Her current research interests include global leadership and learning to learn.

Christina A. Douglas is a research associate at the Center for Creative Leadership. Since joining the Center, she has conducted research on developmental relationships and has recently written *Formal Mentoring Programs in Organizations: An Annotated Bibliography.* She is also a feedback specialist in the Center's Leadership Development Program. Prior to joining the Center, she worked for Xerox Corporation and managed projects related to development and validation of selection systems. She received her B.A. in psychology from Cornell University and her M.A. in industrial and organizational psychology from the University of Maryland. She received her Ph.D. in organizational behavior and human resources from Purdue University.

Wilfred H. Drath is a research scientist at the Center for Creative Leadership. He has studied managers and how they develop and has participated in leadership development design over the last fifteen years. His most recent interest is the changing meaning of leadership and its implications for practice and development. He is coauthor (with Charles Palus) of *Making Common Sense: Leadership as Meaning-Making in a Community of Practice* and *Evolving Leaders: A Model for Promoting Leadership Development in Programs.* He holds an A.B. in English from the University of Georgia.

Victoria A. Guthrie is the director of innovative program initiatives at the Center for Creative Leadership. In this role she is responsible for bringing fresh initiatives to the Center's established programs as well as generative ideas for future program development. She codesigned three of the Center's leadership development programs: LeaderLab, Leading Downsized Organizations, and Leading Creatively. In addition, she has conducted custom programs for international organizations in Europe, Canada, the West Indies, and the United States. She is coauthor (with Robert Burnside) of *Training for Action: A New Approach to Executive Development*. Prior to joining the Center, she was with Xerox Corporation in Rochester (New York) and Philadelphia. She holds a degree in management from Guilford College and an MBA from Wake Forest University.

Michael H. Hoppe is a senior program and research associate at the Center for Creative Leadership. A native of Germany, he has had extensive international experience in the fields of education policy, organizational behavior, and management development. He has lectured and published on leadership and intercultural communications in the United States and Europe. He holds a Ph.D. in adult education and organizational development from the University of North Carolina at Chapel Hill. He also received an M.A. in clinical psychology from the University of Munich (Germany) and an M.S. in educational psychology from the State University of New York at Albany. His current research activities evolve around the development of leadership effectiveness in a multicultural environment.

Martha W. Hughes-James is a research associate at the Center for Creative Leadership. She has conducted research on organizational diversity issues and the influence of race and gender on management development. She has coauthored or coedited several reports and articles on management development, including *Selected Research on Work Team Diversity* and *Making Diversity Happen*. She received her B.S. in psychology from Guilford College in Greensboro, North Carolina.

Lily Kelly-Radford is the director of the Center for Creative Leadership's Greensboro (North Carolina) branch, which conducts public and contract training programs domestically and internationally. Prior to joining the Center in 1990, she was a trainer in the Leadership Development Program for seven years with various CCL network associates. Since joining the Center, she has served as manager of the LDP and as chief assessor, overseeing the quality and integrity of the Center's feedback interventions. She has also trained in several countries and customizes programs to correspond to international business and cultural issues. She holds a Ph.D. in clinical psychology from the University of Georgia.

Cynthia D. McCauley is a research scientist at the Center for Creative Leadership. She received her B.A. in psychology from King College and her M.A. and Ph.D. in industrial and organizational psychology from the University of Georgia. She has been a part of the research staff since 1984 and has coauthored two of the Center's management-feedback instruments, Benchmarks and the Developmental Challenge Profile: Learning from Job Experiences. She has written several Center reports and has published articles in the *Journal of Management, Academy of Management Journal, Nonprofit Management and Leadership, Journal of Applied Psychology,* and *Leadership Quarterly.* She has conducted research on 360-degree feedback, the impact of leadership development programs, learning through job assignments, and developmental relationships.

Dana G. McDonald-Mann is a senior program associate at the Center for Creative Leadership. She manages the Benchmarks certification workshop, facilitates assessment-related workshops at the Center and client locations, and conducts one-on-one feedback sessions for managers and executives. Prior to joining the Center, she worked in both the public and private sectors. Her specialty areas are training design, delivery, and evaluation; selection system design and delivery; and managerial assessment. She received her B.A. in psychology from Wake Forest University and her M.A. and Ph.D. in industrial/organizational psychology from the University of Maryland, College Park.

Russ S. Moxley is director, nonprofit initiatives, and a senior program associate at the Center for Creative Leadership. He is responsible for crafting the Center's strategy for enhancing the practice of leadership in national nonprofit organizations, and he coordinates the leadership development program activities with national and regional nonprofit organizations. As a program associate he focuses on executive coaching, train-the-trainer workshops, and other feedback-intensive workshops in for-profit and nonprofit companies, in the United States and abroad. He also works with organizations to help them put together leadership development systems. Before joining the Center, he worked in several human resource and management development positions at Arco. He has a B.A. in social science and an M.Th. from Southern Methodist University in Dallas.

Patricia J. Ohlott is a research associate at the Center for Creative Leadership. Her research interests include the career development of women, the developmental impact of job assignments, and issues relating to management of diversity in organizations. She has coauthored the Developmental Challenge Profile instrument and several Center reports. She has published articles in the *Academy of Management Journal, Journal of Applied Psychology, Journal of Management Development,* and *Personnel Psychology.* She has a B.A. in psychology from Yale University and is pursuing a Ph.D. in business administration, with a concentration in organizational behavior, at Duke University.

Marian N. Ruderman is a research scientist at the Center for Creative Leadership. Her research focuses on the career development of women and the impact of diversity on management development processes. She is coeditor (with Susan Jackson) of *Diversity in Work Teams: Research Paradigms for a Changing Workplace.* She has written several Center reports and has published articles in the *Academy of Management Journal, Journal of Applied Psychology,* and *Journal of Management Development.* She has also coauthored the Center's feedback instrument, the Developmental Challenge Profile. She has an M.A. and Ph.D. in psychology from the University of Michigan.

Ellen Van Velsor is a research scientist at the Center for Creative Leadership. In this position, she is responsible for research that supports development of leadership assessment instruments and other assessment products. She is coauthor of *Breaking the Glass Ceiling: Can Women Reach the Top of America's Largest Organizations?* and *Feedback to Managers,* volumes one and two, as well as numerous other chapters and articles. She received her B.A. degree in sociology from the State University of New York at Stony Brook and her M.A. and Ph.D. degrees in sociology from the University of Florida.

Patricia O'Connor Wilson is the Center's director of business development and heads the New York client liaison office. In this role, she is responsible for the systems through which CCL constituencies access the varied resources of the Center and for the enterprisewide business development strategy. She also instructs in the Leadership and High-Performance Teams program and serves as a feedback specialist for the Leadership Development Program. She served in sales, finance, and human resource development functions prior to joining the Center. She has recently coauthored (with Eugene Marlow) *The Breakdown of Hierarchy: Communicating in the Evolving Workplace.* Her areas of interest include development systems, high-performance teams, and large-systems strategic change. She holds a B.S. in human resources from the University of Illinois (Champaign-Urbana) and an MBA in management and organizational behavior from Bernard M. Baruch College.

THE CENTER FOR CREATIVE LEADERSHIP HANDBOOK OF LEADERSHIP DEVELOPMENT

OUR VIEW OF LEADERSHIP DEVELOPMENT

Ellen Van Velsor
Cynthia D. McCauley
Russ S. Moxley

The Manager and the Sage

"Is experience the best teacher?" the bright young manager asked the sage. "Can I develop as a leader from experience?"

"Some people have said that experience is the best teacher," replied the sage. "But some experiences don't teach."

"So experience is not the best teacher?"

"Not exactly that," said the sage. "It is just that not every experience offers important leadership lessons."

"So where do I learn? What experiences will be helpful to me?"

"It is the experiences that challenge you that are developmental," the sage responded, "the experiences that stretch you, that force you to develop new abilities if you are going to survive and succeed."

"Oh, I get it," said the manager. "When I am really pushed to my limits by an experience, I will learn. Is that it?"

"Not exactly," the sage said. "Challenge is important. Our limits need to be tested. But even when we are challenged we don't necessarily learn."

"So," the manager said, looking a bit puzzled, "you mean that I can have the right kind of experiences—challenging experiences—and still not learn?"

"That's right," the sage responded. "You only grow from challenging experiences when you have the ability to learn from them. Not everyone does. As T. S. Eliot once reminded us, 'some people have the experience and miss the meaning.' There are some people who learn hand over fist from a challenging experience. Others learn little, if anything. Growth is not automatic."

"I think I'm getting it," said the manager. "I have to have experiences that challenge me plus the ability to learn from them if I am going to develop. Is that it?"

"Not exactly," the sage replied. "We don't learn or grow in a vacuum. Most of us are part of a larger group or organization. Sometimes we have the good fortune of receiving feedback and support for our growth; sometimes we don't. We need to get feedback from others and take the time to reflect on our experiences. Feedback and reflection allow us to assess how we are doing, what's working, and how we need to change. We also need acceptance, advice, and encouragement from others and support from our organizations if we expect to grow. We simply cannot do it all alone."

"Let me see if I understand. When I avail myself of challenging experiences, when I take seriously learning from those experiences, and when I get support and feedback from key people in my company, I can learn the important leadership lessons I need. Right?"

"Right," declared the sage. "As far as it goes. But there is still the question of what develops in leadership development."

"What do you mean?"

"There are some things that are developable and other things that appear to be hardwired or innate. IQ, for example, and certain personality characteristics appear to be set by the time we are adults, remain consistent over time, and provide some limits to our development. But there are certain skills and capacities that can be developed."

"It all seems so complicated," the manager replied.

"It is a bit complicated. Being stretched and challenged is not easy. Diversity and adversity are the keys to growth, and both challenge us. None of us like to operate out of our comfort zone. And it takes time. Years, in fact. And a lot of pieces have to fit together: challenging experiences, organizational support, individual readiness. We used to think it was easier, that single events were developmental—a single event of training, for example. But that understanding was inadequate. Development happens over time as part of a process or a system. There is still a lot we don't know about how leaders develop. But we have learned a lot and we are learning more all the time. And the good news is that we can learn and grow and change."

"Thanks," said the young manager. "Thanks for your time and your insights. I think I understand. Given all that you've said, it's becoming clear that I must understand development in a longer time frame, requiring several elements to support it and having different outcomes in different contexts."

"I do think you understand," said the sage. "Good luck on your journey."

◆ ◆ ◆

The questions asked by the manager in this story are questions that we have asked at the Center for Creative Leadership for a number of years. In the 1970s, the Center began experimenting with feedback-intensive leadership development programs—programs that provide participants with a heavy dose of feedback in a supportive environment. Over the years, we have refined these programs and added new components, we have developed more sophisticated feedback tools and methods, and we have studied the impact of our programs on the participants. We have also tried to understand how managers learn, grow, and change throughout their careers—not just from formal programs, but from the challenges in their working and nonworking lives, the relationships they cultivate, and the hardships they encounter.

We continue to invest energy and resources in efforts to understand and improve the leadership development process. The basic question that underlies much of this work, both in research and in education, is, How can people develop the skills and perspectives necessary to be effective in leadership roles?

Much of what we have learned from examining this question is contained in this handbook. In this introductory chapter, we present a framework for understanding what is to follow. We distill what we have learned into a model of leadership development, and this model serves as scaffolding upon which to place the concepts that are discussed in detail in later chapters. We begin this chapter by sharing our basic assumptions and presenting the model. We then look at the elements of the model more closely. We end the chapter by considering how, given our model, the process of leadership development can be enhanced.

Assumptions and Model

We define *leadership development* as the expansion of a person's capacity to be effective in leadership roles and processes. Leadership roles and processes are those that enable groups of people to work together in productive and meaningful ways.

You should note three things about this definition of leadership development. First, we tend to see leadership development as the development of capacities within the individual. Most of our research and educational programs are directed toward the individual. Even when our interventions are directed at teams or organizations, the primary goal is improving individual capacities.

Second, we try to look at what makes a person effective in a variety of leadership roles and processes (rather than what makes him or her "a leader"). The assumption here is that in the course of their lives, most people must take on leadership roles and participate in leadership processes in order to carry out their commitments to larger social entities: the organizations they work in, the social or volunteer groups they are part of, the neighborhoods they live in, and the professional groups they identify with.

These leadership roles may be formal positions infused with authority to take action and make decisions (for example, a manager, an elected official, or a group's representative at a meeting) or they may be informal roles with little formal authority (the team member who helps the group develop a better sense of its capabilities, the person who organizes the neighborhood to fight rezoning efforts, the whistle-blower who reveals things gone wrong). Leaders may actively participate in recognized processes for creating change (such as serving on task forces or project teams, identifying and focusing attention on problems or issues, getting resources to implement changes) or more subtle processes for shaping culture (telling stories that define organizational values, celebrating accomplishments). Rather than classifying people as "leaders" or "nonleaders" and trying to develop individuals into leaders, we have assumed that everyone can learn and grow in ways that make them more effective in the various leadership roles and processes they take on. This process of personal development that improves leadership effectiveness is what we understand leadership development to be about.

Finally, although it may go without saying, we should note that we do believe that individuals can expand their leadership capacities. That is, a key underlying assumption in all of our work is that people can learn, grow, and change. We do not debate the extent to which effective leaders are born or are developed. No doubt, leadership capacity has its roots partly in genetics, partly in early childhood development, and partly in adult experience. What we focus on here is what our experience has amply demonstrated: adults can develop the important capacities that facilitate their leadership effectiveness.

The core question, of course, is how to go about it. How do people acquire these leadership capacities? How do their organizations (in particular the human resource professionals responsible for this development) help them in the process? The model illustrated in Figure I.1 reflects our attempt to summarize what we have learned thus far about the ingredients that go into leadership development.

FIGURE I.1. LEADERSHIP DEVELOPMENT MODEL.

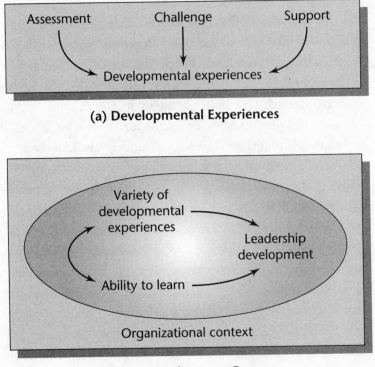

(a) Developmental Experiences

(b) The Development Process

The three factors in Part A of the model—assessment, challenge, and support—are the elements that, when combined, make developmental experiences more powerful. That is, whatever the experience, it has more impact if it contains these three elements.

We know that although leaders learn primarily through their experiences, not all experiences are equally developmental. For example, the first year in a new job is usually more developmental than the fifth or sixth year. Working with a boss who gives constructive feedback is usually more developmental than working with one who doesn't. A training program that encourages lots of practice and helps participants examine mistakes is usually more developmental than one that provides information but no practice. Situations that stretch an individual and are feedback-rich, while also providing a sense of support, are more likely to stimulate leadership development than situations that leave out any of these elements. You can make any experience—a training program, an assignment, a relationship—richer and more developmental by making sure that the elements of assessment, challenge, and support are present.

Part B of the model shows that leadership development is a process that requires both a variety of developmental experiences and the ability to learn from experience. The latter is the element that the individual brings to the development process. In the course of much of our work, we have noticed that people learn from similar kinds of experiences to differing degrees and in different ways. Although such variation is explained in part by the level of challenge that different people perceive in any experience, another part is the individual's ability to learn from an experience. Ability to learn is a complex combination of motivational factors, personality factors, and learning tactics.

Part B of the model also shows that developmental experiences and the ability to learn have a direct impact on each other. Being engaged in a developmental experience can enhance a person's ability to learn, and being able to learn can lead to experiences that are more developmental. Take the case of Joe, for example. He is an American completing a three-year assignment in his company's Singapore office. The assignment is a far cry from his previous five years at corporate headquarters; he rarely sees his boss and often doesn't have a clear sense of what is happening at headquarters. Most of his direct reports are from Singapore or other countries in the Far East. Joe would readily admit that this experience has challenged his abilities and provided a mirror for assessing some of his cultural biases. He has learned a great deal, including how to make quick decisions on his own and how to work across cultural boundaries. Because he has been successful in this developmental experience, he feels very competent and motivated as a learner. His self-esteem has been boosted, and he has developed strategies for learning when encountering strange and unfamiliar new territory. He returns from the assignment seeking new challenges and better prepared to take advantage of the learning opportunities he runs into.

Thus, although in our model we conceptually separate the developmental experience and the learner (the better to discuss them), they are in actuality closely interconnected: developmental experiences can enhance a person's ability to learn, and those with high ability to learn seek out a variety of developmental experiences.

Finally, Part B indicates that any leadership development process is embedded in a particular organizational context: the organization's business strategy, its culture, and the various systems and processes within the organization. This context shapes the leadership development process—how it is focused, how well-integrated and systemic it is, and who is responsible for it.

Elements of an Effective Developmental Experience

Through the Center's research and educational programs, we have begun to better understand the elements that are key drivers of leadership development (assessment, challenge, and support). When we look at any type of developmental experience—from training programs to job assignments—we find that they are most effective when all three elements are present.

These elements serve dual purposes in the development process. First, they motivate people to focus their attention and exert effort toward learning, growth, and change. Second, they provide the raw material or resources for learning: the information, observations, and reactions that lead to a more complex and sometimes quite different understanding of the world. To enhance the development of leaders, we need to help them find, create, and shape a wide range of learning experiences, each of which provides assessment, challenge, and support. Table I.1 summarizes the motivational role played by each element, as well as the kind of learning resource each provides. In the next three sections of this chapter, we look at each of these elements in more depth.

TABLE I.1. ELEMENTS OF A DEVELOPMENTAL EXPERIENCE.

Element	Role in Motivation	Role as a Resource
Assessment	Desire to close gap between current self and ideal self	Clarity about needed changes; clues about how gap can be closed
Challenge	Need to master the challenge	Opportunity for experimentation and practice; exposure to different perspectives
Support	Confidence in ability to learn and grow; positive value placed on change	Confirmation and clarification of lessons learned

Assessment

The best developmental experiences are rich in assessment data. Assessment is important because it gives people an understanding of where they are now: what their current strengths are, the level of their current performance or leadership effectiveness, and what are seen as primary development needs. In the context of their everyday work, people may not be aware of the degree to which their usual behaviors or actions are effective; in the face of a new challenge, they may not know what to continue doing and what to change. Even if they do realize that what they are doing is ineffective, people may believe the answer is to just work harder; it may not occur to them to try a new strategy. But when an experience provides feedback on how they are doing and how they might improve, or provides other means for critical self-reflection, then people are more likely to understand their situation and to capitalize on a learning opportunity.

One important function of assessment data is that they provide a benchmark for future development. Another is that they stimulate people to evaluate themselves. *What am I doing well? Where do I need to improve? What are others' views of me? How do my behaviors impact others? How am I doing relative to my goals? What's important to me?* Still another is that assessment data provide information that helps people answer these questions. The result is an unfreezing of one's current understanding of self, to facilitate movement toward a broader and more complex understanding.

Assessment data can come from oneself or from other people. The sources are almost limitless: peers in the workplace, bosses, employees, spouses, children, parents, friends, customers, counselors, and organizational consultants. The processes for collecting and interpreting the data can be either formal or informal, with many shades of variation in between.

Formal assessment from others includes such processes as performance appraisals, customer evaluations, 360-degree feedback, organizational surveys that measure employee satisfaction with managers, and assessments and recommendations from consultants. Informal assessment data from others are available more regularly through less structured processes: asking a colleague for feedback, observing others' reactions to one's ideas or actions, being repeatedly sought out to help with certain kinds of problems, or getting unsolicited feedback from the boss. Self-assessment can also occur through formal and structured means, as with psychological inventories or journaling, or through informal and often in-the-moment processes, such as monitoring of internal states, reflecting on decision processes, or analyzing mistakes.

Assessment information points out the gaps between a person's current capacities or performance and some desired state or ideal capacity level. The desired level might be based on what the job requires, what someone's career goals demand, what other people expect, or what people expect of themselves. This gap is one of the keys to why a developmental experience motivates learning, growth, and change. If the area is something that is important to them and if they believe in the accuracy of the assessment data, people work to close the gap by improving their current capacities. If the assessment data indicate that there is no gap—that, in fact, the person is quite talented in a particular area—then the outcome of the assessment is increased self-confidence. The person may seek out more opportunities to use and refine the talent.

Good assessment data also help people clarify what needs to be learned, improved, or changed. Having data not only motivates a person to close the gaps but provides clues to how those gaps might be closed. For example, if the leader of a work group learns that part of the reason for low morale in the group is his pattern of not delegating important work to others (which, he comes to understand, is grounded in perfectionism), then improving morale involves learning how to let go of work, including how to be more in touch with these perfectionist tendencies so that they can be better managed. Or if a frustration at work is diagnosed as being partially caused by low tolerance for ambiguity, then the person can focus on how to increase her tolerance or how to shape situations so that they are less ambiguous.

Challenge

Developmentally, the experiences that can be most potent are the ones that stretch or challenge people. Individuals develop certain strengths— ways of thinking and acting—that work for them, become comfortable, and lead to habitual ways of thinking and acting. As long as conditions don't change, people feel no need to move beyond their comfort zone to develop new strengths. In a comfortable assignment, they use their familiar strengths well in serving the needs of the organization, but they do not learn very much from it. The same is true for a comfortable relationship, feedback that confirms, or a training program on skills that have already been mastered. In all such cases, comfort is truly the enemy of growth and continued effectiveness.

Challenging experiences force people out of their comfort zone. They create disequilibrium, causing people to question the adequacy of their skills, frameworks, and approaches. These experiences require that people develop new capacities if they are going to be successful. A task force assignment in which the task is critical to the business, in which success or failure will be known, and in which task force members present a recommendation for action to the senior executives of the organization can be developmental because challenge is imbedded in it; however, it is particularly developmental for people who have not faced these types of challenges before.

People feel challenged when they encounter situations that demand skills and abilities beyond their current capabilities, when the situation is very confusing or ambiguous (that is, when current ways of making sense of the world no longer seem to work), or when confronted with a situation they would rather not have to deal with—for example, when a person is caught in the middle of two divisions who want a conflict resolved in opposite ways, or finding out that the organization isn't going to promote the person into a job he thinks he deserves.

Some challenges are due to a lack of experience; they require the person to broaden and acquire new skills and perspectives. Other challenges require changing old habits: either the situation has changed and old responses are no longer adequate, or old responses were never that effective in the first place.

What kinds of situations stretch, confuse, and confront leaders with difficult tasks? In other words, what are the sources of challenge? One common source is novelty. New experiences usually require new skills and new ways of understanding oneself in relation to others. They are often quite ambiguous, requiring much discovery and sense making by the newcomer. The power of new experiences is illustrated in Linda Hill's in-depth study (1992) of men and women during their first managerial assignment. They found that becoming a manager required more than learning new skills and building relationships. Rather, it was a profound transformation, one that caused them to think and feel in new ways—to actually develop a new identity.

Difficult goals, whether set by oneself or by others, are another source of challenge. People often respond to difficult goals by working harder. But they may also discover that extra effort isn't enough, that they have to work differently in order to reach the goal. Executives report that some of the toughest assignments in their careers are starting-from-scratch assignments, where they have the difficult goal of building something from nothing—and they usually have to do it quickly, with little structure in place, and with little experience (McCall, Lombardo, and Morrison, 1988). To succeed, they have to let go of normal operating procedures and learn as they go, using whoever and whatever is available to solve problems. Leaders who go through formal leadership development programs are often faced with the difficult goal of changing their own behavior—or risk endangering the performance of their groups or their own career goals. Again, this difficult goal is a source of challenge and thus is a potential stimulus for learning and growth.

Situations characterized by conflict—either with someone else or within oneself—are also a source of challenge. Dealing with conflict with another person or group often requires people to develop an understanding of other perspectives and reshape their own point of view. People also experience incompatible demands that cause conflict within themselves, for example, meeting work and family responsibilities, working satisfactorily for both the boss and subordinates, or meeting customer needs in ways that don't overstress the organization. Ron Heifetz (1994), director of the Leadership Education Project at the Kennedy School of Government, Harvard University, sees the surfacing and orchestration of conflict as one of the hardest but most valuable tasks of leadership. In this view, conflict is the stimulus for mobilizing people to learn new ways. He gives the example of an industrial plant that was a major source of jobs for a community but was creating levels of pollution unacceptable to federal agencies. As community leaders were forced to deal with the conflict between jobs and health, they developed new ways of understanding the problem (namely, as an issue of diversifying the local economy), which implied new courses of action for them to take.

Dealing with losses, failures, and disappointments can also stretch people. Losing their jobs, making business mistakes, or damaging relationships can cause a great deal of confusion, often stimulating a search for new meaning and understanding. In the Center's work, we have found that these kinds of experiences, which we have labeled *hardships*, seem to startle managers into facing themselves and coming to terms with their own fallibilities. Hardships also teach managers how to persevere and cope with difficult situations. This is sometimes referred to as the "inoculation effect": undergoing stressful experiences may render similar experiences in the future less distressing, primarily because the person develops better coping strategies.

The element of challenge serves the dual purpose of motivating development and providing the opportunity to develop. Challenging situations motivate by capitalizing on people's need for mastery. So long as the outcomes of the situation matter to people, they are motivated to work toward successfully meeting the challenge. This means becoming competent in new situations, achieving difficult goals, managing conflicts, and easing the pain of loss and failure. Mastering challenges requires putting energy into developing skills and abilities, understanding complex situations, and reshaping how one thinks.

Challenging experiences also provide opportunities to learn. People don't learn how to negotiate without having places to practice negotiation, that is, to test out different strategies and see how people react to them. They don't gain broader perspectives without coming face-to-face with people who have different perspectives or with situations that do not fit neatly into how they think about the world. People don't learn to cope with stress without feeling stress and figuring out how to decrease it. By engaging the challenge, people interact with the environment in a way that produces the information, observations, and reactions needed to learn.

Simply stated, people don't develop the capacity for leadership without being in the throes of the challenge of leadership. Participating in leadership roles and processes is often the very source of the challenges needed for leadership development. Leadership roles and processes are full of novelty, difficulty, conflict, and disappointments. In other words, leadership itself is a challenge that is developmental. Leading is, in and of itself, learning by doing.

Finally, we also want to emphasize the importance of variety of challenge for developing the wide range of capacities that leaders need. We emphasize this because we have found that people learn different lessons from different kinds of experiences. From a "fix-it" job, leaders can learn toughness, the ability to stand on their own two feet, and decisiveness. From leaving a line job for a staff position, leaders have the opportunity to learn how to influence those over whom they have no direct control. From a formal leadership program, participants have the chance to step back from day-to-day routine and develop a deeper understanding of their preferences, strengths, and blind spots. From an effective boss, leaders learn important values, such as fairness and sensitivity to the concerns of others. From a hardship situation people can recognize their limits and learn how to deal with stress. All are important leadership lessons; each is often learned from a different type of experience. Thus, a variety of challenging experiences throughout their careers is an important ingredient for developing versatile leaders.

Support

Although developmental experiences stretch people and point out their strengths and weaknesses, they are most powerful when they also have an element of support. While the element of challenge provides the disequilibrium needed to motivate people to change, the support elements of an experience send the message that their efforts to learn and grow are valued. If people do not receive support in the form of confirming messages, and if other people do not allow and encourage them to change, then the challenge inherent in a development experience may overwhelm them, rather than opening them up to learning. For a sales manager on a key cross-functional task force, beginning to understand and value the dilemmas of the manufacturing engineer on the task force may be the initial step in developing a broader perspective—but what if she is thwarted by a boss who constantly reminds her not to give in to the unrealistic demands of "those bozos in engineering"? As another example, an organization that wants to develop more effective teamwork is unlikely to make progress if it continues primarily to reward individual contributions.

Support is also needed to help people handle the struggle and pain of developing, that is, to actually help them bear the weight of the experience. It is needed to help them maintain a positive view of themselves as people capable of dealing with challenges, who can learn and grow, who are worthy and valuable. Seeing that others place a positive value on their efforts to change and grow is a key factor for people to stay on course with development goals.

Perhaps the largest source of support is other people: bosses, coworkers, family, friends, professional colleagues, coaches, and mentors—even a favorite author. These people listen to stories of struggle, identify with the challenges, suggest strategies for coping, reassure in times of doubt, inspire renewed effort, celebrate even the smallest accomplishments, and cheer from the sidelines.

Different sources may provide different kinds of support. For example, the new managers in the study cited earlier relied heavily on peers to release pent-up frustrations and find emotional support, and those who had developed close relationships with former bosses often turned to them when they were struggling with difficult questions. We have also found that the support of one's current boss is a particularly important factor when trying to change behaviors or learn new skills.

Support can also take the form of organizational norms and procedures. Organizations that are more supportive of development have a closely held belief that continuous learning and development of the staff is a key factor in maintaining organizational success. They emphasize helping people identify development needs and work out plans for addressing them. They use a variety of development strategies, make resources available for learning, and recognize and reward efforts to learn and grow. Feedback, cross-group sharing of knowledge and information, and learning from mistakes are part of the organizational culture.

Support is a key factor in maintaining motivation to learn and grow. Support helps engender a sense of self-efficacy about learning, a belief that one can learn, grow, and change. The higher their self-efficacy, the more effort people exert to master challenges, and the more they persevere in difficult situations (Bandura, 1986). Support also serves as a social cue that puts a positive valence on where people are currently and on the direction in which they are moving. They sense, "If other people support me in doing this, it must be something valuable to do."

Support mechanisms also provide learning resources. By talking to others about what they are struggling with, openly examining mistakes, and seeing to it that the organization reacts positively to the changes they make, people have the opportunity to confirm and clarify the lessons they are learning. They get the sense that they are on the right track, that the feedback they are receiving is legitimate, and that the new ways in which they are making sense of their situations are shared by others.

In summary, the key elements that make any experience more developmental are assessment, challenge, and support. Whether you are designing a training program, providing 360-degree feedback, putting someone in a developmental job assignment, or matching the person with a mentor, you need to ensure that all three elements are part of the experience.

What Develops in Leadership Development

Over the years, we have asked effective managers to identify what they have learned that has made a difference or a lasting change in how they manage. We asked them to think about experiences on the job, outside of work, and in formal leadership development programs, and to isolate the critical lessons. The results are clear: development comes from many kinds of experience. These managers learned from challenging jobs, from significant people, from hardships, from training and coursework, and from a miscellany of other events (McCall, Lombardo, and Morrison, 1988; Morrison, White, and Van Velsor, 1987). The lessons they learned involved new skills, values, abilities, and knowledge. Over time, people who failed to learn became stuck—in their personal lives or in their jobs.

But we also know that some traits, like IQ and certain personality characteristics, are more or less innate and appear to remain stable over time. Development work with adults cannot—as some people fear and others hope—significantly improve IQ or provide a personality transplant.

Over time, we have begun to identify at least some of the capacities for enabling leadership that are developable. In no certain order, here are some of the capacities we believe that leaders can, and even must, learn over time:

- Self-awareness
- Self-confidence
- Ability to take a broad, systemic view
- Ability to work effectively in social systems
- Ability to think creatively
- Ability to learn from experience

Self-Awareness

A key aspect of understanding self is awareness of personal strengths and weaknesses: what one does well and not so well, which situations bring out the personal best and which are difficult to handle, when one has a wealth of expertise to draw on and when one had better look for expertise elsewhere.

But self-awareness also means people must understand *why* they are the way they are—what traits, learned preferences, experiences, or situational factors have shaped their profile of strengths and weaknesses—and understand the impact of their strengths and weaknesses on others, on their effectiveness in various life roles, and on reaching their goals. This broad self-awareness helps leaders understand how they can best carry out their roles and responsibilities, how they can contribute to the group, and what personal shortcomings they need to guard against in working with others.

Self-Confidence

One of the consistent results of our research on the impact of leadership development programs is that frequently the most highly rated outcome is increased self-confidence. As a program progresses, people become more aware of their own abilities and begin to develop a surer sense of what they have to offer others. We have also learned that people develop self-confidence from other challenging experiences, such as succeeding in a key assignment or overcoming a hardship situation. In general, self-confidence tends to be developed any time people feel they have successfully handled a new or difficult experience. This self-confidence enables leaders to act in difficult situations, offer their leadership talents to the group, and take on increasingly complex leadership challenges.

The Ability to View Life from a Broader, Systemic Point of View

Being able to take a broader, more complex view is another capacity that develops, for most people, as the result of many life experiences within and outside of work. The notion, common to many cultures, that people grow wiser (if not smarter) as they mature is a common way of understanding this capacity. People who develop it are able to see organizations and communities as systems, handle ambiguity and complexity, build systems for coordinating and integrating, use multiple frameworks in thinking about problems, and design long-term strategies. Because groups and organizations encounter complex and multifaceted problems, people who have this capacity are better equipped to help the group identify and address these problems.

The Ability to Work in Social Systems

People develop many interpersonal and social skills over the course of their lives. From their experience in organizations, they learn how to motivate others and how to delegate work to them. They learn what bosses are like and learn how to deal with them. Over time they develop the ability to influence peers, build teams, and negotiate with external parties. They learn how to deal with difficult employees and manage conflict. From interacting with people of different walks of life or from different cultures, they can develop the ability to listen to, honor, and work with diverse points of view. Because leadership roles and processes are by their very nature social (meaning that they require interactions with others), the ability to work effectively in social systems is a fundamental capacity for leaders.

The Ability to Think Creatively

People can develop the ability to think "outside the box," to get beyond their own assumptions and the frameworks that limit how they understand problems and issues. Creativity involves seeing new possibilities, finding connections between disparate ideas, and reframing the way people think about an issue. People can learn strategies for innovation, developing novel and useful ideas that help to solve difficult problems. Implementing innovations also requires an element of risk taking, of going into uncharted territory and leaving behind the familiar. The ability to think creatively enables leaders to contribute novel insights that can open up new opportunities or alternatives for the group or organization.

The Ability to Learn

When we say someone has the ability to learn from experience, we mean that the person recognizes when new behaviors, skills, or attitudes are called for, engages in activities that provide the opportunity to learn or test new skills and behaviors, and works to develop a variety of learning tactics in order to acquire the needed skills or behaviors.

Engaging in these activities requires a certain level of cognitive ability, but it also involves personality, motivation, and learning tactics. Cognitive and personality elements are, for the most part, fully developed and stable in adults. Motivation to learn is complex. It is partly dependent on self-esteem; how people feel about themselves influences their sense that they can face the challenge and succeed. It is also related to personality; some people may be, by nature, more oriented to learning than others are. Finally, motivation is related to the timing of a development experience in relation to other life events.

Yet even with these limitations, people can become better learners. The ability to learn is itself developable. People can become more aware of how they learn; they can work on developing new perspectives in relation to learning; and they can add to their portfolio of learning tactics.

Each of these capacities is made up of an array of skills, abilities, and perspectives. To develop any of these abilities, people first have to realize that their current skills or perspectives are inadequate or are not being fully utilized. This alone can be a major step, sometimes triggered by a mistake or failure, a personal crisis, or a piece of feedback from an assessment experience. Next, people have to identify the skill or perspective that they want to more fully develop and begin to try it on for size. Finally, after an extended period of practice, they can begin to feel comfortable with the new skill or perspective and start to use it effectively. This cycle is repeated many times as people expand their abilities in each domain. This is why we say that leadership development takes time.

Enhancing Leadership Development

Certainly we believe that leadership development can be enhanced by intervening in the learning, growth, and change processes of individuals. This is a key assumption underlying our work. If leaders do learn, grow, and change over time, and if we understand the factors that contribute to that growth process, then development can be enhanced by influencing these factors.

The leadership development model suggests three main strategies for enhancing this process:

1. Create a variety of rich developmental experiences that each provide assessment, challenge, and support.
2. Enhance people's ability to learn from experience.
3. Use an approach that integrates the various developmental experiences and embeds them in the organizational context.

Creating Rich Developmental Experiences

There are many types of experience that develop leadership abilities in those who participate. Significant among them are 360-degree feedback, the feedback-intensive program, skill-based training, job assignments, developmental relationships, and hardships. (Each is explored at length in its own chapter in Part Two of this handbook.) The developmental potency of any one of these experiences depends on whether it contains a good mix of assessment, challenge, and support.

For example, although a feedback-intensive program obviously focuses on assessment, it must also challenge the participants and at the same time support them. The element of challenge comes from exercises and simulations used in these programs, which are deliberately designed to take people out of their comfort zones, and from interactions with other participants, who often challenge a participant's point of view. At the same time, these programs take great care to create a supportive environment in which people can be candid and hear negative information about themselves, while the positive information they get shores up their self-confidence.

Job assignments are another example. They can be particularly rich sources of challenge, but if people are to learn from assignments, they must have opportunities to receive ongoing feedback while struggling with the challenge. People in challenging assignments also need others they can turn to for support, as well as needing to feel supported by the organization in general.

Enhancing the Ability to Learn

To repeat, learning from experience involves three separate activities: (1) recognizing when new behaviors, skills, or attitudes are called for; (2) engaging in activities that provide the opportunity to learn or test new skills and behaviors; and (3) working to develop and use a variety of learning tactics in order to acquire the needed skills or behaviors.

It is usually not easy to recognize when new skills or approaches are needed. Sometimes mistakes or failures serve to get people's attention. But often, even in new situations, people tend to stick with the skills and approaches that have worked for them in the past. The temptation to rely on existing strengths can be especially powerful when new situations demand quick response or create high stress for other reasons.

Assessment and feedback are critical if people are to recognize that current skills are insufficient and comfortable approaches are inadequate. Getting reliable information continuously about how they are doing is an important way for people to know that change is necessary; it is, therefore, an important component of enhancing the ability to learn. If they stopped to think about it, most people would probably say that in new situations new approaches to learning might be more beneficial than old approaches. However, when actually faced with a new challenge, most people tend to use habitual ways of learning. For example, some people always jump right in and take action in a new situation, when a more effective approach might be to seek the advice of those who are familiar with the situation at hand. Other people almost always read to acquire new learning, even if the situation might provide the richest learning via a hands-on or action approach.

Relying on comfortable approaches in new situations almost always limits effectiveness and learning. Yet it is possible to develop new learning tactics. When people are given a variety of challenging experiences, the novelty they face demands that they develop new learning tactics. Assessment of how they currently learn, understanding of other ways to learn (perhaps through reading or skill-based training), and opportunity to experiment with new learning tactics (in the classroom or on the job) can help people develop the flexibility inherent in a strong ability to learn from experience. Chapter Eight looks in depth at what is involved in enhancing this critical ability.

Linking Development Experiences

Creating rich development experiences and equipping people to learn are two strategies for enhancing leadership development. A third strategy is to design and implement developmental experiences systemically.

Rather than keeping various development experiences separate, a systemic view treats them as interrelated and building on one another. For example, a training program can be preceded by open conversations about expectations of learning goals and can be timed so that it helps a manager rise to the challenge of a tough new assignment. The assignment is in turn supplemented by ongoing feedback and coaching, as well as opportunities to reflect—alone and with others facing similar challenges—on what and how the manager is learning.

Our major criticism of the approach of many organizations to leadership development is that they do not take this systemic view. Instead, they have an events-based approach to development: How to develop a bright young engineer—clearly gifted, high potential—who needs improvement in interpersonal skills? Send the engineer to a training program, and the shorter it is the better. There is no question of readiness, no feedback prior to training, no planned support or reinforcement upon return. The hope is that training "fixes" people. As you will discover, we have found that training is a powerful intervention, an important part of a developmental system. But it is only one part.

The story is the same with multirater (or, as some call it, 360-degree) feedback. Again the tendency is frequently to use the feedback as an isolated event rather than as part of a process. Multirater feedback is an effective assessment activity, an experience that helps unfreeze people and prepares them to learn from other development experiences. But if you just give someone feedback from an instrument and stop there, little real development takes place.

In addition to linking developmental experiences, leadership development processes also need to be embedded in the organizational context. How is leadership development connected to the business strategy? Who is the organization targeting for development? Who is responsible for development? How will other organizational systems and processes support development? These broad strategies are further articulated and illustrated in Chapter Seven.

Summary

To summarize, let us return to the leadership development model and the assumptions behind it.

First, we define leadership development as the expansion of a person's capacity to be effective in leadership roles and processes. Second, we believe that developing the capacities needed for effective leadership—such as self-awareness, systemic thinking, and creativity—is synonymous with what is often labeled personal development. This development unfolds over time. It is maximized by a variety of experiences that challenge people, support them, and provide them with understanding of how they are doing. It also depends on their having an adequate level of ability to learn. Leadership development processes that integrate various experiences and embed them in the organizational context are likely to be effective.

Finally, if there is one key idea to our view of leadership development—an overarching theme that runs throughout our work—it is that leadership development is an ongoing process. It is grounded in personal development, development that is never complete. It is embedded in experience: leaders learn as they expand their experiences over time. And it is facilitated by interventions that are woven into those experiences in connected and meaningful ways.

PART ONE

LEADERSHIP DEVELOPMENT: EXPERIENCES

CHAPTER ONE

360-DEGREE FEEDBACK

Craig T. Chappelow

Terry Anderson can recall with great clarity the day he received life-changing feedback. From the point of view of this handbook, the unusual thing about Anderson's feedback is that it did not happen in his boss's office, or even in a leadership development classroom. It happened in a jail cell.

While working as a journalist covering the Middle East in the early 1980s, Anderson was taken prisoner in Beirut by Shiite extremists and held for nearly seven years. In *Den of Lions* (1993), Anderson recounts the conditions of his imprisonment. Much of the time he was blindfolded and shackled. Each new day brought with it the promise of being released and the fear of being beaten.

At the time of this feedback event, Anderson and three other captives were being held in a ten-by-twelve-foot room. The captives could not get away from one another, and conflict was high. The tension was particularly difficult between Anderson and fellow captive David Jacobsen. They argued and fought constantly.

Anderson recalls one morning when the guards took Jacobsen out of the cell to use the bathroom. Those trips were the only time in the day when any of the prisoners was away from the others. Anderson used the opportunity to ask the other two captives for feedback:

> This morning, while David was in the bathroom, I asked Tom and Father Martin what was going wrong, what they thought I could do to make it easier. Their answer was a solid blast at me.
>
> "You challenge David all of the time. You seem to want to top him, to prove something to him. It's like a pair of bulls trying to dominate the same herd."
>
> I was shocked. Naturally, I'd assumed the others would agree with me that David was causing the trouble. . . .
>
> I've been sitting here thinking about all that. It's not a view of myself that I like—argumentative, bullheaded, trampling on other people. Especially in a situation like this. It's hard to accept, but I have to, since both Father Martin and Tom agree. . . .
>
> Once again, I'm faced directly with the contradiction between what I believe I am and what others see me as. This place is like living in a hall of mirrors. There's no hiding from the others, and there's no ignoring the reflections they give me of myself. [Anderson, 1993, pp. 138–139]

The conditions under which Anderson received this feedback were more dramatic than what most managers will ever find in their work roles. But his experience illustrates the three critical components of the leadership development process outlined in the introductory chapter: assessment, challenge, and support.

Assessment came in the form of verbal feedback from multiple sources, in this case from his fellow captives. The challenges for Anderson were dramatic and obvious. Changes had to be made for the group to survive their terrible situation, and it was soon clear to Anderson that he was the one who had to take the lead in changing his own behaviors. The support (which Anderson describes later in his book) was provided by the other captives once they saw that Anderson was making an effort to improve their lot. They all worked harder to get along after this confrontation.

What happened was this. Terry Anderson received a simple type of multirater feedback: two opinions about his behavior that he was able to compare to his own. The difference between how he perceived his behavior and the way the others perceived him was startling for Anderson. It was, for him, a blind spot that he wanted desperately to act upon.

In that respect, Anderson is far from unique. People's own views of themselves are often narrow and biased. The enhanced self-awareness created by feedback can help leaders know where to focus their developmental efforts and motivate them to better understand their strengths and improve their weaknesses.

This chapter explores the role of multirater feedback (also known as 360-degree feedback) in the leadership development process, highlighting in particular some of the things we have learned about feedback over the past twenty years, through research and practice at the Center for Creative Leadership. As such, it is not a comprehensive review of the professional literature on 360-degree feedback. Those interested in such a review should consult one of the recently published books on the topic (see, for example, *Maximizing the Value of 360-Degree Feedback* by Tornow, London, and CCL Associates, 1998, or *The Art and Science of 360° Feedback* by Lepsinger and Lucia, 1997).

The chapter is organized in three major sections. The first section examines the purpose and uses of 360-degree feedback: How does it work? Why is it needed? What is its role in the leadership development process? For what purposes do organizations use it? The second section describes the steps involved in implementing a 360-degree feedback process: choosing an instrument, collecting the data, feeding back the data, and creating a development plan. The final section provides guidelines for enhancing the success of a formal feedback initiative and looks at future trends in 360-degree feedback.

360-Degree Feedback: Purpose and Uses

What we call 360-degree feedback is a method of systematically collecting opinions about a manager's performance from a wide range of coworkers. This could include peers, direct subordinates, the boss, the boss's peers—along with people outside the organization, such as customers, suppliers, and sometimes even family members. The benefit of collecting data of this kind is that the person gets to see a panorama of perceptions rather than self-perception, which affords a more complete picture. One critical person from whom opinions are solicited, though, is the manager herself.

When embedded in a larger leadership development process, the impact of formal 360-degree feedback can be great. Research shows that 360-degree feedback can improve performance and lead to behavior change (Hazucha, Hezlett, and Schneider, 1993; Atwater, Rousch, and Fischtal, 1995; Smither and others, 1995).

How Does It Work?

Typically, the person being assessed (identified in this chapter as the *participant*) selects a number of coworkers (who are called *raters*) to participate in the feedback process. Working individually, the raters and the participant complete surveys designed to collect information about the participant's specific skills or specific behaviors that are deemed important to managerial or leadership effectiveness within the organization. A sample page from a feedback survey is shown in Figure 1.1.

After the raters complete the surveys, they return them to a centralized location for scoring. A report is printed and delivered to a feedback specialist (a sample page from a feedback report is shown in Figure 1.2). Then the participant and the specialist get together to go over the report; the specialist, usually someone who has experience with the particular instrument being used, helps the participant understand what the various scores mean. The participant then uses this feedback to establish a developmental plan geared toward increasing effectiveness.

Why Formal Feedback?

In the life of a busy organization, people often find themselves feedback-starved. Two factors play into this. First, people get caught up in day-to-day pressures and responsibilities and fail to pick up the cues

FIGURE 1.1. SAMPLE 360-DEGREE FEEDBACK SURVEY.

	Strength	Development Needed
Getting Information, Making Sense of it; Problem Identification		
1. Seeks information energetically.	○○○○○	○○○○○
2. Probes, digs beneath the surface, tests the validity of information.		
3. Creates order out of large quantities of information.		
4. Keen observer of people, events, things.		
5. Defines problems effectively; gets to the heart of a problem.		
6. Spots problems, opportunities, threats, trends early.		
7. Logical, data-based, rational.		
Communicating Information, Ideas		
8. Adept at disseminating information to others.	○○○○○	○○○○○
9. Crisp, clear, articulate.		
10. Good public speaker; skilled at performing, being on stage.		
11. Makes his or her point effectively to a resistant audience.		
12. Strong communicator on paper; good writing skills.		
Taking Action, Making Decisions, Following Through		
13. Action-oriented; presses for immediate results.	○○○○○	○○○○○
14. Decisive; doesn't procrastinate on decisions.		
15. Troubleshooter; enjoys solving problems.		
16. Implements decisions, follows through, follows up well; an expediter.		
17. Carefully weighs consequences of contemplated action.		

Source: SkillScope®, copyright © 1997 by the Center for Creative Leadership. Reprinted with permission.

FIGURE 1.2. SAMPLE 360-DEGREE FEEDBACK REPORT.

SKILLSCOPE
for Managers
RESULTS

KEY TO SYMBOLS
- ● Strength
- ■ Development Needed
- ○ Strength ⎫
- □ Development Needed ⎬ Boss's feedback

PAT SAMPLE			
SELF	8 others		
	Strength	Development Needed	

KNOWLEDGE OF JOB, BUSINESS

SELF	Strength	Development Needed	
	●●	■■	70. Shows mastery of job content; excels at his or her function or professional specialty.
	●	□■	71. A good general manager.
■	●●	□■	72. Effective in a job with a big scope.
	○●	■■	73. In a new assignment, picks up knowledge and expertise easily; a quick study.
■		■■	74. At home with graphs, charts, statistics, budgets.
■	●	■	75. Understands cash flows, financial reports, corporate annual reports.

ENERGY, DRIVE, AMBITION

SELF	Strength	Development Needed	
●	●●●●		76. Good initiative; continually reaches for more responsibility.
●	○●●●●		77. High energy level.
●	●●●●●		78. Ambitious; highly motivated to advance his or her career.
●	○●●●●	■	79. Goal-directed, persistent; driven to achieve objectives.

TIME MANAGEMENT

SELF	Strength	Development Needed	
■	●	□■■■	80. Sets priorities well; distinguishes clearly between important and unimportant tasks.
●		□■■■■■	81. Makes the most of the time available; extremely productive.
■	●	■■■■	82. Deals with interruptions appropriately; knows when to admit interruptions and when to screen them out.
■	●	□■■■■	83. Avoids spreading self too thin.

from others that provide one source of ongoing feedback. While waiting for the elevator after a tough meeting, a manager gets a pat on the back from his colleague for handling a presentation well. The next day, someone lets him know that his reaction to a sensitive question was unnecessarily defensive. At the end of the week, one of his team members cautions him that his instructions to their assistant sounded patronizing. These small bits of data—informal feedback—float around managers all the time, largely unattended in the rush of business concerns.

Formal 360-degree feedback provides something that informal feedback seldom does: a structured means of collecting and processing data, and an opportunity to reflect on this valuable information. It may be the only time some leaders ever consciously stop to take stock of their performance effectiveness.

Second, giving feedback and receiving feedback are threatening activities for many people, and they may not think doing either is worth the risk. This is particularly true the higher up in the organization one moves (Kaplan, Drath, and Kofodimos, 1985). In the modern organization, much lip service is being paid to the need to increase communication in all directions; at the same time, many people are reluctant to give performance feedback to coworkers, especially to their superiors. When they ask themselves "What do I have to gain by telling my boss about his development needs?" they struggle for an answer.

Formal feedback, by its very nature, helps reduce the interpersonal threat of face-to-face feedback for both parties. The formalized structure and the neutral character of the instruments serve as a shield of objectivity. As one participant in a leadership development program stated: "Normally the thought of having someone give me job feedback is like going to the dentist. Even though I'm glad I did it after it's all over, I have white knuckles the whole time I'm in the chair. Using a 360-degree feedback instrument makes the process easier to take because it is broken down into specific manageable pieces. I can reflect on my data privately, and then talk with someone who knows how to help me understand it."

Why 360 Degrees? The Importance of Multiple Perspectives

There is an old saying: "If one person tells you that you remind him of a horse's backside, you can ignore him. If ten people tell you the same thing, you probably ought to go ahead and get fitted for a saddle."

There is strength in numbers. Remember that Terry Anderson opened to believing the feedback about his behavior only when he saw that everyone else agreed that he was responsible for the tension within the group.

Unanimous agreement, even if less than complimentary, would be easy to understand. Seldom is that the case. It is common for people to be perceived differently by different rater groups. This variance can cause considerable confusion for the participants, unless they are able to think through the reasons. Helping with this analysis is one of the functions of the debriefing session between participant and feedback specialist.

There are many valid reasons why feedback is not uniform (Moxley and McCauley, 1996). It may be that the participant actually behaves differently with various people. The amount of exposure that someone has with different groups also explains variations in perception. Perhaps one group has more opportunities to see the person using the behavior being rated. Also, the observers' expectations come into play. The rater groups may have differing expectations about how the participant will use the specific behavior when interacting with them, and so they have their own opinions as to whether the behavior, or its absence, is a problem. Finally, two observers can interpret the same behavior very differently. For example, a manager is blunt in his interpersonal interactions. One observer interprets the behavior as direct, efficient, and precise. Another observer sees the same behavior as abrupt or even rude.

Even though interpreting their significance sometimes takes work, obtaining multiple perspectives on performance is an improvement over the traditional assessment approach of having only the boss evaluate performance (known as the top-down approach). Multiple views of a 360-degree process are preferable because

- They reflect a more comprehensive representation of a manager's reality, in which a multiplicity of views need to be taken into account. A typical manager may supervise double or triple the number of staff members than she did ten years ago.
- They reduce the potential for bias (London and Beatty, 1993).
- The boss often does not observe the individual's behavior daily, especially if located in another building, another region, or even another country, conditions that make it very difficult to maintain an accurate ongoing assessment.
- The increase in team-based work has also dictated the need for collecting and synthesizing other team members' feedback.
- Previously untapped sources of feedback can be included. Some leaders are in a position of being judged for their effectiveness by how well they work with people outside the organization, such as customers, suppliers, or clients.

The Role of 360-Degree Feedback in the Leadership Development Process

It is a fundamental theme of this handbook that all the separate events and experiences that are part of a leadership development process are more effective if they each incorporate the three key components of assessment, challenge, and support (see the Introduction). Is this true of 360-degree feedback?

The assessment component is self-evident. It can be used to help people answer the question "How am I doing?" by providing the perspective of multiple raters. It can enhance self-awareness by providing new information about existing strengths and key developmental needs.

Using 360-degree feedback is also a source of challenge. As a *Fortune* magazine writer put it, "What your boss, your peers, and your subordinates really think of you may sting, but facing the truth can also make you a better manager" (O'Reilly, 1994, p. 93). The challenges provided by 360-degree feedback come in several forms: a new experience, comparing oneself to a model of excellence, or examining one's previous self-concept.

For some participants, a 360-degree feedback process is the first time they have seriously examined their strengths and weaknesses. This kind of introspection can challenge their comfort zone. Also, sometimes simply seeing strengths and weaknesses compared to a model of behavior is challenging: the model defines leadership and the assessment data show how the person measures up. Many 360-degree feedback instruments provide normative samples so that participants can compare their feedback to an aggregate sample of other managers—which is yet another challenging experience.

Some participants discover that their raters do not agree with their self-ratings of their strengths. This contradiction to the participants' picture of reality can provide a challenge. Feedback from the perspective of others sometimes provides the gentle nudge required to reflect on our strengths and weaknesses. Or it can provide a forceful whack necessary to get our attention and demonstrate the need for immediate behavior change, as it did for Terry Anderson. Perhaps the greatest challenge of all is answering the question, "Now that I have the data, what do I do with it?" In this sense, it serves as a valuable "unfreezing" process.

To provide optimal support (the third component) for the participant's development, various features need to be built into the feedback process:

- Maintaining the confidential nature of the feedback data
- Giving participants access to a trained feedback facilitator for clarification about the data
- Involving superiors, to gain buy-in for the participant's developmental plan
- Allowing the participant and immediate boss to meet beforehand, to discuss their goals for the process
- Offering organizational support for the kinds of assignments that are known to contribute to effective development of leaders
- Strategizing how to receive ongoing feedback
- Following up periodically on the developmental plan

We return to these features later in this chapter.

For What Purposes Do Organizations Use 360-Degree Feedback?

What are organizations trying to accomplish when they implement a formal 360-degree feedback process? As you might imagine, their goals are diverse as organizations frame and focus their efforts in different ways.

Some organizations use 360-degree feedback primarily as part of *developmental processes for individual managers and leaders.* For example, one manager was struggling with the concept of providing direction and vision for his group; he could see the value but wasn't clear how to go about it. In completing a 360-degree feedback instrument that contained the item, "Brings up ideas about the future of the organization," he realized from his raters that this was a specific behavior he was not doing well. Now he meets with his direct reports once a month, and he asks for feedback about how he is doing on this particular task.

Even when people have solid insights about their own strengths and development needs, they may not be aware of how these qualities affect their coworkers day to day. An international high-tech manufacturing organization frequently sends individual managers one at a time to a leadership development program conducted by an outside company. At this program the participants take part in an elaborate business simulation and receive feedback on their behavior from the other twenty people in the program. After the simulation, participants receive the result of their 360-degree assessment from their coworkers back home. More often than not, there is consistency of feedback from these two sources, and it is often quite surprising to the participants. They are not aware of how consistently their behaviors affect others.

The organization may focus 360-degree feedback for individual development on particular subgroups (for example, high-potential managers) or at different times in a manager's career (such as near the completion of a developmental assignment).

Organizations also use 360-degree feedback to *determine group strengths and development needs.* By compiling individual feedback results into an aggregate group profile, one large industrial construction company focuses on the issues that, as a company, they would like to maintain or develop further. The resulting information is built into every manager's development objectives for the upcoming year. Taking this example one step further, some organizations use the group data to establish needs for organizational training activities.

Some organizations use formal feedback initiatives to *broaden employee awareness of valued behaviors.* The simple process of reading and answering the specific items on the feedback instrument puts these valued dimensions out in front of people and usually triggers discussion of them. For example, a large European insurance company decided that the key to their survival was to be less bureaucratic and more entrepreneurial. They searched for and found a 360-degree feedback instrument designed to specifically measure behaviors known to exist in successful entrepreneurial environments. They are planning to implement this instrument with their senior managers.

Another example comes from deregulation of the telephone industry. One service provider decided that, as a market edge, it was going to pursue excellence in customer service. Most of the managers had been hired in the era when telephone customers did not have options and were forced to live with the service they received. This company started a major initiative that included conducting internal customer-service workshops; individual coaching; pushing decision making downward in the organization; and completing 360-degree feedback to focus on decisiveness, customer focus, and responsiveness. As a result, they were able to help the managers see where their skills did or did not match the organization's valued behaviors.

Three-hundred-sixty-degree feedback is particularly useful in supporting three types of organizational values: open communication, valuing employee input, and expectations that people should take charge of their careers. Here are some illustrations:

- A major urban hotel group wanted to encourage open communication among the owners of the company. One part of their approach was to initiate a regular 360-degree feedback process in which each of the six participants was a rater for all the others. This surfaced issues for discussion and helped establish an open-door work environment. By asking others to complete the survey, these leaders are indicating that they are amenable to performance feedback. They are, in a sense, establishing a norm for communication.

- One organization became particularly interested in using a 360-degree feedback instrument as part of its efforts to enhance employees' sense of empowerment. The process of multirater assessment is inclusive; soliciting participation from diverse rater groups indicates that the organization is interested in their perspective.

- An international consumer products company encourages its managers to actively plan their career progression from the day they are hired. The company uses 360-degree feedback to put data in the managers' hands and responsibility for career planning on their shoulders.

Administrative Versus Developmental Use

One question that frequently comes up when an organization considers using 360-degree feedback is, "Should the feedback be used only for the development of the participants receiving the feedback, or should it also be used for administrative purposes?" When feedback is used for development purposes, the data help the participants set in place a plan to increase their effectiveness in the organization. Administrative purposes include decisions about hiring, promoting, or compensating people.

The critical difference between these two approaches is ownership of the data. In assessment for administration, the participant's organization owns the data. The final assessment is shared with the participant, but it is also used by the boss, human resource representative, or others in the organization for administrative decisions. In assessment for development, the individual participants own the data. Although they may be encouraged to share some of the data and their developmental plan with the boss, the feedback report itself is confidential and for the participant. The participants alone decide if, with whom, and how they share the report data.

In our work at the Center for Creative Leadership, we use 360-degree feedback for development purposes only. There is increasing pressure in some organizations to tie assessment to administrative uses, but sufficient evidence shows that rater responses change when they know the resulting data will be made public (London, 1995). In general, raters tend to score people more leniently if they know it could affect their salary or promotion opportunities. Such data are less accurate and therefore not so helpful to people who want to make changes. Ultimately, if the participants own the data, the organization places the primary responsibility for their development squarely on them.

Because the focus of this handbook is on development of leaders, and because the Center's experience is in using 360-degree feedback for development purposes, the feedback processes and practices described in the rest of this chapter assume that the 360-degree assessment is for development.

Implementing a 360-Degree Feedback Process

To ensure that the process goes smoothly and that the participants and sponsoring organization benefit fully, follow these steps.

Step One: Choosing an Instrument

Choosing a feedback instrument involves first identifying the business purpose and the target population for the 360-degree feedback. At the most basic level, HR executives setting out to design and deliver a feedback intervention must be clear up front on these questions: Why do we need this? Who is it for? What outcomes do we expect (Dalton and Hollenbeck, 1996)? Then, when comparing instruments, certain quality standards and features should be examined.

Why Is This Needed? A common mistake that organizations make is to commit to an assessment activity of some kind without clearly defining what they hope to gain from it and without connecting it to specific business needs.

The business purpose should drive the decision about what kind of instrument to select. A manager's performance is defined within the context of a business strategy, and so should the selection of instrument. All too often one particular 360-degree feedback instrument is chosen simply because an HR executive or consultant has an affinity for it and tries to use it in all cases. They would be better off putting their energy into clear definition of the need for the assessment activity, and then finding the best instrument for that purpose. If the purpose of the feedback intervention is to focus the participants on organizational competencies, then the instrument should ask questions that connect to the particular competency model.

Who Is It For? Once the business need for the assessment has been defined, the target population should be identified. This is essential for choosing the right instrument. People at any level can benefit from 360-degree feedback, but care should be taken to ensure that the instrument is appropriate for the participants' particular situation. For example, an instrument containing many questions about managerial and supervisory skills would probably not work well with lower-level staff or individual contributors.

Managers need different kinds of feedback at different times in their careers. Early on, they might use 360-degree feedback to help define what skills are important. Later in their careers, they need to know how their strengths and weaknesses affect others, to make any changes needed. As they continue to move higher in the organization, it may be critical to use 360-degree feedback to evaluate their ability to set and implement a vision for the company's future success.

What to Look For. It is not the goal of this chapter to serve as a detailed guide to selecting from among the scores of 360-degree feedback instruments on the market. A comprehensive source for that purpose is *Choosing 360: A Guide to Evaluating Multi-Rater Feedback Instruments for Management Development* (Van Velsor, Leslie, and Fleenor, 1997). There are some basic steps, however, that can help guide the search.

The first step in narrowing your selection is to find an established tool with psychometric integrity. It should be professionally developed and adequately tested. Some estimates suggest that only one in four tools currently on the market meet this criterion (Van Velsor and Wall, 1992).

Is the instrument valid? Does it really measure what it claims to measure, and are the resulting scores empirically related to effectiveness on the job? Is the instrument reliable? Is it stable over time? Do the items within a scale measure the same construct? Is there agreement within rater groups? The vendor should be willing to answer these basic questions and provide you with this information.

Be a savvy consumer. Ask the vendor for a summary report of the research foundations for the instrument. Obtain samples of the survey and feedback report. The individual items should make sense to you, and they should reflect behaviors that are valued by the organization.

Other things to investigate include accompanying materials and vendor support. Is there a developmental planning guide to help participants sort their data and set a workable plan for change? Does the organization have adequate resources to respond to questions or problems encountered in using the instrument?

Standardized Versus Customized. Organizations have a choice of using a preexisting standardized assessment instrument developed by a vendor (sometimes called off-the-shelf) or having an instrument custom designed for their use. Unfortunately, there is no such thing as the perfect instrument, and there are advantages and disadvantages to both types.

A primary advantage to using an existing instrument is cost; it is significantly less expensive than hiring someone to design and develop an instrument, a scoring program, and supporting materials to accompany it. Also, an existing 360-degree feedback instrument can provide extensive normative data, so participants have the opportunity to compare their scores to many other managers in other organizations.

The advantage to creating a customized instrument is that the questions can be tailored to measure the specific competencies your organization considers important. At first glance, this may seem to be the best route to follow. Organizations are like families: everyone likes to think that theirs is unique—the best, or the strangest—and so no existing instrument could capture the essence of their particular situation. It is usually not difficult to identify a list of behaviors and outcomes that you could call competencies. The difficult part comes in designing the survey, scoring program, and supporting materials that are needed.

More important than the logistical challenge of creating a customized instrument is carrying out the validity and reliability studies to be sure that the instrument is psychometrically sound. Some organizations do not care if the instrument does not meet these standards and therefore never conduct these studies. This is extremely shortsighted. If you are asking participants to be open to the feedback and to make changes in their behaviors based on the results, you are well advised to make sure the results are valid.

A third approach is to customize an existing instrument. This allows you to tailor the content and length of the instrument, selecting competencies from existing individual development instruments and combining them to create an instrument that closely reflects the competencies of interest to the organization. One advantage to this approach is that it ensures the organization of valid and reliable questionnaire items.

In the end, many organizations realize that there are good standardized instruments in existence that already measure the majority of competencies or behaviors that they have identified as important; they conclude that the logistical and cost factors involved with customizing an assessment are not worth it. With the number of 360-degree feedback instruments available, most organizations should be able to find a good tool that matches the business need and works for the particular population being assessed.

Step Two: Collecting the Data

Once an organization selects the best instrument for its use, it must provide the proper structure to help the participants collect the best data possible.

Rater Selection. The participant typically collects feedback from the boss, peers, and direct reports. The instrument vendor usually suggests the optimal number of raters for each group; a typical distribution is one boss, five peers, and five direct reports. The most accurate responses come from raters who have had a chance to observe the manager using a wide variety of behaviors over time. Therefore it is most beneficial for the participants to select raters who know them well and know their work.

Some organizations prefer to control distribution of surveys by selecting the raters for the participant. However, this could deter buy-in by the participant being assessed. A better approach is to let the participant select the raters.

Rater Anonymity. The sensitive nature of personal feedback data requires that care be taken to protect the privacy of the raters. If the raters suspect that their feedback is not anonymous, they may be reluctant to participate in the process, or may answer the questions more favorably than they would if their responses were protected.

Questionnaires should be constructed so that participants have no way to tell who said what on their report. This is typically done by requiring a minimum of three respondents in each rater category. If three or more people from within the same category return surveys, their answers are combined and presented as an aggregate score. If fewer than three people in one category return surveys, then the participant's report does not include item-level feedback in that category. A common exception is with the boss's feedback. This data is frequently identified separately. In this case the materials should give the boss clear notice that her responses are not anonymous.

Some instruments provide a way for raters to add written comments, expanding their feedback to include data that the instrument does not capture. Having these broader, deeper impressions is obviously an advantage, but it comes with a clear disadvantage: loss of anonymity. The participant may be able to identify the rater's handwriting or communicative style. Thus, simply requiring the raters to type their comments offers only a partial shield, as how people express themselves can sometimes identify them as well. Comments reported verbatim make it harder to protect anonymity.

The other downside to using literal comments is the problem known as "verbatim bias." We have noticed that participants give more attention to written comments than numerical or graphical scores. No matter what their scores on the standardized part of the assessment, people tend to focus on and remember the written comments more. As a result, verbatim comments that are inconsistent with the numeric results can unfairly bias the feedback. Feedback facilitators need to help participants put these comments in perspective.

Data Confidentiality. The data collected through feedback instruments belong to the individual participants; they should never be viewed by anyone else without the participant's consent. Breaches of confidentiality and rater anonymity, even if accidental, can jeopardize the feedback process, compromise the integrity of the human resource group, and lead to lack of trust within the organization for any subsequent assessment activities. Take the utmost care throughout the entire feedback process to protect these data.

Preparation for Participants. Every person involved in the assessment and feedback process should be adequately prepared for their role. The purpose for the activity and the expected outcomes should be explained fully, and it should be made clear how the feedback will be used. One regional electric utility holds a half-day session to kick off the assessment phase of the development program for upper managers. The people who are to receive feedback, their bosses, and their raters attend this session together. The president of the company introduces the background and goal of the overall program. The senior HR executive then introduces the 360-degree feedback instrument and discusses its purpose. Raters are given instructions to reduce rating errors, and all materials are distributed on the spot. The bosses or coaches of the participants attend an additional afternoon session that helps them understand how to best support the developmental planning process.

Step Three: Feeding Back the Data

How the feedback is delivered varies depending on the type of instrument being used and the organization's plan for its implementation. The three most common approaches are with a one-on-one session, a group session, or a combination of the two.

In the one-on-one approach, a participant has an individual session with a facilitator that includes an introduction to the background of the instrument, an interpretive session about the participant's data, and further assistance with developmental planning. All of this could, in some cases, be done in one day, depending on the complexity of the instrument and the depth of the developmental planning activities.

The second approach involves participants' going through the feedback experience at the same time in a group setting. They receive the introduction to the instrument, their individual feedback data, and the development planning activities all at once. This is less staff-intensive and affords the opportunity to use small-group activities when appropriate to enhance learning. The disadvantage is that the participants do not have an opportunity to speak privately with a facilitator to discuss their data.

Combining some group sessions and some one-on-one sessions often provides optimal outcomes. In this scenario, the presentations are made once in a group setting but the individuals meet one-on-one with a facilitator to discuss their personal data privately.

Group Feedback Sessions. A group feedback session is most often intended to adequately prepare participants to receive and understand their individual feedback. Here is a basic outline of steps to follow:

1. Clarify purpose, goals, and expectations of the feedback process.
2. Discuss the research that supports the 360-degree feedback instrument being used.
3. Provide a context for receiving feedback, including these points:

> First, feedback is data, and the data are neutral. Data cannot make decisions about you. You make decisions about the data.

This is just one snapshot of you. It does not define you as a person. It is important that you put this snapshot alongside others to see what overarching patterns emerge.

People often make one of two common mistakes when they receive 360-degree feedback: they accept the information too quickly, or they reject it too quickly. Consider it; think it over.

You are the expert about you. You know who filled out the questionnaires, you know your work situation. The facilitator will help you understand the data, but you must decide what they mean.

4. Explain how to read and interpret the report.
5. Allow time for individual reflection on the data, and for Q&A.
6. Introduce any data-sorting exercises included with the materials.
7. Explain the logistics of the one-on-one sessions, if they are scheduled.

It is important to treat the group feedback session seriously. People invest much time and emotion into this process of self-discovery. On the other hand, we have found that after the participants have an opportunity to see their feedback and understand the report format, a light touch can be appreciated. After they receive their scores, participants might enjoy the humor in the list of the "Top Ten Reasons for Rejecting Your 360-Degree Feedback."

Top Ten Reasons for Rejecting Your 360-Degree Feedback.

10. My job makes me act that way; I'm not really like that.
9. This was just a bad time to ask for feedback.
8. All my strengths are right, but my weaknesses are not.
7. Everyone has it in for me.
6. I used to be that way, but I've changed recently.
5. Nobody understands what I'm going through.
4. This must be someone else's report.
3. My raters did not understand the questions.
2. They're all jealous of my success.
1. It's all accurate, but I just don't care.

One-On-One Feedback Sessions. As a condition of sale of the instrument, some vendors require a one-on-one feedback session. Even instruments that are fairly simple and straightforward are enhanced by a private consultation with a facilitator who has experience using the tool. This is particularly true for participants receiving 360-degree feedback for the first time. They typically appreciate the opportunity to open up and discuss their feedback, whether good or bad news, with a dispassionate third party.

The feedback facilitator should have experience with the particular instrument being used; some vendors require they be certified in its use. Ideally the facilitator is outside the participant's chain of command or influence. One large pharmaceutical firm maintains a pool of eight independent consultants to deliver instrument feedback as part of its leadership development program for middle managers. The company finds that this gives the process additional credibility since the organization is investing in these "experts." It reinforces the confidential nature of the data since no company employees (even those in HR) see the participant's report. The organization also benefits from using the same consultants, since they become familiar with the issues and goals of the organization.

It is helpful if the participants have ample time to analyze their data before the one-on-one session. For the sake of efficiency, it is tempting to hand participants their report, give them a few minutes to digest the data, and then shuttle them off to the one-on-one session. When this happens, participants arrive for the feedback session still trying to understand what the numbers, graphs, or tables mean. With no time to reflect on the feedback, they may not yet be ready to consider the full implication of the data.

If some of the feedback is negative or surprising to the participants, it is likely that when they begin the one-on-one session they are still dealing with their emotional reaction to the data or to the raters. It is difficult for the feedback facilitator to move things beyond the emotions, to do the needed analysis of data. It is better to give participants an overnight break between receiving the feedback and having the one-on-one session. If they have a chance to sleep on the data, they usually understand it better, have time to deal with their immediate emotional reactions, and are fresher for the meeting.

On the other hand, feedback data does have a shelf life. Ideally, the one-on-one session should occur within one to four days of receiving the data.

The one-on-one session should take place in a private office or breakout room. The facilitator prepares for the session in advance by reading the person's report thoroughly and making notes. A good feedback facilitator tries to understand not only the data but also the context for the particular person. This is best understood by asking the participant a few short questions at the beginning of the session:

- "How do you want to use the data?" The person who is seeking a promotion to the next level in the organization has an entirely different framework for feedback than does a person who is happy in her current role and wants to enhance her working relationship with her direct reports.
- "What is happening in your present job situation?" There may be something unusual going on within the company that is having an impact on the person's feedback.
- "Were you surprised by any of your feedback? disappointed? pleased?" Sometimes this question alone is enough to get people talking about their reactions to the data.
- "What overarching themes do you see emerging from your data?" Perhaps the most valuable thing experienced feedback facilitators can do is help participants make connections in the data that they do not initially see.
- "How would you summarize your data? What are the key strengths? What are the key development areas?" Helping the participant summarize and focus the data is critical. The session should progress from the global to the most specific.
- "What changes are you motivated to make right now? in the future?" The most critical decision the participant makes about the data is choosing the areas on which to focus and work.

Feedback facilitators should use their expertise about the instrument, but they should resist the temptation to act as an expert on any particular participant's data. The participants are (and must be) the experts, deciding for themselves what to pay attention to and how to make meaning of the feedback. The facilitators are commonly asked, "What do you think my raters meant by this response?" Although they can make an educated guess, they really have no way to know the answer to that question. Effective feedback facilitators consider themselves tour guides to the data, asking helpful questions and helping the participants see connections among their data across the instrument.

Feedback facilitators should consider giving the participants the option to make an audiotape of the session so that they can fully engage with the feedback facilitator rather than writing notes. This also serves as a useful tool when reviewing progress against their developmental plan in the future.

Are Importance Ratings Important? Many 360-degree feedback instruments ask the raters to identify a limited number of competencies that are particularly important for success in the participant's position or organization. The data are tabulated and presented in the feedback report. The participants can then compare their perceptions of what is important to the perceptions of their raters and use those similarities and discrepancies to prioritize development goals.

These importance ratings are typically very well received by the participants. It gives them a way to focus on whatever feedback appears to be most important. For example, Joe received negative feedback from his raters on the dimension that measures managing relationships. However, out of eight raters, none indicated that "managing relationships" was one of the top five, most important competencies. As a result, Joe ignored this feedback and concentrated on other areas for improvement.

The problem is that the accuracy of importance ratings has not been established on most 360-degree feedback instruments. Even for some instruments that contain sound psychometric properties for items and dimensions, the importance ratings have not been subjected to the same scrutiny. Therefore it would be prudent for Joe's feedback facilitator to encourage him not to completely discount his relationship feedback. It could be that every single rater thought that there were six critical dimensions for Joe's job, but the limitations of the instrument forced them to pick five. If that sixth most important item in Joe's case is managing relationships, then he has missed a major part of his feedback. It could be that Joe's raters do not know what is really important for success in his job, either because they do not know his job well or because they are mistaken about the real selection criteria used within their company.

Self-Rater Agreement. Participants tend to pay close attention to the degree to which their own ratings of their performance agree with the ratings from others. In general, there tends to be closer agreement between peers and supervisors than with either self-and-peer or self-and-supervisor (Harris and Schaubroeck, 1988). This would suggest that self-perception of strengths and weaknesses is more out of alignment than the collective perceptions among raters. Does that matter? Besides, who is right?

It can matter a great deal. In their study on executive derailment, McCall and Lombardo (1983) found that when many executives derailed, it was because they had blind spots. They were unaware of or ignored the fatal flaws that had led to termination or missed promotions. Using a sound 360-degree feedback instrument can be a first step in reducing or eliminating these blind spots.

As to who is right, people need to consider whether a discrepancy represents inaccuracy on their part or merely a difference of opinion. Campbell and Nilsen (1993) suggest that when it comes to predicting job performance, the other raters are more accurate than the individual participant's own assessment. Others suggest that although other's ratings may be more *valid* under certain circumstances, they should not be presumed to be more *accurate* (Dunnette, 1993).

Also, does a discrepancy mean a person is unaware of strengths and weaknesses? Fleenor, McCauley, and Brutus (1996) believe that self-and-other discrepancy does not necessarily represent low awareness. Their findings suggest that it could be a reflection of either arrogance (on the part of those who rate themselves higher than others rate them) or modesty (by those who rate themselves lower than others do). That is, overraters or underraters may understand how they are perceived by others but choose not to believe it.

For the participant trying to understand the feedback contained in a 360-degree feedback report, the best approach is to consider that all perspectives are accurate. Even though a divergence of opinion might make the feedback harder to interpret, it does represent the real environment within which people must do their work. One implication for the feedback facilitator is that it is important to hear the participant's reaction to any self-and-rater disagreement on the report, and to use that response to frame a context for the feedback.

Step Four: Creating a Development Plan

A 360-degree feedback process should yield a development plan. Quality developmental planning is more than just an exercise in goal setting. It is a thorough blueprint for achieving and sustaining behavior change by using a variety of strategies proven to enhance learning. Using the feedback collected from a sound 360-degree feedback instrument, a person can choose from several approaches to selecting a theme on which to focus:

- Identify a development need and improve upon it. This is the most obvious strategy for most people and the one most commonly engaged.
- Identify a strength and capitalize on it. This means participants take something they do well and are more visible in their approach to it. They may teach it to someone else or, when appropriate, do it more often.
- Identify a development need and transform it to a midrange skill. Rather than trying to turn weaknesses into strengths, perhaps they only need to tweak a certain issue a bit.
- Compensate for a weakness by owning it and adopting strategies to work around it. Use a strength to tackle a weakness.

- Address lack of experience in an area by seeking out new opportunities. It could be time to gain experience in an area they have spent an entire career avoiding.

Deciding which goals to work on can be difficult. Once participants have considered the approaches listed above and identified a developmental goal, they should ask themselves three questions about their goals:

1. Does the goal motivate and energize me?
2. Will achieving this goal help me be more effective in my current position?
3. Will my organization benefit from this goal?

If the answer to any of the three questions is *no*, then the individual may not be focusing on the right goal.

Once an appropriate goal has been identified, the individual should use a variety of strategies to achieve the goal. For example, those of us who have been responsible for leading a workshop or facilitating a feedback session have all had this experience: an eager participant, sincerely motivated to make behavioral changes as a result of a formal feedback event, sets out to plan for personal change. The first question he asks is, "Can you recommend a good book (or workshop) on this subject?" By using this approach only, the individual is closing himself off to the richest developmental activities at his disposal. One study indicates that reading and classes account for only 6 percent of the events that teach the key managerial lessons (McCall, Lombardo, and Morrison, 1988). It would be much more effective to set a developmental strategy that takes into account a broad variety of experiences:

- New job assignments. When practical, new jobs with different duties—starting something from scratch, fixing something gone wrong, moving from a line to a staff job, or accepting a broad change in scope and scale of responsibilities—can teach a wide variety of important lessons. (See Chapter Four for more on job assignments.)

• Existing jobs. There may be tremendous potential for development in someone's present job. By becoming aware of the challenges in their current role, and how these challenges can teach critical lessons, people are in a better position to capitalize on them and address developmental needs quickly.

• Ongoing feedback. A critical component of any developmental plan is to build in progress checks. This feedback may be formal or informal, but the plan should provide for collecting it regularly.

• Role models and coaches. The best free developmental opportunity most people have is the opportunity to watch someone else do something well. For example, if a person decides to work on delegating more effectively, she should identify someone she knows who does it well. Then she should go out of her way to observe that person in action and try to discover what makes him effective. It would also help to engage that person in ongoing conversations about this subject. (See Chapter Five for more on developmental relationships.)

• Training and reading. Although this constitutes a small part of the sum total of developmental learning, it is an important one. Depending on the individual's approach to learning, this tactic might work well. (See Chapter Three for more on skill-based training.)

Enhancing the Success of a Formal Feedback Initiative

Savvy HR executives understand that a 360-degree feedback activity is not a stand-alone event. The feedback by itself probably does not have a long-lasting effect or lead to behavioral change. In fact, providing assessment without developmental planning and follow-up almost guarantees that the organization does not get its money's worth. As one senior manager from a large bank stated, "We have access to some of the best 360-degree feedback instruments on the market through our human resources office. The problem is, nothing happens afterward. You are on your own to try to guess how best to carry on. Your boss may even hold you back. We even have a name for it; we call it 'drive-by assessment.'"

The way for an organization to realize a return on the money and effort invested in a 360-degree feedback instrument is to make the feedback event part of a larger, ongoing developmental process that is tightly connected to a clear business need within the organization.

Getting the Boss's Support

At a minimum, participants should solicit the buy-in and support of their bosses, or as an alternative an executive coach. Managers who have bosses that support these changes are more likely to achieve the changes in the end (Hazucha, Hezlett, and Schneider, 1993).

An international pet foods company follows a simple model of boss-participant meetings that work well for this purpose.

Meeting One. Before completing the assessment forms, the participant meets with the boss or coach to

- Discuss how the participant plans to use the information collected by the assessment (for example, to get a promotion, to work more effectively with subordinates, to identify the next logical job challenge)
- Set a date for the next meeting, to take place after the participant receives the feedback report and has a one-on-one consultation with a feedback facilitator

Meeting Two. After the participant receives feedback and has had an opportunity to identify developmental goals, the participant meets with the boss or coach to

- Gain any clarification needed (in a nondefensive manner) from the boss about specific questions regarding the boss's feedback. This would apply only when the 360-degree feedback instrument has the boss's scores broken out separately.

- Share with the boss the developmental goals the participant chooses, to elicit buy-in and support of the effort.
- Set a date and time for the next meeting (should be approximately six months later).

Meeting Three. The participant and boss meet after six months to

- Discuss the progress made toward the developmental goals. The goals can be refined or redirected by the participant if necessary.
- Set a date and time for another progress check in six months.

Issues of Sequence and Timing

If the assessment process is to be spread across different levels of the organization, it can be difficult to decide where to start. The recommended approach is to start at a high level in the organization and then move downward.

One medium-sized security equipment manufacturer has had success using this "cascading" approach. The company identified a need to become more action-oriented and decisive. They hoped that having a more entrepreneurial approach to their work would result in shorter delivery cycles. Every individual in the organization was required to participate in a 360-degree assessment process that measured these and other behaviors. This initiative was set in a sixteen-month developmental process within the organization. The president of the company and three vice presidents were the first to complete the assessment and receive feedback. The activity was then delivered to the directors and so on down through the company, until all 250 employees were included.

The organization reported that using this particular approach had at least two clear benefits. First, starting with the top executives demonstrated their buy-in to the process and modeled openness to feedback. The second benefit was that all employees had the opportunity to complete the survey as a rater for someone else before having the assessment done to them. This helped them become familiar with the kinds of questions being asked, helped to demystify the process in general, and allowed them to start the process from the perspective of a rater. This, in turn, helped them not to dismiss other raters' data on them.

Another issue is timing. When is the best time for people to receive feedback? When are they most open to hearing feedback and motivated to make behavioral changes? From our experience, a person in the midst of a career transition such as a significant increase in the scope and scale of the job is usually more motivated to consider 360-degree feedback than someone who is continuing with business as usual. People who sense a need to break out of a rut are often particularly open to performance feedback if they think it will help them make a transition. Finally, people who are being sent messages from the organization that they must change or face derailment may be the most motivated of all.

Best Practices in 360-Degree Feedback Processes

The Center for Creative Leadership's experience in working with organizations as they implement 360-degree feedback processes has yielded the following best practices (Dalton and Hollenbeck, 1997):

- Communicate your purpose. All participants, raters, and supervisors involved should know the purpose of the 360-degree assessment, their role, and the purpose of the developmental program. Some organizations feature the activity in a newsletter.
- Prepare the participants. Orientation to the instrument as well as rater training should be planned in advance.
- Make top management visible players. Many companies have senior executives get feedback first, to model openness to the process.
- Tie feedback data to a larger program. Be clear about how this specific assessment activity fits in to the business need and the overall development plan.
- Clarify ownership of data. Clearly state who owns the feedback data.
- Insist upon integrity. This effort should be the best work the organization is capable of. It is crucial to maintain the integrity of the process through confidential handling of sensitive material.
- Commit to 100 percent accuracy. Implement administrative checklists to ensure that all raters have the correct materials and know how and when to return them.

- Make administration "ASAP" and user-friendly. Find ways to make it simple for people to participate. Plan ahead, give lead time, and use postage-paid return envelopes.
- Provide a safety net. Make sure that there is always a human contact for everyone involved, both raters and participants. Always build time into feedback programs for individual consultation should someone have a strong emotional reaction to the feedback.
- Check the timing. Be sensitive to what else is going on in the organization. Midway through a downsizing is probably not the best time to conduct this activity. Also avoid heavy vacation periods.
- Provide confidentiality and anonymity. A process that permits direct return to the scoring organization gives a greater perception of rater anonymity. Confidentiality of results should be clarified before planning the event.
- Have a sunset clause on data. What is the shelf life of an individual's report data? This varies from person to person, but a reasonable rule of thumb is to not use data that were collected more than a month before.
- Anticipate what will go wrong. Plan for unexpected events such as facilitators becoming ill (have backup facilitators ready), snags in mailing systems, program materials being held up in customs, etc.
- Start small. An organization's first 360-degree intervention should start with a small pilot group, to work out the systems before rolling out a large initiative.
- Integrate with other interventions. Be sensitive to other ongoing activities within the organization that might get in the way of successful implementation. Are there other survey-intensive activities occurring at the same time?

Pitfalls and How to Avoid Them

Just as we have been able to identify best practices, we have noted common pitfalls encountered in creating 360-degree feedback processes.

Not Getting Your Money's Worth. Like most organizational initiatives, purchasing a 360-degree feedback instrument has to get past the accountants. We believe that 360-degree assessment is a cost-effective way for managers to enhance their development. However, at $50–300 per person, organizations must be able to show positive results from this investment. The best way to do this is to plan carefully in advance before purchasing a 360-degree feedback instrument. Make sure the process reflects a specific business issue that the organization is trying to address. For example, if the business purpose is to create more productive work groups, how will success of the feedback process be measured? Is success seen in terms of reduction in the turnover rate, increased customer satisfaction, fewer product defects, or faster service delivery?

Compromised Anonymity or Confidentiality. Quality implementation requires absolute anonymity of raters, so that people feel free to answer the questions honestly without fear of retribution by the participant. The integrity of the instrument and the feedback process also depend upon complete confidentiality of the participant's feedback report data. The sponsoring organization should make the survey return process a secure one. The finished feedback reports should be held completely confidential. The only copies should be seen by the participant and the feedback facilitator. At the end of the feedback session, the facilitator should return to the participant any copies of the report the facilitator used to prepare for the session.

Survey Fatigue. The increased popularity of 360-degree feedback means larger workloads for those completing the assessment forms. This is particularly an issue with intact work groups. In some cases the boss is completing surveys for each person in her group. At twenty to fifty minutes for each form, this can become an overwhelming time commitment. It could also lead to the boss's answering the survey questions as a comparison between participants. The best way to avoid this problem is to allow the boss as much lead time as possible to spread the task out over time, and to inform the boss in advance of how long it takes to complete one survey.

Botched Logistics. Distribution and collection of instructions, surveys, feedback reports, and other supporting materials must go smoothly and on schedule to support the integrity of the assessment process. A group of twenty participants typically has anywhere from six to twelve raters filling out forms, for a total of 120–240 surveys in circulation at one time. HR executives should identify the kind of internal administrative tasks that arise with such an undertaking and assign specific responsibility for those tasks. The instrument vendor should be able to help you understand and plan for this part of the process.

Missed Deadlines. In order to protect the confidentiality of the raters, most 360-degree feedback instruments require that a certain minimum number of instruments (typically three) be returned from each rater group. It is important, therefore, for each rater to complete a survey and return it on time. Announce the schedule with deadlines well in advance. Use e-mail or telephone reminders to contact any nonrespondents as the deadline date approaches.

Bruised Feelings. It is possible that participants could feel hurt by or resent the negative feedback they receive from coworkers, which leads to tension between them after the assessment process is finished. This risk is reduced by using a sound 360-degree process with experienced feedback facilitators, and by conducting participant and rater training before the event.

Nothing Changed; Now What? Using 360-degree feedback is likely to establish expectations among the raters that people's behavior will change just by virtue of having received the feedback. Ultimately it is up to the participants (sometimes in collaboration with the boss or coach) to determine what, if any, behaviors to change. The raters may not notice that the participant is working on new skills, or they may wish the participant had selected different developmental objectives.

The Future of 360-Degree Feedback

There are several interesting innovations being pursued in the use of 360-degree feedback instruments. Two in particular bear mention: increased interest in measuring a person's ability to learn from experience, and use of automated data-collection and feedback processes.

Assessing the Ability to Learn. To this point, we have been addressing 360-degree feedback instruments as they apply to measuring the knowledge and skills necessary for effective leadership behavior. Awareness of these "end state" skills is critical for an individual leader's effectiveness, yet they are limited because they place the focus of feedback on past successes rather than on future challenges (McCall, 1997). As the work environment changes rapidly, these end-state measurement techniques—even though they address the organization's list of expected competencies—ignore the need to measure an individual's ability to learn from experiences that can teach invaluable lessons.

Bartlett and Ghoshal (1997) describe the phenomenon of identifying and developing executives by using only end-state assessments as the "Russian doll" theory of management development. In this classic toy, a series of dolls, each smaller than the one before, are nested within each other. By opening up the largest doll and progressing through the smaller dolls inside, one notices that they are painted to look exactly alike. The smallest doll is an exact copy of the largest, differing only in size. In this analogy, the largest doll represents a mature, experienced leader in the organization. By using only end-state competency assessments, organizations are looking for future leaders who are exactly like (that is, have the same skills and experiences as) the largest doll, the senior manager. The risk is that the organization identifies and develops leaders based on a model of past success rather than on the future challenges likely to face executives.

Organizations benefit from using both end-state assessments and those that help the participants understand their approach to learning. Take the example of a large U.S.-based multinational oil company. The company's leaders were interested in helping a group of promising executives better understand their current performance and enhance their value to the organization for future career postings. Many of these executives were originally hired as engineers or physical scientists, and all had moved up through the company and were considered high-potential. In addition to generating assessment data to help the executives see how they were doing at the time, the organization wanted these participants to understand more about their learning styles. The company was particularly interested in having them depend more on their leadership and influencing skills rather than their original scientific training.

The company chose to use two assessment instruments. One was a popular 360-degree tool designed to help the participants get feedback on skills and perspectives needed to be effective in their current roles. The second was a newer instrument designed to help the participants understand their ability to learn from experience. The feedback facilitators used the first to identify important issues for the participant and then used the learning instrument as a lens through which to view the feedback from the first. For example, one participant received clear feedback that his coworkers perceived him as unapproachable. Overall he was surprised by the areas in which he received negative feedback. When he looked at his data from the learning instrument, he realized that he was not putting himself in situations that provided opportunities for the kind of day-to-day informal feedback that is critical to a manager's job. This was not an aspect measured by the general 360-degree feedback instrument. In combination, the two instruments gave participants a comprehensive array of information.

Automating the Data-Collection Process. One drawback to easy implementation of a 360-degree feedback instrument is the amount of paper distribution and tracking that is involved. This is particularly difficult with global organizations, with participants and raters located all over the world. Diverse mail systems, languages, and time zones make paper-and-pencil instruments even more difficult to track. Some vendors make their instruments available through various electronic platforms, such as telephone keypad response, e-mail response, disk-based surveys, network-based surveys, intranet-based surveys, and Internet-based surveys.

Each approach has its upside and downside. Telephone systems use existing hardware (everyone has a telephone) but are tedious and time-consuming. E-mail systems are becoming more widespread as e-mail becomes more available, but these surveys are difficult to score (and, ironically, are sometimes even printed and hand-entered at the scoring site). Disk-based systems simply replace paper shuffling with disk shuffling. They also introduce the need for virus checking at each stop along the feedback collection route. Network-based assessment systems are generally user-friendly and easily scored, since the system lives on the client's computer system, but they need regular maintenance and can be difficult to change. Intranet systems work much like network systems, since they also live on the client's computer system, but they limit the rater pool to those who work for the client organization.

Internet-based systems show the strongest potential so far, since they can be easily scored and the system can live anywhere. One drawback is that until the Internet is seen as a safe method of transferring sensitive data (as with credit card numbers, so too with someone's perceptions about the boss's performance) some raters may not be comfortable using the technology for this purpose. The best candidates for using automated 360-degree feedback instruments are organizations that already use the Internet to maintain internal secure information.

Summary

There are many reasons for using a sound 360-degree feedback instrument as part of an organization's leadership development efforts. Feedback from such an instrument provides people with formal assessment data from multiple perspectives and challenges them to set developmental goals. Given an organizational context that supports efforts to work toward those goals, the outcomes include increased bench strength in the organization and increased effectiveness in leadership roles. Organizations enjoy better results if the feedback is embedded in a longer-term developmental process. By using the information presented in this chapter, organizations can enhance the benefits of using 360-degree feedback instruments and avoid many of the common problems.

CHAPTER TWO

FEEDBACK-INTENSIVE PROGRAMS

Victoria A. Guthrie
Lily Kelly-Radford

The idea for a feedback-intensive program started (at CCL) with Senior Fellow Robert C. Dorn, who had a vision for a program in which assessment-center-type data would be fed back to participants in a safe, supportive environment for developmental purposes. In his words, "In a feedback-intensive program, development means helping a person to see more clearly significant patterns of behavior, to understand more clearly the attitudes and motivations underlying these patterns, to reassess what makes the person more or less effective relative to the goals he or she wants to attain, and to evaluate alternative ways of meeting these goals." Our Leadership Development Program was the first realization of his vision.

When people think of leadership development, they often think of a program: a structured experience, usually offered at a site away from the workplace, as brief as one day or consisting of two or more sessions over a period of several months. At CCL we have developed a kind of leadership development program, which we refer to as *feedback-intensive*, that in its almost thirty years of operation has been generally acknowledged as very effective.

In this chapter we describe the basic elements of a feedback-intensive program (an FIP) and how they relate to a leadership development process. We also differentiate the defining features and purposes of a feedback-intensive program from those of 360-degree instrument feedback, as well as those of skill-based training programs. Throughout this chapter, we make use of the tripartite notion of assessment, challenge, and support presented in the Introduction.

Our hope is that by acquainting people with the mechanisms and underlying principles of this particular type of program we help them better understand (1) how a feedback-intensive program works and (2) when and how to use one for leadership development. This should make it possible for people to get the most benefit from this type of experience and should provide some essential knowledge for those organizations wanting to design and conduct their own programs.

Feedback-intensive programs are powerful because they combine and balance the three key elements of assessment, challenge, and support. Typically, a feedback-intensive program is a classroom-based experience that takes place away from work. Throughout the program, assessment and feedback are almost constant, immersing participants in rich data about themselves and their interactions with others.

The amount and intensity of feedback, in turn, creates intense challenges: the need to look inward, the discomfort of being rated while engaging in new and demanding tasks, and encounters with different ideas and perspectives.

To help participants cope with these challenges, the program provides intensive support from both the program staff and other participants. The climate in the classroom is relationship-based; over the course of the program, the group becomes a community of learners who grow to trust each other.

By design, challenge and support work hand in hand in an FIP. While on the one hand the elements of challenge encourage participants to call into question their current frameworks, at the same time the elements of support facilitate understanding and build self-confidence.

What Is a Feedback-Intensive Program?

The kind of program we call *feedback-intensive* is intensive in both depth and breadth. Feedback is rich, deep, and comprehensive; it comes from many sources and reflects many attributes. Assessment and feedback focus not only on skills and behaviors but also on underlying values and personality-based preferences. The models and content presented in the program challenge participants to focus on behaviors and perspectives that enhance leadership effectiveness and life satisfaction.

The process of providing a rich and intense feedback experience is grounded in our understanding that people approach leadership with frameworks built on their past experience, their values, and personality-based needs and preferences. Over time, people tend to develop skills in areas that are comfortable for them. Later, as people are rewarded for what they do well, they naturally tend to rely on those strengths. Yet we know that new challenges often demand new approaches. As situations change, strengths can be overused and new development needs can surface. To maintain effectiveness as a leader, an individual must maintain active awareness of current strengths and development needs, including understanding how these are perceived by others. The many tools employed in a feedback-intensive program measure needs, preferences, values, skills, and behaviors from the perspective of many different audiences, all with a dual purpose: to enhance self-awareness, and to begin to think clearly about planning change (see "Defining Features of a Feedback-Intensive Program").

Defining Features of a Feedback-Intensive Program.

- The program is a classroom-based educational experience.
- The program typically takes place away from work.
- Feedback is intense and comprehensive:

    Comes from multiple perspectives

    Uses various instruments and experiences

- Feedback has depth:

  Goes beyond skills and behaviors to values and preferences

  Integrates surface behaviors with underlying personality aspects
- Feedback is constant throughout the program.
- The program provides concepts and models for reflecting on various aspects of leadership.
- The climate is relationship-based and support-intensive.

To summarize, this is what a feedback-intensive program is: an intensive and comprehensive look at an individual's leadership, using many lenses to view many aspects. And this is what it is not: it is not the same as 360-degree feedback; it is also not the same as skill-based training.

FIP Is Not 360-Degree Feedback

In recent years, a specific type of feedback experience known as multi-rater, or 360-degree, feedback has received a great deal of attention in the field of human resource development. Because they are a relatively quick and easy method of providing managers with information on current leadership strengths and development needs, 360-degree feedback instruments have become quite popular. In fact, they are typically used as one critical piece in a feedback-intensive program.

Although a key benefit of both an FIP and use of 360-degree instruments is enhanced self-awareness, the feedback experience in an FIP is both quantitatively and qualitatively different from the experience of using a 360-degree instrument alone. The essential distinction is this: 360-degree feedback presents a person with a full picture of strengths and weaknesses in several work-related dimensions; we say the picture is "full" because it represents the opinions of many (coworkers, direct reports, and the boss, as well as the participant). All these opinions, taken together, describe the individual's leadership skills and behaviors today. By looking deeper into personality, a feedback-intensive program helps the person understand not only their leadership skills and behaviors but also their needs, preferences, and values. For example, although

360-degree feedback might reveal the *fact* that a person is not strong in teamwork, FIP feedback employs many kinds of measures and looks at many aspects of that person to explain *why* that is so (perhaps the person doesn't need to feel included in things, or believes that people should be acknowledged for their individual accomplishments, or has long been successful in independent ventures).

At CCL, we often use analogies of mirrors or snapshots to describe an FIP experience. The analogies also illustrate the difference between using a single 360-degree instrument and an FIP. That is, feedback from a 360-degree instrument is like seeing yourself in a single mirror or in a single snapshot. You see, in other words, one dimension of yourself: the skill or behavioral dimension of who you are as a leader. Feedback in an FIP is like using multiple mirrors or taking snapshots from various angles, each of which shows you a separate, but related aspect of yourself (for example, personality-based preferences, behaviors, values, and skills). In addition, an FIP provides various mechanisms, to be described later in this chapter, that facilitate integration of these various views.

FIP Is Not Skills Training

There is a fairly common misconception that people who go through a feedback-intensive program do so primarily to gain new leadership skills—for example, to become better at listening, conflict resolution, or delegation—and to gain these skills on the spot. Although it is true that participants often *do* become better at using those skills because of new insights gained during the program, this is not the main purpose of an FIP.

Such skills as listening or conflict resolution are valuable, and certainly no one would suggest that an FIP ignore opportunities to focus on skills. But it is important to understand that if the goal is to practice and hone new skills, then the appropriate avenue is a skill-based training program (described in Chapter Three) rather than a feedback-intensive program.

Why Use a Feedback-Intensive Program?

The practical challenge for HR practitioners is to know when a feedback-intensive program is the appropriate course of action. We have, unfortunately, no formula to answer this question, but there are certain guidelines.

Our research shows that a feedback-intensive program is particularly useful for people who have recently taken on management responsibilities, have had a significant change in the scope of their responsibilities, or are facing significantly different job or personal demands because of other organizational (or life) changes (Van Velsor and Musselwhite, 1986). In general terms, three circumstances appear to call for a feedback-intensive program:

1. A time of career transition, either to a new organization or to new responsibilities in the present job. Integrating feedback from many sources can help a manager recognize that new challenges require additional skills and new behaviors.
2. In developing the careers of people identified as high-potential. Organizations often feel that full and complete assessment of the strengths and weaknesses of their future leaders is a valid investment.
3. When someone shows signs of potential derailment. Being passed over for promotion, faltering in performance in normally strong areas, and interpersonal difficulties are all signs pointing to a need to take stock, with the sort of comprehensive assessment that a feedback-intensive program provides.

In addition to the very real constraints of budget, you would recommend an FIP only after looking at the totality of a situation. What are the new role demands? How central is the person's role in the organization? How severe is the difficulty? How significant is the future potential?

How Does a Feedback-Intensive Program Work?

In broad terms, a feedback-intensive program has three phases: (1) pre-program activities, (2) the program itself, and (3) postprogram activities. To help you visualize what happens during a program, these three phrases are described here in overview. To make the descriptions concrete, this overview is based on a program format we often use at CCL. There is, of course, room for virtually endless variation.

Preprogram Activities

In a very real sense, the program begins with the materials participants receive and complete several weeks before the program. These preprogram activities might include

- Responding to open-ended, essay-type questions
- Interviewing their boss about how he or she views effective leadership in their organization
- Completing a variety of personality inventories, attitude surveys, questionnaires about their current leadership challenges, and self-ratings of their skills and abilities
- Rating forms, completed by their bosses, peers, and subordinates (the multirater or 360-degree feedback instruments discussed in detail in Chapter One)

Some time before the program itself, all the completed forms and questionnaires are returned to the program site for scoring. Program staff then use the data as raw material for feedback reports that are then delivered at appropriate times during the program.

Completing these preliminary activities usually has the effect of stimulating people to reflect on their own leadership behaviors. Participants frequently report that they began noticing a certain way of doing something as a result of filling out a particular questionnaire or answering a specific question on an essay-type survey. This process is similar to what McCarthy and Keene (1996) define as the heart of assessment. *About Learning* describes assessment as the conversation that takes place first within the individual as he or she receives information from the world, then with others as they share their worlds, then between the teacher and the participant as the person learns the world of the "experts," and finally between the individual and his or her work.

The Program Itself

An FIP is generally a weeklong event. At CCL we commonly use the six-day format illustrated in Table 2.1. To give you a view of how a program works, let us look in on one.

The first day is a time for getting acquainted. In some programs, it also affords time for further assessment. In the morning, participants and staff introduce themselves to each other, and participants tell why they are there and what they hope to gain from the experience. Many report they are there to better understand themselves, learn about their strengths and weaknesses, or develop a better understanding of leadership. Some are there to learn how to work more effectively with a new team or in a newly merged organization. A few are sent for interpersonal skill development.

TABLE 2.1. A SAMPLE DESIGN FOR A FEEDBACK-INTENSIVE PROGRAM.

Day 1	Day 2	Day 3	Day 4	Day 5	Day 6
Morning					
Program opening	Call to leadership model	Decision making	Enhancing the learning process	Feedback (staff)	Goal setting and action planning
Afternoon					
Group and individual assessment activities	Performance development	Building effective teams	Activity-based learning	Feedback (peers)	Evaluation and closing

In the afternoon, participants are put into small groups for experiential exercises. The exercises have a dual purpose: they serve as icebreaker and assessment mechanism. The exercises are chosen for the qualities and behaviors that they reveal; as people work through the exercise, trained staff observe and record their behaviors. The exercises are of many types, including leaderless group discussions, targeted experiential exercises, and small-scale simulations (these and other assessment methods are discussed in more detail later).

The first day can be stressful for participants. They have already spent a good deal of time completing questionnaires before the program, and then they are further assessed once they arrive. They may not acknowledge it until later, but many participants report feeling like the person who confided, "I'm about to be exposed. I've made it successfully to this point, but I know this time I won't be able to cover this flaw."

After the first day of introduction and assessment, an FIP is segmented into modules, each usually half a day in length, that relate to various challenges faced by people in leadership positions. For example, a module may focus on the extent of involvement of people in decision making, or on the issues of tradeoffs and ethics in decision making.

Some form of feedback is embedded in each module. Either the module itself has some form of assessment built in, or at some predetermined point one of the questionnaires completed in the preliminary packet is brought into the discussion. Usually the feedback relates to the content of the module. For example, in a module on group decision making there is a place for introducing the feedback collected earlier from the participants' direct reports (opinions of their bosses' decision-making style). Or a module on ethical decision making might include an experiential exercise (observed and later debriefed by staff) on the tradeoffs often present in decision making.

The participants themselves also provide feedback, on themselves and on each other. Time is structured so that people learn how to give constructive feedback in small groups and discuss issues important to each individual.

The next-to-last day is an intensive, concentrated period of consolidating feedback. This is often the most meaningful day for participants. They use this time to consolidate and understand the information they've received from various sources, summarize their current strengths and development needs, and point themselves in the direction of setting development goals and creating action plans for accomplishing them.

Goal setting and action planning typically happen on the last day of the program. The entire week has been building to this day. Given all the feedback they have received during the week and the discussions they have had with staff, feedback specialists, and their classmates, the participants begin setting goals for their continued development and strategies for attaining them.

Postprogram Activities

The process is not over when the participants depart at the end of the sixth day. It is important that they be given some structured support as they continue to reflect on what they have learned about themselves and to pursue goals and action plans.

One form of support is goal letters. On the last day of the program, participants indicate when they wish to be contacted about their goals. At that time, program staff follow up by writing the participants and asking about goal completion or modification. Another process uses an instrument designed to assess change as a result of the program. We have developed one such instrument, based on our impact assessment research, and often use this tool to follow up with participants and help them monitor their own development and progress toward goals over time.

Another process uses a peer group, formed during the program. People who go through a feedback-intensive program together often form strong bonds by the end of the week. Staying in touch through the peer group not only reinforces these bonds but provides a strong source of ongoing support as people work on their goals. A more extensive list of postprogram activities is included at the end of this chapter, in a section addressing the issue of intervention over time.

Assessment Methodologies

Assessment is a major element in a feedback-intensive program. It comes in many forms and from a variety of sources: formal feedback from a supervisor, feedback from peers and subordinates, observations from trained observers during the program, and participants' own assessment of their values and preferences. Together they create an intense and thorough assessment experience, an experience enhanced by the opportunity for people to informally compare themselves with other participants.

To produce the many kinds of assessment, a feedback-intensive program takes advantage of different methods and techniques. As mentioned earlier, these methods act as a sequence of mirrors, each reflecting back to the individual a piece of information that can be linked with other pieces to form a comprehensive assessment.

Many of these assessment techniques produce data in the form of "scores," or ratings, to be fed back to people. It is critical that these ratings be reliable and valid (for more information, see Leslie and Fleenor, 1998). Participants deserve ratings that they can take seriously and use productively to create plans for change. If program facilitators cannot say with certainty that the scores are reliable and valid, then they do not know that the instrument or rating scale is constructed well enough to produce consistent, stable scores; they do not know whether scores are measuring what they claim to be measuring or whether higher scores are really related to greater effectiveness. People have many reasons for rejecting tough feedback; the quality of the assessment tools should not be one of those reasons.

This section describes some of the psychometric and behavioral assessments that are a major part of a feedback-intensive program, in particular structured experiences (leaderless group discussions, simulations, and targeted exercises), self-assessment of preferences, and assessment of skills and behaviors (360-degree feedback and structured feedback from fellow participants).

Structured Experiences

Structured experiences are group activities that provide assessment data through goal-directed, live-action, task-based interactions. They may be done by small groups, or the entire group as a whole. Unlike instruments (discussed later in the chapter), which display a person's strengths and development needs numerically on paper, structured experiences reveal strengths and weaknesses in real time. Three common types of structured experiences are leaderless group discussions, simulations, and targeted exercises.

Leaderless Group Discussions. This technique has a long history in assessment-center research and practice. The basic idea is that a small group of people, four to eight, is assigned a task; the group as a whole, rather than an individual leader, is accountable for the outcome. Participants are given a time limit for completing the task and may be instructed to use collaboration, competitive positioning and persuasion, or any of a number of other perspectives. Staff members trained to rate certain individual leadership behaviors observe the group and rate participants on a number of variables, such as motivating others, leading the discussion, task orientation, interpersonal skills, and verbal effectiveness. These observations are compiled for feedback later. Earth II is an example. In this competitive exercise, participants are told to imagine themselves living on another planet, one without a designated leader. They must accomplish three tasks in a short period of time: (1) create their own description or resume for an ideal leader, (2) convince other group members that their candidate is the one best suited to lead Earth II, and (3) as a group choose a leader and rank-order the remaining candidates.

As they try to persuade the others in the group to support their candidate, participants reveal much about their leadership traits. One person may create an excellent candidate, but because of her interpersonal style or verbal effectiveness she is unable to sway the group her way. Another may recognize during the discussion that his candidate is not as strong as some of the others and offer to pull his candidate in favor of another. For some participants, the tough issue is balancing the need to have their own candidate win with the group's need to have the best possible leader—the very common conflict between competition and collaboration. Later in the program, people receive feedback on factors such as how well they helped the group stay on task, how often they led the discussion, and how well they were able to see the short-term and long-term issues involved in candidate selection.

Placed early in a program, a leaderless exercise can provide feedback, boost self-confidence, help group members begin to get to know one another, and provide a valuable source of corroborative data to compare to the feedback they receive later in the program.

Simulations. Simulations are exercises that in some way replicate aspects of people's real-life jobs. They can be as small as fashioning a manager's in-basket, or as large as a full-scale simulation of two organizations working together. In-basket simulations are often done by individuals working alone and scored with respect to a "book solution" (for example, how many "correct" choices were made within a specified period of time).

In somewhat larger simulations, lasting from half a day to several days, small groups of people interact to solve a series of problems, such as finding a better way to respond to customer complaints. These simulations may involve twenty or more people. The participants are asked to represent leaders in the top team of a large corporation, or employees in two or more organizations that are in some sort of working relationship, such as customer and supplier or joint-venture partners. They take on roles in marketing, operations, or international human resources in their respective "companies," complete with in-baskets, telephones, and fax machines. They are presented with a complex, realistic situation and a fairly intense timetable for solving it.

Watching how people perform in simulations, staff accumulate feedback on individual issues such as how quickly someone finds information and how well he or she communicates it to others, and also on group concerns such as how thoroughly problems are treated or how effectively group members work together toward a goal.

Targeted Exercises. Short, experiential exercises, done in small groups, provide assessment data and also serve to reinforce a point made in the classroom or a theme that is central to the program. Unlike simulations, targeted exercises do not attempt to replicate the actual work environment; instead, they focus on a smaller aspect of a leader's responsibilities or one specific issue that is particularly relevant.

People usually enjoy these exercises, since they are designed to encourage participants to put forth their experience and strengths. At the same time, they find the exercises quite challenging for the same reason; those comfortable behaviors that have made them successful in the past may not serve them well as they wrestle with the exercise.

Simulations and exercises provide an opportunity to work in real time on realistic projects and dilemmas. Both afford a laboratory for learning about current leadership behaviors and styles, and for practicing new ones. In many exercises, people are encouraged to choose a behavior they are considering changing and experiment with it in the safe environment of the classroom.

Three Methods for Facilitating Learning from Structured Experiences

All three types of structured experience (leaderless group discussion, targeted exercises, and simulations) have in common that they force people to deal with concentrated periods of challenge. They have to work within severe time constraints, or make decisions based on conflicting data, or behave in ways that go against the grain for them, such as responding with more patience, acting upon incomplete data, or surrendering leadership to another member of the group. Whenever people are forced to move out of their familiar ways of doing something, they are challenged to step back and assess their effectiveness. This often leads to a sense that performance isn't what it could be; as a result, they come away feeling frustrated. In many debriefing sessions after such exercises, participants protest, "Well, this wasn't a real situation. In real life I would have. . . ."

In such situations, learning doesn't happen without reflection; here (much as in real life), people are in the position of needing to act in the moment. Three methods are good at enhancing learning in structured experiences: group observation, videotaping, and facilitated debrief. They are effective because they help individuals see the impact their behavior has on others and more clearly understand what it means to be effective in a group.

Group Observation. One way of helping people see the strengths and accept the limitations of how the group (as well as each individual) goes about its task is for individual members to observe the group in action (for example, from behind a one-way mirror) and then carry on group discussion of the activity at its conclusion.

An exercise called Hollow Squares, sometimes used early in a six-day program like the one presented in Table 2.1, illustrates the use of group observation and discussion. This is an interactive team exercise in which the group is divided in two; one half is assigned a project that the other half must complete. The exercise reflects what occurs in a team when some members are given the task of planning an event while others must implement the task. Time constraints, untested assumptions about what information can or cannot be shared, somewhat ambiguous directions, and lack of communication all tend to get in the way of effective group problem solving.

Typically, those given planner roles focus intently on deriving the best plan for the implementers to carry out. Implementers, meanwhile, know only that they are waiting to be told about a task they need to complete under a tight deadline. They usually spend their time anxiously trying to figure out what is going on. Several participants are asked to be observers of the exercise, taking their place behind a set of one-way mirrors that allow them to observe simultaneously both the planners and the implementers at work. The observers are told to make note of behaviors and actions that help and hinder the group in accomplishing its task. They are asked to be charitable, remembering that they would probably make the same "mistakes" that their fellow classmates will make.

After the exercise, participants debrief the experience in teams. The observers are asked to summarize for the group what they saw from behind the one-way mirror, without identifying specific people by name. Having these observations come from a fellow participant, rather than from a staff member, makes tough feedback easier to hear, especially when the exercise is used early in a program. Through the ensuing group discussion of this experience, those who were on the planning side look at the behaviors that come into play when people are asked to plan something that others must carry out. The implementers assess what happens to people who are to be charged with carrying out a task they didn't plan, looking at the behaviors they exhibit as they wait to be instructed. The exercise allows each subgroup to examine its own assumptions and behaviors, and to give feedback to the other group on the impact of its members' behavior.

Videotaping. Another tool for helping people learn from a structured exercise is to videotape the event. The video recorder does not evaluate; it simply records what actually occurred. After completing an exercise, the participants view the videotape, observing how each person in the group—including themselves—went about task behaviors such as seeking or giving information or testing consensus, and how well or how poorly they interacted with others to accomplish the task. They can witness themselves and others in the subtle behavioral "acts of leading": their habits of eye contact, how they use the space around them, whether they tend to sit in with the group or always pull back, how they get their ideas out, or what happens to their voices when they feel frustrated.

Facilitated Debrief. When the structured exercise is a simulation, the live action of the simulation itself is followed by a facilitated debrief of the experience. In larger simulations, the debriefs can span one or two days. In these facilitated discussions, participants can express their feelings of frustration, talk about their insights, get feedback on group performance from staff, discuss their own views of how they did as a group, and give each other individual peer feedback.

Self-Assessment of Preferences: The Use of Personality Instruments

Personal preferences are one underlying source of people's behavior on the job and elsewhere, so a comprehensive assessment process should also include data on preferences. The data are typically collected through personality questionnaires completed by the participants themselves, usually before they come to the program. These questionnaires focus on the person's preferred ways of interacting with the world; they have no right or wrong answers, no good or bad scores. Although the scores may be compared with norms, the comparison is only a way of showing participants how their own preferences differ from those of other participants, or from those of the population as a whole.

The Myers-Briggs Type Indicator (MBTI) is a good example because it is probably the most widely used instrument of this kind. It assesses preferences in how people gather and process information, reflecting those preferences on four bipolar dimensions: extroversion (E) and introversion (I), sensing (S) and intuition (N), thinking (T) and feeling (F), and judging (J) and perceiving (P). Based on their scores on these four dimensions, people are assigned one of sixteen "types" (ESTJ, INFP, ENFJ, ISFP, etc.). People of the same type share many of the same preferences and frequently have similar strengths and development needs. When this instrument is used in groups, people learn that there is a great deal of hidden diversity in any group and that each person, even those with the same type preference, brings to the group unique and valuable assets.

Assessment of Skills and Behaviors

In a feedback-intensive program, assessment of skills and behaviors is accomplished in several ways: through structured exercises (which have already been discussed); through 360-degree feedback from the participant, the participant's boss, peers, and direct reports; and through structured feedback from fellow program participants.

360-Degree Feedback. Multirater (360-degree) instruments are typically used in an FIP to collect and compare self-perceptions to perceptions from "back home," that is, how a manager's boss, peers, and direct reports view that manager's leadership skills and behaviors. Because 360-degree feedback is the topic of Chapter One of this handbook, it is not covered in any detail here. Suffice it to say that in a feedback-intensive program, 360-degree feedback is sometimes presented as part of an in-class module on leadership and sometimes as part of a structured session with a trained facilitator. These sessions may be with a small group of participants, or just one individual and the facilitator.

Feedback from back home is particularly useful and powerful in an FIP because it rounds out the feedback experience. Participants then have three strong sources of information about themselves: knowledge about skills and behaviors (from the 360-degree feedback), data on personality, and observations of other participants and facilitators during exercises or simulations. All these types of information support and reinforce each other, providing the strength and stability seen in the analogy of a three-legged stool. Because feedback from back home often mirrors feedback received from staff and fellow participants in the program, it can provide compelling closure to the awareness being developed during the week.

Powerful feedback is fraught with potential for misunderstanding, so care needs to be taken in its presentation and delivery. See Chapter One for guidelines on feeding back information from 360-degree instruments.

Structured Feedback from Fellow Participants. During a feedback-intensive program, participants receive a constant stream of feedback. Much of it comes from the others in the program. Some of the exercises have a feedback component built in; those who have just worked through the exercise together share with their fellow members what they observed. The focus in this section, however, is on a structured time for participants to give each other wide-ranging feedback based on their experiences together during the program. There are two ways this can happen: peer observations and peer interviews.

In peer observations, each participant is assigned to observe one or two others throughout the course of the program. The goal is to be able to give those participants constructive feedback on the impact of their behavior, both during classroom activities and outside of class. Observers are taught how to watch for patterns of behavior that might help their fellow participants become more effective. These observations are consolidated and fed back, one participant to another, during a specific program module devoted to peer feedback.

In addition to being another source of valuable feedback for each participant, peer observations provide a learning laboratory for giving and receiving feedback. People learn how to give specific, behavioral examples in their feedback and how to solicit feedback on specific points they wish to work on themselves.

Finally, peer observations also provide people with an excellent picture of first impressions. Creating favorable first impressions can be critical for managers, who often interact with multiple people in rapid succession. The remembered behaviors of first impressions can color perceptions long after an initial meeting, and negative impressions, even long after an individual exhibits stellar performance.

Peer interviews are structured conversations between participants, often used early in a program. Participants are given an interviewing guide and then interview each other in pairs. The interviews can be typed up, for use in the feedback sessions that take place later in the program. Peer interviews serve several important roles: they help members of the class get to know one another better, allow staff to begin to know the participants as individuals, and give staff members a way to evaluate a participant's ability to conduct an interview when the purpose is to help another person feel at ease.

Processes like these are especially valuable because peers provide breadth and variety of experience and have no hidden agenda in providing feedback (especially in an open-enrollment FIP; more on this issue later). Program peers usually have a sincere desire to help one another learn.

Confidentiality and Anonymity: Two Key Issues in Assessment

A feedback-intensive program is meant to stimulate a positive process of growth, to enable people to see what they are currently doing and acknowledge, without defensiveness or fear of negative impact, areas in which their behavior may not be as effective as it could be. For this to happen, people must trust the data they get in feedback and must trust the process used to deliver those data to them.

Confidentiality is a major part of building a nonthreatening environment for learning. People need to know that the assessment data belong to them and that no one else (outside of program staff) has access to those data without their permission.

Rater anonymity is also important. When back-home raters know their identities will not be revealed, they usually answer questions as honestly as they can, often providing feedback that they could not or would not give face-to-face.

Elements of Challenge

In a feedback-intensive program, there are at least four sources of challenge. The assessment and feedback process, by its very nature, provides one source of intense challenge: that of looking inward, the discomfort of being observed and rated by others, the fear of having weaknesses exposed. Because the assessment element has been discussed in the previous section, it is not covered here in more detail. Other sources of challenge are the conceptual framework itself (the classroom content), engaging in unfamiliar activities (such as artistic activities, writing in a journal, and participating in a simulation or an outdoor activity), and encountering different ideas and perspectives.

Conceptual Framework: Content and Models

A feedback-intensive program usually uses a model of effective leadership to provide both a framework for understanding what leadership is and a backdrop for the assessment that occurs throughout the program.

Leadership models often cover a broad domain, including communications, interpersonal relationships, coaching, teamwork, decision making, and dealing with ambiguity and turmoil. The underlying intent of presenting a model is to enhance the challenge of the program by providing a new framework for understanding leadership and for self-assessment.

The content of a program may vary, to some degree, depending on the participants, because different groups of people face somewhat different leadership challenges. For example, a program for students might be aimed at helping them assess which kinds of leadership roles they want to pursue. A program for senior executives would more likely focus on changing the ingrained behavior patterns that have helped them move up in their organizations but are becoming less effective.

The art in designing a program is in constructing content that matches, as closely as possible, the challenges faced by the target population. The students are likely to need modules that help them develop a sense of individual purpose or learn to take initiative. Senior executives may need to explore how they react to organizational changes such as a turbulent business environment or globalization.

In an effective FIP, content and models are presented simply and directly. If the content is too complex, people may be overwhelmed and spend the entire program struggling to understand the material, rather than putting it into action. People need to be able to take in the conceptual material smoothly, so they can make a connection between what they hear in the classroom and what they do in their jobs and in their lives. The content and models should be connected to people's everyday experience, so they can take what they learned in the class and put it to work back home.

Engaging in Unfamiliar Activities

Challenge also comes from engaging in new kinds of activities that force people to move out of their comfort zone. For some, the challenging activity might be a simulation or an exercise in group problem solving under tight time constraints. For others, it may be an artistic activity, or an outdoor challenge course. All these activities challenge by taking people out of their element, introducing ambiguity, and demanding that they use untested skills and behaviors. Simulations and structured exercises have already been described in this section, so we now discuss exercises that use dramatic movement, acting experiences, and outdoor exercises.

Dramatic movement or dance can shed new light on troublesome situations. A participant in one CCL program talked about her difficulty in coping with multiple demands from her boss, coworkers, and family. She described herself as being pulled in too many directions at once. In a module involving dramatic movement, she asked several of her classmates to help portray her situation. She "sculpted" them into position, creating a frieze depicting the tugs she felt from these demands. She gave each of her feedback participants a phrase to say, and then she put herself into the picture. The verbal and visual effect on the entire class was powerful. Next we suggested that she reshape the frieze as she would like her situation to be, again assigning short phrases to each character. The group members were then asked to reflect on the two scenes without group discussion, to find a way to move themselves so as to get from the original scene to her ideal one.

Typical of most people, she was uncomfortable "performing" in front of the class, and she was skeptical that the exercise had legitimate connection to her problem. She later acknowledged the insights she found through this process. Not only did she gain some specific ideas about how to deal with her situation, but her self-confidence also got a big boost.

An acting experience is another effective way of learning about leadership. While acting out a role, one's tone of voice, body language, and gestures can be examined; this helps leaders understand how they naturally tend to convey different emotions. These elements can also be developed and expanded, thereby enabling leaders to convey the messages they intend.

As another example, programs incorporate exercises based on nature and the outdoors. Many people report that spending time outdoors gives them an opportunity to reflect on issues they are facing or on feedback they have received. One participant, who entered a program after being passed over for a promotion, used an outdoor experience to develop a "sustaining metaphor." She felt her career was dead-ended unless she acted to change herself. To compound her anxiety, the feedback from home was worse than she had expected. She reported that the nature walk during the program was the key for touching her heart and allowing her to put recent events in perspective. On the walk, she found a tree that had split in half at a wound but had survived. The tree became a metaphor for her, about making a conscious choice to grow beyond her setbacks.

These are but a few examples of nontraditional methods. They not only provide different avenues for assessing strengths and needs but also are challenging to people who have become comfortable with doing things in traditional ways.

Meeting Diverse People with Different Perspectives

Finally, people are challenged when they encounter others with ideas and perspectives different from their own. In an FIP, this type of challenge may come from participants' being intentionally selected so as to maximize racial, gender, or cultural diversity in the classroom. Challenge also comes from interacting with people who are different in terms of the functional, professional, or industry perspectives they bring along. Sharing personality data during the program, too, challenges people to see the diversity that is often hidden, even in a group that appears on the surface to be homogeneous.

In sum, a feedback-intensive program provides challenges in several arenas. The program moves from lectures, which can be intellectually challenging, to experiential exercises, which can be interpersonally and cognitively challenging, to 360-degree feedback, which can be challenging to assumptions about self and others.

Support Elements of an Effective Feedback-Intensive Program

People usually enter a feedback-intensive program expecting, even wanting, to learn more about their strengths and weaknesses as leaders. But understanding the links between the leadership challenges one is facing at work and one's own strengths and development needs is a complex task. Actually getting feedback that suggests there are areas in need of improvement can create significant anxiety, because it requires that people examine where they feel less competent and therefore vulnerable.

To hear and accept feedback in these areas, and to be motivated to change behaviors or add new skills, people need a good deal of support. They need to be in an environment that helps them

- Appreciate their strengths and see themselves as worthwhile and successful
- Feel accepted, cared about, and respected
- Understand and value the feedback as relevant and useful, and believe they can learn to use it
- Feel responsible for defining what is important in their feedback and the extent to which they will work on self-improvement
- Develop a workable plan for the changes they decide they want to make

As one participant said, "Even though I was really nervous and didn't know what to expect in this group of successful and very assertive people, from the moment we entered the room the staff seemed to provide an anchor and comfortableness that let me not just put a toe in the water but jump right in. It was magic, and I am so glad it was there for me."

The "magic" to which this person is referring is the power of a well-constructed learning community in the classroom.

Creating a Learning Community

In an FIP, a learning environment is created primarily through formal and informal processes and behaviors enacted by program staff. These processes and behaviors include

- Staff enactment of norms that support learning
- Consciously integrating (in real time) elements of each participant's situation into program activities
- Sharing participants' perspectives with each other
- Teaching methods that meet the needs of all learning styles
- Opportunities for consolidation of feedback through individual and group reflection

Although the content of a program is important in helping people cognitively frame their feedback in a wider leadership context, the "process" side is what enables people to deal emotionally with their feedback and to connect it meaningfully to their work and personal lives. Support processes can be nearly invisible to participants. Yet when done correctly, participants begin to enact these attitudes and behaviors with each other and provide one another with ever-more-constructive feedback as the week unfolds. As they become comfortable sharing deeply with one another, a bond of trust forms. At that point, as people learn that they each have the ability to help and teach others, the classroom truly becomes a community for learning. The participants themselves become supportive threads in the elegant tapestry of their own program experience. However, it is the program staff who are responsible for setting these processes in motion.

Staff Behaviors That Facilitate Participant Learning. The program staff contributes much more than solid knowledge of the content and shepherding of a variety of stimulating activities. Staff members also consciously enact attitudes and behaviors that facilitate participant learning.

To create a community where participants feel safe, attempt self-disclosure, and are willing to listen to uncomfortable feedback and to give it constructively to others, program staff have to be able to

- Relate to each participant with personal authenticity
- Be comfortable with self-disclosure
- Understand and acknowledge each participant's unique needs, as well as their own definitions of themselves and their situations
- Be nonjudgmental and nonprescriptive in working with participants

For staff members, being authentic means acknowledging that, even though they are up in front of the class, potentially in a position of "authority," they don't have all the answers. This is not easy. Most staff people care intensely about providing a good experience, and for some staff this may mean being able to always have the answer. But when asked a question for which they do not have an answer, experienced program leaders freely admit it and immediately take the opportunity to create a sharing atmosphere by asking others who may have the knowledge to share their opinions. This attitude is critical to creating a good learning environment for participants in that it sets a tone that it is acceptable not to know everything, that one can have value as a person in spite of having weaknesses.

Beginning each program with appropriate self-disclosure is another important staff behavior. For most people in this culture, self-disclosure is a reciprocal activity. Done in the right doses—neither too personal nor too distant—self-disclosure by a staff member helps participants open up and allows them to show those behaviors to one another. Being able to discuss personal issues openly is a key factor in a participant's ability to make sense of the feedback he or she receives during the course of the program.

To create the best possible learning experience for each individual, program staff must be willing and able to get outside of their own needs and expectations as staff members and respectfully meet the participants where they are, developmentally and emotionally. In order to meet the participant's need to feel accepted, respected, and cared for, facilitators must find a way to connect personally and nonjudgmentally with each individual: the quieter ones, those who emerge as leaders in the group, and even the rudest person in the group. That means that, in the classroom, a staff member makes eye contact with each participant, acknowledges the contributions made by each one, recognizes when a participant may not understand the material or has a question, remembers which person asked a particular question or made a specific contribution, and takes whatever time is necessary to ensure that each participant is having a valuable learning experience every day of the program. It means taking the time to get to know the participants and understand their unique ways of looking at the world and their special areas of expertise. Finally, to support the participant's need to feel accepted and respected just as they are means that staff must have a sincerely nonjudgmental attitude about each individual's way of understanding self and others.

In order for people to effect positive change, they need to be able to take responsibility for their own development. To best help people assume this responsibility, program staff need to be able to take a nonprescriptive stance in working with participants. Taking this stance can sometimes be difficult, for staff and for participants. For example, when participants examine their personality profiles or feedback from back home, they frequently ask, "What's the best way to be?" The only possible answer for the staff to give is that there is no one best way to be—just different ways for different situations and different people. This kind of response can be hard for some people to hear, especially those who are in the midst of turbulent change (either in their external environment or within themselves) and who are seeking some solid ground upon which to stand. When participants insist on getting the "right" answer, staff need to guard against the very human temptation to want to be "helpful" and provide those answers. Similarly, staff members must refrain from diagnosing participants' issues. Instead, the role of staff is to facilitate the processes whereby participants themselves can decide what their developmental needs and issues are and how best to go about working on those.

Here is an illustration of these processes in action. It reveals a staff member able to remain nonjudgmental, use her personal authenticity and willingness to be vulnerable, and self-disclose in order to help turn a defiant group into individuals willing to learn from their program experience.

The class was a mixture of successful, highly intelligent academics and researchers brought together to function as a leadership team for a set period of time. They viewed themselves as different from "corporate types" and thought of the Center as a corporate training facility catering to business "fat cats." They constantly demanded statistics, research, and hard facts, and it was little consolation to the staff that these participants carried the same challenging attitudes and limited respect for their fellow classmates as they did for program staff.

The group became especially resistant when it came to receiving 360-degree feedback. Their attacks on the credibility of trainers, the instruments, and the data became a safe and persistent retreat from taking a serious look at their behaviors or considering the negative feedback they might have received from their back-home observers.

One of the loudest protestors was a gentleman who claimed that he already knew how to learn, as evidenced by his degrees and the positions he held. He already knew the human side of leadership, he insisted further, since he was a writer of short stories and poetry.

During a program break, one of the instructors privately shared with this person that she, too, wrote poetry and asked if he would look over some of her work and give her some pointers. He agreed, offering to do so at the end of the day. Later, during the instructor's presentation, he challenged her for failing to be open with the whole class about her ability to write, and demanded that she share her poetry openly, since they had been asked to share their reactions to feedback and he felt that this was equally private.

Although surprised by his outburst and feeling quite vulnerable at his request, the staff member agreed to read one of her poems. A long silence followed the reading. Then one participant said, "What these people [the staff] have been trying to help us see is what we do to ourselves and to others. We're supposed to be here to develop better ways of interacting with each other so as to help our communities. I think there is something we all can learn here."

If any learning was to occur for this group, the instructors had to find ways to be patient, nondefensive, honest, authentic in their attitudes, and respectful of where the participants were coming from regardless of how difficult it felt. After days of struggling with this group's unwillingness to learn, the behaviors and attitudes employed by this staff member facilitated the group's learning how to better monitor itself and move away from destructive critiques of people and situations. For them, this was a critical first step.

Enhancement Techniques for Staff Use

Beyond setting the learning processes in motion through their attitudes and behaviors, program staff use several other techniques to enhance the learning environment in the classroom.

Integrating Elements of Each Participant's Situation into Program Activities. In the most effective feedback-intensive programs, staff take the details of the participants' back-home situation (such as industry or market issues) and make them an integral part of the program content. This does not happen by accident. Good facilitators stay alert for brief tidbits of conversation or nonverbal behavior that reveal the issues and challenges the participants bring with them. It also happens because the facilitators do their homework. Prior to the start of a program, they review the biographical information on all the participants, along with the preprogram questionnaires and scored feedback reports. Once the program begins, they listen and watch closely for clues about the participants' interests, concerns, and differences. As the program progresses, they are quick to use arising opportunities to weave appropriate pieces of this information directly into the program, as examples or as prompts for group discussion.

Encouraging the Sharing of Perspectives. Participants bring with them a wealth of experience and knowledge. Skilled facilitators look for ways to pull that expertise into the discussions, so the larger group can benefit from shared information. To stimulate the sharing of perspectives, facilitators might ask participants to describe how the content is connected to their experiences, to brainstorm ways of using the content, or to talk about some of the assessment issues that arise during the discussion. This sharing of perceptions and expertise helps participants understand that everyone has something to offer and that people all have something to learn from each other, no matter how different another person seems to be—an important norm that the program fosters.

Teaching to All Learning Styles and Abilities, Using a Variety of Methodologies. If a program is to provide a good learning environment for participants, every individual must be able to learn in the ways that suit him or her best and at a rate that feels comfortable.

It is well known that people do learn in different ways (see Chapter Eight for more on learning tactics). Many learn best within a conceptual approach, such as listening to lectures and discussions. These folks learn the most when they are sitting in a classroom listening to program staff present ideas, or reading materials related to the concepts. Others learn better by doing something than by spending time hearing or reading about it. These action-oriented people prefer exercises, simulations, and hands-on learning. Still others learn best in interaction with other people, by seeking advice or discussing issues in a group setting. Finally, most people need time to reflect on the information they receive, if they are to integrate it into their thinking and future behavior. For these reasons, staff build FIP designs to maximize the variety of learning vehicles and methodologies (using lecture, structured exercises, instruments, informal discussion groups, etc.).

We also know that people learn at different rates. The light bulb may come on for any individual at any time during a program, since people pull distinct learnings from common experiences. This is another reason for encouraging groups to share their individual perceptions and their own expertise. Doing so works to help participants become more open and accepting of others' points of view.

Creating Opportunities for Reflection and Consolidation of Feedback.

As we've said throughout this chapter, an FIP is an information-rich experience. By the second or third day, people have been given multiple pieces of feedback from a variety of sources. In order to draw learning from all this information, an FIP provides many opportunities for individuals to consolidate the feedback they have received using processes of both solitary and group reflection.

One process that is very effective and highly valued by participants is use of feedback specialists, coaches, or process advisors. In highly interactive, confidential sessions, the participant and the specialist work one-on-one to learn as much as they can from all the accumulated feedback the participant has received throughout the program: preprogram assessments; classroom experiences; observations during exercises, discussions, and simulations; and personal observations from staff and fellow participants. Together the two explore the implications, settle on some possible areas for change, and discuss various action plans for the changes. It is an educational experience, designed to be an exciting process of discovery, confirmation, and action. The process is founded on honesty and openness, and facilitated by a thoroughly trained specialist.

Depending on how the FIP is designed, the structure of this coaching session varies. Some sessions occur during the program itself, perhaps a three-hour block near the end of the week. Sometimes the coaching is an ongoing follow-up between the participant and the coach over a period of months.

Another process used for enabling people to reflect on their experiences and more effectively learn in the present is journaling. A learning journal can be used in many ways: at the end of each learning segment, following feedback from the group or from an assessment, after a discussion. Sometimes thought-provoking questions are asked, to stimulate participants' journaling. Or they might simply be instructed to summarize the event and write down what they were feeling as it unfolded.

Journals can be useful in discovering patterns of behavior, for planning future actions, or simply as a way of working through issues. When the program calls for ongoing contact between the participant and a feedback specialist, a journal serves as a useful communication tool.

A third way that an FIP provides opportunity for consolidation of feedback is by using processes of group reflection. In processes of this type, small groups of three to six people spend time together at various points in the program, discussing their feedback or other issues. Participants provide encouragement to each other and share wisdom about issues they may have in common. They are also in a unique position to provide each other with honest feedback about behaviors and skills they have seen among themselves during the week. Because these group discussions allow participants to begin sharing more deeply with one another, a bond of trust forms in the group, enhancing even further the climate for learning that participants experience.

The Outcomes of a Feedback-Intensive Program

With more than fifteen years of research, we at the Center for Creative Leadership have learned a great deal about the impact of a feedback-intensive program. Key elements of the research are summarized here; a more detailed discussion of how impact can be assessed is the subject of Chapter Nine.

Learnings from Our Research

From our work in evaluating programs that are feedback-intensive, we have learned that there are potentially five main areas of development and change: knowledge acquisition, change in self-awareness, change in perspective, goal attainment or reframing, and behavioral change. Some kinds of change begin during the program itself; others are not likely to occur until much later.

Knowledge Acquisition. One area of knowledge gained during an FIP is leadership, for example, what the skills of effective leaders are, or which dimensions of personality affect leadership style. Participants also describe learning new information about themselves (scores on personality dimensions such as extroversion or dominance) and about how others perceive them. The learning often sparks another kind of change, in self-awareness.

Self-Awareness Change. Self-awareness is the most frequent and powerful area of impact from a feedback-intensive program. Often, new self-awareness is sparked by a discrepancy between self-assessments and those of others, on 360-degree feedback and in classroom exercises.

We know from our research that it is typical for managers to come into a feedback-intensive program seeing themselves more favorably than they are seen by others. In one study of a five-day leadership program (Van Velsor, Ruderman, and Phillips, 1992), we found that only 10 percent of the managers saw themselves as others saw them on all the dimensions measured by a 360-degree feedback instrument; 45 percent had a significant discrepancy, and most of those tended to rate themselves higher than others rated them. Yet when asked to rerate their leadership capacities soon after the program, the vast majority of people (80 percent) revised their self-view to be more in line with feedback they received in the program.

In a feedback-intensive program, participants tend to enhance self-awareness in a variety of ways. People who feel less than competent because of the complexity and scope of their responsibilities often become aware that they are reasonably good managers. Some gain awareness about skill deficits or about how they are perceived by others. Some gain personal insights about how they see themselves or about their own needs.

Transformational Perspective Change. Perspective change is similar to awareness building in that it refers to a change in attitude or outlook, rather than change in observable behavior. It differs from self-awareness building by referring not to a changed view of self but to new understandings about others, about the challenges people face, or about other significant aspects of the context in which they live and work. The two work hand in hand.

A few examples may serve to illustrate. Two men, one black and one white, were involved in a peer feedback discussion. The white man described behavior he had observed in the other as "aggressive." The other man's startled reaction, and the discussion that followed, helped the former realize, much to his surprise, that he would have classified the same behavior in a white male as "assertive." It was not the behavior that was different, but how he experienced it. This one incident was profoundly revealing; it opened his eyes to information about himself, and it also changed his subsequent view of behavior in others.

At the start of another program, a manager received feedback on her comfort level with change and learned that her style tended in the conservative direction; she preferred to make small changes at a slower pace. In the classroom, she interacted with others who view change differently. From their stories, she learned that change doesn't always mean disaster. This new perspective was reinforced when, through structured exercises, she was forced to experiment with other approaches. By the end of the week, she began to incorporate the idea that it is possible to view change as opportunity.

Goal Attainment and Reframing. Over the years, our follow-up on the goals participants set has shown that three to twelve months later most people either are still working on their goals or have accomplished them. We also know that people are more likely to accomplish their goals when they have adequate postprogram support or when they are participating in an FIP that extends over a period of time (more about this in a later section of this chapter).

In research done by Young and Dixon (1996), we took an in-depth look at how participants approach goal setting in an FIP and found that there are at least three approaches.

The first is the traditional goal-setting approach. This style is characterized by the view that a person sets goals and tries, in a fairly linear pattern, to carry them out. If obstacles to goal attainment arise, they are overcome, or the person abandons the goal, or he fails to attain it. Whether the person succeeds in these goals or fails, he considers the exercise closed after that. This approach is similar to that taken by many program evaluations, which seek only to see whether the goals set have been achieved (see Chapter Nine for more on assessing the impact of development experiences).

A second approach views goals as visions or ideal outcomes, with the path to get there subject to change as events unfold. This more flexible approach takes a longer view of goal accomplishment and allows the participant freedom to create new strategies for goal attainment as circumstances change and obstacles arise.

Finally, a third group of participants in this study took what was described as a process view of action planning. They appeared to set out on a journey leading them through a series of goals and action plans, success or failure, each culminating in some learning and a resetting of goals. This group probably got the most from the goal-setting or action-planning process, since they tended to set and achieve many goals and learn from both successes and failures.

Behavior Change. Although change in awareness is probably a necessary precondition to behavior change, it appears not to be a sufficient condition. In the self-awareness change research described earlier, only about one-third of the participants were seen by others as having accomplished significant behavior change six months after the program ended. However, this program was a five-day experience with no follow-up and to our knowledge was not used as part of a systems approach.

More extensive behavior change was found over time in the Young and Dixon study (1996) of a program with an extended design and significant follow-up. This feedback-intensive program spanned six months, included two classroom sessions three months apart, and extended work with process advisors between classroom sessions, back-home partners in change, and on-the-job "learning" projects. In this program, alumni were seen by coworkers as having made change in thirteen of the fourteen areas measured. When participants were rated as having changed in a particular area, they were rated as more effective as a result. Compared to the results of a control group of managers who did not participate in the program, this was still impressive, as program participants showed significantly more change than control group members in eight of the fourteen areas.

Program Design Issues with Consequences for Impact

Obviously, a number of factors determine the effectiveness of a feedback-intensive program. Three external factors, somewhat interconnected, stand out: variations in program length, intervention over time, and whether it is an open-enrollment program or an organization-specific program.

Variations in Program Length. Behavioral change does not just happen, nor is it something that can be "done to" someone. In order to behave differently, people first need to recognize the need for change. Then they need to understand how to do things differently and to become comfortable with the new approaches. Doing all this takes time.

From our research and classroom experience, it is evident that shorter programs (three days or less) can do an excellent job of raising awareness of different perspectives and ideas, but they teach more at the cognitive level (knowledge acquisition and limited self-awareness change) than the behavioral level (significant change in awareness and behavior). Participants tend to show an attitude of "that was interesting; now let's get back to work." We have found that it typically takes five or six days to bring a person through the full process of self-awareness and even longer to effect significant behavior change.

Intervention over Time. A feedback-intensive program that spans time (such as those where the experiences and processes are introduced in two three-day sessions over a six-month period, often with some form of coaching included) seems to have a greater impact (Young and Dixon, 1996) than a single-session program. People move beyond that's-good-to-know cognitive frameworks and beyond "how does this fit with my values perceptions and situation" and "so what will I do about it?" to actually being able to effect change in their approaches and perspectives.

It is therefore important to supplement a single program and turn it from an event into an ongoing developmental process for a participant, by adding activities that continue to reinforce action plans or provide support for change. Here are some possible postprogram activities:

- Debriefs for participants with managers or with a human resource support person, as well as for program faculty. Have people ask themselves such questions as "How did it go? What did we learn? What would I do more of, or less of, or differently?"
- Alumni groups to expand learnings. Bring past participants together to build a network and share insights and developmental experiences so as to benefit one another. This is a method of reinforcing learning.
- Helping pairs or learning partners reinforce and support behavior changes. Pairs or partner arrangements can be created with fellow classmates or by selecting colleagues in the work environment. Generally these are three-person teams that are asked to provide input to one or two specific actions or changes a participant wishes to make. The partnership consists of someone who is willing to give support and encouragement, someone else who provides honest feedback on how the individual is doing, and someone who can offer experience and knowledge around the issue the individual is working on.
- Goal-setting reports. This process gives ongoing accountability to the actions set in a program. Each round of reports affords the participants an opportunity to establish additional or new goals.
- Individual consultations and follow-up. These forms of coaching continue the work done in the program. They generally focus on an action plan and the individual's situation. Follow-up or an ongoing coaching process allows the participant to continually refocus action plans as the situation changes.

Open-Enrollment or Organization-Specific Programs. A feedback-intensive program can be offered as an open-enrollment program, where individual managers come to a program attended by people from different companies (such as the public programs held at CCL). It can also be offered as organization-specific, by which we mean programs developed and run for a single organization by a vendor (such as CCL) or those developed and run by organizations for their own employees. Whether the group is open-enrollment, mixed, or made up of people from the same organization is a significant issue from the point of view of impact. Each kind of program offers benefits; each has its drawbacks.

In an open-enrollment program, people have access to what all the other participants know; this creates a miniature version of partnering. That is, everyone has access to the breadth of experiences and best practices occurring in a number of organizations. For a fair percentage of participants, the interactions do not end at the close of the program. Further, in an open-enrollment program there is a greater sense of trust and confidentiality, and the ability to learn increases because of the variety of viewpoints and people's lower sense of vulnerability in discussing their ideas and their feedback.

On the other hand, an organization-specific program affords the greatest leverage. When eighteen to twenty-four people from the same organization experience a program simultaneously and develop a common language, the impact on the overall organization outweighs sending a few people at a time over an extended period. The organization-specific program is effective when the intent is to increase communication and team building, as with an organization that is geographically dispersed. It is also effective with an identified high-potential group who may be the next leaders of the organization, where the intent is both to develop each person and to enable them as a group to develop a network and more effective work relationships.

There is, however, a significant difference between the classroom environments of open-enrollment and organization-specific programs.

In every organization-specific program, there is a "giant" in the room—namely, the culture of the organization—and it exerts an enormous influence on what is learned and how. For example, one participant group in a CCL program worked for an organization that had just been through a major reorganization. They arrived feeling confused, overloaded, frightened, and frustrated. In their organizational culture no one spoke directly to issues; hallway conversation was rampant but during meetings no one dared rock the boat. In the program classroom, they behaved the same way. Between sessions, private grumblings could be heard, but when the facilitators asked people to talk about their organization and what might need to change, not one person would address the giant. They were all in the program for an individual developmental experience, but before that could begin to happen an intervention was required that allowed them to address their organizational issues.

Guidelines for Selecting or Using a Feedback-Intensive Program

Assessment, a variety of challenges, and developmental support—the key ingredients for continuous personal development—are all present in good measure in any effective feedback-intensive program. Table 2.2 summarizes guidelines to assist you in selecting, using, or designing a feedback-intensive program for leadership development.

What can a manager or human resource practitioner do? In selecting a program, you can

- Find out what staff members do to create and maintain a safe learning community in the classroom
- Find out whether assessment tools have known reliability and validity

When people return from a program, you can

- Create networks or alumni groups to facilitate continued learning
- Encourage discussion, coaching, and ongoing development planning between the participant and his or her manager

TABLE 2.2. WHAT TO LOOK FOR OR INCLUDE IN AN FIP.

Assessment	1. Use of multiple assessment methodologies (for example, personality instruments, 360-degree leadership instruments, targeted exercises, simulations, etc.)
	2. Variety in sources of assessment data (self-ratings; feedback from boss, peers, subordinates, customers, fellow participants, program staff)
	3. Integrity in assessment processes (for example, reliability and validity of assessment methods, confidentiality for participants, anonymity for raters)
	4. Program methods and experiences that surface participants' leadership strengths and development needs in real time
Challenge	5. Teaching methodologies that address various learning styles (for example, lecture, experiential, one-on-one discussions)
	6. Adequate time and processes for reflection
	7. Program content that is based on real issues and challenges that participants face
Support	8. Program staff who understand learning and support needs of participants
	9. Structure in which development needs and goals are defined with participant learning needs in mind, rather than prescribed by program content or staff
	10. Program staff who have the process facilitation skills necessary to link program content to feedback and feedback to action planning, in a way that protects confidentiality and promotes openness and learning
	11. Ways of extending the individual's learnings about self beyond the program, for individual benefit and for better coaching and development of others
	12. Processes for program follow-up through goal report forms; telephone calls; or other methods of support, encouragement, and assessment of development and change over time

- Allow for mistakes and failure as the participant begins to try new approaches

You can also identify other mechanisms your organization has in place to continue and expand the participant's learning (see Chapter Seven in this handbook, on development systems, for more information).

Finally, you can help people create long-term development plans that incorporate the FIP assessment by linking their development goals to next-step development experiences, such as skill-based training, a developmental relationship, and the like.

CHAPTER THREE

SKILL-BASED TRAINING

Dana G. McDonald-Mann

For most people reading and using this handbook, the concept and practice of skill-based training are very familiar. What may be something of a new idea is the specific use of skills training as part of a leadership development process.

From research and practice we have learned that when skill-based training is appropriately designed and implemented it can play a valuable role in leadership development; that is the focus of this chapter. We take advantage of this opportunity to present some of what we at CCL have learned about planning good training, but the main concern in this chapter is training as it relates to leadership development. In particular, we delineate the specific leadership capabilities that can be learned through training, and we look closely at what is involved in incorporating training events into the leadership model presented in the Introduction.

Skill-Based Training: What Is It?

Often the word training is used in a very generic sense. This chapter deals with just one type of training, called skill-based training, which is a development experience in which individuals gain knowledge and practice behaviors necessary to hone present skills or develop new ones.

The range of knowledge and skills that can be learned through training is vast; we are concerned here with the specific skills that leaders need. Conger writes that "Skill-building approaches to leadership assume that through a series of step-by-step instructions and demonstrations, managers can learn the skills and techniques of leaders" (1992, p. 128).

This chapter elaborates on the distinction between skill-based training and the feedback-intensive program, introduced in Chapter Two (a distinction that is summarized in Table 3.1). A feedback-intensive program assesses current skill level, increases self-awareness, changes perspective, and clarifies values and goals. It is designed to develop the person as a whole, by helping people understand their strengths and development needs. In the process, a feedback-intensive program may provide some skill-based training, but skill development is not its primary focus.

Two Domains of Learning

Skill-based training encompasses two types of learning: knowledge and skills. Knowledge is the cognitive domain (Nadler and Nadler, 1994); for example, participants in a training program acquire knowledge when they receive a lecture on the principles of strategic planning. Knowledge is a necessary first step, but by itself it is not sufficient for changing leadership behavior. The new knowledge must be put into action. Skills encompass the action domain of learning. To fully learn a new skill, people must practice it and get feedback on their performance; for example,

TABLE 3.1. SKILL-BASED TRAINING
VERSUS FEEDBACK-INTENSIVE TRAINING.

	Skill-Based Training	Feedback-Intensive Program
Purpose	To improve performance in specified skill areas	To gain in-depth understanding of strengths and weaknesses; develop increased self-awareness
Focus	Narrow focus on only specified skill areas	Wide focus on a broad range of potential strengths and weaknesses
Use of feedback	Feedback is used as a tool for assessing pre- and posttraining skill levels and for increasing skill level during training	Feedback is used to understand how one is viewed from multiple perspectives and how one's behavior has an impact on others
Use of practice	Ample opportunity to practice new skills through experiential activities is central to good skill-based training design; practice is necessary to improve skill levels	Little, if any, practice of new skills; experiential activities are used to generate data about oneself, one's behaviors, and how these behaviors are viewed by others
Content	Design includes prescriptive information: specific models, "how-to's," and tactics for use	Design includes information that helps participants organize their experiences (rather than prescriptive information); typically includes general models and concepts

those same participants learn to develop strategic planning skills by actually creating strategic statements and having them critiqued.

An effective skill-based training environment, then, is one that allows participants to (1) learn conceptual information or necessary behaviors, (2) practice using the new information or behaviors, and (3) receive feedback on their performance.

A Well-Designed Program: The Case of Joanne

Rather sophisticated examples of skill-based training are evident in higher levels of many organizations. Meet Joanne, a midlevel manager in the corporate headquarters of a retailing chain we call, for the purposes of this chapter, You-Shop. Joanne has been identified as a person of high potential within the organization and thus has been selected to participate in You-Shop's leadership development process. This is an on-going process that includes skill-based training, a coaching program, and 360-degree feedback; it is also linked to the organization's succession-planning process.

Although Joanne has learned many of her leadership skills on the job and expects to continue that path, she now decides, as part of transition into a new position, to participate in a skill-based leadership training program. The four-day program includes modules on systematic thinking, critical evaluation, and building interpersonal skills. Each module provides both knowledge and skills in the specified content area. For example, one module in the interpersonal-skills section focuses on teaching participants how to give feedback. First, they are presented with a brief lecture on positive and negative feedback and a conceptual model on constructive feedback (all in the knowledge domain). Then they begin to learn the skills, first by observing role modeling of effective and ineffective methods. Finally, through various role-play exercises they practice giving feedback and receive an evaluation of their performance.

Leadership Training: What Can It Teach?

Over the years, researchers have identified specific capacities that are linked to effective leadership, such as visioning and motivating others. Some of them are considered developable; people can *learn* self-awareness, self-confidence, systematic thinking, creativity, critical evaluation, empowerment, and effective interaction with others (Conger and Kanungo, 1988). Of these, the first two (self-awareness and self-confidence) are best developed through a feedback-intensive program. But the others can be learned in a skill-based training program: the abilities to interact socially, think systematically, make critical evaluations, think more creatively, and empower others.

At this point we often hear a common refrain of protest: those capabilities are too widespread, too subtle, too deeply rooted to lend themselves to ordinary training programs. Those who make this protest usually define these leadership capacities in very broad terms, and in that sense they are correct. What can be done is to dissect those broadly defined qualities and separate out the specific underlying skills. At that level, skill-based training is eminently possible.

Table 3.2 shows some of the skills that we believe define the five leadership capacities discussed in this chapter. Although this is not an exhaustive list, it does clearly demonstrate that there are skills, important to leadership effectiveness, that can be learned in a training program.

Ability to Interact Socially

Being able to interact socially is one leadership capacity that is critical for success. Many of the specific skills encompassed within it can be learned on the job, but they can also be practiced and honed via skill-based training.

Let us check in with Joanne. From past experiences she has developed good basic interpersonal skills, particularly in the area of com-

TABLE 3.2. SKILLS THAT DEFINE LEADERSHIP CAPACITIES.

Leadership Capacity	Skills
Ability to interact socially	Conflict management
	Negotiation
	Influencing
	Team building
	Active listening
	Ability to give feedback
	Communication
	Adaptation
Creativity	Ability to see alternate solutions
	Ability to question assumptions
	Ability to explore ambiguity
Critical evaluation and systematic thinking	Ability to think analytically
	Ability to detect problems
	Problem solving
Empowerment	Ability to motivate others through participative decision making
	Goal setting

munication. She has strong active listening and presentation skills, and they served her well in her initial supervisory and management jobs. But Joanne's present position requires a new set of interpersonal skills. She now needs to be able to build a team, confront problem employees, and manage conflict. All these are skills that can be developed in training. As Joanne practices those skills in her new assignment, integrating what she learns in the classroom with the daily challenges of the job, she will become even more effective in this area.

Ability to Think Creatively

To help people develop their ability to think creatively, to think outside the box, a training program teaches them to find novel approaches to situations they might encounter as leaders. First, they would *un*learn the tendency to follow conventional patterns, and then they would learn how to come up with new and unconventional approaches. They would gain knowledge about how to develop alternate solutions, and they would have opportunities to practice and receive feedback on their new skill.

Systematic Thinking and Critical Evaluation

Systematic thinking and critical evaluation are two closely related skills that work hand in hand. Systematic thinking refers to the ability to analyze a situation in a logical, orderly manner; critical evaluation means using this analytical thinking to sort through the situation and detect problems. Creative thinking, in contrast, looks for new ways to solve the problems once they are uncovered. To see how these skills can be developed in a training program, consider the experience of Mike, an up-and-coming young leader. His training program in systematic thinking and critical evaluation first provides knowledge, using lecture and role-play, about how to analyze situations, integrate information, and use deductive reasoning to diagnose problems. The next part of the program gives Mike opportunities for practice and feedback. If he links this information to his earlier training in creative thinking, he will be able to evaluate situations and develop innovative solutions.

Empowerment

As organizations find themselves trying to do more with fewer people, empowerment skills become ever more important. Empowering leadership practices include participative decision making and goal setting, two skills that are trainable.

What About Learning on the Job?

Leadership capacities learned through skill-based training overlap with those that can be learned on the job. It is not an either-or situation. Learning from one experience is reinforced by learning from other experiences. Each approach has its advantages and disadvantages.

To its advantage, skill-based training gives participants information in an organized and succinct manner and offers them a safe environment in which to practice new skills and receive feedback. Unfortunately, skill-based training must always confront the issue of transfer of training. When the training environment feels contrived—which, to varying degrees, it does by definition—some people find it difficult to take what they learn and use it in their job setting. They sometimes tend to leave the new skills at the classroom door.

Transfer of training is not an issue when learning comes from an actual job experience. On the job, people have the opportunity to learn and practice new skills in real-life settings. They also learn firsthand the consequences of success or failure. Another advantage is that learning through job experience may be most efficient because it doesn't take people away from work.

A downside to learning on the job is that people are on their own to gather information from a variety of sources and must practice new skills on the fly. Learning through experience allows people to understand the consequences of success or failure, but at the same time they must also account for the costs of any mistakes, which obviously are greater than mistakes made during a training program. Finally, on the job, people do not always receive feedback immediately, and perhaps not until a performance appraisal. Obviously, this inhibits learning.

Training Methods: How Can You Do It?

Five different methods are often used in skill-based training: lecture, case study, role-play, behavioral role-modeling, and simulations. This section describes all five, organized in order of the amount of interaction provided (see Figure 3.1). This sequencing reflects the theory that active experience facilitates learning better than passive techniques and that participants learn better through interactive methodologies (Thiagarajan, 1996).

Although each method is discussed separately, please note that most training programs use all or some combination of them. A multimethod approach is always preferable, for it helps to maximize learning. Also note that the discussion here focuses on off-site training because this is the way most managers experience skill-based training.

Lecture

A lecture efficiently presents content-specific information to a relatively large group of people in a relatively short amount of time. Even the

FIGURE 3.1. INTERACTIVITY OF FIVE TRAINING METHODS.

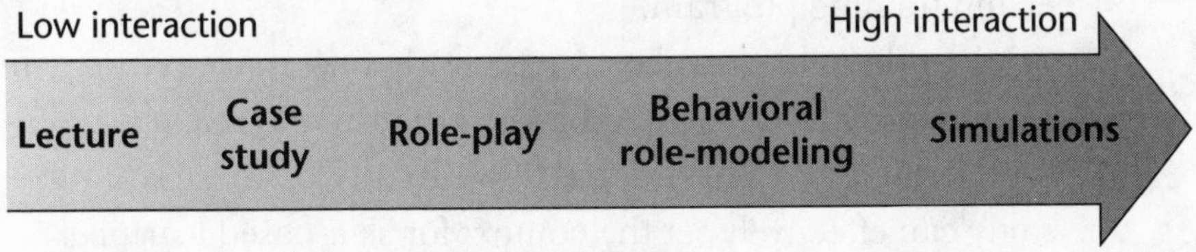

Low interaction   High interaction

Lecture | Case study | Role-play | Behavioral role-modeling | Simulations

most dynamic and experiential training program uses some amount of lecture to convey the knowledge base.

The traditional lecture format, familiar to anyone who ever sat in a classroom, uses one-way communication. An interactive lecture, however, is much more effective, especially for adults. In fact, some insist that "responsible" participation by the audience is critical in training (House, 1996).

An interactive lecture presents content-specific information but also engages participants in discussions and explorations of that information. An interactive approach stimulates questions, generates group discussions, and even encourages open discussion of disagreements (House, 1996). Depending upon the amount of interaction encouraged, participants may or may not be able to tailor the information to their needs.

Case Study

A case study presents participants with information describing an organization, a situation in the organization, how the situation was handled, and the outcome. The trainer instructs participants to critique the situation and outcome in light of information they have learned, to decide whether the action taken was appropriate and what could have been done differently.

Case studies serve several functions in training programs: they are icebreakers, they provoke thought and vicarious learning, they afford practice opportunities, and they test participants' learning (Alden and Kirkhorn, 1996). Of these, two—provoking thought and providing practice opportunities—are particularly relevant in a skill-based leadership training program.

As a thought provoker, a case study may make participants aware of previously unrecognized issues, their need to learn a new skill, or both (Alden and Kirkhorn, 1996). In any of these situations, a case study can effectively set the context for skill-based learning.

However, the highest value for case studies is the opportunity they offer for practicing skills, once the knowledge base is in place. They are particularly useful for practicing complex skills, such as the abilities to see alternate solutions, question assumptions, explore ambiguity, think analytically, and detect and solve problems. These skills underlie the leadership capacities of creativity, systematic thinking, and critical evaluation.

Role-Play

Role-plays are defined as exercises in which "players spontaneously act out characters assigned to them in a scenario" (Thiagarajan, 1996, p. 521). They work something like this: once participants understand the theories, principles, and techniques underlying the topic at hand—effective conflict management, for instance—they are divided into pairs. The trainer distributes a short description of a scenario in which a manager must resolve a conflict he or she is having with another manager in the organization and that has affected interactions between the two work groups. The partners take on the role of the two managers and act out the situation, practicing what they have learned about conflict management to resolve the problem.

By design, role-plays reflect reality but provide the participants only limited details about the hypothetical situation. Because of this, the range of behaviors that might unfold during the exercise is almost unlimited. Responding appropriately to whatever evolves, using the knowledge gained, is an inherent part of the exercise.

As a rule, role-plays are most useful for practicing interpersonal skills: conflict management, negotiation, influencing, team building, active listening, giving and receiving feedback, and communication (Thiagarajan, 1996, p. 521).

Behavioral Role-Modeling

Behavioral role-modeling, an elaboration of the role-play technique, is based on social learning theory (Bandura, 1986). It first presents participants with models of appropriate behavior, after which they role-play the behavior and receive feedback on their performance. For example, in learning effective negotiation skills, participants start by watching a videotape of an effective negotiation. At the end of the videotape they are reminded of the key steps necessary to complete a negotiation successfully. They then receive role-play materials and practice negotiating with partners, using the key steps that have been modeled and described.

Like role-plays, behavioral role-modeling is useful for learning interpersonal skills. In fact, researchers Goldstein and Sorcher (1974) used the approach to improve interpersonal and managerial skills, and at one point behavioral role-modeling was cited as one of the more effective training methods (Burke and Day, 1986).

Simulation

Simulations usually offer a realistic representation of one or more aspects of the leadership role: setting direction, acting on values, building relationships, or acting strategically. Simulations are like role-plays in that they mimic aspects of work reality. However, unlike role-plays, simulations provide detailed information and more structure for the participants.

In a typical simulation, participants receive a packet of detailed information about a fictitious company: an organizational chart, detailed background on the company's financial status, descriptions of the various departments, and the challenges facing both these departments and the organization as a whole. They are assigned, or they self-select, a role as one of the organization's leaders and receive additional information about this person and the specific problems and opportunities the leader faces. Once roles have been assigned and materials have been reviewed, participants run the fictitious company. They set priorities, make decisions (or fail to make them), work with disgruntled customers, and solve personnel problems. At the end of the exercise, participants give and receive feedback on the *what* (the content) and the *how* (the process) of their performance.

Which Techniques to Use?

For those charged with designing a skill-based leadership training program, the challenge (and the art) lies in matching content areas with the most appropriate training methods. It is to be emphasized that for greatest effectiveness, multiple methods should be used. For example, lectures are needed in most skill-based training because they are the most efficient way to deliver large amounts of information and theory. But no matter how well done, lectures alone are never sufficient.

Throughout this handbook we stress that leaders learn by doing. The same principle holds true in training. Learning new leadership skills means acquiring knowledge—through lectures—and then practicing that new knowledge. In skill-based training, the doing can come in case studies, role-plays, behavioral role modeling, and simulations.

Table 3.3 illustrates the appropriate matches between knowledge and skills on the one hand and methodology on the other to maximize effectiveness.

TABLE 3.3. TRAINING METHODOLOGY AND EXAMPLES OF SKILLS LEARNED.

Training Methodology	Examples of Skills Learned
Lecture	Conceptual information such as theories, models, principles, and techniques
Case study	Complex skills such as ability to see alternate solutions, question assumptions, think analytically, and detect and solve problems
Role-play	Interpersonal skills such as conflict management, negotiation, influencing, team building, active listening, giving and receiving feedback, and communication
Behavioral role-modeling	Same as role-play
Simulations	Problem solving, interpersonal skills, and analytical thinking

The Role of Training in Leadership Development: How Can You Use It?

In this chapter training has been defined as a planned event; in earlier chapters leadership development was defined as an ongoing process. The question now is how skill-based training, as an event, fits into a leadership development process.

The leadership development model described in the Introduction suggests that the presence of three elements (assessment, challenge, and support) is important to a successful developmental experience; it also suggests that development is optimized when one development experience is linked to another. This section examines the relationship between skill-based training and the model from both perspectives: how assessment, support, and challenge improve the effectiveness of skill-based training; and how training can be integrated with other developmental experiences.

Skill-Based Training and Assessment, Challenge, and Support

How can assessment assist in developing new skills? Here is one scenario.

Arthur, a manager in a computer software company, attends a skill-based leadership training program. The program is highly interactive and performance-based. Before the program, Arthur believed that he had good conflict management and delegation skills, but after the first short simulation he realizes that he needs to learn and grow in both areas. Throughout the weeklong program, Arthur continues to receive feedback on the improvement he makes as a result of continued opportunities to practice. At the end of the program, participants share impromptu feedback on each other's learning during the week. Arthur returns to his job with better awareness of his current skill level and his continued development needs. This is informal assessment; it was not explicitly built into the program design as pretraining and posttraining measures.

An alternate scenario illustrates a more formalized approach. Imagine that Arthur attends the same training program, but this time it includes pretraining and posttraining measures of his skills in the specific content area. On the first day of training, Arthur completes a series of assessments on his current skill level. The program design includes lectures, short simulations, and ongoing feedback. On the last day of the training, Arthur again completes a formal assessment of his skill level. He receives feedback on the results of the two assessment measures and on his improved skills and returns to his job with specific assessment information.

In the first scenario, Arthur has a sense of his areas of improvement and need for further development. In the second scenario, he has specific data.

Assessment in the form of ongoing feedback improves the effectiveness of skill-based training. As participants practice new skills, immediate feedback helps them adjust their learning if necessary. Pretraining and posttraining assessment also serve a motivational role. Assuming that participants are motivated to successfully perform their job, pretraining assessment of skills (compared to skill levels required by the job) highlights skill gaps, which in turn can motivate participants to learn. Once participants have successfully learned the training content, posttraining assessment can validate their efforts. If they have not, posttraining assessment highlights the need for either further training or a different approach to developing the skills.

Challenge

By definition, learning something new takes people out of their comfort zone and into new waters. Leaving this comfort zone is a challenging experience, but it is necessary if learning is to take place. In most skill-based leadership training programs, participants leave their comfort zones.

Skill-based training has the necessary challenge embedded in it whenever participants are presented with new information and unfamiliar ideas, and when they are required to learn and practice new behaviors. Role-plays, behavior modeling, and simulations are relatively safe ways to put individuals into situations where they can try out new skills, with relatively little consequence from mistakes.

Support

What can be done to support people as they attempt to develop new skills? In relation to training, this question is most often discussed in terms of people getting the support they need to use on the job the new skills they learned in the classroom.

Transfer of training is the extent to which training content is applied on the job. One factor that strongly affects transfer of training is the degree to which the organization has a supportive climate, where people are allowed and encouraged to use new skills on the job.

Rouillier and Goldstein (1990) identified two major components of a supportive climate: situational cues and consequences. An example of a positive situational cue is giving participants the opportunity to use the training content immediately. Another is if supervisors relieve pressures on the participants for a short time to allow them to practice new skills on the job. Examples of positive consequences include participants' receiving acknowledgment and being rewarded (for example, with choice assignments) when they use their new skills.

Conversely, the organization's normal practices can have the effect of prohibiting a supportive transfer climate. In organizations where time constraints do not permit a performance decline while learning happens, where risk taking is punished, and where particular skills and perspectives are not valued in the culture, participation in training programs is often a hollow exercise.

Learning takes time, and the organization must provide this time. When participants return from a training program and start to work on incorporating their new skills into their job, they may experience a drop in performance (Bunker and Webb, 1992). An organization must provide support and time for new skills to be fully integrated. A supportive organization rewards a manager for practicing and learning new skills. A nonsupportive organization punishes a manager for the work not done during the learning phase. The second manager may dutifully attend a training program and learn the content but continue to use the old behaviors on the job to avoid any drop in performance.

In addition to time, learning also requires taking risks. Organizations must support this risk taking in order for transfer of training to occur. Trying new skills and mastering them involves practice, and performance usually drops during the learning process. A risk-averse organization wants a guarantee that the first attempt at learning will result in success. Seldom is that the case. An organization typically needs to tolerate several learning attempts before success is achieved.

Consider the managers who are attempting to learn a more creative leadership style. They may need to try several different approaches before finding one that works effectively. Then the new style needs to be fine-tuned so it fits the work group and the organization. If such risk taking is punished by the organization, the managers simply revert to an old style and do not realize the benefits of development.

Finally, even if it is willing to provide time for learning and supports risk taking, an organization typically provides this support only for the skills valued by its culture. To some extent, this point is related to the relevance of the training content.

The organizational value system may be enacted in a variety of ways. Again, Joanne, the young manager at You-Shop, provides an example. She attends a weeklong executive development training program at an out-of-state university. During the week, Joanne learns new theories of leadership, employee motivation, and organizational behavior. She also learns ways to apply this information on the job and receives ample opportunity to practice the new skills.

When she returns to work, Joanne begins to use her new skills. Three weeks later, she is called into her vice president's office and questioned about her behaviors. He tells her that members of her workgroup have complained about her recent changes. Joanne enthusiastically relates what she learned during training and explains her goals for implementing the new skills. The vice president brusquely interrupts. "Are you kidding? Everyone knows that the New Age stuff they teach at that place will never fly around here." Although these new skills are relevant to Joanne's job, they are not valued by the organization.

Skill-Based Training Connected with Other Developmental Experiences

When skill-based training is thoughtfully and purposefully linked with other development experiences, development is optimized.

Let us look in on Joanne one final time. Her experience in a leadership training program is part of her transition into a new job. She successfully completes the program and makes the tough decision to continue with her development, even in the face of criticism from the vice president. At the end of the first year in the new job, she attends a feedback-intensive program. Here she gains many insights from her experiences and decides to improve her leadership capacities in the arena of critical thinking and evaluation. Several months later, she attends a skill-based training program to help improve her analytical thinking. However, she feels the program simply provides the basics. To supplement the training experience, Joanne establishes a coaching relationship with her immediate supervisor, who also provides her with several task force assignments that require critical-thinking skills.

This example illustrates the interplay among several development strategies, in this case a *feedback-intensive program, skill-based training, assignments, ongoing coaching,* and *feedback.* The feedback-intensive program highlights Joanne's need to develop her abilities in critical thinking. The skill-based training provides basic knowledge and skill practice, but the assignments, coaching, and feedback are necessary to allow Joanne to refine those skills. No one of these experiences by itself fully facilitates Joanne's development. Together, they have tremendous leverage. Skill-based training reinforces other development experiences and is in turn reinforced by them.

Improving Effectiveness: When to Use Skill-Based Training?

To ensure that any skill-based training program is as effective as possible, as we have already mentioned it should include the three core elements (assessment, challenge and support) and should be linked to other development experiences. In addition, two other characteristics are particularly critical: timing and relevance.

Training Program Timeliness

The most effective training program presents content that is needed at that time and is immediately used. For example, a team of executives about to negotiate a new agreement with joint venture partners would find a workshop in negotiation skills particularly timely. Someone who has just been promoted to general manager and who is now, for the first time, managing and leading people who have more technical expertise would find workshops in building teams and delegation to be timely.

Career transitions, new challenges added to present jobs, and organizational change mark times in an individual's career when skill-based training is likely to be timely. In these situations, skill-based training is perceived as instrumental in successfully navigating the change-related situation.

What is needed, then, is just-in-time training, training that provides people the skills they need when they need them.

Relevance of Training Content

In skill-based training, content that is directly relevant to participants' jobs is learned better than content that is not. An upper-level manager knows she needs empowerment skills because she has just acquired a group that has been downsized from two levels of management to one, and her new direct reports now have many more direct reports and a much broader range of responsibilities. Skill-based training is relevant to this aspiring leader if it provides knowledge and skills in empowerment. Another young leader moves into a position that requires viewing the entire organization as a system; it is no longer sufficient to take care of things in only one functional area. Skill-based training is relevant to this leader if it provides knowledge and skill in thinking and acting systematically.

In one sense, timing and relevance work hand in glove, so much so that at times they look the same. But in fact, skill-based training can be relevant but not timely (needed but too late to be effective) or it can be timely but not relevant (provided soon after a career transition but not on relevant topics). Obviously, both are needed. One way to ensure that both are provided is through a training needs assessment.

The Importance of Training Needs Assessment

Before undertaking any type of training, an organization should first conduct a training needs assessment to determine what development needs exist, whether training is an appropriate response, and, if so, what type of training is needed.

A training needs assessment has three large components: organizational analysis, task analysis, and person analysis (Goldstein, 1993). The first examines factors within the organizational system that have an impact on a training program. Through this examination, management should articulate the outcomes expected from the training program. Task analysis closely examines the job performed by the people targeted for training; the goal is to clearly identify the skills that they should acquire by the end of the program. Finally, person analysis identifies the participant's current skill level. If there is a gap between the skills needed (task analysis) and the current skills (person analysis), training is called for.

In this section, we have focused particularly on organizational analysis, for it is here that integration of skill-based training and other development experiences can be considered. The organizational analysis should examine the goals of the organization, its resources, the climate for transfer of training (discussed earlier in this chapter), and the internal and external constraints on training (Goldstein, 1993). At the same time, senior management should also articulate the link between training outcomes and organizational goals. Conflict between them usually results in an ineffective training program, confused participants, and a frustrated human resource practitioner.

Conclusion

This chapter has described skill-based training, enumerated specific leadership capacities that can be developed through training, discussed the role of skill-based training within the broader context of leadership development systems, and outlined when and how skill-based training can be most useful.

What can be done with this information? If you are an HR practitioner planning to use skill-based training as part of an overall developmental system, the information here can help you ensure that the program has the most favorable design and that training is transferred as smoothly as possible.

You can increase the relevance of the training content using assessment information. Specifically, a training program can provide a pre-training assessment of the specific skills to be taught. Also, either before the training program or at the beginning, participants should receive information on the levels of specific skills required by their job. Any gap between their current skill level and what they need on the job should make the training content more salient. Look for ways to emphasize perceived job relevance. The training environment both in the classroom and on the job should maximize the link between the training content and future rewards.

You should also pay attention to the characteristics of the training program. Appropriate characteristics can be achieved through a training needs assessment and program design. Specifically, the needs assessment helps ensure that the training program is teaching skills that are immediately needed on the job or will be needed in the near future.

It also helps ensure that the training content is consistent with current or future directions in the organization.

Finally, you must consider transfer of the training content into on-the-job behavior and work to be sure that the job environment supports (and preferably rewards) application of newly learned skills. One step toward this goal is making sure that organizational expectations, supervisor expectations, participant expectations, and training objectives all match.

CHAPTER FOUR

JOB ASSIGNMENTS

Patricia J. Ohlott

Take a few moments and reflect back over your career. Try to identify at least one job (or an assignment that was part of a job) that you think was an important developmental experience for you as a leader, a job experience from which you learned a great deal. It probably was a job from which you learned more than just new business content; something about this experience changed the way you lead. Ask yourself what it was about this job that was so difficult or challenging for you:

- Was it a promotion or a move to a different part of the business?
- Did you have to deal with difficult customers or clients?
- Did you have to manage something with which you were unfamiliar?
- Did you have to build an effective team from scratch?
- Were you responsible for a downsizing?
- Was there a great deal of risk involved?
- Was it a high-visibility task?

Now ask yourself what you learned from this experience. What do you do differently today, because of your experiences in that job or assignment? Perhaps you learned about persuading others, strategic thinking, perseverance, delegation, or coping with ambiguity.

Did you realize you were learning at the time? Was it planned? Was it difficult? Do you think you could have learned these things in a classroom?

Job assignments are one of the oldest and most potent forms of leadership development. They give leaders the opportunity to learn by doing—by working on real problems and dilemmas. However, systematic and deliberate use of job assignments for development purposes is a more recent phenomenon in most organizations. Until the 1980s most organized leadership development efforts focused on classroom education and training.

A number of research studies conducted at the Center and elsewhere in the 1980s support the notion that many managers consider job experiences as *the* primary source of learning (see, for example, Broderick, 1983; McCall, Lombardo, and Morrison, 1988; Morrison, White, and Van Velsor, 1987; Wick, 1989; Zemke, 1985). Although the studies are based primarily on retrospective accounts and are therefore subject to all the biases associated with memories, these studies are noteworthy in that their conclusions are drawn from actual stories related by successful executives. Executives were asked to identify crucial events in their development as leaders. Their stories showed that they felt they learned more from influential people at work and from the challenges inherent in their jobs than from formal training programs and other nonwork experiences.

In the 1990s, in both the theory and the practice of leadership development, there has been increasing recognition that on-the-job experiences play a critical role. Although formal training and development programs are still important, organizations are becoming more and more aware that they can no longer rely only on these formal programs if they are to develop executives who are effective and adaptable.

One technique used informally by many companies is job rotation, to teach technical skills and broaden business knowledge. Less common, although in our view far more effective, is systematic use of job assignments as a development experience. Two notable examples are Citicorp and General Electric. At GE, an important factor in determining consideration for executive positions is who will benefit the most from the experience in terms of their development (Sherman, 1995). Citicorp tries to place high-potential managers in jobs for which they are no more than 60–70 percent prepared, thus giving them the new challenges they need to continue development (Clark and Lyness, 1991).

Citicorp and GE are somewhat unusual in their policies. In most organizations, the ideal candidate for a position is someone who already has the skills to do the job and thus can hit the ground running. Organizations tend not to make assignments for development purposes. Perhaps another reason assignments are not often systematically used for development purposes is that organizations don't really understand why and how to do it.

That is the goal of this chapter: to outline for human resource professionals working with managers, executives, and other future leaders the types of experience from which people learn and the kinds of learning that typically result from various experiences. Although most of the work at the Center has been conducted with managers and executives, we believe that developmental assignments provide important opportunities for growth for all types of leaders.

What Constitutes a Developmental Job Assignment?

We use the term *job assignment* because it can refer to an entire job, such as opening a new facility or redesigning a system, or a piece of a job, such as dealing with a difficult employee or serving on a temporary task force to solve a particular problem. A new assignment might be an entirely new job (via a promotion or transfer), or it might mean responsibilities added to an existing job, such as working on a short-term project team while also doing the day-to-day work of the normal job.

An important distinction is that assignments are not necessarily work someone is "assigned" to do; a person may seek out and volunteer for assignments, such as heading up a task force to study the efficacy of a new software package, handling a negotiation with a customer, or serving as liaison with a community group.

What makes a job assignment developmental? Essentially, it must be something that stretches people, pushes them out of their comfort zones, and requires them to think and act differently. It may involve roles that are not well defined, and it usually contains some elements that are new to the person. These assignments place people in a challenging situation full of problems to solve, dilemmas to resolve, obstacles to overcome, and choices to make under conditions of risk and uncertainty.

Thus, the key element in a developmental assignment is challenge. By tackling unfamiliar tasks and seeing the consequences of their actions, people learn from the challenges in their assignments. This learning may produce changes in how managers make decisions, take actions, handle risks, and approach problems.

Although developmental assignments are, first and foremost, challenging, the assignments that are *most* developmental also incorporate assessment and support (the other elements of the leadership development model presented in the introductory chapter). New assignments provide assessment data if they reveal strengths or deficiencies in someone's current skills. Until they face situations that call for a particular competency, leaders may not know to what degree they have the competency. For example, a manager who is in charge of building a new team discovers for the first time how good (or bad) she is at it. This points her toward areas where she needs to improve. If the context is feedback-rich as she tries different strategies, if she gets multiple sources of input on how well she is doing, then her learning in this new assignment is enhanced.

Being given a developmental assignment can in and of itself be experienced as supportive. It is a signal that the organization believes the person can successfully handle the assignment and learn from the experience. This boost to self-confidence motivates the person to learn. But the challenges of an assignment can be particularly difficult, requiring additional support from others as the work unfolds (we return to this point later in the chapter).

Challenges Inherent in Developmental Jobs

Research into what makes a job developmental has identified five broad sources of challenge related to learning:

1. Job transitions
2. Creating change
3. High levels of responsibility
4. Nonauthority relationships
5. Obstacles

Within these broad categories are a number of specific challenges, characteristics of assignments that have been found to be particularly developmental (McCauley, Ruderman, Ohlott, and Morrow, 1994). These challenges, summarized in Table 4.1, stem from the roles, responsibilities, tasks, and context of the job.

This section describes how and why the five sources of challenge affect learning and suggests specific types of jobs that are likely to present these challenges. Table 4.2 provides other specific examples of job assignments.

Job Transitions. A transition involves a change in work role, such as a change in job content, level of responsibility, or location. Specific job transitions that have been shown to be particularly developmental include changes in level, function, or employer (Nicholson and West, 1988); vast increases in the scope of the assignment (McCall, Lombardo, and Morrison, 1988; Valerio, 1990); and moving from a line to a staff job (McCall, Lombardo, and Morrison, 1988).

Transitions place people in new situations where the responsibilities of the job are to some degree unfamiliar and where the usual routines and behaviors are no longer adequate. Transitions require people to

TABLE 4.1. SOURCES OF CHALLENGE IN JOB ASSIGNMENTS.

Transitions	1. Unfamiliar responsibilities: the leader must handle responsibilities that are new, very different, or much broader than previous ones.
	2. Proving oneself: the leader has added pressure to show others he or she can handle the assignment.
Creating change	3. Developing new directions: the leader is responsible for starting something new in the organization, making strategic changes in the business, carrying out a reorganization, or responding to rapid changes in the business environment.
	4. Inherited problems: the leader has to fix problems created by a former incumbent or take over problem employees.
	5. Reduction decisions: decisions have to be made about shutting down operations or staff reductions.
	6. Problems with employees: employees lack adequate experience, are incompetent, or are resistant.
High level of responsibility	7. High stakes: clear deadlines, pressure from senior leaders, high visibility, and responsibility for key decisions make success or failure in this job clearly relevant.
	8. Managing business diversity: the scope of the job is large and includes responsibilities for multiple functions, groups, products, customers, or markets.
	9. Job overload: the sheer size of the job requires a large investment of time and energy.
	10. Handling external pressure: external factors that have an impact on the business (for example, negotiating with unions or government agencies, working in a foreign culture, coping with serious community problems) must be dealt with.
Nonauthority relationships	11. Influencing without authority: getting the job done requires influencing peers, people in higher positions, external parties, or other key people over whom the leader has no direct authority.
Obstacles	12. Adverse business conditions: the business unit or product line faces financial problems or difficult economic conditions.
	13. Lack of top management support: senior leaders are reluctant to provide direction, support, or resources for current work or new projects.
	14. Lack of personal support: the leader is excluded from key networks and gets little support and encouragement from others.
	15. Difficult boss: the leader's opinions or management style differs from those of the boss, or the boss has major shortcomings.

TABLE 4.2. DEVELOPMENTAL CHALLENGES AND EXAMPLES OF ASSIGNMENTS WHERE THEY MAY BE FOUND.

Challenge	Examples of Assignments
Job transitions	Being the inexperienced member of a project team
	Taking a temporary assignment in another function
	Moving to a general management job
	Managing a group or discipline you know little about
	Moving from a line job to a corporate staff role
	A lateral move to another department
Creating change	Launching a new product, project, or system
	Serving on a reengineering team
	Facilitating the development of a new vision or mission statement
	Dealing with a business crisis
	Handling a workforce reduction
	Hiring new staff
	Breaking ground on a new operation
	Reorganizing a unit
	Resolving subordinate performance problems
	Supervising the liquidation of product or equipment
High level of responsibility	A corporate assignment with tight deadlines
	Representing the organization to the media or influential outsiders
	Managing across geographic locations
	Assuming additional responsibilities following a downsizing
	Taking on a colleague's responsibilities during his or her absence
Nonauthority relationships	Presenting a proposal to top management
	Corporate staff job
	Serving on a cross-functional team
	Managing an internal project such as a company event or office renovation
	Working on a project with a community or social organization
Obstacles	Working with a difficult boss
	Working in a situation where there is little or unclear direction from senior management
	Responsibility for a business or product line that faces intensely competitive markets
	Starting a new project with few resources

find new ways of thinking about and responding to problems and opportunities. In addition, people who have been moved into dramatically different assignments are motivated by having to prove themselves all over again to an entirely new group of coworkers.

The extent to which a job transition is developmental is person-specific; that is, it depends on how similar the new job is to the previous one. A job amounting to a great stretch for one person may be developmental, but the same transfer would not be so for someone who has already had a job with similar responsibilities and tasks. A job move is likely to be less developmental if there are few new elements in the job (Davies and Easterby-Smith, 1984; McCauley, Lombardo, and Usher, 1989; Nicholson and West, 1988) or little increase in the amount of discretion the manager has to define the job (Brett, 1984), or if differences from previous positions go unnoticed by the incumbent (Brett, 1984; Nicholson and West, 1988).

Listen as one manager describes his first key transitional assignment:

I was considered one of the best electricians at the site. Most of the guys and managers were coming to me when they needed answers, and the crew was rather close. They knew me and knew how I functioned. One of the guys I even went to high school with. Then I was promoted to electrical foreperson. When I got the job it was like I had to reprove myself. The guy that surprised me the most was the one I went to high school with. He expected because he was my friend he should receive special treatment. I learned that there is a transition period when you move from the labor force into management. The testing that goes on from below and above is a feeling-out process to determine boundaries, not only for them, but for me. At the time I didn't understand what was happening to me and took the actions as an attack on my authority.

Another example of a transitional assignment is moving from a line job to a corporate staff role. Line managers assigned to staff roles often must relocate to corporate headquarters and report to executives they have not worked with before, while struggling with technical areas that are new to them. A line-to-staff move challenges people to learn to think strategically as well as tactically. It can also teach important relationship lessons about what top leaders are like and how to work effectively with them. In summary, this particular assignment provides opportunities to learn how to influence those over whom one has no direct control.

Task-Related Challenges

The second, third, and fourth sources of challenge that were listed earlier are task-related and stem from the responsibilities, requirements, problems, and tasks inherent in the job itself. They are relatively more objective than transitions, so it may be easier to determine whether or not they are present in a given assignment. For example, it is clear that an English-speaking American manager assigned to open the company's first new plant in Mexico faces a number of challenges.

We have found three types of task-related challenges to be particularly developmental: those resulting from the need to create change, those stemming from a high level of responsibility, and those related to negotiating nonauthority relationships.

Creating Change. Jobs that require a person to create change call for numerous actions and decisions in the face of uncertainty and ambiguity. A leader with a mandate to create change may be responsible for starting something new in the organization, carrying out a reorganization, fixing problems created by a predecessor, or dealing with problematic employees. Often the assignment has a clear goal, such as reducing the workforce by 20 percent, but the role itself is not clearly defined and the leader has some freedom to determine how the goal should be achieved. The more uncertain and complex the changes are, the bigger are the learning challenges of the job.

Starting a business from scratch and turning around a business in trouble are classic examples of this type of developmental assignment. Although the two assignments are very different in focus and can teach some distinct lessons, they both hold opportunities to learn some of the skills important to effectively creating change. Among other things, leaders in such assignments often learn important lessons about agenda setting, such as decisiveness and shouldering responsibility for their own actions. They also learn more about relationships with employees, such as leading, motivating, and developing, as well as confronting those who are problematic.

One manager gave us an example of an assignment where she was required to create change:

> I was assigned to manage a brand that needed to be repositioned. I worked with my boss on a new campaign that capitalized on our research and development findings as well as our consumer research data. I assembled a core team of members from the majority of areas to share the brand's objectives and how they could achieve those goals. Within the first year we reversed a five-year decline and grew volume by 35 percent. From this experience, I learned that when people feel a part of a process or decision, there is greater team effort and positive end results. The key was to listen to what they were saying, then empower them to act upon the information. I also learned to truly set clearly defined goals that are measurable and achievable. Once people feel valued and appreciated, they are willing to go the extra mile for the project and/or the manager.

High Levels of Responsibility. Leadership assignments with high levels of responsibility have greater breadth, visibility, and complexity; they also require more external interfaces than jobs with less responsibility.

Moving to a job with a high level of responsibility may involve a leap in the scope of the job; larger budgets; more people; and more diverse responsibilities, as with different functions, groups, or areas. With a higher level of responsibility can come higher stakes, greater business diversity, and more pressure from external factors. There may also be a danger of overload because the job requires a large investment of time and energy.

Jobs of this sort provide potent opportunities for learning such lessons as resourcefulness in knowing how to adapt to changing and often ambiguous circumstances; being able to think strategically and make good decisions under pressure; and building and mending relationships with subordinates, coworkers, higher management, and external parties. Dealing with broader and more complex problems provides a setting for learning about integrating different perspectives, prioritizing, and making trade-offs.

Leaders in high-level jobs are in a position to have significant impact on the organization. At the same time, they do their work with greatly increased visibility. The combination of the opportunity to make a difference and being in the spotlight may encourage people to work harder to enhance their leadership skills and abilities. There is also evidence that learning is reinforced and supported when the actions people take in a significant context are successful (Kelleher, Finestone, and Lowy, 1986; Wick, 1989).

Here is one manager's account of his company's innovative use of a developmental assignment with a high level of responsibility: "The CEO specifically requested me to work with him to develop a strategic plan to curb the drug problem in our metropolitan area. I worked closely with him and with an executive director in the community. They taught me how CEOs think, process information, and view success. I worked closely with impoverished communities: gathering information, identifying their issues and needs, and working with them to accomplish real tasks. This assignment strengthened my strategic planning skills and polished my interpersonal skills, from one [socioeconomic] extreme of people to the other."

Nonauthority Relationships. Most leaders are accustomed to managing downward. When they find themselves in situations where they must achieve cooperation among people over whom they do not have direct authority, they come face-to-face with another source of challenge. Typical situations might be working with clients, peers, or joint-venture partners, serving as part of a project team or task force, or negotiating among different departments. Managers in these situations learn a great deal about building relationships, handling conflict, and being straightforward with others. To get all parties to work together effectively, leaders have to learn new skills in effective negotiation, communication, and conflict management.

Among the most common examples of assignments that challenge leaders to manage nonauthority relationships are leading or participating in a cross-functional project team or task force. As organizations become flatter, make greater use of cross-functional teams, and rely more on alliances and partnerships to accomplish their work, this type of assignment is increasing.

One executive told us about his experience and what it taught him. In addition to his normal managerial role, he was selected to work with the company's complaint department to find a better way to handle customer problems. To identify the different types of calls and decide who would handle them, he had to work with people who did not formally report to him. There was constant finger-pointing and disagreement between departments as to who should handle which types of calls and who would pay for overtime or incentives for improved performance. From this experience, he reported learning how to build and sustain relationships in other departments, how to deal professionally with people who had different management styles, and how to disagree while maintaining professional respect for one another.

Obstacles. A fifth type of developmental opportunity derives from the contextual features of the job. The basic tasks and responsibilities of the job may remain constant, but the challenges of the job change if a contextual feature is altered. These contextual features generally represent difficult situations, or obstacles, with which managers have to deal in the course of fulfilling their job responsibilities.

Obstacles may result from situations within the organization such as a difficult boss or unsupportive group of top managers, or from external factors such as adverse economic conditions. When people work to reduce the psychological discomfort that occurs in such situations, learning usually results.

Here is one manager's story:

> My boss had been with the company for thirty years. He was extremely demanding and expected a lot, but at the same time he gave no direction, guidance, or clear vision on what he wanted or where he was going. Due to his knowledge and experience, I was always uncomfortable and was not willing to challenge him. Today, we are peers and still talk frequently. I see him as a man facing some of the challenges I have. Over time, I have come to realize that I should have challenged him. He was oftentimes proven to be wrong, and I should have spoken up.

Successfully dealing with these difficult situations leads not only to learning about strategies for handling them but also to increased perseverance and self-confidence. However, we have found that generally people see the positive side of these negative situations only when thinking about them in retrospect. It may be that while they are in the midst of the situation, the discomfort predominates, masking any sense of positive outcomes. It is also possible that learning cannot occur until the obstacle has diminished. Thus, self-reflection may be especially important in helping people learn from obstacles, and people dealing with difficult situations may need special coaching to become aware of the opportunities for learning that they provide.

Learning from Assignments

Talking about assignments for development purposes begs the question, "Development for what?" What kinds of things can people learn from the challenges in a developmental assignment?

In a word, developmental assignments teach practical knowledge and skills that enhance and expand the ability to be effective. Burgoyne and Hodgson (1983) call this type of development "natural managerial learning" because it requires people to draw conclusions independently on the basis of their own experiences and to apply those lessons to help meet current and future challenges.

The Center has conducted extensive research into the challenges inherent in developmental assignments and the types of lessons they teach. The initial study of 191 managers and executives by McCall, Lombardo, and Morrison (1988) identified thirty-three important lessons executives reported they had learned from challenging experiences. These lessons do not reflect qualities such as intelligence or common sense; rather, they reveal fundamental leadership skills and ways of thinking. Although derived from a study of executives, these lessons are important for all kinds of leaders, as they represent a wide range of skills, abilities, insights, knowledge, and values. McCall, Lombardo, and Morrison (1988) grouped these lessons into five themes: handling relationships, setting and implementing agendas, basic values, personal insight, and executive temperament.

1. *Handling relationships* encompasses a variety of lessons about working with other people who may have different ideas, outlooks, and agendas. Central to this skill is the ability to understand other people's points of view. The lessons in this category reflect the recognition that different skills may be required for dealing with all types of people in varying situations. Examples include how to handle political situations, understanding the perspectives of others, dealing with conflict, and motivating and developing others.

2. *Setting and implementing agendas,* as distinct from formal strategic planning, is often how managers actually determine direction. In John Kotter's study (1982) of general managers, they describe agendas that cover a broad range of business issues over many time frames. As they use the term, *agenda* encompassed both goals (specific and vague) and plans, which were often not closely related to formal plans. The types of lessons that enhance a leader's ability to set and implement agendas involve finding alternative solutions to problems, structural and systemic

design skills, business and technical knowledge and skills, accepting responsibility for the direction one sets, and strategic thinking.

3. *Basic values* are the underlying principles that guide leadership behavior. New values may be formed, and established values tested and shaped, by organizational experiences. Examples of these lessons are understanding the importance of credibility, learning how to treat people with respect, being sensitive to people's needs, acting with integrity, and relying on others (rather than managing everything oneself).

4. *Personal insights* are lessons of self-awareness, as when people see a need to balance work and personal life, learn their own wants and needs, and recognize their weaknesses and blind spots. The most effective leaders are self-aware, while a lack of self-awareness is strongly related to derailment. Knowing what they want to achieve helps leaders identify opportunities for growth in that area. Knowledge of their own strengths, weaknesses, and goals helps them recognize further areas of development while maintaining the confidence to withstand the feedback and criticism entailed in achieving their goals.

5. *Executive temperament* refers to the personal qualities necessary to cope with the demands and ambiguities of a leadership role. Important lessons in this category involve knowing when to be flexible versus when to stand firm, when to be tough and when to be compassionate, and being able to tell the difference between situations that can and cannot be controlled.

These five categories represent general types of skills and abilities that can be learned from challenging job experiences. Researchers McCauley, Lombardo, and Usher (1989) found that these skills differentiate between effective and ineffective managers.

Another key finding is that, although not in one-to-one correspondence, assignments with different challenges teach different types of lessons. For example, while working on a task force where a key challenge is to influence others without formal authority, a person is likely to learn important lessons about resourcefulness, building and mending relationships, and putting people at ease. From a turnaround assignment where a reduction in workforce is required, a leader can learn more about how to confront problem subordinates and how to build and mend relationships.

Leveraging Assignments for Development Purposes

To systematically use assignments for development, an organization needs to focus on five tasks: (1) creating a shared understanding of how assignments can be developmental, (2) helping individuals see the learning opportunities in their current jobs, (3) using development as a criterion in giving assignments to individuals, (4) maximizing individual learning during a developmental assignment, and (5) tracking developmental assignments over time.

The following section discusses these tasks in greater detail and includes examples from a few organizations that are more systematic and intentional in their use of assignments for leadership development than is the typical organization.

Create a Shared Understanding

To be active partners in their own development process, people need to understand what competencies contribute to effectiveness in their organization and which job assignments help develop those competencies. There are a number of techniques organizations can use to identify these assignments.

One strategy is to use existing, published general resources. *Lessons of Experience* (McCall, Lombardo, and Morrison, 1988) provides some valuable tools, including checklists, tables, and summaries, that may be helpful in linking assignments with potential outcomes. Its authors provide a particularly useful matrix of types of job challenge and the management lessons most often associated with them. Lombardo and Eichinger (1989) offer eighty-eight developmental experiences that can be added to existing jobs. Some examples are to represent concerns of nonexempt staff to higher management, deal with a business crisis, do a competitive analysis, design a training course, carry out a project with another function, supervise outplacement, and run the company picnic.

Organizations also conduct informal, internal "developmental audits" to determine where developmental assignments tend to occur and what kinds of things people typically learn from them (White, 1992). For example, a human resource manager can survey current and former job incumbents and their coworkers to see what they perceive to be the job's major challenges. White also suggests interviewing senior managers to determine which assignments they feel have been most developmental for them and what they learned from those assignments. Valerio (1990) used this strategy to customize a taxonomy of developmental assignments for NYNEX. In addition to asking about key developmental assignments, she presented the managers with the thirteen competencies used by the company to assess managerial performance and asked them to describe on-job and off-job tasks that contributed to development of each competency.

From this type of information, a few organizations have created their own unique matrix of developmental assignments and learning outcomes. Such a matrix can be part of career development information shared with employees. NCR Corporation (1992) provides this information to its engineers and engineering managers in a career development manual. The manual explains the levels and types of jobs in various career paths for engineers within the company, the competencies needed in these jobs, and which key assignments help develop these competencies. The key assignments are fairly specific and are tailored to the organization. For example, "working on a customer hotline" and "serving on a quality deployment team" are among the assignments that help develop negotiation skills.

A few innovative organizations systematically collect information about the challenges in their job assignments and what individuals are learning from them and make that information widely available in their organization through an online database. As part of a special assignment or before moving on to a new job, people complete a computerized questionnaire that asks about the tasks of the assignment, challenges faced, and what they learned or in what ways they have grown. Tasks, challenges, and lessons learned are categorized in a framework that is available to others throughout the company. Thus, a leader who needs to expand the ability to build a team could go to the database and see in which jobs or special assignments others in the company reported learning a great deal about team building, and then look for similar opportunities.

Help People See the Learning Opportunities in Assignments

People are more likely to learn from their current job assignment if they are aware that the potential exists to do so. Most people recognize that they learn a great deal on their jobs, but when asked to plan for their own development, they tend to think more about training and education programs. They need to be encouraged by bosses, mentors, and coaches and by the human resource staff to think about the challenges in their jobs and see the potential learning opportunities.

To approach these challenges as opportunities sometimes seems unnatural. The things that are challenging in jobs may also be particularly stressful, and people's first reaction may be to avoid them. Thinking about jobs as developmental requires a change of mind-set. Sometimes this change in mind-set can be achieved simply through a discussion with a boss, mentor, coach, or HR person. Other times, however, it is difficult for people to think about an assignment in terms of development because they are more focused on meeting deadlines, completing tasks, and accomplishing goals. Often a formal approach is necessary.

Organizations wishing to take a formal approach to conversations about developmental opportunities can use a survey instrument such as the Developmental Challenge Profile, or DCP (Ruderman, McCauley, Ohlott, and McCall, 1993). The DCP can be used to assess the developmental aspects of existing jobs. This short questionnaire asks people to what extent specific challenges are present in their jobs, using the framework of transitions, creating change, high levels of responsibility, nonauthority relationships, and obstacles presented earlier in this chapter. Some sample items:

> For you, this job is a dramatic increase in scope.
>
> Your business or unit must operate under adverse business conditions.
>
> The people reporting to you are more senior or more experienced than you.
>
> You have to lay off large numbers of your people.
>
> If you fail, serious business losses are likely.
>
> Your boss is opposed to something you think is important to do.

DCP feedback provides individuals with an improved overall understanding of how jobs contribute to development. It also helps them recognize the specific developmental opportunities in their own jobs and encourages them to take advantage of and learn from these challenges.

Maria's experience provides an example. Her new assignment brought changes both in boss and in job responsibilities. Before the new job, Maria had for several years reported to the same vice president, a very hands-on kind of person who was heavily involved in all aspects of her work. Her new boss was exactly the opposite. This gave Maria the freedom to independently manage the activities of her area. At first, this independence was frightening. Not only was she managing in a less familiar area but now there was no one looking over her shoulder to catch mistakes. In a conversation about the new assignment, Maria's boss pointed out that mastering the unfamiliar parts of her assignment and working more independently were the developmental challenges in her job. This learning orientation provided Maria with a new level of enthusiasm toward the job. She developed new insights about how to effectively manage in the new area and gained confidence in her decision-making ability.

Looking back on her assignment some time later, Maria told us, "I gained a renewed appreciation for the value of change and the exposure to new challenges. Now the importance of job rotation and change is a more common element in planning my career and that of my staff." This positive experience encouraged Maria to seek out further challenges and also led her to emphasize challenging assignments with her staff.

Use Development as a Criterion in Giving Assignments

To make the most of their developmental assignments, organizations need to ensure that development considerations are included at all levels of the staffing process. At the individual level, leaders can use assignments in planning for their own development or for developing their subordinates. Organizationally, the developmental potential of assignments should be given careful consideration in charting succession plans and in planning development of high-potential managers.

Encourage Use of Assignments in Individual Development Plans.
Increasingly, people are taking more responsibility for their own development. As you help aspiring leaders with their development planning, encourage them to set development goals based on feedback they have received about their strengths and weaknesses. The development plan should focus on a few domains toward which to direct improvement efforts. Once areas for improvement have been identified, you and the individual can work together to create an action plan to meet the development goals.

Assignments can play a key role in the action plan, although the plan may also include other elements such as coaching, coursework, and regular feedback. Encourage people, when outlining their plan, to think about the types of challenges they need to help them reach their goals. If those challenges are not present in the current job, help them strategize ways to gain access to some of the needed challenges, such as through new assignments or adding responsibilities to the current job. Without this emphasis on assignments as a development strategy, many people think about development only in terms of training opportunities.

Leaders at all levels can be educated about how to use assignments in development planning for their subordinates. The process used by one national retail store chain is a good example. A task force worked along with senior managers to identify leadership competencies that are important to success in the organization. To help managers develop these core competencies, a detailed development plan is created for each of them. The plan includes the development issue, learning objectives, and expected outcomes of the assignment for the organization, such as a new sales initiative or better financial performance. It encourages the managers and their bosses to consider such questions as

- What are the individual's learning and development needs?
- What are three to five leadership challenges in each job?
- How can the learning need be matched with the appropriate challenge?
- How can assignments be structured to make them more developmental?

Additionally, as part of the organization's performance management system, bosses are evaluated on how well they develop others (Sutter, 1994). They are encouraged to take an active role in helping their direct reports meet their development goals.

Use a Developmental Perspective in Succession Planning. Traditional approaches to succession planning attempt to fit the most highly qualified candidate with the job, in the hopes that candidate then carries out the responsibilities of the job most efficiently and effectively. Currently, a pitfall of many succession planning systems is that they focus primarily on identification and assessment of talent and pay less attention to development. What results is a list of candidates who might fill particular positions should they become vacant, with less consideration as to what experiences the candidate might need to be prepared for the job, or how the job itself might fit the individual's development needs.

However, organizations today are becoming increasingly aware that it is important for job placement decisions to incorporate developmental considerations. In one recent study, 31 percent of executive promotion decisions were developmental in nature (Ruderman and Ohlott, 1994). In these promotions, executives were being prepared for further advancement, groomed for specific key positions, or given the opportunity to improve in order to prevent derailment. Other research suggests that incorporating individual development needs into succession planning decisions is related to improved organizational reputation and financial performance (Friedman, 1986).

The recent experience of one organization illustrates the value of this approach. A critical executive position in this organization—head of a rapidly growing division—would be opening up within the next nine months. At about the same time, because of retirement and transfers, a number of key people would be moving out of the division, so one of the challenges for the new person was to put together a new management team for the division. The team charged with selecting the new leader followed the company's basic philosophy of succession planning: Who is most likely to learn from the assignment? Of the potential candidates, who has not had the opportunity to deal with some of the challenges in this assignment? Whose talents can be further refined by the assignment? Who has developmental needs that can be addressed by the assignment?

Three potential candidates were being reviewed, all of them with outstanding strengths. For one candidate in particular, however, the job would clearly be developmental. Her last several job assignments had involved fixing parts of the business that were in trouble, and now she needed an opportunity to work in a growing business that would allow her to build and expand, rather than downsize. In particular, she needed to learn how to size up talent and hire a team of people who could complement each other and work together. This assignment would provide just the experience she needed to continue growing as a leader.

Identify and Target Key Assignments for High Potentials. Organizations often identify key competencies needed by their leaders for achieving the organization's strategic goals. As an example, increased emphasis on international markets calls for leaders who can work across cultures. Or a focus on creating new products requires leaders who foster innovation. Key assignments for developing these competencies should be identified, and people with a high level of leadership potential should be targeted for those assignments.

For instance, a company that wants to compete globally may decide that it is important for its future leaders to have international experience early in their careers. The company then pinpoints specific overseas assignments that can develop the necessary skills. In recent years 3M has provided an example of this strategy (see Seibert, Hall, and Kram, 1995). Knowledge of international operations has been identified as an important skill for 3M's future leaders. To this end, the company uses international experience, in the form of managing a subsidiary in a foreign country, to develop its high-potential managers. These international assignments are especially designed to encompass appropriate experiences deemed necessary for advancement within 3M.

Another example comes from Citicorp (Clark and Lyness, 1991). The organization was growing rapidly, becoming flatter, and facing intense competition. As part of their response to these organizational challenges, they identified interpersonal and strategic skills as important competencies to develop in people targeted for senior-level jobs. A major component of the development process for these high-potential managers is to undertake two assignments of three or four years each. One assignment involves a major strategic challenge, and the other exposes the manager to heavy people-management challenges.

Implementing a system that targets key assignments for high-potential managers requires significant organizational investment and top leaders who are committed to individual development, realizing that it can have organizational benefits as well. Involvement at every level of the organization and tight collaboration between the human resource department and top management are critical success factors (Cobb and Gibbs, 1990; Clark and Lyness, 1991).

Maximizing Learning from Assignments

As we have discussed, just because the opportunity for learning is present in an assignment doesn't mean the individual can or will take advantage of it. Preparation and support are important steps organizations can take to increase the chances the desired learning will occur.

Prepare People for Learning from New Assignments. Telling people who are chosen for a developmental assignment that they are being given the assignment as an opportunity to learn often motivates them to take advantage of the opportunity.

One way to prepare people for a developmental assignment is to have them complete a checklist for learning (Dechant, 1990, 1994). Such a checklist includes questions about what strengths and limitations a person brings to an assignment, what aspects of the job and its context might prove to be particularly challenging, and what learning outcomes the person expects. See Table 4.3 for an example of a checklist.

Whether or not an actual checklist is used, thinking about such questions helps raise people's awareness of themselves as learners and helps them make the most of new opportunities. Setting developmental goals, providing access to coaches, and scheduling regular feedback on developmental progress are other ways organizations help people prepare for learning.

Support Individuals Throughout the Developmental Assignment. Perhaps the most important success factor is organizational support. People in developmental assignments are placed in situations in which some of their abilities and skills may be deficient. Support increases their confidence in their ability to learn, increases their sense of permission to experiment, and relieves the stress that can inhibit learning. Support for learning can mean the difference between failure and success.

Support takes a variety of forms: an outlet for stress relief, a sense of collegiality with coworkers, understanding there is permission to fail, endorsement of one's ideas and actions, or acceptance and approval from others. Models or mentors who have experienced similar challenges themselves can help guide people through their new assignments. In a job-swapping program at Greyhound Financial Corporation, for instance, managers are coached by the previous jobholder (Northcraft,

TABLE 4.3. QUESTIONS THAT FACILITATE LEARNING FROM A DEVELOPMENTAL ASSIGNMENT.

About yourself

1. What strengths do I bring to this job? What will help me?

2. What are my development needs? What might hinder me from being effective and successful?

3. What aspects of this job may be particularly challenging for me, given my background, experience, strengths, and development needs? (Is the role clear or ambiguous? Will I have the formal authority to do what I need to do? Are there obstacles, and if so, how might I overcome them?)

4. What can I learn from this job? What do I want to learn?

5. What do I need to know to be able to do this job effectively?

6. What might make it difficult for me to learn?

About the assignment

1. What are the organization's objectives for me in this job?

2. What are my own personal objectives in this job?

3. How does this job fit with the organization's mission, values, and goals?

4. What do I know about this job? What are the tasks, responsibilities, and requirements? What are the key leadership challenges?

5. What are my subordinates like?

6. What is my boss like?

7. Am I likely to encounter any resistance? What steps might I take to overcome it?

8. Who can help me? Where can I turn for support?

9. What other resources do I have available to me?

10. Is there anything I would like to change about this assignment?

During and after the assignment

1. How can I monitor my learning progress? (For example: keep a journal, find a person to be a "learning partner," seek feedback often, either formally or informally)

2. What am I learning? Anything I did not expect?

3. What am I not learning that I thought or hoped I would? Why?

4. How will I know I have learned what I wanted and needed to learn?

Griffith, and Shalley, 1992). Support may also come in the form of compensation and other means of public recognition.

People learn more effectively when they have support and encouragement from above. Bosses have a positive impact on development through their special abilities or because of the relationships they form with their employees. Supportive bosses can foster development in a number of different ways: giving subordinate managers the latitude to try things on their own, providing visibility and recognition, opening doors, giving advice, buffering their people from the system, providing useful feedback, and delegating exciting and challenging tasks.

Support plays an especially important role in helping overcome obstacles. For example, 3M corporation pairs senior, U.S.-based executives with managers in overseas assignments to help provide ongoing support and advice throughout the assignment (Seibert, Hall, and Kram, 1995). Chapter Five provides a more in-depth discussion of the importance of relationships for development.

One important form of support is follow-up. At some point during the assignment, human resource staff work with the individual to assess whether the developmental challenges expected to be part of the assignment are actually present. This assessment serves as the basis for a discussion with a coach or boss about whether the assignment is working out as planned, unexpected challenges have arisen, there is enough support for learning from the assignment, and the right balance between using existing talents and stretching has been achieved. At one organization, for example, the development guide emphasizes follow-up on the development process by including timetables for reports and review meetings with the boss.

Central to the process of supporting the person is providing specific ways of capturing what is learned from the assignment. Many of the methods of support discussed here also provide avenues for reflection. Research into the adult learning cycle of planning, doing, and reflecting emphasizes that when lessons are learned in active learning experiences such as job assignments, they have deeper, more practical, and longer-lasting meaning.

Tracking Developmental Assignments over Time

Human resource information systems should track the kinds of developmental assignments people are given and how they respond to the challenges. In terms of job assignments, human resource functions normally track only changes in job titles, organizational levels, business units, or locations. This type of information provides little insight into the developmental history of the individual. Tracking developmental assignments and what is learned from them provides decision makers with

- A way to assess whether they are providing people with a breadth of challenge over their careers
- Insight into which individuals are particularly effective learners and thus have high potential for continued development
- In-depth knowledge of how to create assignments that are effective for developing certain capacities

In particular, organizations should monitor the developmental track records of women and other nontraditional managers, because succession plans have been less successful in advancing them than in advancing white males (Curtis and Russell, 1993). Limited variety in career assignments is one explanation for the career blockages experienced more frequently by nontraditional managers. Chapter Ten provides a detailed discussion of the role of challenging assignments in developing nontraditional managers.

Some Issues in Using Assignments for Development

This chapter has briefly touched upon some of the issues inherent in using assignments for developmental purposes. Here we investigate these issues in greater depth. These are questions we are frequently asked by human resource practitioners who are grappling with the idea of an assignment-based development system.

On Whom Should We Focus Developmental Assignments?

Admittedly, some of the most powerful developmental assignments, such as major start-from-scratch or turnaround jobs, have limited availability. Who is given a developmental assignment depends partly on the organization's strategy for leadership development. Organizations with traditional approaches limit developmental opportunities to a select group of people, such as those who are considered high potentials. These are people who have been carefully identified and selected as candidates for future top leadership positions. Current leaders closely follow their careers, and developmental assignments may be allocated to them as the organization deems necessary. We recommend that these organizations search broadly and deeply for their talent and reassess people often, to lessen the possibility of overlooking talent.

Other organizations choose to create a range of developmental opportunities and make them more widely available. They investigate ways to add some developmental elements to existing jobs as well as systematically place selected individuals in highly developmental jobs (such as starting up a new business or revitalizing a poorly performing existing business).

Finally, as previously mentioned, significant tension exists between finding the "right" person for the job and finding the person who will learn most from the job. Hollenbeck and McCall (forthcoming) characterize this tension as finding the balance between "maximum performance" and "maximum development." Every assignment, no matter how small or insignificant it seems, has the potential to be developmental for someone. Clark and Lyness (1991) caution decision makers to differentiate smart from dumb risks when deciding who gets a developmental assignment. A smart risk has two components: the manager has most of the competencies and skills to help the person succeed in the job, and the stretch is not overwhelming. Learning is undermined if the challenging part of the assignment is overwhelming.

How Can We Use Assignments Developmentally While Downsizing or Restructuring?

People often equate a developmental assignment with a move to a position with higher levels of responsibility. However, most organizations lack enough big developmental assignments to adequately develop all the future leaders they need. As organizations downsize and become flatter, they are no longer able to rely on promotions and high-visibility assignments to meet all their development needs. To compensate, the developmental component framework presented in this chapter can be used to identify opportunities in assignments other than promotions and to add developmental opportunities to existing jobs without moving people.

A lateral move, for instance, can be just as developmental as a promotion, provided there is some aspect of the job that is challenging to the new incumbent. Lateral moves still involve transitions if they are moves to a different function, business, or product. Consider this example described to us by one manager: "I was on the threshold of being promoted into a sales and proposal-writing role in one of the most successful businesses in the investment area. Instead, I was transferred to HR, at a level which was really a lateral move for me. I learned that you can make lemonade out of lemons. I took the job and redefined it into one of the most influential positions in the organization."

Other avenues for development when high-level assignments are few and far between are (1) redesigning jobs to include more developmental features, (2) giving special task force or project responsibilities, (3) creating joint projects across functions, and (4) giving special troubleshooting assignments (Baldwin and Padgett, 1993; Lombardo and Eichinger, 1989; Sutter, 1994). Lombardo and Eichinger (1989) also list a number of small developmental assignments that can be added to existing jobs.

Transition and task-related challenges (defined earlier in this chapter) can readily be added to existing jobs, as in assigning a manager to lead a cross-functional project that involves people over whom the project leader has no direct authority. Contextual challenges are not as easily added;

indeed, we do not recommend attempting to add challenges derived from obstacles to anyone's job. Difficult contextual job features are not the most desirable stimuli for learning. However, it is important to recognize when these features do exist and to help people view them as positively as possible, by pointing out opportunities for learning.

Aren't Some Jobs Too Important for Developmental Assignments?

The answer to this question, generally, is a simple, blunt *yes*. Some assignments are definitely too critical to the continued success of the organization to risk placing people who might not be able to handle them. The business risks of the candidate's failure are usually easy to identify; the business will lose money or customers, for example. However, to err on the side of caution has its risks, too. An organization that does not place people in challenging assignments where they can learn and grow never develops its executive bench strength.

A large oil company, for example, relied on one man as their specialist in oil field start-ups. They never allowed him to do anything else, and they never allowed anyone else to open a new oil field. Eventually he felt stifled and left the organization to take a job with another company that offered him opportunities to broaden his skills. The oil company was left with no one who was even partially competent to open a new oil field.

In contrast, a consumer products organization purposely holds onto a small area of the business that is not profitable. The company continues to fund the business because it is headquartered overseas and provides a valuable international assignment used to help develop potential senior managers, with relatively small risk.

How Long Should People Stay in a Developmental Assignment?

This is a controversial subject in many organizations. If people are kept in jobs too long, they experience few opportunities for learning and become bored. At the other extreme, if people are moved too quickly, they lose the opportunity to complete an assignment, as well as the chance to reflect on, consolidate, and refine what they have learned from their experience. To optimize learning, people need to remain in an assignment long enough to be able to see the consequences of their actions and decisions.

John Gabarro's research (1987) suggests that it can take three and a half years for a person to glean the important lessons from a developmental assignment. At first, managers tend to deal with the most familiar problems, as when those with financial backgrounds concentrate on the numbers. Then they begin to learn other aspects of the job, and eventually new problems surface that weren't apparent in the initial assignment. Gabarro also found that managers did not learn at a deeper level until after the first eighteen months in a job.

Summary and Conclusions

Job assignments undoubtedly provide the bulk of developmental opportunities in today's organizations. Unfortunately, these potent sources of leadership development are often ignored or used haphazardly. This chapter provides a framework for using assignments for development purposes.

Once an organization has identified its potentially developmental jobs and the strengths and weaknesses of the people it wants to develop, there are several ways it can proceed. At one end of the spectrum, where organizational involvement is minimal, it can provide people with information about developmental opportunities in their current jobs and allow them to take charge of their own development, including adding the challenges they believe they need.

Other organizations choose to develop a systematic program of job rotation, in which they identify future leaders and their strengths and development needs and then create a development plan where the individuals are given particular jobs intended to improve their skills and abilities. The organizations may decide to systematically expose early career managers to a variety of key assignments, or look at specific individual development needs and attempt to address them by one assignment or a series of assignments. Some organizations also choose to conduct assignment-based development on a small scale, or they choose an informal rather than a formal system. They may encourage widespread developmental opportunities or limit opportunities to a select group of people.

Rather than limit developmental assignments to select groups, we believe it is important to keep in mind that most jobs with leadership requirements can be shaped to increase their developmental potential so that more people encounter developmental aspects in their work (McCauley and Brutus, 1998). Thus assignments can be used to grow future senior leaders or to provide opportunities for stretching and growth for solid performers not targeted for top-level positions.

Challenging job assignments are perhaps the most potent form of leadership development that exists. However, learning from challenging assignments is much more difficult than learning from a typical leadership development program. Simply because an opportunity for development exists doesn't guarantee learning will happen. Developmental features of jobs are not objective; whether or not they provide learning depends on how they are experienced by individual managers, who have varying backgrounds and experiences, interpret jobs differently, and even shape their own jobs.

To further complicate matters, development for its own sake is seldom the primary objective when placing a manager in an assignment. It may not be appropriate to place people in developmental assignments where the stakes are very high because the costs of failure are too great. However, using job assignments for development purposes provides an additional benefit beyond achieving task objectives and may even result in competitive advantage for the organization. Leaders can learn essential practical skills and perspectives that help them function more effectively.

In an organizational environment where the structure of the employment relationship is changing and lifetime employment is no longer taken for granted, providing employees with a variety of developmental opportunities from which they can round out their repertoire of leadership skills is one way organizations help their people remain employable, even if their business should experience a downturn. It also helps ensure that they always have a core group of competent leaders to count on.

CHAPTER FIVE

DEVELOPMENTAL RELATIONSHIPS

Cynthia D. McCauley
Christina A. Douglas

Ask someone to describe the people who have influenced his or her personal development, and you can expect a long conversation. Beyond all the stories about parents and grandparents, there are favorite teachers, classmates, teammates, siblings, and coaches. Then there's the first boss, the great boss, the horrible boss, special coworkers, mentors, spouses, and children. And don't forget the people who influence from afar, through their writings, their art, or their activities as reported by the media.

That relationships shape people's lives is both a commonly held notion and a phenomenon widely studied in the social sciences. Two broad topics in particular have received a great deal of attention in the psychological literature: (1) social learning theory, a framework for understanding how people learn by observing others (Bandura, 1986); and (2) socialization, the process by which individuals internalize the norms and values of the groups they become part of (Van Maanen and Schein, 1979).

We would like to thank Steve Noble, vice president with the Development Resource Group, for providing access to the Mandel Executive Development Program.

In addition, research-based advice on almost any topic related to learning and development also entails a relationship strategy:

- How do schools increase learning in the classroom? Allow students to work in cooperative learning groups (Johnson and Johnson, 1989).
- How does a workplace support the development of new knowledge? Build relationships and community around the work (Institute for Research on Learning, 1993).
- How can people enhance their career development? Seek a mentor (Zey, 1991).
- How can people learn to cope better with stress? Develop a social support network (Aldwin, 1994).

Within this larger framework of learning through others, we focus in this chapter on relationships in work settings that are particularly developmental, that is, relationships individuals point to as their key sources of assessment, challenge, and support. We begin by describing the various roles other people play in the leadership development process and then suggest how people can maximize their use of these relationships. The remainder of the chapter is devoted to organizational strategies for enhancing access to relationships for leadership development.

The Role of Other People in the Leadership Development Process

Because relationships are so central to the learning and development process, they affect each of the elements—assessment, challenge, and support—in the leadership development model described in the Introduction. To better understand how relationships serve these functions, let us examine the various developmental roles that people in relationships play for one another. These roles are grouped by the major elements of the model, in Table 5.1. Note that although each role represents just one aspect of a relationship, most developmental relationship are made up of multiple roles. At the end of this section are illustrations of how roles are combined to form different types of developmental relationships.

TABLE 5.1. ROLES PLAYED BY OTHERS IN DEVELOPMENTAL RELATIONSHIPS.

Element	Role	Function
Assessment	Feedback provider	Ongoing feedback as person works to learn and improve
	Sounding board	Evaluation of strategies before they are implemented
	Point of comparison	Standards for evaluating own level of skill or performance
	Feedback interpreter	Assistance in integrating or making sense of feedback from others
Challenge	Dialogue partner	Perspectives or points of view different from own
	Assignment broker	Access to challenging assignments (new jobs or additions to current one)
	Accountant	Pressure to fulfill commitment to development goals
	Role model	Examples of high (or low) competence in areas being developed
Support	Counselor	Examination of what is making learning and development difficult
	Cheerleader	Boost in own belief that success is possible
	Reinforcer	Formal rewards for progress toward goals
	Cohort	Sense that you are not alone in your struggles and that, if others can achieve their goals, you can, too.

Assessment

Assessment, the formal and informal processes for receiving data about oneself, is an important element of an effective development process. One key developmental role in assessment is that of *feedback provider*: a source of day-to-day, ongoing feedback data on how a person is doing in seeking to learn new skills or perspectives. An in-depth feedback-intensive program or data from a 360-degree feedback instrument might be the impetus for taking on particular development goals (see Chapters One and Two), but it is the continuous feedback that people get as they work to achieve those goals that becomes critical.

Someone acting in the role of feedback provider observes as a person is working to improve and provides in-the-moment feedback. For example, after getting feedback that she dominated meetings, Melissa set a goal of giving others an opportunity to share their views and influence the group. She asked two coworkers who were often in meetings with her to give her feedback on how well she was achieving this goal. For the next six months, she checked in with them after each meeting to get feedback and any suggestions they had for improvement.

People also need feedback on strategies and ideas before they are implemented. In other words, they need *sounding boards*. People bring their ideas to a person acting as a sounding board for reactions and fine-tuning: What should I do in this situation? What would be the likely consequences if I took this action? Which of these three options is the best? George, a manager of a nonprofit organization, was about to lead his board in a strategic planning process for the first time. He contacted a manager in another organization who was considered an expert in strategic planning and asked for help; the two met regularly to debrief and plan next steps. For George, engaging in a new challenge while having access to a knowledgeable sounding board made the experience a particularly developmental one.

People also gain informal assessment data by comparing themselves to others. In this type of relationship, the other people take the role of *comparison points*. There are two types of comparison points: comparing oneself to someone who is seen as a model or expert (How do I compare to the best? How do I compare to someone who is doing what I want to be doing?) and comparing oneself to people in similar situations (Am I doing as well as others? Have I been able to achieve as much as others?).

Comparing themselves to a model helps people see how they measure up and where improvement is needed. After spending several days shadowing a top executive in a major organization, a younger executive running a smaller company noted that although her own work required tackling problems that were just as big, a major difference was the number of problems the other executive had to juggle at once. She realized that this skill of managing multiple problems and finding their interconnections was what she needed to develop if she ever hoped to occupy a similar position.

Comparing themselves to others in similar circumstances gives people insights about how well they are doing. A small group of employees who are going through a yearlong leadership development program get together periodically to update each other on their progress toward development goals. These meetings provide a sounding board for addressing the obstacles they are encountering, but they also serve as a context for judging how well each person is accomplishing his or her goals relative to the others.

Finally, other people serve in the role of *feedback interpreter.* As such, they usually don't provide assessment information directly but instead help people make sense of the feedback data they receive. In one feedback-intensive program, all participants spend half a day with a feedback specialist who helps them (usually in a private meeting) discover themes in their data, connect those themes to their current context, and begin thinking about next steps. Many organizations that use 360-degree feedback provide recipients with access to a professional who can help them interpret the feedback. But this role does not have to be a formal one; people often turn to a trusted colleague to help make sense of feedback received informally from a boss or direct report.

Challenge

Challenge—being pushed beyond the normal comfort zone—is another important element of a development process. One way other people push individuals beyond their comfort zone is by challenging their thinking. We refer to people in this role as *dialogue partners.* They expose people to different perspectives and help each other explore these differences by questioning, prodding, and reflecting on underlying assumptions. This exploration of different perspectives is often the first step in developing more complex and adaptive frameworks for understanding and acting in the world. For example, members of a cross-functional team addressing a major business issue reported that, in the process of digging beneath their differences and learning together, they shed some of their functional biases and developed more of an integrated perspective on the problem.

Other people also play important developmental roles when they provide individuals with assignments that stretch their capacities; we call this role *assignment broker.* These assignments can be new jobs, new responsibilities added to the current job, or temporary assignments outside of a person's normal job responsibilities (see Chapter Four).

Another way that people motivate others to learn and grow is by holding them accountable for the developmental goals they have set; this is the role of *accountant.* Bosses are often expected to play the two roles of assignment broker and accountant simultaneously. For example, as part of many performance management systems, employees decide with their bosses on development goals for the coming year. Part of the boss's responsibility is to find the challenging experiences that help move the employees toward those goals and then monitor their progress in the assignment.

Individuals are also challenged when they attempt to emulate *role models.* They step outside of their comfort zones, trying new or more complex skills and behaviors. Rita, a high-potential manager who had been assigned a mentor as part of a leadership development program, observed a style of supervision in her mentor that was different from her own. The mentor used a style Rita termed "hands-in" (occasionally auditing a subordinate's work), while Rita herself tended to more hands-on (looking over the subordinates' shoulders while they are doing the work). She was attracted to her mentor's style, but trying it out was a stretch for her.

Sometimes people unknowingly act as negative role models: people whom others observe and make a conscious effort *not* to be like. In their study of developmental experiences in executives' careers, McCall, Lombardo, and Morrison (1988) found that reports of negative role models occurred almost as frequently as those of positive role models. They were often bosses whose behavior was described in unflattering terms (pompous, pigheaded, dictatorial, and vindictive) and—more importantly—led to negative reactions in others (anger, sabotage, mistrust, and bitterness). These negative role models create a different kind of challenge for people: the challenge not to become like them. People who must work directly with a negative role model also have the considerable challenge of learning to cope with a situation that is probably beyond their control.

Support

People need support to help them effectively deal with the struggles of a developmental experience; that support often comes from other people. There are a variety of support roles that people play for each other.

One is the role of *counselor*, providing emotional support during the difficulties of the learning process. Counselors encourage people to explore the emotional aspects of the learning situation: fear of failing, anxiety about leaving behind the familiar, stress in trying to learn and change while carrying a heavy workload, frustration at not making progress, or anger with others who do not support development.

In a relationship with a strong counseling component, people can vent frustrations and negative emotions without feeling judged. They know that there is someone they can turn to if they need to, and this alone can give them the confidence to take risks or try new things. Michael had a tendency to redo the work of subordinates if the work didn't meet his standards, rather than giving them feedback and coaching. He lived in a constant state of frustration and finally shared those feelings with a trusted and more experienced colleague. The colleague helped Michael see that he was contributing to his own frustration by his perfectionist tendencies and his fear of giving negative feedback. With a better understanding of his emotions and a colleague who cared enough to help him reach this understanding, Michael felt he could begin trying to change his behaviors.

Support is also provided by people who play the similar developmental roles of *cheerleader* and *reinforcer*. Cheerleaders are on the sidelines, encouraging learners, expressing confidence in them, and providing affirmation. Reinforcers reward people for making progress toward development goals. Julie, an R&D project leader, shared with her mentor her desire to become more assertive and forceful with her ideas. Knowing Julie's reserved nature, her mentor knew that the change would require a long and sometimes difficult learning process. So she became Julie's cheerleader, helping her celebrate small wins along the way and assuring her that the changes she was making in her attitude and behaviors were indeed valued by the organization. As Julie improved, her mentor reinforced the changes, giving her opportunities to represent the organization at several important external forums and writing a letter to her divisional vice president that praised Julie for the progress she had made and pointed out the resulting positive benefits for the company.

There is a final role that provides invaluable support to the learner, albeit a more passive form of support. We refer to this role as *cohort*. These are people who are struggling with the same challenges and thus can empathize with each other. People find great comfort in connecting with others facing similar challenges, realizing that they are not alone. Members of a network focused on managing innovation in organizations cited this type of support as a major reason for remaining in the network. Back in their companies, they often felt alone, struggling to make innovation a priority. However, connecting with like-minded people during network meetings left them reinvigorated to face their challenges again.

Cohorts can also provide people with the living proof that they can learn to master the challenges of the journey. Seeing others doing it, people believe they can do it, too. Brad, a school superintendent who was working hard to be more delegating and giving his direct reports authority to make major decisions, got an unexpected boost from Jack, another superintendent he knew well. While they were both away at a national convention, a crisis arose back home in Jack's district. Assuming Jack would rush back home to handle the crisis, Brad offered to take over his friend's remaining responsibilities at the convention. To his surprise, Jack replied that he had touched base with the key leaders back home and was confident they could handle it, so he would be staying at the convention. Brad suddenly felt renewed in his own development efforts: if Jack could delegate the responsibility for handling a crisis, surely he too could learn to delegate and trust the decision-making capacities of others.

From Roles to Relationships

Each developmental relationship in a person's life provides a mixture of roles. A boss might be both accountant and assignment broker. A former colleague might act as both a sounding board and a cohort. A spouse may play many roles at different times: role model, counselor, accountant, dialogue partner. Note that these kinds of relationships provide differing developmental roles. There is no prototypical developmental relationship, no one role or combination of roles that have to be present in order to make it developmental.

However, some relationships are more developmental than others. At least two factors seem to be at work here. First, some relationships are more developmental because they provide more such roles. Mentoring relationships, for example, are usually long-term, and the two individuals develop a personal closeness. Over time, mentors are likely to play a number of roles: sounding board, counselor, feedback provider, assignment broker, cheerleader, reinforcer, role model. Mentors usually end up having a profound influence on the protégé's learning and development (Kram, 1985; Levinson, 1978).

Second, a relationship can be especially developmental because it provides just the right role that the person needs at the time. Having someone in a counseling role may be particularly developmental during a hardship experience (see Chapter Six). Someone to provide feedback and encourage from the sidelines may be exactly what a person needs the most as he or she tries to change an ingrained habit. The superintendent in the earlier example cited the brief experience with his fellow superintendent as *the* turning point in his struggle to develop a new leadership style. The lesson is that at various times, depending on the developmental need, different types of relationships are seen as the most essential.

Individual Strategies for Using Developmental Relationships

To capitalize on the developmental power of relationships, how might people go about it? What steps should they take? If you are involved in helping people in your organization plan their development, here are some strategies you might suggest to them.

1. *Seek out multiple relationships for development.* It is unlikely that one person can provide all of the roles needed in ongoing leadership develop-

ment. There are just too many diverse roles for one person to handle them all, and no one person should be burdened with all those expectations. Even people identified as mentors are unlikely to meet all the developmental needs of the individual. Instead, people should cultivate a range of relationships. Exposure to a breadth of viewpoints and experiences is important, and overdependence on one individual can actually limit a person's career progression (McCall and Lombardo, 1983).

2. *Figure out which roles are needed for the current development goals and find the right people for those roles.* What is actually needed: a role model who can demonstrate the skills and behaviors this person wants to develop? Encouragement, to stay motivated? Ongoing support to change an ingrained habit? A dialogue partner to move the person beyond accustomed ways of looking at issues?

Once needs have been clarified, the question becomes who can best meet those needs. As with all human capacities, people excel in different developmental roles, perhaps because of their innate gifts. For example, certain people seem naturally meant for a coaching relationship. They are motivated to teach others; they may be keen observers, enabling them to give clear and specific feedback; they know when to give stretch assignments and how to encourage without pressuring. Others are much better in the role of counselor. They are good listeners, sense the personal issues underlying development problems, and are comfortable with close relationships in the work setting.

Other differences are due to the nature of formal roles in organizations. For example, bosses are often in a better position to provide stretch assignments, hold individuals accountable for development, and reinforce learning through the formal reward system. Peers in someone's work group might be the best source of comparison points; people in other functions or even outside the organization might be the best source of fresh perspectives.

The point is to strive to understand which people—because of their personal strengths or the nature of their relationship—have high potential to fulfill particular developmental roles. Table 5.2 presents a series of questions that help people reflect on the roles they might need and the kind of person who could best play those roles for them.

TABLE 5.2. QUESTIONS FOR EXPLORING POTENTIAL DEVELOPMENTAL RELATIONSHIPS.

What Is My Development Goal?

What developmental roles do I need as I work on this goal?	Who could provide this role?
Feedback provider: Will I be practicing new behaviors that need to be refined based on feedback?	Who is in a position to observe me practice these behaviors? Who is good at observing and assessing the impact of behaviors? Whom do I trust to be straightforward with me?
Sounding board: Will I encounter dilemmas and choices that I need to think through before acting?	Who is good at thinking out loud and considering alternatives? Who has faced these same sorts of choices before? Who am I willing to share my uncertainties with?
Comparison points: Would it help to gauge my progress against others?	Who would be a relevant comparison point? Who would be willing to share his or her progress with me? Whose successes would be easy for me to see?
Feedback interpreter: Will I need someone else to gather feedback for me and help me make sense of it?	Who is good at making sense of complex data? Who am I willing to share feedback with? Who will others trust as a gatherer of feedback for me?
Dialogue partner: Do I need to understand new and different perspectives?	Who has a perspective different from my own? Who is good at engaging in dialogue, at examining underlying assumptions? Who is good in the role of devil's advocate?

TABLE 5.2. QUESTIONS FOR EXPLORING
POTENTIAL DEVELOPMENTAL RELATIONSHIPS, cont'd.

What developmental roles do I need as I work on this goal?	Who could provide this role?
Assignment broker: Will I need help in gaining access to stretch assignments?	Who can sponsor me when certain jobs become available? Who can help me add needed challenge to my job? Who can help me find stretch opportunities outside the workplace?
Accountant: Am I more likely to succeed if someone holds me accountable for making changes?	Should my boss hold me accountable in some way for achieving this goal? Are there others who want me to achieve this goal?
Role model: Do I need to closely watch someone who is already very skilled in the area of my development goal?	Who would be a great role model for me? Whom should I watch or talk to, to get strategies for achieving my goal? Whose ability in this area has always been an inspiration to me?
Counselor: Will this goal be very difficult for me? Will I likely encounter a personal frustration?	Who can be my confidante as I struggle with this goal? Who can be both empathic and objective? Who understands me enough to see through my excuses and procrastinations?
Cheerleader or reinforcer: Do I need a lot of encouragement and reinforcement to succeed?	Who is always able to make me feel competent? Who can I share my small successes with? Who is in a position to reward me for success?
Cohort: Will this be easier if I can connect with others in the same boat?	Who would understand what I'm going through? Who are my peers in this situation? Who would be "good company" for this journey?

3. *Fully use lateral, subordinate, or external relationships.* People often look upward in organizations for the developmental relationships they need. The hierarchy gets narrower toward the top, and higher-level managers are often difficult to access. An experienced colleague, a peer in another division, or even the retired executive who lives down the street may serve your development needs just as well. Learning partnerships can also develop with subordinates; a supervisor coaching a direct report in one area could easily receive coaching in another area in return.

4. *Don't assume that relationships need to be long-term or intense to be developmental.* Because of the dominance of the mentoring concept, people have a certain type of relationship in mind when they think of learning and development. They might miss or underestimate the opportunities to learn from relationships involving only modest contact. We have found that people can learn a great deal from shadowing a role model for several days, from working on a short-term project with a cross-functional team, from bosses that they weren't particularly close to, or from colleagues they see twice a year. Instead of focusing on the length or depth of the relationship, the real question is whether the experience with the person brings a different perspective, new source of knowledge, willingness to engage, belief in one's capabilities, insightful nature, or talent for keeping people motivated.

5. *Be especially aware during times of transition.* It is particularly important for people to reassess their developmental needs during times of transition; this includes reassessing the kind of developmental relationships they need. Going through a transition is challenging in and of itself and may require special advice and support from others. Developmental relationships become more important during times of restructuring or downsizing, for example, because they act as an antidote to the stress (Kram and Hall, 1989). Also, being in a new situation puts new and different demands on people, which is likely to require development in new areas. This in turn calls for new role models, new sources of support, and people with expertise connected to the challenges in the new setting. For example, managers in expatriate assignments need role models for how to work in the new culture and advisors to help them interpret and make sense of their new environment.

Creating Developmental Relationships in Organizations

Shelley is a manager in the marketing department of a large organization. She's known as a consistently high performer. She works well with people throughout the organization, and she's also extremely bright, quickly learning new technical and business information as she takes on new projects. Her boss sees her as an asset to the company and wants to encourage her continued development. Earlier in the year, the two of them had a long discussion about her development goals. They identified two specific areas for her to work on: learning to be more comfortable making decisions amid ambiguity, and developing a broader organizational perspective.

When the boss heard that the vice president of public relations was looking for someone to work with her on a short-term assignment, he secured the assignment for Shelley. He felt that the assignment would stretch her in ways that would help her develop in the areas they had identified and that the vice president would be a good role model. As Shelley was planning for this temporary assignment, she thought of a fellow member of the international group (an informal network in the organization that meets monthly) who had previously worked for this particular vice president. She asked if he would be willing to act as a confidant and sounding board for her during this assignment, and he agreed.

Shelley's boss was also able to get her into one of the organization's formal programs for high-potential managers. As part of this yearlong program, she was assigned to a learning triad with two other managers at her level but from different functional areas. The three worked together on various tasks and exercises given as part of the program and debriefed their experiences together, but there was an additional mandate: each person brought to the group a problem he or she was struggling with at work. The threesome helped coach one another as they worked on their problems throughout the year.

Shelley works in an organization that is rich in developmental relationships. The richness isn't just in the number of relationships and the roles they play for Shelley, but in the various ways they came about. We might say that the developmental relationship with the boss evolved naturally. It was part of his role as a manager; he saw her development as part of his responsibility. Other relationships—with the vice president of public relations and with her former subordinate—were more intentional. They were consciously sought out to fill a developmental need. Finally, the peer learning group was brought about by a formal organizational initiative. The organization created the structure that brought these three people together for the primary purpose of learning and development.

There are, then, three bases for developmental relationships: some arise naturally, some are intentionally sought out by the individual, some are structured by the organization. We use this framework to think about how organizations enhance access to developmental relationships in the workplace, using three proactive strategies:

1. Enhance the developmental power of natural relationships within the organization.
2. Encourage employees to intentionally seek out the developmental relationships they need.
3. Create formal relationships for the purposes of learning and development.

Enhancing the Developmental Power of Natural Relationships

Organizations pursuing this strategy work to develop the mind-set that making the most of the organization's people resources is a manager's responsibility (Waldroop and Butler, 1996). They spell out the payback to managers for spending time developing their subordinates: they get stronger teams that deliver better results, become magnets for talent, and—as subordinates move to other positions in the organization—develop a network of support (Peterson and Hicks, 1996). Most important, they hold managers accountable for the development of direct reports through their performance review and reward systems.

To make this work—to give managers responsibility for developing others and then hold them accountable—organizations also have to develop managers' skills in this area. Many organizations have framed these as "coaching" skills.

Being a good coach means being competent in many of the roles described earlier in the chapter: giving feedback, acting as a sounding board, providing the right kind of developmental assignments, and providing encouragement and reinforcement for learning. Managers may need help here, because being a coach sometimes runs counter to typical behaviors (Waldroop and Butler, 1996). A coach must adopt the attitude of a teacher, not a competitor; must be willing to explore ideas and issues rather than make quick evaluations and judgments; must think long-term rather than about the immediate task at hand; and must slow down enough to develop a relationship rather than work with the subordinates in frantic sound bites.

Just like any other leadership competency, coaching skills are best developed using a multiple-strategy approach: feedback on coaching behaviors, skill-based training, opportunities to practice coaching in work situations, and access to others who can give advice and support. In addition, a focus on improving coaching skills is most likely to meet with success if it is part of a larger development effort. One organization developed a five-day coaching-skills program as part of a salesforce improvement initiative (Graham, Wedman, and Garvin-Kester, 1993). Sales managers completed the program and were expected to use the coaching skills as part of their role in the improvement process. The course material was tailored specifically for coaching salespeople and included tools (such as a behavioral checklist for observing interactions with clients) that managers would begin using in their jobs.

Similarly, a division of Mobil Oil implemented an on-the-job development program for its engineers in which supervisory coaching was a key component (Cobb and Gibbs, 1990). All the supervisors attended a coaching workshop with one of their engineers. They were introduced to effective coaching practices and engaged in skill development as a pair. Together they developed a plan for the supervisor to coach the engineer in a work assignment after the workshop. The two also worked together to implement coaching between the supervisor and other members of the workgroup who were not at the workshop. The lesson here is the critical importance of integrating any formal program on coaching with the real work of coaching in the organization.

Some organizations have carried this strategy of enhancing the developmental power of existing relationships one step further. They see developing others as a shared responsibility across the organization, not just a managerial responsibility. They want staff members to know how to coach not only subordinates but peers and superiors as well. In other words, they want the skills of a coach to be a part of the skill repertoire of all employees.

One financial organization has launched an initiative to develop more of a "coaching culture." As one part of this effort, they identified employees who are particularly good coaches and set out to understand the mind-sets and skills of these people, the tools they use, and the impact they have on "coachees." They are using this knowledge to develop a coaching model and a workshop to teach the skills of coaching to others throughout the organization.

Another organization expects each manager and his or her direct reports to be a workteam and also serve as a "coaching group," sharing responsibility for giving feedback and supporting the development of each member of the group (Palus and Rogolsky, 1996).

There has been an explosion recently in the resources on coaching available to the HR professional and line manager. At the end of this chapter, we offer some key resources for learning more about the strategies and practices of coaching in the workplace.

Encouraging Employees to Intentionally Seek Out Needed Developmental Relationships

The first strategy, enhancing the developmental power of relationships, focuses on creating more people who have the skills and motivation to develop others in the workplace. This next strategy focuses on the other half of the relationship equation: creating more people who want to access others as part of their development efforts.

The most straightforward way of implementing this strategy is in the development planning process. As employees are setting development goals and steps for reaching them, they should be educated about the role of other people in learning and development and encouraged to include relationship strategies as part of their development plan. The questions in Table 5.2 can help. In our earlier example, Shelley felt she would need a sounding board as she took on the special assignment with the VP of public relations, but not just any sounding board—someone who had worked with this VP before and could give her particular insights. She intentionally sought out someone who could play this role.

Once the need for a developmental role has been established and a potential candidate identified, the next step is to explore whether the person is willing to serve in the role. Sometimes the candidate is someone the individual already knows well and can informally approach on his or her own. If not, an introduction from a third party may be best, or the person might need to set up a formally recognized developmental relationship with the chosen candidate, such as asking that person to serve as a formal advisor to a project or a formal coach in a special assignment.

However formal or informal the resulting relationship, clear expectations, time frames, and intended outcomes should be discussed. A strategy for working together and clarity about confidentiality need to be established. Potential obstacles or downsides to the relationship should also be explored.

Another way that organizations encourage employees to seek out developmental relationships is to purposefully broaden their access to other people, particularly people who might help them in their development efforts. One technique is to solidly support the formation of networks. Some organizations have created networks for women managers or for particular ethnic or racial groups (Barclay, 1992; Morrison, Ruderman, and Hughes-James, 1993). Others have created networks to link people at similar levels across functions. Some networks extend across organizations, providing a forum for people with similar responsibilities to connect with each other. For example, the Association for Managers of Innovation (AMI) is a network of people from different organizations who are responsible in some way for innovation within their company. They learn from each other using a process they label "beg, brag, and what if." This means a large part of the agenda is devoted to individual members' bringing problems to the group that they would like input on, sharing a successful initiative or project with the group, or engaging the group in exploring a future scenario.

An additional way of broadening people's access to others they can learn from is to designate special developmental roles within the organization. For example, after defining its core competencies (the areas of expertise that are critical to the success of the business), one company designated particular individuals as mentors in each of those areas. These mentors were highly skilled and knowledgeable in a particular core competency and were given the responsibility of keeping the organization at the forefront on that competency. Then, if employees needed to develop more expertise in a certain core area, they immediately knew who to seek out for coaching and guidance.

Creating Formal Relationships

A more direct strategy for enhancing access to developmental relationships is to intentionally create them—to formally match people for the purposes of learning and development. Why do organizations do this? From the organization's perspective, there are times when people need *extra* developmental attention. Formal relationships are most often created for

- Socialization of new managers
- Preparing high-potentials for more responsibility
- Developing women and people of color
- Meeting development needs of senior executives
- Organizational change efforts

We have found that about 20 percent of organizations with at least five hundred employees have at least one initiative that makes use of a formal developmental relationship (Douglas and McCauley, 1997). These initiatives were found in many kinds of organizations, with different geographical locations, employee size, sales volume, and types of product or service.

Socialization. Starting a new job or a new assignment is typically a stressful time for a manager. From the organization's perspective, getting new managers acclimated quickly is vital to productivity. Companies also find that turnover is very high among new employees; they are continually searching for socialization tactics that retain qualified people. Formal relationships are a very effective solution. In one large manufacturing organization, people who are promoted to a management position are routinely assigned to an experienced peer (called a peer coach) in a similar managerial role to facilitate their transition. These assignments typically last about six months and include shadowing, coaching, and weekly meetings. Peer coaches are nominated for these assignments by a committee of senior managers; they receive bonus pay through the company's performance-appraisal system.

High-Potentials. Louis, a thirty-two-year-old operations manager, has been on the fast track within his company for three years and is expected to make the vice-presidential level within the next five years. He and twenty-three other high-potentials have been selected by a management committee to participate in a two-year development program that includes training, rotational assignments, workshops, lectures, action learning, and broad exposure to strategic management issues.

As part of the program, Louis and his colleagues are each matched with a senior manager for a one-on-one mentoring relationship. These senior managers have been carefully selected and matched with prospective protégés based on the developmental needs and competencies of the participants. Although some structure is placed on the relationships (for example, the pairs are asked to meet at least twice a month), there is a lot of flexibility in terms of roles and activities.

This program at Louis's company exemplifies a common approach. Many organizations frequently find that high-potential, fast-track managers need some extra developmental attention to facilitate their rapid progression through the management ranks. Formal developmental relationships provide that attention, in the form of support, exposure, and developmental opportunities.

Developing Women and People of Color.

The number of women and people of color in management positions has been steadily climbing in the last twenty-five years, but their upward progression through the organization is still a major problem. There are indications that women and people of color face major barriers as they attempt to advance, as evidenced by their small proportions within the top ranks of U.S. companies. (See Chapter Ten for a more in-depth discussion of this issue.)

Informal mentoring relationships, frequently identified as a key source of development and support for people seeking higher levels of leadership responsibility, are largely unavailable to women and people of color because of the small number of potential mentors within the executive ranks. Therefore, organizations have turned to formal developmental relationships as a strategy for these groups. A large financial corporation has implemented a one-year program for African American managers that includes formal mentoring relationships and structured networks. All African American managers within the middle-management ranks are asked to participate in the program. Each participant is assigned to a network of seven to nine other African American managers; each network meets monthly to discuss career issues and to provide support for one another. In addition, each participant is also assigned to a formal mentoring relationship with a senior manager from a different function or division.

Meeting Development Needs of Senior Executives.

Organizations frequently find that top executives require extra development attention to address specific needs, involving perhaps specific skills, performance issues on the job, or broader changes in behavior (Witherspoon and White, 1997). Because of their level and the nature of their jobs, these executives often have difficulties developing and maintaining developmental alliances. Therefore, organizations often create formal developmental relationships to provide these executives with that extra development attention when attempting to remedy a particular skill deficit.

For example, a midsized, diversified service organization has spent over one hundred thousand dollars in the past two years improving the communication and interpersonal skills of several executives within the top management team. The organization has hired three highly respected consultants to provide intensive one-on-one coaching in these important skill areas. The pairs meet every two or three weeks for a six-month period; together, they complete behaviorally specific development plans to improve these skills.

Organizational Change Efforts. Finally, formal relationships are sometimes created during times of organizational change, to help managers develop the skills and behaviors they need to facilitate the transition. For example, a large manufacturing company has undergone a major reorganization that included setting up self-managing workteams. Each workteam is assigned a coach, a senior manager nominated for the role by an executive committee. The coach is to provide support and sponsorship to the workteam and to each individual on that team. The coach works closely with the team's immediate supervisor, to formalize development goals for the team and its members.

Types of Formal Developmental Relationships

In addition to having a range of purposes, formal developmental relationships also vary in form or structure. The examples we have cited thus far illustrate this variety. These variations, however, can be grouped into four basic, commonly used forms:

1. One-on-one mentoring
2. Peer coaching
3. Executive coaching
4. Coaching in groups

When should an organization opt for a particular type of formal relationship? What are the potential problems associated with each type? These questions are addressed in the descriptions below, and guidelines are summarized in Table 5.3.

TABLE 5.3. FORMS OF DEVELOPMENTAL RELATIONSHIPS: WHEN TO USE THEM, AND POTENTIAL PROBLEMS.

Form	When to Use It	Potential Problems
One-on-one mentoring	Senior managers have time, experience, and expertise to share with junior managers Junior managers need exposure to perspectives and job demands of senior managers	Lack of integration with other management development strategies in organization Senior managers may not have skills or motivation to teach others Potential for role conflict between boss and mentor May narrow opportunities for other developmental relationships May cause resentment for managers who have not been asked to participate
Peer coaching	Individuals need familiarity with issues and perspectives in other functions or parts of the organization Individuals need coaching to get up to speed in a business knowledge or technical area Improved cross-group communication is desired Peers going through similar experiences need opportunities to learn from and support each other	Coaching needs of the targeted managers may not complement each other Organizational climate may not promote open communication between colleagues Managers may feel resentful at being asked to coach and assist other managers Managers may not have the time or motivation to participate
Executive coaching	High-level executive has no peers or boss who can serve as coach Need expertise of professional skilled in behavioral change strategies Want a concentrated period of coaching on a particular skill	Experience and skills of coach may not meet needs of executive May be too expensive May undermine others' confidence in executive if coaching not kept confidential
Coaching in groups	Potential coaches are in short supply Anticipate that peers can learn and benefit from each other Increased cohesion among group members is desired	Some managers may need more individualized developmental attention Potential coaches may lack skills, time, or motivation to mentor group Requires a fair amount of time and planning to be effective Potential for conflict between group coach and supervisors of participants

One-On-One Mentoring. A one-on-one formal mentoring relationship typically entails a junior manager being assigned to a senior manager outside of his or her direct reporting line. This type of formal relationship is usually directed toward a particular group of junior managers (high-potentials, new managers, people of color) in the hopes that these relationships will provide some of the same important career and personal development supports as do informal, long-term mentoring relationships. By formalizing the process, the organization is ensuring that all of the identified junior managers have equal access to a mentor, and it focuses the mentoring effort within a specified time frame. One-on-one formal mentoring relationships should be considered by organizations if junior managers need additional exposure to the perspectives and job demands of senior managers and if senior managers have particular experience and expertise to share with junior managers.

A national restaurant chain uses a formal mentoring program to train and socialize new managers. Every new store manager is assigned to a senior manager (at another store) for a yearlong mentoring relationship. The mentor is expected to spend at least six hours per week in the new manager's restaurant, providing coaching and support. The mentoring role has been integrated into the company's performance appraisal system, and each mentor is held accountable for the protégé's store performance.

Although one-on-one formal mentoring provides junior managers with wonderful opportunities for learning and development, there are also some cautions to be considered before making the decision to implement a program. For one, formal mentoring relationships, if they are to be effective, need to be integrated into the larger management development strategy and clearly linked to business strategies and personnel practices (Kram and Bragar, 1992).

Another caution concerns the people selected to act as mentors. Not all senior managers have the time, motivation, experience, and expertise to share with junior managers. It is also important to assess the potential for role conflict between the mentor and the junior manager's boss. Other potential drawbacks include creation of a climate of favoritism, resentment by nonparticipants, and negative experiences (Kram and Bragar, 1992; Kizilos, 1990; Murray and Owen, 1991; Noe, 1991).

Peer Coaching. In peer coaching an employee is assigned to a colleague at the same level within the organization. It is based on the assumption that peer relationships are important vehicles for learning and growth (Douglas and Schoorman, 1987; Kram and Isabella, 1985; Kram and Bragar, 1992; McCauley and Young, 1993). Commonly used in educational settings (as with peer coaching among teachers or principals), it has gained popularity within corporate settings only in recent years.

In the corporate world, peer coaching is typically used to help people develop specific skills in their current positions. One organization, citing poor communication between functions, instituted a peer coaching program in which each employee was matched with a colleague in another function; they were to share information, help each other develop skills, and support one another. National Semiconductor has instituted a coaching process in which managers receive 360-degree feedback and then create a "performance partnership" with a peer, a partnership for new behavior and enhanced personal productivity (Peters, 1996). The partners attend a coaching workshop together and create a contract on how they will work together.

Peer coaching is called for when employees need familiarity with issues and perspectives in other functions or parts of the organizations, when they need help getting up to speed in a particular skill or knowledge base, or when cross-group communication needs improvement. An organization considering a peer coaching initiative has to take the time to fully understand the developmental needs of the potential participants and their ability to help each other with those needs.

There are some potential drawbacks to a peer coaching program. There may be times when the coaching needs of the targeted individuals do not complement each other. The organizational climate may not promote open communication between colleagues. Some people may feel resentful at being asked to help others. Some people may not have the time or motivation to participate in the peer coaching program if they do not see any career or personal benefits.

Executive Coaching. Executive coaching is usually used to help chief executives, board members, and senior managers in particular skill areas that have been identified as needing improvement. The senior executives are paired with external coaches (outside consultants specializing in executive coaching), who work with them on identified weaknesses for a short period, usually about six months. Executive coaching initiatives are normally highly confidential and tend to be used as needed.

Anna, a fifty-two-year-old executive vice president in a global manufacturing company, had decided to focus on improving her communication skills after receiving feedback from several peers and her manager that this was an area that needed improvement. With some advice and encouragement from her manager, she participated in a six-month program of executive coaching. Her coach, an external consultant, interviewed several people, including her manager, mentor, peers, subordinates, and family members. Then, based on this data and Anna's own introspection, he worked with her to formalize a behaviorally specific development plan. Once the plan was in place, he stayed in contact with her for several months to help her make some important changes in work behaviors.

Witherspoon and White (1997) have identified four roles that executive coaches may play: coaching for skills, for performance, for development, and for the executive's agenda. Coaching for skills focuses on improving the skills needed in a person's current task or project. Coaching for performance also emphasizes a person's present job, but the learning is more broadly based; it typically revolves around some performance issues. Coaching for development addresses preparing someone for a future job. Coaching for an executive's agenda refers to broadly based learning that revolves around the executive's perceived needs; this type of coaching tends to be long-term and evolving.

Executive coaching should be considered when people need coaching on a particular skill and have no peers or managers who can provide it. They may prefer a concentrated period of coaching by a professional skilled in behavioral change strategies. Organizations considering this approach need to carefully check the credentials of the potential coach.

Coaching in Groups. Philip, a thirty-four-year-old human resource manager, has been asked by his company to participate in a one-year career development initiative. He and five other managers from different functions are meeting every month to share career issues. Cherie, a financial vice president, has volunteered to act as their guide and learning partner. In addition to sharing her own perspectives and experiences, Cherie helps the group develop their meeting agendas, provides active support, gives feedback to individual members, assists the group in obtaining desired learning projects and needed resources, and affords them some visibility within the organization.

Philip and his colleagues are also participating in another type of formal developmental relationship: coaching in groups. It is a combination of the basic processes involved in one-on-one mentoring and peer coaching. Organizations may want to consider group coaching when potential coaches are in short supply, when it is anticipated that peers can learn and benefit from each other, and when increased cohesion among group members is desired.

Group coaching typically involves a learning group of four to six individuals who meet regularly and are assigned to a senior manager. The senior manager's role within the learning group is to act as a learning partner by helping the managers understand the organization, guiding them in analyzing their experiences, and clarifying career directions. The senior manager strives to create an environment wherein participants can learn from each other as well as from the senior manager (Kaye and Jacobson, 1995).

Among the potential drawbacks is the concern that some managers need more individualized attention than group coaching can realistically provide. Finding the right coach is also a concern. Group coaching requires a great deal of commitment from a senior manager and a different set of skills from those in coaching a single individual. Potential coaches might lack the necessary skills, time, or motivation to mentor a group. The participants' immediate supervisors may also feel resentful toward the group coach. Finally, group mentoring requires a fair amount of time and planning by all participants.

Key Characteristics of an Effective Formal Initiative

With all the shapes and forms that formal relationships take, how can organizations be sure the ones they are considering will be effective?

The literature on this subject cites well over one hundred characteristics or components of successful programs, but they all seem to cluster into five overarching themes (Douglas, 1997):

1. Organizational support for the program
2. Clarity of purpose, expectations, and roles
3. Participant choice and involvement
4. Careful selection and matching procedures
5. Continuous monitoring and evaluation

Organizational Support. Organizational support is defined as the degree to which an initiative is encouraged and supported by the organization as a whole. Specifically, it means the program should be integrated with strategic business needs, organizational systems (performance appraisal process, reward systems, communication systems), and other management development efforts. There should be visible support from top management and a supportive organizational culture. In fact, support of top management is probably the most frequently mentioned success characteristic within the literature. Finally, adequate resources need to be available.

Clarity of Purpose, Expectations, and Roles. The program goals and objectives must be clearly defined, and the choice of program must be driven by those objectives. The goals and objectives need to be fully communicated to everyone involved—program participants, potential mentors, top management, nonparticipants, program coordinators, and others—so that they have realistic expectations of what the program can and cannot achieve. They should also receive, in an orientation session or similar format, a clear description of their roles and responsibilities. Finally, participants in the program should clarify their expectations with the partner in the match. Questions that help with this clarifying process are presented in Table 5.4.

Choice and Involvement by Participants. The more participants feel they have decision-making control over their involvement in a program,

TABLE 5.4. CLARIFYING THE FORMAL RELATIONSHIP: TOPICS TO REVIEW.

Goals and intended outcomes	What does each person hope to gain from the relationship?
	What would a positive relationship look and feel like?
	What are the measurable goals of the relationship?
	What are the "softer" goals and expectations (less able to be measured)?
	What is the expected time frame for the relationship?
Activities	What will discussion and meetings focus on?
	What are some activities that might best serve the goals of the relationship?
	What will the plan of action be?
Communication and frequency of contact	How will you communicate (for example, phone, meetings, e-mail, and so on)?
	How often will you communicate?
	When will you communicate?
Responsibilities	What are the responsibilities of each person in the relationship?
	What does each person have to offer to the relationship?
	Who will take initiative for setting up contacts?
Issues of confidentiality	How will you handle issues of confidentiality?
	What issues that evolve from the relationship will be kept confidential?
Fears	What are the drawbacks of the relationship?
	What are you afraid might get off track in the relationship? How can you guard against this?
Evaluation	Do you need a process for following up on the terms of the contracted relationship?
	Does the relationship need to be evaluated? How? How often?
	If expectations are not met on either side, what actions should be taken?
	How will the partners be held accountable to each other?

the more effective it is likely to be. In particular, people need to feel that they have something to say about how the process is structured and about their individual roles in it.

Careful Selection and Matching Procedures. *Selection and matching* refers to thoughtful and predetermined processes for identifying and pairing participants in relationship-based initiatives. If it is to succeed, the program needs participants who are committed to its goals and motivated to participate wholeheartedly. This means the participants need to be carefully selected, based on program objectives and a predetermined set of criteria. Then they must be matched with their relationship partners through procedures that are well thought out and consistent with the goals of the initiative. The procedures should address both how the matching happens (whether through voluntary matching, matching by a committee, by a program coordinator, etc.) and what criteria are used (similar interests, accessibility, position, functional areas, strengths, etc.).

Continuous Monitoring and Evaluation. Effective relationship-based programs typically have established processes for monitoring the program while it is under way, assessing effectiveness, and making improvements. The strategies used for monitoring should be worked out while the program is being designed, well before it actually starts. Periodic assessments can be made through focus groups, interviews, or surveys (Kram and Bragar, 1992). The choice of strategy may depend on existing mechanisms in the organization's human resource area, but it is important to make sure that the chosen strategy assesses both process and outcome variables and is linked to business strategies.

Formal Developmental Relationships as Part of a Developmental Process

Two promising trends we see in formal developmental relationships are assigning people to more than one relationship and linking the relationships with other leadership development strategies. These practices help integrate formal relationships into an overall developmental process.

One such program is being implemented in a regional financial organization. The goal is to prepare fast-track employees for key management positions. Participants must apply for the program and go through an extensive screening process by top management. Those who are accepted spend their entire time focusing on learning and development; during the program they are actually employees of the organization's corporate university. Over the next nine months, they take formal training classes and are involved in rotational assignments. They also are assigned to a business mentor, a senior manager who provides business, technical, and political advice. They usually have just one business mentor, but they may have more than one if the required exposure to expertise cannot be met by a relationship with a single individual.

Participants also have a formal developmental relationship with the university's director of trainees, who provides them with ongoing feedback. The director garners input from the various supervisors on the participant's rotational assignments and from the business mentor, feeds their observations and impressions back to the participants, and helps them plan changes and improvements based on the feedback.

A second example is the two-year executive development program sponsored by the Council of Jewish Federations (CJF). The council is an association of 189 Jewish federations, local organizations that raise money to help each Jewish community respond to people in need and populations at risk. CJF helps strengthen the work of its member federations by developing programs to meet changing needs; providing an exchange of successful community experiences; establishing guidelines for fundraising and operations; and leading joint efforts to meet local, regional, and international needs. The executive development program was designed to develop high-potential professionals who are projected to attain the most senior level positions in major federations throughout North America. The program is funded in large part by the Mandel Associated Foundations in Cleveland, and participants are called "Mandel Fellows."

Over the course of two years, the fellows engage in a variety of development activities. They begin the program with a weeklong feedback-intensive program (see Chapter Two). They spend a two-week period in Israel, working with emerging Israeli leaders to understand various issues in the Jewish community worldwide. Throughout the program, there are also several two-day meetings focused on particular managerial issues, as well as opportunities to engage in distance-learning events focused on Judaic history and philosophy.

The fellows are assigned to two formal relationships during the program: they are matched with an "executive mentor," and they choose one or more "leadership coaches." The executive mentor is a successful large-city federation president. The major purpose of this relationship is to help the fellow see the issues and challenges faced by a senior leader in a major federation (the type of position the program is preparing them for) and the strategies used to lead such organizations. The relationship is built around a visit by the fellow to the mentor's organization. A typical visit consists of shadowing the mentor during normal work activities, debriefing and discussion time with the mentor, meeting with other staff (and getting their views of the mentor's leadership behaviors and styles), and being included in the mentor's nonwork activities. The connection could also foster an ongoing informal relationship, one in which the fellows get advice and input as their careers progress.

The leadership coaches are recognized leaders in the participant's own local community, usually leaders in corporate or public sector organizations. These relationships are intended to help the fellows understand the leadership complexities, dynamics, styles, and strategies in a markedly different institution. The expectation is that they will be exposed to new perspectives of effective leadership in a large-scale organization. Additionally, fellows often look for leadership coaches who are particularly strong in an area where they want to learn and improve.

The pairs engage in a wide variety of activities. Coaches are shadowed, are used as sounding boards, or serve as consultants on a project the fellow is working on. They share with the fellow their experiences, philosophies, leadership models, things they have read, etc. They open up their organizations for observation and discussions with staff. They are asked to observe activities in the fellow's organization or share their expertise with a particular group in the organization. The type of activity depends on what the fellow wishes to get out of the relationship.

In addition to these two one-on-one relationships, the program also produces valuable relationships among the participants. They learn from one another by sharing their experiences, getting and giving feedback, and providing advice. They are also sources of support for each other, thus strongly fulfilling the role of cohort. Because of the length of the program and the intensity of many of their shared experiences, these relationships are likely to continue once the formal program is over.

Summary

Developmental relationships are an important strategy for enhancing the leadership development process. They are a source of assessment information and a resource for interpreting and understanding that information. They challenge an individual directly or provide access to challenging assignments. And they are a primary means of support for development.

Some people seem naturally to access others in their efforts to learn and grow, and some people are natural coaches. Generally, these people tend to find each other without much organizational intervention. However, organizations that want informal developmental relationships to occur regularly for more people need to (1) develop coaching skills in the organization and reward people for using those skills, (2) encourage people to seek out the developmental relationships they need, and (3) provide ample opportunities for people from across the organization to meet and develop relationships.

In addition to creating the context in which informal developmental relationships are likely to flourish, it is often appropriate for organizations to create formal relationships directed toward specific development agendas: developing employees new to their roles, preparing high-potential managers, developing women and people of color, meeting the development needs of senior managers, and supporting organizational change efforts. These relationships can take the form of one-on-one mentoring, peer coaching, executive coaching, and coaching in groups.

Successful formal initiatives are those that have organizational support; clarity of purpose, expectations, and roles; choice and involvement by participants; careful selection and matching procedures; and continuous monitoring and evaluation. Formal initiatives are most effective when they are integrated into a larger process of leadership development.

Resources on Developing Coaching Skills

Chiaramonte, P., and Higgins, A. "Coaching for High Performance." *Business Quarterly,* Autumn 1993, pp. 81–87.

Evered, R., and Selman, J. "'Coaching' and the Art of Management." *Organizational Dynamics,* Autumn 1989, pp. 16–32.

Geber, B. "From Manager into Coach." *Training,* Feb. 1992, pp. 25–31.

Hargrove, R. *Masterful Coaching.* San Francisco: Pfeiffer, 1995.

Hendricks, W., and Associates. *Coaching, Mentoring, and Managing.* Franklin Lakes, N.J.: Career Press, 1996.

Kinlaw, D. *Coaching for Commitment: Managerial Strategies for Obtaining Superior Performance.* San Francisco: Pfeiffer, 1993.

Mink, O. *Developing High-Performance People: The Art of Coaching.* Reading, Mass.: Addison-Wesley, 1993.

Orth, C., Wildinson, H., and Benfari, R. "The Manager's Role as Coach and Mentor." *Organizational Dynamics,* Spring 1987, pp. 66–74.

Peterson, D., and Hicks, M. D. *Leader as Coach.* Minneapolis: Personnel Decisions, 1996.

Waldroop, J., and Butler, T. "The Executive as Coach." *Harvard Business Review,* Nov.–Dec. 1996.

CHAPTER SIX

HARDSHIPS

Russ S. Moxley

We were sitting around a conference table at a beautiful resort in Manchester, Vermont. I had asked these executives of a large consumer products company to reflect on their careers and identify one or two significant events that had changed the way they managed. The president sat quietly, very pensively, while his colleagues talked about the critical incidents they had encountered and what they learned from them. They described many of the experiences detailed in other chapters of this book: challenging assignments, difficult bosses, their first job as a supervisor, training courses attended.

Suddenly the company's chief legal counsel, realizing that the president hadn't spoken, turned to him and said, "Jim [not his real name], what do you have on your list?" Jim demurred. "Mine are different," he said. "They're not like yours." The attorney persisted, gently nudging Jim to share his experience.

Finally Jim spoke. "Sometimes I guess you really have to get your nose bloodied before you learn. I've had a great career. Lots of good jobs, and on each of them I've done fairly well. Along the way I developed a lot of confidence in my ability, to the point that I pretty much thought I always knew what needed to be done. So I didn't delegate very well, didn't rely much on the other members of the team. Then I had a heart attack. It was like running into a brick wall. I realized that I was finite, that I couldn't do it all. It was a humbling experience. It was only then that I realized that I'd better learn to delegate, to really trust the experience and expertise of people like yourselves. I think I've been a different kind of leader since then, not so much of a one-man band."

Jim's story is a good example of the sort of lessons people can learn from life's curveballs. From the challenging and important assignments Jim completed during his career, among other things he learned self-confidence. He learned to trust his own judgment and have confidence in his decisions. These are important lessons for a leader to learn. But as is true with every other strength, if self-confidence is taken to an extreme it becomes a weakness. Self-confidence that goes unchecked becomes arrogance. By his own account, Jim had become arrogant. He thought he could do it all. He didn't need to delegate; he didn't need a team of strong subordinates.

What's the best antidote for arrogance? Often it is a hardship. After his heart attack, Jim learned to balance self-confidence with humility. In the process he became a more well-rounded leader. He was able to act with flexibility, maintaining confidence in his own judgment but also relying on the judgment of others.

A Different Kind of Developmental Experience

When people mentally list types of experience that would be included in a definition of *developmental*, they think of training, challenging jobs, coaches and mentors. But they usually don't think of hardships. Yet hardships are important to the development of well-rounded leaders. Learning is not random. Specific experiences teach specific lessons, and hardships offer lessons not attainable elsewhere.

Hardships are a different kind of developmental experience because *they are not planned*. People encounter them, ready or not, during the course of their career and their lives. Also, the lessons learned from hardships are learned *after* the experience, after people have gotten through them, had time to reflect on them, and gained perspective on and from them.

Hardships are also different because *the challenge imbedded in them is different.* The challenges described in other chapters of this handbook are external to the person: a challenging assignment, a difficult boss, challenge built into a training program. Challenge is an important part of these experiences, but it is not the direct result of something the manager did or didn't do. Hardships are different in that the experience—the business mistake, or being passed over for a promotion, or a heart attack—is one's own. Even when caused by something outside the person's immediate control, such as a downsizing, the hardship is experienced in an intensely personal way. This is the challenge of facing adversity, and it is internal to the person.

At the core of any hardship experience is a sense of loss: of credibility, a sense of control, self-efficacy, a former identity. *The dimension of loss* is another way in which hardships are different from other developmental experiences. The loss provokes confrontation with self, and in dealing with loss and the pain accompanying it, learning results.

This sense of loss causes people who usually live in an external world to turn inward. *What did I do wrong? Do I not measure up? What could I have done differently? Could I have done anything to prevent it?* This is a time of taking stock, reflecting on strengths and weaknesses, considering what's important in life and work, giving up an old identity while transitioning to a new one. As with other losses, people go through stages of denial, defensiveness, and anger before working their way through to some level of acceptance.

How people respond to this loss drives learning. As reported in *Lessons of Experience,* a book that describes the results of one Center research project on how and what leaders learn from experience, "These hardships can provoke several types of lessons . . . the executives learned about themselves in relationship to others, their career aspirations, their capacity to overcome fear and defeat, and their ability to adapt in a sometimes arbitrary world. In each confrontation they came up short. Therein lay the lesson. As research has shown, the acceptance and recognition of limitations, followed by an effort to redirect oneself, are characteristic of successful people in general. It was how the executives responded, then, not the event itself, that is the key to understanding the value of these hardships" (McCall, Lombardo, and Morrison, 1988, pp. 88–89).

Hardships and the Lessons They Teach

From several research projects done at the Center, five types of hardship events, and the lessons taught, have been identified. The five types are summarized in Table 6.1. This is of course not an exhaustive list of the hardships people experience, but it is fairly representative. Other hardships usually fit under one of these types.

TABLE 6.1. FIVE TYPES OF HARDSHIP AND THE LESSONS THEY TEACH.

Hardship	Lessons Learned
Business mistakes and failures	Handling relationships Humility How to handle mistakes
Career setbacks	Self-awareness Organizational politics What one really wants to do
Personal trauma	Sensitivity to others Coping with events beyond one's control Perseverance Recognition of limits
Problem employees	How to stand firm Confrontation skills
Downsizing	Coping skills Recognition of what's important Organizational politics

Mistakes and Failures

According to IBM legend, in the early days of the company a young engineer made a mistake that cost the company thousands of dollars. Embarrassed and afraid, the engineer approached founder and president Tom Watson, told him of the mistake, and offered to resign. Watson is reported to have said, "Resign? I can't afford for you to resign. Look how much I have already invested in your development."

Like that young engineer, all managers and executives make mistakes. Contracts are negotiated poorly, business deals go sour, opportunities are not seized, a relationship with an important client is mismanaged, the boss does not get what she wants when she wants it. The question is not whether mistakes are made and failures experienced but whether they are seen as opportunities to learn, grow, and change.

The sense of loss that often accompanies mistakes and failures involves loss of self-efficacy (loss of confidence in doing a particular thing) and loss of confidence from others at work. When people help others "save face" after a mistake, they are trying to make sure they don't add to the sense of loss already being experienced.

Executives tend to learn from their mistakes if three conditions are present (McCall, Lombardo, and Morrison, 1988):

1. *Cause and effect are very clear.* If people are unsure of their responsibility for the mistake or feel they couldn't have done anything to prevent it, few lessons are learned. On the other hand, if cause and effect are clear, if people know they are culpable, the chances are greatly enhanced that lessons will be learned. As soon as someone says "I blew it" or "I had a part in it," openness to learning is present.
2. *The cards must be on the table.* It is easy to downplay mistakes, pretend they did not happen, and deny their consequences. It is harder to put the mistake on the table, discuss it openly, and pull learnings from it. But discussing mistakes honestly and openly is the best way for managers and executives to assess their contribution to the mess and learn from it, and the only way to encourage broader organizational learning.

3. *The organization's position on how mistakes are treated must be clearly under-stood.* Many organizations proclaim they encourage appropriate risk-taking behavior as a way of becoming more innovative, but few have clearly defined how they handle the mistakes that are bound to happen when people take risks. The best way for companies to show they really mean what they say is to implement a mistake system.

Like a reward system, an organizational mistake system specifies what employees can positively expect if they take appropriate risks but don't succeed, if they move into difficult assignments and make mistakes, or if they agree to test untested skills in managing a difficult employee and don't handle it adeptly. For instance, the existing performance-appraisal and compensation systems might be expanded to include specified rewards for good, determined efforts that are not successful. Or a program of special public acknowledgment can be instituted for those who attempt herculean tasks but fall short.

If these three conditions are met, the lessons that can be learned from mistakes are quite potent.

Mismanaging relationships is a frequently cited mistake, and learning how to better handle them is one of the most important lessons. This includes learning more about what senior-level executives are like and how to work with them; how to deal better with direct reports on issues such as delegation and decision making; and, in a general sense, how to understand other people and their perspectives better.

A second lesson often learned from mistakes is humility. Mistakes have the capacity to teach people about their flaws and limitations. One executive told us the story of doing a poor job of negotiating a contract with a major international client that caused his company thousands of dollars: "I didn't ask for help. I didn't think I needed it. I learned very quickly how much I didn't know. I learned it the hard way."

Finally, making mistakes and learning from them teaches the very important lesson of how to handle them. There appears to be a real difference in how leaders who succeed and those who don't handle mistakes. People who try to cover up or whitewash their mistakes, who blame others when mistakes surface, and who do not warn others that the consequences of a mistake might affect them are candidates for derailment. Conversely, people who acknowledge their mistakes, own their responsibility for them, and let others know who might feel the consequences continue to be seen as effective. The difference is not that one group makes mistakes and the other doesn't. All leaders make mistakes. The difference is how mistakes are handled.

Career Setbacks

Jan had been identified as a high-potential manager in her organization. She rose very quickly, completing one challenging assignment after another. She was on a fast track. Then it happened. A promotion that she expected went to someone else.

Calvin was moved from his line job to a corporate staff position. He was told that the new job (long-range planning) was important; he was not told that it was seen as a developmental experience for him, that there were particular leadership skills he could learn in this new assignment. But Calvin came to hate the new job; he felt he was on the sidelines looking on while others were making important operational decisions.

Helena was put in a new assignment that entailed a significant change in scope and scale. For the first time, she was managing people who had more technical expertise than she, and many were older. The company knew it would be a stretch assignment for her, that she was going to be in over her head. They thought she could do it, but she couldn't; it was too much of a stretch. After a year of struggle, Helena was demoted. But she also received a lot of support, so that after having time to catch her breath she got her career back on track.

These stories illustrate three types of career setbacks: missed promotions, unsatisfying jobs, and demotions. Being fired is an obvious fourth type.

What's the sense of loss from a career setback? For some it is a loss of control, especially control over their careers. For others it is loss of self-efficacy, a sense that they might not measure up in certain critical skill areas, a realization that they don't have all the leadership capacity they need. For others, especially those fired, it is a loss of professional identity.

Whatever the sense of loss, career setbacks are usually wake-up calls. They offer people a chance to learn others' perceptions about themselves. Executives who experience a setback may already know that they have weaknesses, but now they learn that others also recognize the weaknesses and that the weaknesses matter. They learn that without significant change in their leadership skills and perspectives, they can derail—if, in fact, they haven't already done so. For people who are open to learning, career setbacks are unfreezing experiences, opening them to new insights about their strengths and limitations and enhancing their readiness to learn from other developmental opportunities.

Not all setbacks result from limitations of the individual. Reorganizations, reengineering, and mergers and acquisitions all lead to less-than-desirable opportunities for otherwise outstanding performers. It is easy at times like these for people to become cynical and blame their situation on organizational politics. Development happens if people are able to see career setbacks as opportunities to learn.

Another lesson that leaders can learn from career setbacks is what kind of jobs they like and don't like. The reality check that comes with the setback often leads people to take stock of themselves. As they do, they learn about what type of work is satisfying and meaningful, and they decide to take more responsibility for managing their careers and choosing work that is meaningful.

Learning positive lessons from career setbacks is aided by the right kind of support from significant others in the organization. If wounds are to be healed, an appropriate intervention, one that includes lots of listening and sorting of feelings, is crucial. Someone needs to work with the person, taking on the role of counselor (see Chapter Five for more on this developmental relationship). Unfortunately, in most organizations it is exactly at such times that an effective intervention is least likely to happen. The managers of those who have experienced a setback are often unable or perhaps unwilling to help the wounded person through the sense of loss.

Personal Trauma

One surprising developmental experience that people continue to report to us is personal trauma: illness, death, divorce, children in trouble. Our surprise is not that executives experience these hardships but rather that they learn such powerful and lasting leadership lessons from them. The bad news is that it sometimes takes a traumatic experience to wake people up; the good news is that they *can* wake up, and learn, grow, and change.

One organizational leader talked about his experience of his wife's six-year battle with cancer. Before that, he had been a "take no prisoners" type of leader: confident, challenging, forceful, task-oriented. He acknowledged that he had not been sensitive to others, that he did not stop long enough to see things from their perspective. The important leadership lesson he learned from this trauma was that he could balance toughness with sensitivity and be more effective as a result.

Another executive told us how reality broke through his years of denial when he realized his teenage son was an alcoholic. When the boy was arrested for DWI and a police officer asked if he wanted to call his father, the son answered bitterly, "He probably isn't home, and if he is, he won't care." Stopped dead in his tracks, the executive was able to admit to himself that he had spent too little time being a father and a husband. He also realized, once this experience started him on a journey of introspection, that work was not bringing the kind of meaning and satisfaction for which he longed. The result: he eventually created a better balance between his work and his personal life and, in a long and tough process, rebuilt a relationship with his son.

A third person told us about the anguish of losing her teenage daughter to leukemia. This leader held a high position in her organization and was used to being in control, but here was an event that she could not even influence, much less control. She could do nothing to make the fear go away. There were times, she told us, that she wasn't sure she was going to make it, that it was just too hard. The leadership lesson in this? She learned how to cope with things beyond her control. She learned that even when she could not control the events in her professional and personal life, she could control her reaction to them. She also learned how to persevere, how to go deep inside and embrace her fears as a way of getting through them. She developed mental and emotional toughness, learned that wading into is the best way of getting out of, and learned that she had the ability to hang in there in tough situations.

As these stories illustrate, executives experience loss of control in these personal and traumatic events. For men and women used to being in charge and maintaining control, these personal traumas seem like earthquakes shaking the very foundations of life. How they cope with this loss of control is what drives learning.

Problem Employees

Difficult employees come in many guises. Those that are most obvious—people guilty of theft or fraud or deceit, or whose work is clearly below standard—are not the hardest to deal with. Company policies, or common sense, provide a ready solution for those. The hardest to manage are the situations where the decision of what to do is not clear cut.

Take, for example, the employee whose behavior is inconsistent. When he is "on" he is one of the best workers in the company, charming and competent. But when he is "off" he is serious trouble: deceptive and manipulative, doing things he knows are wrong, and then trying hard to cover his tracks.

What should his manager do? Here's a talented employee, with important skills and abilities the company needs. Most managers would like to develop him and shore up the downside, rather than fire him. So they spend an inordinate amount of time talking with him, influencing, coaching, and even cajoling him. They keep thinking that if they just work hard enough, well enough, and long enough they can turn the situation around. Some executives report working with problem employees for several years before moving them to a more suitable position or, as a last resort, firing them.

What can leaders learn from this situation? They can learn about the importance of standing firm and being forceful. And they can learn how to confront problem employees. This learning fits one of the over-all themes of this handbook: leaders learn by doing.

Before joining the staff of the Center, I was manager of management development for a major oil company. I was promoted into this position over a group of peers, one of whom felt he deserved the promotion and had, in fact, been promised it. He spent the next several years attempting to prove that he knew more about the division, and more about the management and organization development function, than I. He was bright and talented, a capable consultant, and he had a good sense for organizational politics. But he let his ambition blind him; he became so politicized that he lost credibility with me and with other important managers in the organization.

Dealing with him was a going-against-the-grain experience for me. I had not experienced quite such a difficult subordinate in other managerial jobs. What did I learn? I learned that trying to work with someone over a long period of time, trying to win that person's support, isn't always the right way to go. I also learned that although confrontation is still not easy for me, it is sometimes important—to the other person and to my image of myself.

Downsizing

Sometimes events conspire. No matter how hard and well some people work to develop their leadership capacities, no matter how much they try to meet the company's expectations, no matter how loyal they have been, there are times when none of that matters because they fall victim to corporate downsizing. They lose their jobs through no fault of their own, but even knowing this does not lessen their sense of loss.

Because executives so often identify themselves with the work they do, there is first and foremost loss of identity. This is compounded by loss of relationships and community, and loss of security. As much as with any other hardship, men and women who experience downsizing need an opportunity to work through their fear and insecurity, their frustration and anger, their sadness and their distrust.

Yet most organizations, and the executives in them, are not prepared to help men and women work though the healing process following downsizing. As David Noer (1993) has so eloquently taught us, downsizings are done from the head (not the heart) of the organization's executives. Although some downsized individuals seek out professional counseling and others rely on support systems outside of work to help them sort out their feelings, almost none find the kind of support they need inside their organization. The element of the development process that we have called support is too often lacking exactly when it is most needed.

If support is available, either inside or outside the company, powerful lessons can be learned. People learn that they have the ability to cope with things beyond their control. One executive said to us of his experience of downsizing, "I learned that nothing is guaranteed. I decided to take advantage of every opportunity to maximize my marketability. I also learned not to be overwhelmed with anxiety, especially in situations where I have little or no control."

People can use the time after being downsized to take stock, consider anew what's important in life and career, and make new decisions about how to invest talents and energy. Again, how one responds to the hardship drives learning.

Being downsized is one kind of hardship; being responsible for a downsizing is another. One district operations manager told us, "Because of a reduction in the number of districts in our company, some 250 people were being displaced or laid off. I had the unpleasant duty of telling people how this reorganization affected people in my district. The hardest task was telling this one manager he was being laid off. He took the news extremely hard. I was not prepared for his reaction—he cried."

What did this manager learn from the experience? "This experience awakened me to the real world of management in dealing with people. I became more compassionate and understood people's feelings better. I think it made me stronger and equipped me to handle difficult situations when managing people."

The Lessons Learned from Hardships

In the previous section the individual lessons learned were described; here they are linked together into five general themes or patterns. Together, the themes focus on the important issues of personal awareness and personal attributes.

Recognition of Limits and Blind Spots

Hardship experiences *unfreeze* people, by which we mean open them up to new awareness. When unfrozen, leaders tend to realize, perhaps for the first time, that they have limits. They understand that they do not always have to be strong and heroic. They also become aware of their blind spots, what others know about them but they themselves do not. This is significant because our research and experience, as well as the research done by others, show that self-awareness is a key attribute of effective leaders.

Sensitivity and Compassion

Being sensitive and compassionate is the "soft" side of leadership. Sensitivity and compassion are very valuable attributes for everyone, in personal and work life, yet many people find them hard to express. People who hold positions of great power and authority often find them particularly hard. Experiencing a personal hardship teaches empathy, concern for the hopes and aspirations of others, and understanding of another person's perspective.

Coping with Circumstances Beyond One's Control

Events do conspire; leaders cannot control everything, but they can control how they respond to those events. In turbulent times, when the organizational ship is being tossed to and fro, this attribute is especially critical.

Balance

Deciding what really matters and getting clear about life and career aspirations is another lesson that hardships teach. It is often a hardship that forces executives to create a more appropriate balance in their work and family life, to invest more energy in spouse and children.

Flexibility

So often people think of behaviors as either-or. They can be tough or compassionate, self-confident or humble, a strong individual leader or a good team player. In fact, really effective leaders learn to act with flexibility. They learn to be "both-and" people. They are tough, stand-on-their-own-two-feet, forceful leaders; at the same time, they are empowering, sensitive, and compassionate.

Using Hardships for Development

Even though people realize they can learn positive lessons from difficult experiences, there are reasons they don't usually include hardships when they think of development. They work hard to avoid embarrassing gaffes, minimize the possibility of failure, avoid derailing. Managers don't choose to hire difficult people just so new skills will be tested. People don't look upon personal trauma (such as a heart attack) as being relevant for work-related development, and they don't think of stressful situations as developmental. For all the right reasons, people seek to minimize the possibility of experiencing hardships.

Managers also tend to go out of their way to keep their direct reports from experiencing hardship. Even the worst ogre of a boss would not go to someone and say, "You need a good developmental experience that will teach you humility. I suggest a heart attack." Rather, managers are likely to structure work in a way that avoids hardship. They give their direct reports safe assignments, for instance, jobs they have proven they have the skills and abilities to handle. They promote people in small, incremental steps, usually in the same area of their technical specialty, so they won't experience failure.

This is very human and very understandable, but shortsighted. If managers want assignments to be developmental, they must understand that comfort is the enemy of growth. They must make sure that jobs or tasks stretch employees and force them to operate outside of their comfort zone. Assignments given for developmental reasons always involve some risk, and one of those risks is that the person doing the work might make mistakes, might even fail.

Hardships, after all, are unavoidable; the trick is to make sure the hardships that do happen are eventually seen as developmental. How does this come about? What can individuals, and their bosses and HR managers, do to make sure that the lessons of hardship are not buried by the trauma?

What Individuals Can Do

There are several things that people can do for themselves to maximize the likelihood of learning positive lessons from difficult experiences. First, they must accept the reality that during the course of their careers and lives, hardships will happen. They are built into the fabric of life. Mistakes are made while learning the ropes in new and challenging assignments; employees occasionally make life difficult for others; plum assignments go to someone else.

Whenever there is a choice, people must be willing to embrace hardships rather than shy away from them. They must accept assignments that challenge and test them, even though chances are great they will make mistakes. They must be willing to try out untested skills, such as the ability to confront a difficult employee, even though the process is uncomfortable. It is easier to avoid these challenges and the hardships that often accompany them, but that only ensures that people miss out on the leadership lessons they offer.

People must be intentional and purposeful about finding the constructive leadership lessons in hardship. Learning positive lessons is not automatic. It requires that people be willing to look inward and face whatever they find there. This kind of introspection goes against the grain for most people. Yet without reflection and careful attention, it is too easy to become cynical, to feel victimized rather than learn positive and enduring lessons. After his heart attack, Jim, the executive in the opening story of this chapter, confronted himself with the hard questions; only then did he find the positive lessons.

People must also learn how to move beyond the hardship. One difference between leaders who are effective and those who are not is that effective leaders learn to face up to their hardships, acknowledge their effect, and then let go. They don't wallow in them or continue to berate themselves for them.

What HR Managers Can Do

There are at least four specific things that HR managers or professionals can do to help individuals and organizations use hardships developmentally. First of all, help the organization create and implement a mistake system. Not all companies treat mistakes as opportunities to learn: "In some companies even the executives believe that 'one mistake and you're out'. . . . If managers are not given opportunities to learn from their mistakes, there would be no one left to manage anything more testy than the company picnic" (McCall, Lombardo, and Morrison, 1988). As a first step, HR managers can work to avoid the downside, by seeing that people don't get punished if they fail at a stretch assignment or if a decision known to involve risk doesn't quite work out. On the upside, they can build into HR systems (such as performance appraisal) recognition for taking on difficult assignments or people, even if in the end a business mistake or failure results or the problem employee has to be fired.

Second, help ensure that hardships are not avoided. HR managers can encourage line managers to add challenge to people's present jobs and occasionally select someone for an assignment based on what that person can learn, even though the assignment will be a real stretch and mistakes will be made. HR professionals can also work to ensure that other development experiences (for example, classroom training) are designed to stretch the capacities of participants.

Third, help make sure that hardship experiences are linked to other developmental experiences. Hardships often provoke informal but intense self-assessment. The lesson learned can be enhanced from a formal assessment process, such as use of a 360-degree feedback instrument. (Other suggestions for linking hardships to developmental experiences are in the next section).

Finally, intervene when necessary. Left alone to stew in their own juices, people often do just that. HR professionals may have to step in at the right time and in the right way to give employees the support and encouragement they need and help them learn positive lessons from the experience. Willingness to suspend judgment, ability to listen deeply, and ability to facilitate learning are the skills most needed to help others in making sense of a hardship.

To be sure, there is a boundary issue that must be carefully considered. It is appropriate to intervene during a work-related hardship—after a business mistake has been made, during a downsizing, while an executive is struggling with a difficult employee—to offer the executive a chance to vent, reflect, and process learning. Intervening during or after a personal trauma raises the boundary issue. Personal experiences can be powerful forces for professional growth, but they are also personal. Perhaps the best rule of thumb is for the HR professional to help an individual reflect on, and pull learnings from, a personal trauma only when that person initiates the conversation.

What Line Managers Can Do

There are also specific things that line managers can do to help their employees learn positive lessons from hardships. They must first of all understand mistakes and other hardships as opportunities to learn and not as a failure or a sign of a fatal flaw.

Line managers must also make sure that they do not directly or indirectly punish people for experiencing hardship. Conversely, a line manager can help create the norms in an organization that reinforce people for good-faith efforts even if those efforts do not produce the desired results.

A line manager can also intervene at the right time and in the right way to help an employee learn the right lesson from a hardship. Again, the key role is to listen, help a person learn his own lesson, and not teach. But the manager must also make sure that cause and effect are clear. Once an employee has made a mistake, he or she needs and deserves an honest and forthright discussion of the mistake and its effect. Likewise, someone who has suffered a career setback deserves an honest discussion of the reasons. Anyone having trouble with a direct report caused partly by his own poor management must be shown how he is contributing to the problem. Putting the cards on the table is a hard but important task of the line manager.

Hardships and the Leadership Development Model

In the introductory chapter we identify the elements of an individual leadership development system and present our thinking that all development experiences are stronger if all three elements of the model are present. This is true even of hardships. This section looks at how the elements of assessment, challenge, and support relate to hardship experiences, and how hardships can be linked to other developmental experiences.

Assessment

Perhaps more than any other experience, hardship causes people to stop and reflect, take stock of their strengths and weaknesses, and think about what's important personally and professionally. Intense, informal self-assessment comes with the territory; it is woven into the fabric of a hardship experience. For executives used to living in an external world, this type of introspection can be difficult and painful.

Challenge

The challenge built into hardship is the challenge of adversity. Adversity means being stretched in new directions. It means being uncomfortable in new and difficult roles, being tested by fire, learning by doing in tough and demanding circumstances.

Support

Two kinds of support are critical if a leader is to learn the right lessons from a hardship: support from a boss or another significant person in the organization, and support from the organization itself.

The first thing a company needs to do to help turn hardships into development experiences is to create a "mistake system." As mentioned earlier, a mistake system encourages, reinforces, and even rewards individuals for taking on challenging experiences that are rich in learning but ripe for mistakes and failure.

The second type of support needed if people are to learn important leadership lessons from hardship is that from key individuals. The person from whom support is most needed is often the individual's manager, but an HR professional or a designated coach or mentor can also provide helpful support. Specific suggestions for supportive actions are given in the previous section of this chapter.

Hardships Linked to Other Development Experiences

Learning from hardship can be enhanced when hardships are linked to other development experiences.

Left to her own devices, an executive passed over for a promotion might glean the wrong lessons about herself. She might conclude that she doesn't have the right stuff, the right combination of strengths, for a more senior-level position. But if she asks her boss for feedback, she can learn that there is just one particular skill deficiency that stands in the way, a skill that can be learned from the challenges in her present job and from a skill-based training program. The career setback provokes intense self-assessment (which in turn starts the process of learning), the self-assessment is contrasted with more formal assessment from the boss, and the formal assessment leads to a combination of learning on the job and in classroom training.

Another executive is having difficulty with a problem employee. His perception, based on months of their working together, is that the employee simply isn't up to the job. The manager participates in a feedback-intensive program and learns, among other things, that he is conflict-averse. He realizes that he has never had a clear, direct conversation with the errant employee about the unacceptable work. As one of his development goals, he decides to develop his skills at conflict and confrontation. He plans to do it by working with a development coach who is external to the organization, and by seeking 360-degree feedback later. Once again, the development experiences link to enhance the learning that comes from the single event of a hardship.

Hardships: A Final Word

The goal in leadership development, it is important to remember, is to develop well-rounded leaders, ones with the skills and personal attributes needed to adapt, act with flexibility, and combine what appear to be opposites: toughness and compassion, self-confidence and humility, strong individuals and good team players. The goal is not to develop ideal leaders, ones of mythic proportions, but rather women and men who have the ability to better handle things thrown their way in these times of "permanent whitewater."

Well-rounded leaders are developed by experiencing and learning from the diverse challenging experiences presented in earlier chapters of this book and from the adversity discussed in this one. Although they are unlike the development experiences described in other chapters, hardships are an important source of lessons that help develop better leaders.

PART TWO

LEADERSHIP DEVELOPMENT: PROCESS

CHAPTER SEVEN

A SYSTEMS APPROACH
TO LEADERSHIP DEVELOPMENT

Russ S. Moxley
Patricia O'Connor Wilson

Through our work with a wide array of organizations, we have seen significant changes in recent years in how companies view leadership development. They are changing the way they think about the very complex process by which people develop leadership effectiveness, the role the organization has to play in that process, and how other systems can be designed to support it. In a word, we see that organizations are beginning to practice leadership development more systemically.

Shifts in Perspective

Underlying this change in approach are several significant shifts in perspective.

Development as a Process

The first shift is temporal in nature, from practicing development as an event to supporting it as a process over time:

FROM

I have this manager who desperately needs development. She has been given feedback that her performance is not up to par, and the turnover in her department is increasing to levels we can no longer tolerate. She needs to get the message—if you know what I mean—pronto! Which program would you suggest to help remedy this situation?

TO

I'm interested in engaging one of our high-potential managers in a process of development over time—*not* a single development experience like a training course. In about five years' time, there is a strong possibility that she will be the leading candidate to head up our largest division. We feel the need to craft a long-term strategy for preparing her to make the leadership contributions we know she will someday be capable of making. Where do we begin?

Today's business environment creates in many organizations a sense of urgency to produce short-term results, and thus short-term solutions. In that sort of climate, those advocating a long-term systems approach to development face a real challenge from colleagues with a bottom-line orientation. But the fact remains that development, by its very nature, occurs as a process over time. There is no such thing as a quick fix.

The Experiences That Develop

The second shift in perspective centers on the basic question of what kinds of experience provide development. What is the "stuff" of which development is made?

FROM

I've been asked by my manager to call you. As part of my performance plan, I'm required to engage in a developmental activity each year. What course would you suggest?

TO

I'd like to talk with you about experiences that can round out my development plans for the year. What's lacking for me is the skill of thinking and acting strategically. I'm already engaged in a mentor relationship and was recently given a highly sought-after assignment that will require me to be more strategic. But what other experiences might I integrate with these two?

For some time, many organizations have believed that training was the "stuff" of development, and that the organization's role was simply to provide training. Increasingly, they are viewing training as but one component of the development process. They are expanding their portfolios to include targeted stretch assignments, developmental relationships, and 360-degree feedback—in short, the full range of development experiences we describe in this handbook.

Integrated Development

A third perspective shift is also emerging, one that seeks to integrate development into the daily work of the organization:

FROM

I'm the human resource executive responsible for creating a learning experience for a group of our managers. I'm experiencing considerable resistance from their unit leaders to release them from work for more than a day. How can I better convince them that development is critical?

TO

I'm the human resource executive responsible for creating richer learning experiences for a group of our managers. I've been working in partnership with one of our line managers to explore ways to build more development into the day-to-day experiences of his work group. Do you have resources that can help us design assignments for these people that are developmentally powerful?

In the past, development was viewed as something separate from the day-to-day work of the organization, something that requires sending people to off-site learning situations. Increasingly, however, organizations are finding rich sources of development under their own roof. They are creating developmental experiences within employees' regular, ongoing work, using such strategies as adding challenges to people's present jobs so that they are more developmental; giving people special, short-term assignments as new developmental opportunities; making selection decisions for new positions with at least one eye on whom it might serve as an important development experience. Today, development does not mean taking people *away from* their work. It means helping them *learn from* their work.

Complexity of Development

A fourth perspective shift centers on the complexity of development:

FROM

I have a manager who needs to better understand how to communicate with his team.

TO

The leader of this cross-functional team has to learn how to influence other areas without position power, garner support from colleagues in siloed divisions, and deliver a higher level of innovation, despite a lot of ambiguity that is currently present in the organization.

In an environment where businesses face continual change, rapid innovation, and increasing globalization, complexity has been accepted as the norm. People charged with managing this complexity have complex development needs of their own. The learning challenges are frequent, steep, and multidimensional. Although clearly defined training objectives were the focus in the past, today's environment requires meeting developmental goals that are continually evolving, an unstable mix of clearly defined benchmarks, ambitious stretch goals, and broad competencies for an ambiguous future.

Responsibility for Development

Finally, the perspective of who is responsible for development is shifting:

FROM

Our employees are responsible for their own development. No one understands their needs as well as they do, and of course no one can develop for them.

TO

Our employees have a lot more responsibility for their development, maybe more now than ever before. But we also recognize that development is a shared responsibility, that other people in the organization have critical roles to play.

With the decay of the old paternalistic organization and the advent of the new employment contract, the issue of employee responsibility looms large. Gone are the days when employees abdicated active responsibility for their careers in return for the implicit agreement that the company would take care of them. Today, employees are being asked to take on greater responsibility for their own development. But in some organizations, the pendulum has swung too far, to the point that employees are held responsible for their development but must do so in a virtual vacuum.

Organizations with a systems perspective know that all levels—individual employees, their managers, senior executives, and the organization at large—must be closely involved with all aspects of development, from planning to implementation, ongoing support, and continuous evaluation of the chosen processes.

Forging Systemic Links

The preceding chapters of this book provide detailed information about the pieces of the development puzzle. In this chapter, we begin to put the puzzle together.

All the specific experiences described earlier (assignments, developmental relationships, and the like) develop leadership capacities. Each experience, in and of itself, can be effective when well designed. However, any one particular experience has greater impact if it is linked to other experiences, and if all these experiences are embedded in a supportive, carefully designed system.

We define *leadership development system* as that confluence of interdependent organizational and management processes that work together to provide maximum impact for leadership development experiences. The purpose of this chapter is to describe some of the important links that need to be made:

- Between development experiences and the key elements that make them powerful (assessment, challenge, and support)
- Among development experiences
- Between the leadership development process and other management processes within a particular organization

To illustrate these links, we share stories from several organizations that are putting into practice systemic approaches to development.

The First Link: Experiences and Elements

As a reminder, an *experience* is a particular event (360-degree feedback, a task force assignment) from which people can learn important leadership lessons. An *element* is the specific attribute that makes the experience effective. We have identified three elements that any well-designed development experience needs: assessment, challenge, and support.

The developmental impact of any single experience is enhanced if all three elements are built in. Take a training program you are designing or are considering participating in, as an example. You want to make sure it has impact. You can tell that it is designed for impact if it includes opportunities for an assessment of strengths or skills, if it provides the kind of challenge that stretches participants, and if participants get support for learning and making progress toward developmental goals before, during, and after the training.

The Second Link: One Development Experience to Another

No single development experience, no matter how well designed, leads to maximum development. Leadership lessons are learned best when one development experience is reinforced by other experiences. Change is hard, and it is sometimes painful. People need to work on change through several development experiences somewhat simultaneously.

Furthermore, learning is not random. Certain specific leadership lessons are easier to learn from some experiences than from others. If a person is to have opportunities to learn all the lessons needed to become a well-rounded leader, over time he or she must be exposed to multiple development experiences that are linked together and reinforce one another.

Taking all this into account, we propose an equation for the leadership development process:

Feedback-intensive program + Skill-based training + 360-degree feedback + Developmental assignments + Developmental relationships + Hardships = Leadership development

To be sure, a person does not need all six experiences to meet a particular development need. Someone who needs to think and act more strategically might work on the change through an *assignment* that requires the use of these skills, with the help of a *coach*, and with some formal *360-degree feedback* along the way. This person is on the road to developing a new skill through just three experiences.

Also note that the experiences do not have to be undertaken in the exact linear sequence that the equation seems to suggest. The person learning strategic thinking uses three experiences that are integrated but not done "in order." Another example is an executive who gets passed over for a promotion (a *hardship*). She realizes that it is time to take stock of her strengths and weaknesses and decides to participate in a *feedback-intensive program*. After the program, she solicits support from a *developmental coach* who can help her learn the skills she needs. The lessons of each experience are reinforced by the others.

Not all organizations see the importance of linking development experiences. In too many cases, executive education and leadership development are still centered around single events. Not long ago, we received a call from a manager in a large corporation. He was troubled about one of the company's young engineering managers. The engineer was described in superlatives: bright, great analytical skills, quick, resourceful, persistent, willing to do whatever it takes to finish an assignment. In the past year this gifted engineer was moved into his first supervisory position, and it was here that the problems began. He had trouble delegating important work, and when he did he tended to micromanage. He was impatient when others did not analyze a problem as quickly as he did, and responses often demeaned the direct reports and made them feel stupid. He worked the long hours required to finish assignments, and he expected others to do the same. The people in the department were becoming demoralized and deenergized.

"So," our caller asked, "what kind of training do you think would be good for him?"

The faulty assumption underneath the question is that training is *the* answer to the young manager's development needs. It is not an unusual assumption. Many managers and executives still operate on the mental model that training equals leadership development: send a person who needs to improve his leadership skills to a workshop and hope that the one experience fixes him.

There are at least three flaws with this assumption. The first is that not all development experiences have built into them the elements of assessment, challenge, and support, and thus they are not designed to ensure maximum development. The second is that one experience—in this case, training—is almost never sufficient by itself. Finally, it assumes that development needs can be fixed, and fixed within a predetermined length of time. In truth, underdeveloped leadership skills are a bit like underused muscles. To develop them, one must actively and continuously work on them, over time, through a variety of development experiences until the weakness becomes a strength (or at the very least, no longer an impairment).

Some people report significant change from a single event or experience, especially when the event provokes startling self-insights. More often, though, actual behavioral change happens slowly and over the course of a career; it happens when one experience is linked to another as part of a larger, continuous development process.

The Third Link: Leadership Development and Organizational Context

The third and final important link is to make sure development experiences are embedded in a supportive organizational context. There are several key aspects to this issue.

Business Context. The development process must be *embedded in a business context.* Development processes are not generic; they must support the strategic direction of a company and, in turn, be supported by that strategy. Indeed, a developmental component is inherent to an organization's strategic priorities. To meet the challenges of the future, to achieve the growth and continuous improvement that most strategic initiatives call for, employees must stretch beyond current capabilities.

Embedding leadership development processes in the business context means two things: understanding the strategic direction of the company, and identifying those behaviors and perspectives that individual leaders must develop if they are to effectively support that direction. A leadership development process, and all the components of it, must help individuals learn those behaviors and develop those perspectives.

A major oil and gas company makes a strategic decision to move aggressively from being a domestic producer of hydrocarbons to an international force in its field. Knowing that this is the strategic direction gives all those responsible for leadership development a good sense of the skills and perspectives that must be learned: leading a cross-cultural workforce, leading by remote control, maintaining a perspective that allows people to adapt and change, and being able to live with ambiguity and honor differences, to name but a few.

As another example, a large chemical company decides that its future requires it to become more technology-driven. As part of this shift in strategy, the company wants to make sure that its R&D scientists—people "on the bench"—develop the skills and perspectives they need to be effective general managers. To help that happen, the company identifies the behaviors that the scientists need to develop to be effective GMs in a new and changing environment. They have to make the transition from managing projects to managing people and in the process learn a host of skills related to delegation, influence, confrontation and conflict management, and team development. They need to learn to think and act strategically, and to make day-to-day decisions with the longer-term goal in mind. They must learn how to see organizations as systems. With strategic direction set and behaviors identified, the company is able to put together a leadership development process that supports the strategy and is in turn supported by the strategy.

Still another example comes from the utility industry, where the changing business landscape is requiring companies to rethink their business strategies and the behaviors needed to support them. They understand that moving from a regulated to a deregulated environment requires their managers and leaders to hone their present skills or test untested ones—skills in being more entrepreneurial, more decisive, more action-oriented. Any leadership development system put together within a utility company must take these profound changes into account. Understood in this way, leadership development has two goals:

developing the leadership skills and perspectives of individuals in the organization, and advancing accomplishment of the organization's strategies and business goals. The focus of leadership development for a particular individual may be based on that person's specific needs, but the overall development process is linked to the organization's strategies and goals. This linkage has two significant results, which are themselves linked together: the impact of development is maximized, and corporate support for the development process is greatly enhanced.

Target Population. An organization must decide for whom leadership development is to be targeted. Is leadership development for all employees? For managers and executives? For those women and men who have been identified, either formally or informally, as high-potentials?

To be sure, most people at some time in their careers engage in the majority of the developmental experiences we have identified. They have a challenging job, get here-and-now feedback from a trusted peer before it is asked for, experience an unplanned hardship from which they grow and change, or participate in a training program where they learn new skills. Some people learn easily and naturally from these events, especially those who actively learn from any experience. But active learners appear to be a relatively small percentage of the adult population (Bunker and Webb, 1992). For most people, leadership development needs to be planned and the learning process needs to be supported.

The inherent challenge is that, in many companies, there are too many employees for all of them to be targeted for this kind of holistic and purposeful leadership development. Thus, most companies still must decide whom to target for the development experiences described in this handbook.

A second reason companies must make these decisions is the practical consideration of availability. Consider assignments, for example. Assignments are a powerful source of leadership lessons (see Chapter Four). People learn how to be leaders on the job. But to be developmental, assignments have to be challenging, they have to push people out of their comfort zone, and they have to require them to develop new skills or at least try out untested ones. This means there is at least some risk that an individual will not successfully navigate the new job. A consequence of this for organizations is that not all jobs can be used as developmental assignments; some are too important, with the risks from failure too great. For individuals, the consequence is that there are not enough stretch assignments for everyone. Similarly, practical considerations require that organizations selectively deploy other developmental strategies: identifying participants in a feedback-intensive program, the target audience for 360-degree feedback, candidates for developmental relationships, and so on.

So for the important question of whom to target, there is no single answer. We must respond with a somewhat unsatisfactory "It depends." It depends on the strategic direction of the company, the company's growth and its anticipated needs for future leadership, the developmental culture of the company, and the talent available in the labor market. In answering these questions, some organizations focus developmental processes on a select group of high-potential individuals; others focus on a broad range of employees.

Shared Responsibility for Development. There must be shared responsibility for leadership development. Development, and the environment within which it is occurring, is too complex to be sufficiently managed by the individual alone. Responsibility must be shared by the individual employee, the manager, the person's team, those in human resources who help structure developmental experiences, and the senior executives of the organization, whose support for development is crucial.

Supportive Business Systems. Other organizational systems must support the leadership development process. To be fully effective, a development system must be integrated with the organization's other processes: management planning, performance management, job selection, reward and recognition systems, and even mistake systems (how an organization handles mistakes and failures; see Chapter Six). The confluence of these processes determines the relative effectiveness of any one developmental activity.

If these processes are not interwoven into an integrated system, the effort expended is not fruitful. For example, one organization's leadership development program focused on helping people develop the skills needed to effectively operate in a flatter, more team-based environment. Yet the performance-appraisal and compensation system put more emphasis on individual performance. The reward system undermined the goal of developing a team-based work environment. Other organizations understand in theory that assignments can be used developmentally, but they make selection decisions based on who already has the skills needed to hit the ground running. There is risk involved, of course, but unless some selection decisions are made for developmental reasons, the organization misses an important opportunity. (It should be noted that there is also risk involved in the "safe" course. Without the use of assignments as developmental experiences, organizations limit their ability to develop their bench strength.)

Human resource accounting systems are also used to support the process of leadership development. Organizations can define job assignments not only by title and job responsibilities, but also by the challenges embedded in them. Ready access to such information helps in development planning discussions between employees and their managers. Knowing what challenges people have experienced in past job experiences offers the employees, their managers, and HR professionals insight into which leadership lessons might have been learned and which leadership skills and perspectives developed.

Even budgeting processes either support or undercut leadership development. In general, budgets reflect organizational priorities; as such, they help build a development culture or else communicate that development is not an important emphasis.

Imagine an organization where line managers see themselves as responsible for leadership development and understand that one of their key roles is to be developmental coaches, where at least some selection decisions are made for developmental reasons, where individuals are not punished for making mistakes in trying out new skills and behaviors, and where the skills and perspectives assessed on the annual performance-appraisal process are in alignment with the skills and perspectives people need to be effective at their jobs. In this organization, leadership development is not only a priority but understood—and practiced—systemically.

Stories from the Field

There is much to be learned from what other organizations are doing. A few organizations have already developed an overall systems approach to development; they have linked together several of the development experiences described in this book, integrated those experiences with other management processes, and used those experiences to develop individual leadership ability *and* accomplish business results. Other organizations are moving toward a systems approach by linking two or three development experiences, but they haven't created a fully supportive development system by embedding the experiences in a business context.

We offer stories here to illustrate each situation (pseudonyms are used).

"Retail Stores of America" (RSA)

RSA, best known by its chain of stores in shopping malls across the country, has implemented an entire system for developing their leaders.

A leadership development process is more nonlinear than linear. But to understand more easily what RSA has done, let us list the component parts of the system they implemented in an oversimplified, step-by-step way:

1. The executive vice president, who is primarily responsible for leadership development and who designed the company's system, first made sure that leadership development at RSA was linked to the strategic needs of the business. In her words, the process had to be "need driven," and the outcome to the organization had to be clear and important. At

RSA, leadership development was seen not as extracurricular but rather as a key to accomplishing business objectives.

2. Based on internal and external research, RSA knew what behaviors were needed to accomplish the company's strategy; it created its own leadership success model, with factors such as problem solvers, organizers and planners, achievers, team builders, communicators, and developers. These success factors were then weighted for each manager's job based on the importance of the behavior to success on the job.

These first two steps created the all-important organizational context for RSA's leadership development process. Specific experiences in the developmental process—assignments, developmental relationships, 360-degree feedback, and so on—could now be directed toward developing the skills, behaviors, and perspectives important to the company's business success.

3. A 360-degree instrument was developed to give feedback on the skills and behaviors already identified as important at RSA. With this feedback, individual executives learned how their profile compared to the profile for success at RSA and identified new behaviors they needed to develop.

RSA reinforced its system of leadership development by linking it to performance, using the same success profiles. One-half of the managers' performance appraisal was based on the *what* of their job: how well they met their goals. The other half was based on the success factors, or *how* they met those goals.

4. After the 360-degree feedback process was complete, a review board, composed of members of the executive committee, met for a day and a half to complete the management assessment process and to focus development for the next year. Their purpose was to ensure that the right message and challenges were given to help leaders grow, and that a major job challenge was matched to an individual's development need. The end result was that a measurable assignment was created for many managers, particularly those identified as high-potential.

What RSA called a "measurable assignment" is the same as what we describe as a developmental assignment (see Chapter Four). Three important aspects to what RSA did need to be underlined: the company understood the potency of jobs as developmental experiences, it was willing to make selection decisions about some jobs based on the development needs of its high-potential employees, and it individualized development by matching an individual's need to a measurable assignment.

5. Another important strategy in any leadership development process is a developmental relationship. At RSA, members of the executive committee, the individual's boss, and human resource professionals all saw themselves as providing developmental relationships. They played several of the roles described in Chapter Five: feedback giver, counselor, and coach.

Thus, three development experiences were carefully linked at RSA: 360-degree feedback led to a measurable assignment, which in turn was supported by a developmental relationship. Each of these experiences reinforced the others, and all three were reinforced by other organizational systems and processes.

RSA's executive vice president later reflected on the lessons she had learned from implementing a leadership development system at her company (see "Lessons from 'RSA' Leadership Development System").

Lessons from "RSA" Leadership Development System.

1. Leadership and organization development must be tied to the strategic needs of the business . . . the payoff for the business must be clear.
2. A crystal-clear strategy is critical. Specifically, what is the desired result of the development system?
3. The senior executives must "own" the process. They must demonstrate, through attitude and behavior, that development is important.
4. Forget the textbooks. Understand the concepts, but tailor the process to meet the needs of the organization.
5. There must be a *total system* that becomes part of the fabric of how the business operates.
6. Leadership development is a *process*; there must be a systematic method for development to occur on the job.
7. Accountability, accountability, accountability. There must be a commitment by the supervisor and employee to action and follow-up.

"Global Shipping Inc."

Global Shipping, a major international shipping company, began implementing its own development system in 1990.

A snapshot of GSI taken in 1989 would have shown a company operating on traditional business practices severely in need of modernization. Cooperation between different offices was lacking. Information technology was primitive. Customers were demanding world-class service, yet GSI had no formal quality system. Managers were well versed in the technology of shipping, but they were trapped in a rigid managerial hierarchy and seldom made any overtures toward leadership.

Into this situation stepped a new CEO. He was brought in from the outside, with an emphatic mandate for change. His background included extensive experience with organization development, and he used that experience to collaborate with his senior management team to build a new model for leadership development. This model is shown in Figure 7.1.

FIGURE 7.1. "GLOBAL SHIPPING" MODEL FOR LEADERSHIP DEVELOPMENT.

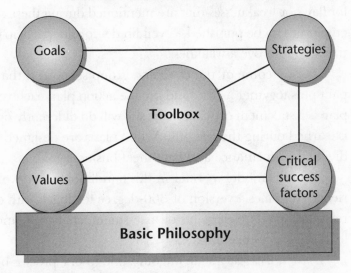

Source: Reprinted with permission from Ingar Skaug.

The four cornerstones of the model are GSI's goals, the strategies for accomplishing them, the business factors critical for success at GSI, and the values that are core to running the business. Each cornerstone provides part of the framework for GSI's leadership development processes, but two of the core values, honesty and openness, provide the bedrock for the processes. The processes simply do not work unless these values are acted upon.

In the middle of the diagram is the "Toolbox." At GSI, leadership development is designed to foster business results. The tools are intended to support the company's business goals, and the tools themselves are designed to be mutually supportive. Three of the tools relate specifically to individual leadership development: coaching groups, employee dialogues, and the leadership development program.

This is learning in a public forum. *Coaching groups* are workgroups meeting in intense sessions so that members can provide each other with direct feedback related to working effectively. Every workgroup, and thus every employee in the company, does this three times a year.

In these sessions, all the people on a workteam are expected to give feedback to everyone else, including their boss. The values of honesty and openness are particularly important here. No one can be punished for flaws or weaknesses that are mentioned during these sessions, but an employee can be punished—even fired—for not participating or for not trying to improve a weakness.

One outcome of the coaching group sessions is that each participant puts together a clear and precise action plan each year. The action plan is a statement of what he or she will do differently because of what is learned during the sessions. Action plans are designed to improve individual performance and help meet business goals.

From the model we offer in this handbook, this development experience combines a version of 360-degree feedback with developmental relationships. The elements of assessment, challenge, and support help lend the experience impact.

Employee dialogues are an ongoing, one-to-one process between all employees and their supervisors. The two people discuss performance in the broader context of functional job descriptions, employee development, and career progression. Honesty and openness are demanded during the conversations, and the expected product is an individual improvement plan. In these conversations the supervisor engages in several types of developmental relationship: feedback provider and interpreter, sounding board, assignment broker, and reinforcer.

At GSI, the coaching groups provide feedback that informs the action plans, and the action plans are then refined during these employee dialogues. The two experiences support and reinforce each other.

All managers from middle level on up attend an off-site *leadership development program*. The program is a six-day residential, public-enrollment program, an example of the strategy described in Chapter Two as a feedback-intensive program. During this intense experience, individuals get rich feedback from a variety of sources on their leadership strengths and weaknesses, and they develop a deeper awareness of the impact of their leadership style on others.

As with the other two development experiences mentioned above, a detailed action plan is generated at the end of the leadership development program, a plan designed to increase individual effectiveness and to meet business goals.

"Delta Products"

Delta Products knew well the leadership development pressures they were facing. Their demographics suggested that they would have significant leadership turnover in the next five to ten years. They were underrepresented by women and minorities in senior leadership positions. Supervisors and managers did not possess sufficient development coaching skills to help the underrepresented employees. Employees did not have a good framework for managing their careers.

With the help of external consultants, Delta Products developed an architecture for development that included learning assignments, learning groups, and learning forums; it also established a process for selecting employees for development.

Delta decided to target its formal leadership development on one particular group: high-performing learners. The first step, then, was to identify these learners. They were pulled from the pool of high-potential employees that had already been identified. All were seen as potential leaders; they were perceived as active learners; and they were diverse in education, race and gender, function, and career interests.

Delta Products was also clear about the attitudes and abilities expected from these learners during the development process. They were to be willing to experiment, look for alternative ways of doing things, become more self-observing, move from knowing to learning, suspend judgment, and think and act with a global perspective. In short, Delta expected the participants in this process to demonstrate that they had the ability to learn from experience.

Delta used several types of assignment to help learners develop the skills and abilities they needed: in-place assignments that had significant challenge and thus important lessons to teach, plus rotational and cross-cultural assignments that offered different lessons.

To reinforce the leadership lessons that people were learning from their assignments, Delta provided the "learners" with two different types of developmental relationships: learning leaders and learning managers. Learning leaders were outside the learner's chain of command; two or three levels higher than the learner; and also diverse in background, experience, race, and gender. The learning leader played three of the roles described in the discussion of developmental relationships (Chapter Five), by meeting with the learner to listen to frustrations (the counselor role), discussing what was being learned on the job and from other development experiences (dialogue partner), and, when asked for advice, responding with a story from their own experience (cohort). Each learning leader received four hours of training.

The learning manager was the supervisor of the learner; he or she offered day-to-day support and encouragement as the learners tried out new skills and behaviors. The learning manager played two of the important roles in developmental relationships: feedback-giver and cheerleader.

In addition to the one-to-one developmental relationships, the learners also got support from learning groups and learning forums. The learning group served as the equivalent of an organizational home-room. Here learners met to debrief their experiences, chat face-to-face, and practice new behaviors. The emphasis was on learning from and with peers in a safe environment. While they were in the learning group, the learners agreed to promote openness and trust, encourage new perspectives, realize that all points of view are flawed, listen between the lines, and seek understanding rather than agreement.

Learning forums, by contrast, were occasional gatherings in which all the learning groups came together for the specific purpose of storytelling. The stories dealt with acquisition, globalization, work-and-life balance, technical choices, and current events. The belief underlying the use of these learning forums was that the culture of Delta Products, and other important lessons of leadership, were communicated through the stories told by its employees.

Who was responsible for the development system at Delta Products? The learner was responsible for a high degree of self-management, development of a learning plan, and execution of the plan. Top management was responsible for providing support and focus, and for providing learning leadership. Line managers were responsible for on-the-job coaching, sponsorship, feedback, and being learning-minded managers. Human resources was responsible for implementing the development strategy and mobilizing resources.

In sum, Delta Products developed a reasonably sophisticated leadership development process for a subset of its high-potential employees. Each experience of the process had the elements of assessment, challenge, and support. One development experience was linked to another, and the whole process was developed to meet the business needs of Delta and the individual needs of participants.

Short Stories

Understandably, very few companies can implement an entire leadership development system at one time. In fact, two of the three actual companies we have just described implemented their system one step at a time. What happens most often is that companies begin by linking two or three developmental experiences and embedding them in their own particular business context.

In the short stories that follow, we offer examples of what several companies are doing, to demonstrate that a system for leadership development can be built in small steps. Note that there are many variations on the theme. The important aspect of each story is that the company is using more than one development experience and is beginning the move toward a systems perspective.

• An insurance company sends an employee to a leadership development program and then makes sure that she gets appropriate coaching when she returns to her job (linking the strategies of assessment for development programs and developmental relationships). This same company begins to use the ability to learn as one important criterion in identifying high-potential women and men.

• A bank provides 360-degree feedback to all of its senior managers and then trains another group of senior managers to be development coaches (linking 360-degree feedback and developmental relationships). This formal mentoring relationship is structured to last several years.

• A large consumer products company decides to make more effective use of assignments as part of their leadership development process. In the past this company hired the best and brightest MBAs and threw them in over their heads. The company learned appropriate ways to intervene during these challenging work experiences to enhance the learning of the MBAs. Jobs are still used as a primary developmental experience, but now learning has been enhanced by the use of developmental relationships.

• A pharmaceutical company develops an all-day preprogram workshop to prepare employees and their managers for an upcoming feedback-intensive program. In the morning, participants and their managers discuss the expectations of the company and the manager, including explanation of why this particular developmental opportunity was chosen at this time, and areas of development that the manager suggests the participant focus on. The participant and manager also schedule a review meeting one week after the program, to review learnings and developmental goals, design experiences (such as further training, assignments, and developmental relationships) for reaching those goals, and define explicitly the support the manager is willing to provide toward those ends. In the afternoon, managers learn more about their role in supporting development of their direct reports. They review some of the typical reactions after the program and how best to manage each, and they learn how to conduct the very important pre-program and postprogram dialogues with the participant.

The Challenge of Implementing Development Systems

As with other complex business processes, creating a full-fledged development system is a considerable undertaking. This helps explain, in part, the gap within some organizations between rhetoric and practice of integrated leadership development. To fully appreciate the challenge inherent to implementation, consider the following.

First, commitment to development systems implies practice of certain values and beliefs that compete with seemingly opposing organizational priorities. This chapter rests on certain beliefs related to development, the practice of which may or may not be a priority within a particular organization. For example, even those managers who believe that people can learn, develop, and change over time (and should be given the opportunity to do so) allow day-to-day business pressures to take precedence over development. Maximum performance becomes more important than maximum development.

Another common belief is that ongoing development of individuals, teams, and the organization itself is a solid business investment. In practice, though, the priority of creating a better ROI for shareholders or attaining 100 percent customer satisfaction most often determines allocation of resources. The challenge for organizations is to understand that focusing on development and focusing on the bottom line are both part of the same ongoing business process.

Second, development systems redefine the nature of managerial work—significantly. Building a development system represents real work, work that requires time, resources, and changes in perspective and skills, particularly for managers. The more an organization comes to practice development systemically, the more pronounced is the centrality of the manager's role as coach, gatekeeper to developmental opportunities, and interpreter of the developmental implications of organizational decisions. This represents a very different expectation of managers than is currently found in organizations and is a key challenge to implementing development systems.

For example, in a fully supportive development system, the role of coach is a critical competency for success as a manager. It requires skills that have not been fully developed to date through education or experience. Practicing development systemically also requires that managers weigh the developmental aspects, as well as the financial aspects, of business decisions.

Third, once created, development systems must work against the inertia characteristic of most complex organizational systems. A development system, perhaps more than any other business system, is organic. As individuals develop, so too must the framework that defines, supports, and integrates this development. But any move to change that framework often meets great resistance. Partly this resistance is logistical; the changes can have a significant impact on other systems, which creates ripples of inconvenience. Another reason, more subtle and more human, is that the status quo represents a measure of stability that people have come to depend on to help counterbalance rapid change in the environment.

If development systems need to be responsive in order to be effective, how can one be designed to overcome the inertia? It is done perhaps by first recognizing the fluid nature of development and experimenting with structures designed up front to be constantly modified and improved. Clearly, this is a challenge with which we continue to struggle.

Fourth, the design of development systems should emulate the customized nature of development: nonlinear and specific to each developmental challenge. Closely related to the challenge of inertia is the tension that arises from the multidimensional aspects of individual development. Clearly, development experiences do not come one-size-fits-all, and the system that supports them cannot be, either.

We are witnessing a great need for development to be available both on-demand and in customizable forms. This reflects the shift toward steeper developmental challenges in most of today's leadership roles. Like other organizational processes, customization of development systems yields greater impact on those it serves. Unlike other organizational processes, development systems must support the confluence of individual, team, and organizational learning and development, areas those of us working in the field are still striving to understand.

A Brief Look Ahead

This chapter has focused on the individual employee moving through a system of developmental experiences, each complete with the three elements of assessment, challenge, and support, with one experience linked to another, and with all experiences embedded within a supportive organizational context. It has presented the stories of some organizations that are experiencing success in integrating these processes into the overall development system. For countless others, the struggle continues.

Managing and supporting a system of development processes for individuals takes on even greater complexity when we consider linking them to other forms of development within organizations. Though not the focus of this handbook, we believe integration of individual, team, and organization development is one of the primary challenges facing us in the future.

Linking all forms of development requires new ways of thinking and acting, including new ways of thinking about leadership and new ways of practicing development systemically. We at the Center for Creative Leadership are slowly moving into these uncharted waters (uncharted at least for us). In Part Three of this handbook, we share some of our ideas on new ways of thinking about leadership, along with ideas on other current and emerging issues.

CHAPTER EIGHT

ENHANCING THE ABILITY TO LEARN FROM EXPERIENCE

Ellen Van Velsor
Victoria A. Guthrie

As quickly as the world is changing, the capacities needed by its leaders also change. To maintain their effectiveness, people in positions of leadership must be able to learn, actively and continuously.

This is no simple task. Learning is neither easy nor automatic. In Part Two of this handbook, we describe at length a number of specific experiences that can develop leadership. But simply going through the experience does not guarantee that one learns from it.

In fact, according to our research (Bunker and Webb, 1992), most managers are *not* active and continuous learners. Most people learn easily within their comfort zone but find it much more difficult to learn when operating under new challenges. Most people prefer to stay with the behaviors that have made them successful in the past, even if the conditions of the past no longer apply. A type of inertia develops. We have come to call the experience of overcoming this inertia "going against the grain." To go against their grain, leaders must let go of proven strengths and comfortable ways of learning long enough to acquire new ones. They must be strong and secure enough to make themselves vulnerable to the stresses and setbacks in the learning process.

Some people are naturally active learners. By virtue of their personalities or early life experiences, they have the personal resources and skills to learn easily. But they are the exceptions. Most people require considerable support for their learning.

We believe that people can learn to become better learners. This chapter focuses on helping managers and the human resource professionals who work with them improve their ability to learn from potentially developmental experiences. It begins with a discussion of what it means to learn from experience, as well as the factors that appear to be operating for people who learn easily. We then turn to what can be done to enhance the ability to learn from experience (for oneself or in working with others) and present a set of guidelines for practitioners wanting to develop managers as active and continuous learners.

The Ability to Learn from Experience

What is the ability to learn from experience, and why does it feel so hard? In our view, the ability to learn from experience involves being able to

- Recognize when new behaviors, skills, or attitudes are called for, which involves being able to see when current approaches are not working
- Engage in a variety of development experiences to learn new skills or test skills that are previously untested, and to try new approaches or reframe points of view (as opposed to avoiding the situation or denying the need)
- Develop and use a variety of learning tactics to acquire the new skills, approaches, or attitudes (four specific learning tactics are described in detail in a later section of this chapter)

Each of these activities or capacities plays an important role in the ability to learn from experience. We believe these skills can be developed and that the ability to learn from experience can thereby be enhanced. Yet for many people, these skills do not come easily or naturally.

Learning from experience can be difficult because it is a different way of thinking about learning. Most people think of learning in the mode of classroom activities, like reading and listening to lectures. They do not consider current experience as being the best teacher. It does not occur to them to spend time reflecting on their experiences and extracting from them the lessons contained within. They do not consider how they could do better at learning from experience.

Learning from experience is also difficult because of the sense of inertia referred to earlier. Inertia holds people back. Doing things how they've always done them, using skills they already have, and continuing to see the world as they've always seen it is a comfortable way of being. People like to use their strengths and get positive feedback on their achievements. This inertia gets worse the older people get—and the higher they go in organizations. If they have been successful, it is harder than ever to let go of what has worked for them. It is usually not until they face demands seriously out of line with their skills and perspectives that they begin to admit that the old ways may not be working.

Learning from experience can feel risky, too. Recognizing the need for new learning is stressful because it requires that people admit to themselves (and possibly to others) that what they are now doing is not working or that their current skills are inadequate. For most people, such an admission provokes some level of anxiety. It often seems easier to respond by shutting down, giving up, or denying the need for new ideas or behaviors.

To make matters worse, there is an active tension in most organizations between producing bottom-line results and developing people. Rather than give employees a developmental assignment where failure is a possibility alongside learning, most organizations prefer to put proven performers in key roles, doing what they already know how to do well. This only reinforces the tendency to stay with what is known and comfortable because it is safer.

Finally, learning from experience is difficult because it requires a level of support that many people do not have in their organizations. Support for the risk of learning (and failure) is one kind of support, but support also includes processes and relationships that help people receive and hear the information they need to hear, understand the meaning of that information, create development plans, persist in their efforts to learn and grow new skills, and have the courage to change outmoded behaviors and attitudes.

Individual Differences in the Ability to Learn

The model of leadership development described in the Introduction argues that people are more likely to learn from an experience if three elements are present: assessment, challenge, and support. However, the model incorporates a fourth element in the leadership development process: the ability to learn. Assessment, challenge, and support are elements of the development event itself; the ability to learn is a characteristic of the person involved in the event. Some people do not learn from a potentially developmental experience even if each of the first three elements is in place in just the right proportion. Others gain tremendous benefit from even the most minimal experience. The explanation lies in their varying abilities to learn. What accounts for these differences, and is there any way to bring about change?

Over the years, an extensive body of research has accumulated on personality, much of which relates to learning. Although it is not the purpose of this chapter to provide comprehensive coverage of that literature, we touch briefly on several factors that seem relevant to working with people who want to improve their ability to learn. It is also worth mentioning that, although many might consider some of these characteristics as hardwired aspects of personality, we believe that most of them can indeed be developed or enhanced through development experiences that are rich and balanced in assessment, challenge, and support. We return to a discussion of how this can happen later in the chapter.

The Role of Intelligence

We address intelligence first not because it is the most important quality but because it is the one that, for most people, comes to mind first in connection with learning. We believe that intelligence, as traditionally defined, plays a relatively small role in a person's ability to learn from experience in adulthood.

Although many people think of only one kind of potential when they hear the word *intelligence*, experts in the fields of psychology and education are now presenting the case for multiple forms of intelligence, each in itself complex, and each important in certain areas of life.

Howard Gardner (1993) defines seven intelligences: linguistic, musical, logical-mathematical, spatial, bodily-kinesthetic, interpersonal, and intrapersonal. What most North Americans mean by *intelligence* is the combination of linguistic, logical-mathematical, and spatial intelligences as defined by Gardner. Because of its long history in U.S. school systems, this combination is probably the first thing most people think of as learning. Yet it is doubtful that superior power in these three areas is a prerequisite for the kind of learning from experience that is important for long-term leadership effectiveness (Argyris, 1991). Very "smart" managers often derail because they are unable to recognize the need for personal change or new behaviors.

On the other hand, the two types of "personal" intelligence seem likely to affect and be affected by leadership development experiences. Gardner describes interpersonal intelligence as the ability to understand other people, and intrapersonal intelligence as the ability to form an accurate model of oneself and to be able to use that model to operate effectively in everyday life.

Obviously, interpersonal intelligence is critical to effective leadership. It is also an important capacity in leadership development because learning from developmental experience often means learning from other people, sometimes directly (as in a developmental relationship) and sometimes indirectly (through interacting with others in a training program or in an assignment). Intrapersonal intelligence is closely aligned with the concept of self-awareness. Many formal leadership development experiences have as a key goal enhancement of self-awareness; that is, they work toward enabling people to form and then use a more accurate or comprehensive view of self.

Self-Esteem and Self-Efficacy

Self-esteem can be defined in two ways, one global (feelings about self as a good person in general), and one specific (feelings of worth in relation to a specific task or category of tasks). Specific self-esteem is sometimes referred to as self-efficacy. Although self-efficacy may be most relevant to specific learning situations, global self-esteem also plays a significant role in the ability to learn. For example, although my feelings about how good a manager I am may have much impact on my reaction to feedback about my strategic skills, how I feel about myself in general is still a factor in learning the new skills. Generally, if I believe I'm a reasonably good manager and an intelligent and acceptable person overall, those beliefs enable me to seek and face critical feedback on strategic skills with the motivation to learn those skills. If, on the other hand, I feel that I'm a good person but a poor manager (or if I feel I am not a very worthwhile or capable person overall), I will probably have greater difficulty being motivated to learn these new managerial skills.

Self-esteem is a well-researched aspect of personality, yet much of the research has focused on self-esteem in relation to task performance rather than learning. We know that people with high self-esteem are less likely to be affected by various kinds of stress and more apt to work harder in response to negative feedback than people with low self-esteem. It seems reasonable to believe that self-esteem has a similar relationship to learning—that having a strong sense of self-worth and a good measure of confidence in their abilities helps people face the possibility that their familiar skills are no longer adequate to the new challenges they face. For people with relatively high self-esteem, engaging in a new and challenging opportunity seems like less of a risk. Research has shown that high-self-esteem individuals seek more feedback because they feel they have less to fear in it (Ashford, 1986).

Yet research has also shown that people with very high self-esteem (overconfidence) may be less susceptible to influence by others or to cues from their environment (Brockner, 1988) and may therefore have difficulty noticing that new skills are needed. Overconfidence can be a serious stumbling block to learning, especially if a person has been rewarded over time for many successes and strengths. We believe openness to feedback is a first gateway to development; people with very high self-esteem may tend not to open that door wide enough, on their own.

People with relatively low self-esteem have different issues—they tend to be highly affected by feedback. They are more likely to be actively looking for information as to "what I may be doing wrong" and less able to do anything constructive with negative feedback when they do receive it. If people with low self-esteem receive negative feedback on task performance, they tend to focus on themselves (what's wrong with me), rather than on the task (what would be a better way). Performance may continue to decline as a result. Although in leadership development work a critical task is to understand self (that is, awareness of strengths and development needs), the individual receiving developmental feedback needs to be able to turn the focus on self outward to the task of setting development goals. So, although people whose self-esteem is low may be well aware that new skills and behaviors are needed, they need more help and encouragement to engage in opportunities to learn.

With regard to learning and feedback, research has shown that the *stability* of self-esteem may be even more important than its level (Kernis and others, 1993). Compared to people with stable self-esteem, those with unstable self-esteem are more likely to perceive that their self-worth is on the line in any situation related to performance or personal feedback and therefore may be more likely to avoid or react defensively in feedback situations. Unstable self-esteem may make it very difficult for people to admit that new skills or behaviors are called for.

Openness to Experience

In the past ten years, researchers have come to agree that one of several stable factors in personality is "openness to experience" (McCrae and Costa, 1985, 1987). People who are open to experience tend to see life as a series of ongoing learning experiences and seek out the new and relish the opportunities it brings (rather than the problems). They appear to have a sense of adventure, to enjoy trying out new ideas, having novel experiences, or meeting new people.

Openness to experience has been found to be correlated with training proficiency (Barrick and Mount, 1991). A key component of success in training is the attitude of the individual going into the event, and people who score high on openness tend to have positive attitudes toward unfamiliar (learning) experiences in general and a greater willingness to engage in them.

Conscientiousness or Need for Achievement

Research (Young and Dixon, 1996) has also shown that openness to experience is not all a manager needs to get the most out of training, or other potentially developmental experiences. In other words, openness to experience appears to be a necessary factor in learning or change, but not a sufficient one.

In addition to openness to new experience or information, a learner needs to be willing to take responsibility for using the new information to modify perspectives or behaviors, and for the persistence to work through difficult issues to accomplish the desired changes. This responsible persistence is related to another stable personality characteristic, called conscientiousness, and to one's need for achievement.

These two characteristics are important because they tell us something about how likely a person is to seek out and accept responsibility for learning, work hard to learn as a result of feedback, and persist in pursuit of difficult learning goals.

Beliefs About Learning and Orientations to Change

Beliefs can be hard to change. The manager who firmly believes that you can't teach an old dog new tricks is not as likely to learn from a development experience as one who sees learning as a lifelong activity and a string of interesting opportunities. Similarly, the person who believes that outcomes are a result of luck, fate, or other factors is less likely to take initiative in leadership or in leadership development.

The term *locus of control* has been used to describe a person's view of self as responsible for and able to effect outcomes. Locus of control can be internal (people believe that outcomes are a direct result of their own efforts) or external (people see outcomes as resulting more from luck, fate, or other factors not under their control). Locus of control might influence people's reaction to assessment feedback, what they believe about the relation between effort and mastery, and how they feel about the rewards they can expect from a learning effort. Trainees with internal locus of control are more likely to act on feedback and remain committed to difficult goals longer because they see themselves as in control of their own development and are likely to believe that their efforts will bring improvement.

For people who are internally focused (as are most U.S. managers), locus of control may not be an issue in their development. But for those whose locus of control seems to be external, who believe that whatever happens is a result of factors outside of their control, what we would call development experiences may be less likely to bring about individual change. External locus of control may be more likely in managers from areas of the world other than the United States, among people who do not so readily subscribe to the view that adult development is a worthwhile end toward which to strive (see Chapter Eleven for more on this issue).

Understanding Feelings and Managing Anxiety

For most people, recognizing that they do not know how to do something and then responding to the challenge in a learning mode produces considerable anxiety. Managing this anxiety is, therefore, critical to learning from experience. Although it is an ability that comes naturally to some people, it is also a skill that can be developed. We explore this skill in the following section.

Developing Learning Skills and Strategies

People approach learning in different ways. The approach that someone takes to learning is partly a matter of personal style, influenced by acquired skills and reinforced by habit. Some people prefer to learn from direct experience, where action-oriented experimentation strategies can be employed; others are more comfortable learning from reflection, reading, conversations with other people, or classroom training.

In our research and practice, we have made some effort to categorize the variety of ways in which people learn. Our expectation is that if people have reference to a behavioral taxonomy, they are able to expand their own repertoire of learning tactics and thus eventually master a greater variety of learning challenges. Implicit in this statement is the belief that particular challenges are best approached in certain ways and that people who use the greatest variety of tactics are the best learners.

We have categorized learning tactics in four major groupings:

1. *Thinking* tactics are solitary, internal cognitive activities. This includes recalling the past to search for similar or contrasting events; imagining the future through such activities as visualization; or accessing knowledge, facts, and wisdom through sources such as the library or the Internet.
2. *Taking action* comprises all the behaviors that have to do with direct, hands-on experimentation, jumping in with little hesitation to learn, in the moment, by doing.
3. *Accessing others* involves activities such as seeking advice and support, identifying role models and coaches, and seeking their help.
4. *Feeling* tactics are those activities and strategies that allow people to manage the anxiety associated with trying something new so that

they can take advantage of an opportunity to learn. Rather than being paralyzed by fear of failure, an individual might talk through his fear with a trusted peer (or write about it in a journal) before moving to a new and challenging assignment.

We believe that in approaching an unfamiliar task—an opportunity for learning—people not only use a preferred approach to learning but also tend to move in a pattern, beginning with their most preferred tactic and moving to another tactic only if the first doesn't work. For example, if I am likely to confront a new situation with a preferred tactic of taking action, I will do this even in those situations where it would be better to read the directions (the thinking tactic) or ask for help from others. Once I become sufficiently frustrated, I might stop and use my feelings to deal with that frustration and then look for someone who might provide help or advice. But I will probably go through this preferred sequence (action, then feeling, then accessing others) regardless of whether it makes the most sense to do so or not. It is all too easy to become stuck using one tactic, or one sequence of tactics, over and over, even if it is not working. In fact, "blocked" learners (Bunker and Webb, 1992) do just that, trying harder and harder without changing their approach.

The problem is, of course, that the preferred approach isn't always the most effective approach. It may be the one that people are most skilled in applying because they have used it the longest, but it may not be what is needed at the moment. In our view, maximizing the ability to learn from a variety of experiences means learning to expand the variety of learning skills or tactics people are most comfortable with, or at least learning to work (for short periods) outside the personal comfort zone. New skills and behaviors are often learned only by using different approaches to learning.

To illustrate, consider the case of Fred, who started his career during the early days of the do-more-with-less wave that followed downsizing and reengineering. He has learned to be quick, opportunistic, and action-oriented. He can think and act on the fly. However, he has received feedback that sometimes he is perceived as sloppy and slapdash, presenting uninformed and ill-conceived plans, and favoring the tactical over the strategic. To develop as a leader, he needs to learn to be more thoughtful, reflective, solitary, and integrative. Yet his action-oriented style (of working and learning) does not lend itself to learning these skills. The "just do it" approach won't make Fred more reflective. Being more reflective probably doesn't appeal to him. It has not been important to his success in the past, and in truth he may have been frustrated in the past with reflective people since he sees them as slow to make decisions. The first thing Fred has to do is deal with his feelings about what is being asked of him; then he needs to find a very different way of learning this skill.

In general, our research suggests that effective learners are facile in their use of all tactics. Consider next the example of Sarah, who graduated with a high GPA from an excellent school. She joined an organization where she established a record as an extraordinary achiever (as an individual contributor). She was thoughtful, reflective, thorough, and assertive. Unfortunately, in leadership roles she was not good at spanning boundaries and working with others to accomplish a task. Having received consistent feedback to the effect that she was perceived as an abrasive loner—albeit a smart one—she set a personal goal of becoming better able to accomplish tasks with others in a group setting.

The "thinking" approach to learning felt natural to Sarah: reading and reflecting. So she set forth energetically on her goal by getting the best new books on leadership and teamwork. Once she felt she had read and thought about the problem enough, she took action, trying to apply what she'd learned to her everyday interactions with people. Things did not go well. She soon realized that her old style of learning (reading and reflecting) would not be sufficient; she would have to learn from others how to best work with others. That is, she would also have to use the "accessing others" tactic to complete her learning goal. She would have to share her goal with peers, find role models, and seek feedback on her attempts to change. She realized that this would be a new and uncomfortable learning style; the mere thought of talking to others about her issues generated considerable anxiety. To be successful, she would also need to employ a "feeling" tactic to manage the anxiety.

The development of feeling tactics may be the most important step one can take in becoming a better learner, because facing new challenges—adopting new learning tactics to develop new skills—often creates significant psychological discomfort. Dealing successfully with this discomfort is a critical first step in being able to go against the grain and learn from experiences.

Finding the Courage and Developing the Skills

People are faced with new challenges whenever the context in which they work and live changes: globalization of markets, promotion, move to a new function or business, marriage or divorce, the birth of a child, and so on. It takes a certain amount of courage to recognize the need for new skills, behaviors, or attitudes and then use what are uncomfortable learning tactics to learn those skills.

People sometimes do not find that courage, staying instead with what is known and comfortable. Yet the results of failing to learn are serious. Over time, people feel caught in a rut, doing the same thing with the same results over and over. Or, as change overtakes them, their performance suffers. Derailment from the career they intend or desire is usually the result when a person's skills and perspectives do not fit what the job is demanding of the person. Someone who is at first well suited for a position or role can, over time, become ill suited, as the job or the organization's demands outpace the person's ability to develop requisite skills. Sometimes, derailment happens because managers continue to use or overuse their strengths, when new skills are required.

How can we, as human resource professionals, go about helping people find the courage and develop the skills to learn? From the model of leadership development presented in the Introduction, two of the three elements seem most important: (1) assessment and feedback, and (2) support. (As may be obvious, challenge is built into the process of learning new skills.) Another factor involves using a variety of development experiences to help people learn. Finally, we have found through our research that the timing of a development experience in relation to other career or life events is relevant to the ability to learn from experience.

Assessment and Feedback. To know whether their current skills fit well or poorly with the challenges they face, people need good information: about themselves (current strengths and development needs) and about the challenges. They need various kinds of information, delivered to them in various forms, and not just once but continuously over time.

Information about self comes from assessment and feedback. In the introductory chapter of this handbook, assessment is named as a key component of the model of leadership development. The premise is that for development to occur, people need to get feedback, either formally or informally, on current skills and perspectives, to take stock of where they are and what they need to learn. In this sense, assessment has two related purposes: to be a vehicle for delivering information on current strengths and weaknesses, and to help people recognize that the need for new skills exists.

Assessment takes various forms. A feedback-intensive program (see Chapter Two) usually provides a variety of opportunities for assessment and feedback, including personality inventories (to enhance understanding of self), experiential exercises or simulations, and 360-degree leadership surveys (to improve understanding of how others see your strengths and weaknesses and to compare your self-ratings of skills and perspectives to ratings made by others). The 360-degree instruments can also be used outside of a program, as an efficient and cost-effective way of helping people monitor their performance and stay in touch with their development needs over time and through different work situations (see Chapter One for a full description of this kind of assessment).

A key benefit of both a feedback-intensive program and 360-degree feedback is that they improve the accuracy or comprehensiveness of people's views of themselves. Being presented with the views of significant others (bosses, peers, direct reports, fellow participants in a program) to encounter shades of contrast and similarity to one's own self-view, is a powerful experience and can be a step toward understanding behavior from other points of view.

Both the feedback-intensive program and 360-degree feedback can work to unfreeze people, giving them the opportunity to take a look at themselves and decide that development is necessary or desired. Part of what happens in an unfreezing process is that a person's self-efficacy is enhanced by affirmation of strengths. We know from our work in evaluating feedback-intensive programs that a key benefit is enhanced confidence and self-esteem (Van Velsor, Ruderman, and Phillips, 1989; Young and Dixon, 1996). Therefore, it is often true that people who, by virtue of personality or motivation, may not seem ready for a development experience can benefit from feedback on a 360-degree instrument or a feedback-intensive program; the experience provides just enough support to motivate the person to dig deeper, set goals for improvement, and build interest in further development.

Sources and Importance of Support for Learning. With all its inherent difficulties—the need to go against the grain, the risk of exposing weaknesses, the fear of failure—learning is hard. Most people need support during the process.

Support can take a variety of forms. There is the support, described in the model in the introductory chapter, that constitutes one element of any good development experience. For example, if the development experience is a new assignment, the learner-manager can be put in touch with a network of others currently doing similar work in such assignments, or benefit from a supportive relationship with a senior manager who is a veteran of that type of work. If the developmental experience is feedback on a 360-degree instrument, the support comes in the form of a well-designed process for administering and delivering the feedback (Tornow, London, and CCL Associates, 1998), competent specialists to interpret the results, and good development planning materials (Leslie and Fleenor, 1998).

People often think of support in the form of one-on-one relationships, and this kind of support is usually essential for learning. Even though people with low self-esteem may have some difficulty in learning from challenging experiences, our research shows that a supportive boss moderates the effects of low self-esteem on learning (Ruderman, Ohlott, and McCauley, 1996).

Using a Variety of Development Experiences. People learn from a variety of development experiences, and development experiences enhance their ability to learn. For example, an individual can learn important leadership lessons from a developmental relationship, and the experience of being effectively coached can contribute to development of the learning tactic we've called accessing others. There is often a reciprocal relationship between a development experience and the learning tactics, whereby each reinforces the other (see also the Introduction).

The best approach in helping managers develop the wide range of leadership skills and learning tactics they need is one that combines multiple kinds of experience over the course of their career. For example, if a manager is facing a challenge (perhaps in an assignment) that she has never faced before (as was the case with Sarah, in our earlier example), she may need to adopt learning tactics that are unfamiliar and uncomfortable for her. In that case, what she learns in the assignment itself (which is one development experience) is enhanced by other development experiences occurring at the same time, say, a coaching relationship with a seasoned manager who is good at the learning tactics she needs, participation in a skills-based training program focused on learning tactics, a teamwork or working-with-others workshop, or a supportive relationship with someone who models the teamwork behaviors and skills she is trying to learn.

Timing of Development Experiences. In a recent research project conducted at the Center, we interviewed a group of senior executives about successful and derailed managers in their organizations. This comment came out of one of those interviews: "I was coaching her. We had many sessions together where the problems were identified and we tried to come up with an action plan. Some problems she owned, others she didn't. She really didn't change. She would change for a week or two, then return to baseline."

This executive was describing a person whose career in their organization was soon to be cut short. Is she permanently unable to change? We don't know, from this one description, but we suspect not. All people can make changes if they feel motivated, and all people can widen the scope of the tactics they use for learning. However, there are times, for everyone, when facing new challenges and learning in them is easier or more difficult than usual (Van Velsor and Musselwhite, 1986). Timing, in other words, is a critical piece of the puzzle.

When things are going well, many people tend not to seek out input from others on how they are doing, and they may not even be open to it. Regardless of whether they are avid or resistant learners in general, most people are readier for information or feedback when things are not going well for them, when they see that they may be in danger of failing. If people have reason to question their present ways of understanding, their perspectives or approaches, or their own competence, they usually want to know why things aren't working and are open to hearing that change of some kind is in order.

In particular, managers' need for new knowledge or skills tends to be higher during periods of transition, and so they are more open to learning from development experiences during these times. For example, when starting a new assignment, many people are keenly aware of how much they do not know and are eager to build the strengths that will help them succeed. They are very receptive to such experiences as a good coaching relationship. Once they have had some time to get their feet wet in the new assignment, they usually benefit from a comprehensive assessment experience (Conger, 1992).

On the other hand, there do seem to be times when people cannot and probably should not take on new developmental challenges—periods of high work overload or intense personal trauma, for instance. If they are emotionally overloaded, most people are unable to process new information about self or performance, even with additional support.

In summary, the timing of a development experience can have a significant effect on ability to learn. People all but lose their ability to learn (temporarily) in response to life events that significantly affect motivation. So, despite the stable influence of personality and the acquisition of various learning tactics, people's ability to learn can be higher at one point and lower in another, based on the need they perceive for new learning and based on the stress of other significant life events.

We close this section with the following example, taken from *Lessons of Experience* (McCall, Lombardo, and Morrison, 1988). It illustrates how powerful learning can be when people are ready, when new learning tactics are acquired, and when the timing is right.

> When I first became a supervisor of a group of development engineers, I looked at management like an engineer would. I read all about performance reviews, and boy, was I ready to give performance reviews! I told them in detail all the things they did wrong, and all the things they did right. No one had ever given them that kind of feedback before. But I just about killed those engineers, and nearly crushed the morale of that organization. I was clearly not a skilled coacher of people. So I went out and got some help. I finally learned that just as you had to know the laws of physics to be a good engineer, you had to know the laws of psychology to be a good manager. This was a tremendous lesson for me: that you can't just translate the skills of one profession into another. When you're going into a new profession, you'd better learn as much as you can about it before you jump. Take as much time as you can learning the differences so that you don't use your own experience when it really doesn't apply [p. 28].

Learning from Small Events

For the most part, we have focused in this chapter (and in this handbook) on the larger, more dramatic events and strategies that stimulate learning and development. We have not paid much attention to the smaller, day-to-day experiences that affect people both at home and in the workplace. Yet a very practical way to accomplish personal development is seeing the small and midsized events and challenges that everyone regularly faces as opportunities to practice new ways of learning (Lombardo and Eichinger, 1989). Common challenges such as having an annual performance-appraisal conversation, supporting a coworker through a family crisis, or negotiating with a spouse over child rearing or household planning provide a means to develop a comfort level with new learning tactics and competence with change (Lee, Guthrie, and Young, 1995). These more or less ordinary events can build self-esteem while simultaneously letting people try on new behaviors.

Guidelines for the Practitioner

To help others enhance their ability to learn from experience, and to increase the quantity and quality of that learning, we recommend the following:

1. Help managers focus on how they learn, as much as where and what they learn. Do they tend to begin a learning process by reading and reflection, moving into action only after an extended period of time spent thinking? Do they jump right into action, trying this and that on their own without ever seeking information from others who may have more expertise or experience? How do they feel about using other tactics, and how might they use current skills to manage the anxiety they feel when trying new behaviors?

2. Help managers expand their repertoire of learning tactics. Coaching can help managers who do not naturally tend to access others; it also helps prod the reflective learner into action. The use of a journal can help the action-oriented learner get more from the development experience (although it may require coaching to get this kind of learner to journal).

3. Do all you can to enhance self-esteem and other individual aspects that affect the ability to learn. Self-esteem enhances people's abil-

ity to learn from experience because it builds their ability to see new perspectives without threatening their current perspectives. It also increases the motivation to learn by decreasing people's anxiety about their weaknesses (it is OK to need to learn) and by building on the belief that people can learn and improve. Self-esteem is a cornerstone to learning from experience. A feedback-intensive program is a good way to boost self-confidence and build self-awareness, both of which motivate people to want to develop new learning skills. Be sure that people have the support they need if self-esteem might suffer (for example, during any development experience, including hardships).

4. Review development systems and programs currently in place, as well as assignments that are or could be used for individual development. Do they reflect a balance of assessment, variety of challenging experiences, and mechanisms for support? A good assessment enhances ability to learn in people who are already motivated, by showing them where to start. It also helps motivate people who do not appear ready for a development experience. Challenge enhances ability to learn by creating the demand for and opportunity to develop new skills and new ways of learning. Finally, ability and willingness to learn are nourished by coaches, mentors, and work partners who provide encouragement and support in the form of honest feedback, knowledge, and experience.

5. Help people find ways to get more regular and more informal feedback, including feedback on the ability to learn, from coworkers and others. It is very difficult, in the press of everyday business, for managers to keep in touch with the need to develop a new skill or use a different approach. For the same reasons, their opportunities for formal feedback and assessment (performance appraisals or structured developmental feedback using personality or 360-degree leadership instruments) are relatively infrequent. Informal feedback in the context of even small-scale development events can provide the bulk of a person's opportunities for development.

6. As much as possible, create a learning environment in your organization that permeates each and every development experience so that managers need not inhibit learning for fear of short-term mistakes or setbacks.

CHAPTER NINE

ASSESSING THE IMPACT OF DEVELOPMENT EXPERIENCES

Ellen Van Velsor

Many organizations today spend significant amounts of time and money on leadership development. They do this because their executives believe that leadership is something that can be developed and enhanced, and that good leadership makes a difference in the company's overall performance. But these executives also insist on accountability. They want to know that leadership development is, in fact, happening as a result of the experiences that have been designed and the systems that have been created.

At the Center for Creative Leadership, we have been working with leadership development programs for more than twenty years. For all those years, we have struggled frequently with questions of evaluating results. Were the programs meeting their intended goals? How can we evaluate the impact of our programs? What is the best way to measure individual change? Can bottom-line results be accurately documented? Clearly, all these questions are vitally important to organizations planning their development systems.

This chapter focuses broadly on what we at CCL have learned about assessing the impact of leadership development experiences. Although most of our formal evaluation research has been on feedback-intensive programs, we also have a large body of data on what people report learning from other development experiences, including job assignments, hardships, and relationships with other people.

The Goals of Evaluation

If you are charged with responsibility for evaluating the impact of leadership development strategies, it is important first to understand the goals that stakeholders in your organization (senior executives, human resource professionals, training staff) hold for those strategies. What leadership capacities do they consider desirable? Are these capacities that can be learned and developed from experience? What kinds of behavior change are desired?

It is also important to understand, from the outset, what can reasonably be expected from the kind of development event you are evaluating. It is not reasonable to expect the same kind of learning from different kinds of experience (McCall, Lombardo, and Morrison, 1988; Van Velsor and Hughes, 1990; McCauley and others, 1994; Ohlott, McCauley, and Ruderman, 1993). It is also not reasonable to expect the same quantity or quality of outcome from a single event as from a series of events linked together over time.

Finally, be clear on why you are doing the evaluation. An assessment of the impact of a development experience could have one or more goals:

1. Understanding a person's development as a result of the experience
2. Evaluating and fine-tuning an intervention so that it better meets its goals
3. Documenting whether participation in development experiences is affecting the bottom line

The goal of understanding individual development is usually a primary one in assessing the impact of a development experience.

Therefore, some of the most important questions focus on how, and how much, people learn and change as a result of the experience. If an impact study also has the goal of evaluating or fine-tuning the event itself, you want to know how the various aspects of the intervention contribute to individual development. If a goal is to assess impact on the bottom line, you need to focus on both individual change and change in the workgroup, attempting to link both of these to data on financial outcomes.

In the usual course of events, organizations are interested in all three goals. A large-scale study of impact examines all aspects, using both formative and summative evaluation (two classic approaches described later in this chapter) and then going beyond them, to a broader focus that promotes organizational learning. More about this later.

Outcomes of Leadership Development

Although most leadership development efforts are focused on individuals, when these efforts are applied to many individuals in the same organization, the morale or productivity of whole groups may be affected. Under these conditions, an assessment of impact might focus on both individual and group or organizational outcomes.

Individual Outcomes: A Model with Five Domains

We have found it useful to differentiate types of learning, development, or change and find ways to measure them separately. This approach is useful for two reasons: because the various types of development do not happen in the same way for all individuals, nor at the same time for a single individual; and because once we understand the conditions under which the different types of learning occur, we can make adjustments in development processes and events.

The model presented in Figure 9.1 is a simple representation of five areas of possible change, what we call "domains of impact." Keep in

FIGURE 9.1. MODEL OF DOMAINS OF IMPACT.

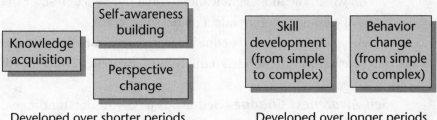

Developed over shorter periods
of time or in single events

Developed over longer periods
of time or through multiple events

mind that any one kind of development experience does not necessarily affect all the domains. In fact, for many people, the impact of a specific development experience may be concentrated in just one domain. For example, a feedback-intensive program focused on helping a person better understand leadership strengths and weaknesses primarily affects the domain of self-awareness. At the same time, feedback alone does not develop new leadership skills in that person; it should be supplemented by coaching or skills training (the skills domain) along with a job assignment that allows the person to practice the new skills and change behavior (the behavior domain).

Knowledge Acquisition. New knowledge is acquired in almost any development event, from feedback-intensive programs to skill-based training to job assignments. One purpose of developmental relationships, for instance, is to transmit knowledge (see Chapter Five). Multirater (360-degree) questionnaires are usually based on models of effective leadership or on skills that are linked to an organization's strategic direction. Those who use a 360-degree instrument not only learn about themselves but simultaneously learn what it takes to be an effective leader in their organization.

The knowledge acquired through all these experiences takes various forms. People gain new information about themselves or about how others perceive them; or they learn new concepts about leadership itself, such as the components of transformational leadership, the cultural values on which the most significant national differences rest, or the dimensions of personality that affect leadership style.

As you might expect, acquisition of new knowledge often sparks the next element in the model, namely, new awarenesses about self.

Self-Awareness Change. Self-awareness—understanding your own strengths and weaknesses, and the impact your behaviors and attitudes have on other people—is enhanced primarily through experiences that are rich in feedback from others. It is natural, then, that a feedback-intensive program (Chapter Two) primarily affects the self-awareness domain, but other types of experience can do that as well. Developmental relationships are good sources of feedback, as is participation in a 360-degree feedback process.

Increased awareness can be global ("I am a reasonably good manager") or more specific ("I am not seen as listening well to others"). After participating in an intensive-feedback program, some people report gaining personal insights about how they see themselves ("I judge myself too harshly") or about their own needs for inclusion, achievement, or acceptance ("I want to be involved, and sometimes my requests for involvement overload me" or "I need substantial issues to keep me driven") (Van Velsor, Ruderman, and Phillips, 1989).

It makes sense to think that new awarenesses about self—becoming aware that change is necessary—have to precede behavior change. In addition, new self-awareness often motivates development of new skills. (See Chapter Eight for additional information on the elements of learning from development experiences.)

Transformational Perspective Change. Perspective change is similar to awareness building in that it is a change in attitude rather than an observable behavior. But it differs in its focus: instead of a person's own strengths and weaknesses, attention is paid to insights about others and the environment in which the person lives and works. Significant perspective changes usually happen more slowly than new self-insights, but they can happen as a result of a single powerful event.

Perspective change, like self-awareness change, can be the result of knowledge acquisition. For example, the realization that "it is possible to manage an organization without becoming a technical expert" is a change in perspective. The person may come to this understanding by acquiring more information about what management involves.

Perspective change, again like self-awareness change, can underlie a change in behavior. In fact, perspective changes are transformational because how the person views an aspect of reality is fundamentally changed, thus facilitating and often resulting in changed behavior. The person who recognizes that managerial work is different from technical work finds it easier from that point on to let go of his need to remain in hands-on mode with his subordinates.

Transformational perspective change is revealed in comments from a person who participated in a feedback-intensive program: "The program got me to thinking that people are different—and that they are motivated differently, their priorities are different—and to start looking for it. When I came back, I started analyzing the people who were working directly for me, and then I started managing differently—not just one big blanket 'Here it is, folks.'"

Here, the perspective change (that people are different from him and from each other) is prompted by new knowledge about situational leadership (the idea that people need to be managed with a style that matches their job competence). The perspective change, in turn, prompts new self-awareness ("I need to manage differently").

Of course, actually learning to manage people differently requires a fairly complex set of skills. It is unlikely that the manager finds a chance to develop those skills simply as a result of one program. To capitalize on the potential for change, follow-up is needed, perhaps coaching or skill-based training.

Skill Development. Thus we come to a fourth area of change. Intentional skill development or improvement often begins after an assessment experience (such as a feedback-intensive program or 360-degree feedback) has created awareness of the need for improvement. Skills can, of course, be developed or improved without formal assessment, as often happens when one takes on a new assignment or challenge. Skill-based training and on-the-job learning are probably the two most frequently used methods for developing new skills.

Mastering new skills often takes time and exposure to multiple experiences. This is particularly true for skills that involve significant personal change in perspective or self-understanding, such as empowerment or learning tactics. Skills that are dependent on learning a process, such as giving constructive feedback or conflict resolution, can be acquired more quickly.

Behavior Change. Behavior change involves acting and reacting differently to situations and problems. It is often an outcome of other types of change.

Behavior change is like skill development in that both take hard work and practice. Similarly, both can be thought of as having simple and complex varieties. Simpler behavior change may follow from new awarenesses gained during assessment, or from learning new skills, as when a person decides to stop interrupting others, to schedule regular meetings with staff, or to spend more time with family. More complex behavior changes, such as collecting further data before making a decision or really allowing the perspectives of others to influence one's own, are only achieved with more time, more work, and higher motivation.

Real behavior change is not usually the result of any single development experience. It happens only over time, through repeated efforts; ongoing feedback; and the use of multiple, preferably linked, development events.

Group and Organizational Outcomes

Some organizations use individual leadership development to foster change in groups. Usually, the expectation is that managers who are given opportunities for development become more effective group leaders and that enhanced leadership generates increased productivity or profitability in the workgroup. If managers are being sent to development events

FIGURE 9.2. EXPECTATIONS FOR LEADERSHIP DEVELOPMENT.

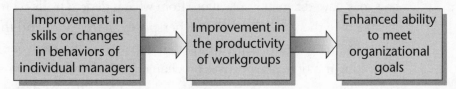

in large numbers, there is often a hope that the impact will be felt throughout the organization. At this level, the desired impact is normally financial as well. This set of expectations is pictured in Figure 9.2.

One way to assess change at the group level is to use climate surveys or other measures of group satisfaction. Another is to take advantage of measures of productivity or group output that already exist in the organization's accounting systems.

Some General Principles to Apply When Looking for Change

There are at least six principles that should always be applied when designing an assessment of the impact of leadership development events.

Examine Development from Multiple Perspectives

In the same way that it is valuable to collect assessment information from a number of sources on a person's current behavior or skill level, it is also valuable to get multiple perspectives when measuring how that behavior or skill level has changed.

It is almost always the case that rater groups (bosses, peers, direct reports, self) disagree on the amount and even sometimes the direction of change, just as they agree or disagree on skill levels at the start of the process. Also, rater groups view change through diverse lenses. For example, a manager may disagree with her boss over how closely her direct reports should be supervised. Change in the direction desired by the boss may have different implications from what is desired by direct reports.

We take the view that all rater perspectives are valid, and that the whole picture is significantly more insight-provoking than any one piece. Collecting multiple perspectives on change gives significantly more and richer data than relying on a single source. Conclusions drawn from only one perspective are often incomplete, if not seriously misleading. It goes without saying that self-report data should always be compared to data from other sources. People working hard at improvements are most likely to see evidence of change first. In fact, they are sometimes likely to see change where others cannot see it, because they want to believe their efforts are paying off or want to justify the expenditure made on their behalf.

Assess Multiple Domains

Developing even a single leadership capacity can involve change in all five domains of impact. In addition, it is entirely possible that any one development experience affects people differently; some people experience a change in some domains and not others. Therefore, it is important to develop appropriate ways of measuring each relevant domain of potential impact and to assess change in each area.

Use Multiple Methods

Because the impact of a development experience on individuals takes various forms, you want to be able to measure different kinds of impact: improvement in skills, enhanced self-awareness, and so on. Also, there may be several reasons for evaluating the experience: understanding how individuals have been developed, fine-tuning the program itself, or assessing impact on the bottom line. Therefore, the most powerful impact study includes multiple methods of assessing impact.

For example, if your goals are to assess the quantity and quality of leadership development in a feedback-intensive program as well as look at how the program itself can be improved, then combine self-reported learnings with a "post-then" assessment of change over time (described later in this chapter), and also use in-depth interviewing to gain information on how different parts of the program are being received. (All of these methods are described more fully in the next section.) Or, if you are looking at the impact of a mentoring program to determine both individual development and impact on the bottom line, take a two-pronged approach. For the individuals, you can rely on interviewing and self-reported learnings, and then follow up on goals set by participants. To understand impact on the bottom line, interview the participants' coworkers, collect data on the group's productivity or morale, and then link these data to financial outcomes over time.

Look at Change over Time

Although any development experience has some relatively immediate effects (such as increases in knowledge or enhancement of self-awareness), other effects (such as mastery of complex skills or changes in leadership style) often occur over time, especially in organizations that take a systems approach to development (see Figure 9.1). Further, as the business environment changes and people's jobs are restructured, a different set of leadership strengths becomes relevant. All these factors make it important to take a long-term approach, both to development itself and to measuring the impact of individual development experiences.

Assess Individual and Group-Level Change

There is usually some level of expectation that group outcomes, such as changes in productivity, satisfaction, or climate, result from leadership development efforts focused on individuals. The same dynamic also works in the obverse: it is possible that development efforts focused on teams (which this chapter does not cover) can have important impact on the individuals on those teams. Therefore, to understand why and how development efforts are, or are not, having a wider organizational impact, it is important to look in all directions, assessing not only individual change but also change in workgroups and any changes in the bottom line that can be documented.

Use Control Groups for Comparison

If there is significant change going on in an organization during or following a leadership development intervention (for example, large numbers of managers participating in a mentoring relationship or in a feedback-intensive program), you cannot assume a direct connection between the development experience and subsequent learning and change. Changes in the business environment—which all modern organizations face almost daily—may be affecting people's behavior. The only way to know if changes in people's behavior are attributable to the development experience is to compare those who participate in the experience with a group of people who do not—in other words, a control group. For the truest results, those in the control group should be like the participant group in all other respects, such as job characteristics, organizational level, tenure, gender, and race.

In the same way, if people are participating in several potentially developmental experiences (which is the case if their organization takes a system view of development), you cannot know that change is attributable to any particular event without using a control group.

Seven Ways to Assess Change

We now turn our attention to seven specific methods for evaluating how various kinds of development experience have an impact on individuals. Although much of what we have learned comes from our experience in evaluating classroom-based programs, we believe that all of the techniques described here are useful in evaluating any set of development experiences. The information provided by each of these methods and the problems with their use are summarized in Table 9.1.

TABLE 9.1. METHODS FOR ASSESSING
THE IMPACT OF DEVELOPMENT EXPERIENCES.

	Information Provided	Problems with Method
End-of-event evaluations	Immediate participant reactions to event in terms of value and enjoyment; can be useful when focus is on the event	Does not assess actual learning or development
Self-reported learning	What people are learning from the experience; goes beyond "reactions"	Captures only the perspective of self; does not assess real change
Questionnaires	Can relate to many domains of impact; provides hard (quantitative) data on change and can be from multiple perspectives	Data can be misleading because of multiple problems with measuring change using "pre-and-post" methods
"Post-then" assessment	Can overcome some problems with measuring change; provide data directly on change	Change in job or raters can still be a problem; relies on rater's memory of past performance
Follow-up to goals or action plans	Assesses accomplishment of goals and plans; points more directly to a bottom-line result	Goal accomplishment can be narrow focus
In-depth interviewing	Deeper understanding; can complement other methods	Time consuming, labor-intensive
Journals	Deeper understanding of long-term impact; can complement other methods	Can limit impact by restricting what participants include; confidentiality issues

End-Of-Event Evaluations

Often called "smile sheets," these evaluations are meant to capture the participants' immediate reactions to the event they have just completed. They are most commonly used with classroom-based programs, and the information they solicit from participants is usually limited to whether they enjoyed the experience or found it valuable.

End-of-event evaluations are useful as a way of helping the presenters gauge participants' immediate satisfaction level. Studying these evaluations over time provides one way of evaluating the competence of the training staff. But in terms of measuring actual impact on the participants, they are of limited value. Neither enjoyment nor perceived value means that someone has engaged in significant development.

These ratings do not answer the important questions of how well the content or learnings transfer to the job; how well participants are able to accomplish their goals; and how much is achieved in terms of knowledge acquisition, new self-awareness, perspective change, skill improvement, or behavior change.

In fact, some research has shown that end-of-event evaluations are wholly unrelated to actual change on the job. In a study of twelve hundred trainees in a large manufacturing organization, Dixon (1990) reports that there was no correlation between posttest scores on knowledge acquired and subsequent performance on the one hand, and participants' ratings, on the other hand, on enjoyment, relevance of the course, how much they learned, or instructor skill.

Self-Reported Learnings

One way to go beyond end-of-event ratings to capture data on knowledge acquisition, new self-awarenesses, and new perspectives is to collect self-reported learnings directly from people participating in development experiences. In general, if an intervention is having the desired impact, individual learnings should be in alignment with the goals for the intervention.

The method is simple: ask people to list several things they learned about themselves, others, or leadership as a result of the experience. If you do this for a group, you can then sort through the data for themes. Also, repeat the process after some time has passed to see how learnings grow or change. This is a rich source of information about the new knowledge or awarenesses that people acquire.

At times, we have used these self-reported learnings as raw material for questionnaires that are then administered to larger groups of people. If these questionnaires are made computer-scorable, they can be used more efficiently, thereafter eliminating the need for content analysis of responses.

People's responses are also useful in developing frameworks and tools for goal follow-up. We have found that data-based learning questionnaires that incorporate a post-then response format are especially useful in looking at change over time.

Use of Questionnaires

Questionnaires are a classic way of collecting data, and they have many legitimate uses. Many organizations, as well as all types of leadership development programs, use questionnaires or 360-degree instruments to give people feedback on their skills and perspectives. It is also conceivable that a 360-degree instrument could be used to assess the match between a person's skills and the demands of a particular job, as well as to identify areas needing development that can be addressed in the context of that job.

Using a follow-up questionnaire to measure change after some time has passed seems the next logical step. Whenever people use the feedback they get from the questionnaire to set development goals or action plans, follow-up measures using the same questionnaire are particularly relevant. This two-step process, often referred to as pre-and-post questionnaires, indeed provides useful follow-up information—as long as the time frame for retesting is appropriate, the same people are involved, the person's job has not changed, and the respondents' framework does not change (Terborg, Howard, and Maxwell, 1980; Millsap and Hartog, 1988; Bedian and Armenakis, 1989; Golembiewski, 1989; Tennis, 1989). We now look at these conditional problems in detail.

Time Frame for Retesting. Any one development experience can produce various kinds of change in people (review the model in Figure 9.1). Some changes (such as knowledge acquisition and new self-awareness) are likely to happen almost immediately, and are therefore measurable immediately after, or even during, a development experience. Others, such as perspective change or relatively simple behavioral changes, can take place over a relatively short period. But still other changes—for example, those requiring practice, deeper change, or complex skill development—take much longer (six to eighteen months), even with good support and coaching.

Depending on when it takes place, reassessment is likely to pick up a different sort of development. Reassessments done in three to six months may pick up changes in knowledge and awareness, which can be reported only by the individual participant. On the other hand, reassessments done at twelve to eighteen months are more likely to pick up change in some of the complex skills and behaviors required of leaders. These longer-term changes are the ones likely to be observed and reported by others.

Change in Raters. Although waiting to assess change captures more, and more varied, change, there are trade-offs. The longer you wait to do a reassessment, the greater the likelihood that the makeup of the group of raters will change. At least some of the people who provided feedback on the first round of questionnaires are likely to have been replaced by a new set of people, so that the ratings from time one and time two might not be entirely comparable.

Change in Job Responsibilities. To further complicate matters, the longer you wait to do the reassessment, the more likely it is that the person is now in a different job. The person's skills may remain stable or even increase, but the value of those skills may be different in the new job. For instance, being highly accessible to everyone, which is rated as a strength in the initial job, may be a liability in the next job, where deadlines are tight. This could be frustrating for someone who is trying to compare, line by line, the feedback received at time one and time two.

To allay confusion and frustration, most people need as much facilitation and support for a reassessment as they had for the original assessment. If it is well facilitated, even potentially confusing feedback offers an opportunity for the person to reflect on what has changed in terms of job challenge and what new adjustments and development plans can now be put into place.

Change in Raters' Framework. Finally, even if the person's job and the raters remain the same, under certain circumstances the feedback from a retest questionnaire is misleading. It is quite common to see retest ratings that are the same or lower when in fact the person being rated has actually improved. In our research, we have often found, for example, that people rate the individual lower in the second questionnaire, yet take the time to write in the margins how much the person has changed.

What is behind this contradiction? This is a phenomenon called "response shift bias," which itself is caused by several circumstances related at least in part to the fact that raters are asked to rate other people's skills and behaviors without being trained to do so.

Sometimes, on the second round, raters cannot do a good job of assessing change because they cannot remember how they rated the person the first time. The questionnaire itself provides a learning experience, since it lays out the specifics of good leadership skills and behaviors. On the second pass, raters may feel clearer about what to observe. Also, because people know that the person being evaluated is actively engaged in making change, they have higher expectations for that person's performance, which unconsciously raises the bar and creates the ironic situation where improved performance actually gets a lower rating than before.

In spite of these drawbacks, the use of pre-and-post questionnaires will undoubtedly continue. They are relatively simple to administer, present a retest opportunity for participants, and produce quantitative results that seem unambiguous to stakeholders. (For additional suggestions on how 360-degree feedback can be used in measuring impact, see Martineau, 1998.)

Post-Then Assessments

One attempt to get around some of the problems presented by pre-and-post assessment comparisons is a response scale that we call *post-then* and others have called "retrospective posttest." Essentially, the post-then questionnaire, administered some time after a development event, asks raters to compare the person's performance at two time points in reverse chronology: currently (whether three, six, twelve, or eighteen months after the event) and at a specific time in the past, usually just before the development event. Raters must think back to what the person was like at the earlier time and record their ratings on two separate scales on the same form. Typically, the response scale has more choices (nine or ten) than a traditional questionnaire (with a five-point scale); this allows people to record smaller amounts of change (see Figure 9.3).

The advantage to this technique is that it eliminates one major drawback to the more traditional pre-and-post procedure: the possibility of a changed frame of reference if two ratings are made at two different times. Although a downside might be that one is being asked to "trust" that the retrospective ratings of past skill levels are valid, change is being measured more directly this way. In using the data, you can focus on specific parts of the ratings, looking at just the difference (change) scores or at both change and current ratings of skills. Keep in mind that *when* the data are collected influences what data you get. Some kinds of development are observable and measurable over shorter time periods (say, three months), while others take longer (perhaps a year or more).

At this point, there has been limited use of this method (Hoogstraten, 1982; Collins and Horn, 1991; Howard, 1993; Henry and others, 1994; Young and Dixon, 1996) and limited research on its reliability. But it seems to hold promise.

Follow-Up to Goal Setting or Action Planning

Some development experiences have goal setting or action planning built into them, but even those that do not can still have specific goals. Indeed, they should; according to recent research, development experiences

FIGURE 9.3. EXAMPLE OF POST-THEN RATING SCALES.

Follow-Up Assessment (Rater Form)

Give the rating that appropriately describes the extent to which the person

**Improving
Self-Awareness**
1. Learns how others perceive him or her
2. Understands how his or her management style impacts those with whom he or she works
3. Is aware of the impact of his or her behavior on others

**Improving
Self-Confidence**
4. Is self-assured
5. Believes he or she can make valuable contributions to the organization
6. Recognizes and appreciates his or her talents and abilities

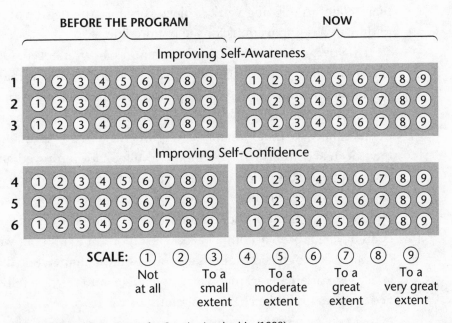

Source: Excerpted from Center for Creative Leadership (1998).

that incorporate goal setting have more impact than those that do not (Kluger and DeNisi, 1996). A natural way to collect impact data on these experiences is to follow up on the plans or goals, by telephone, by mail, or in person.

A goal follow-up can assess (1) how much of the plan has been completed, (2) to what extent and in what ways it has been revised, and (3) what obstacles to implementation have been noted.

The usual approach is to ask people, three to six months after the event, about their progress and to draw conclusions about impact based on how fully they have accomplished their goals. That is, most assessment attention is given to the first question: how much of the plan has been accomplished. This is certainly understandable, particularly if the plan relates to ongoing work projects, because the degree of accomplishment has implications for the bottom line.

However, the other two questions must not be overlooked. One conclusion we have drawn from our research on goal setting is that learning a process for creating goals and becoming skilled at adjusting them when circumstances change are as important as accomplishing them—perhaps more so. In addition to asking whether specific goals and plans have been accomplished, you should also look for improved ability to revise those goals to meet changing circumstances.

This requires of the evaluator not a new set of research methods but a changed framework and a new set of questions. If the original goals have not been accomplished, it is important to find out why. Has the person recognized that circumstances have changed or that how goals were originally framed was inadequate, and purposefully modified the plans to fit the changed circumstances? If so, it would be a mistake to conclude simply that goals were not achieved. (See Chapter Two for more on approaches to goal setting.)

In-Depth Interviewing

Used alone or as a supplement to other, more quantitative methods such as questionnaires, in-depth interviews provide greater depth and broader perspective. An example of an in-depth interview format is presented in Table 9.2.

TABLE 9.2. EXAMPLE OF IN-DEPTH INTERVIEW FORMAT.

Instructions: Listed below are the questions we would like to address in our interviews with you. We hope you have time to look them over and perhaps make a few notes to yourself before your scheduled time with us. It is important to keep in mind the purpose of these interviews: we want to have a better understanding of how participating in [the development experience] has helped you and how we can work to improve the [development experience] for people in the future. Your frank and honest responses will help us in this endeavor. Your responses will be completely confidential.

Overall impact	1. What are the two or three most important ways [the development experience] has had an impact on you?
	2. If we asked those who work with you what you are doing differently compared to a year ago, what would they say? How much would you attribute these differences to [the development experience]?
	3. Has any aspect of [this development experience] helped you bring about change in your group?
	4. What has been the highlight of [this development event] for you?
Individual goals or action plans	5. Would you have set your individual goals and worked toward them if you had not been involved in [this development event]?
	6. What, if anything, got in the way of your working on these goals (or implementing your action plan)?
	7. How did working on these goals stretch your capabilities or enhance your learning? Did this work require that you change your behavior? If so, how?
	8. In retrospect, were these the most appropriate goals to set?
Working with a coach	9. How much and what kinds of interaction have you had with your coach?
	10. What benefits have you derived from that relationship?
	11. Was there anything that got in the way of that relationship being successful? Were there ways your coach could have been more effective?
Process improvement	12. Is there any way that [this development experience] can be improved?

Source: Adapted from McCauley and Hughes-James (1994).

Interviews can be limited to the participants themselves or, if resources allow, expanded to others, including their boss, direct reports, peers, customers, or family members. The varying perspectives gained with this method add richness to the interpretation of other data and help in understanding why desired levels of impact were or were not achieved.

Journals

If journaling is used within a development experience, the journals themselves can serve as a source of rich data on what people are learning, how they understand the experience, and how their perspectives are changing over time. There is, however, a very important trade-off. To be most effective for the participant, the journal should be a private diary of thoughts, emotions, and learnings. Knowing that an evaluator will eventually have access to the journal may keep people from writing freely and fully, which limits its usefulness. It may be better in many situations to encourage journaling as a tool for reflection (and thereby a way of enhancing impact), but to forgo the evaluation data it provides.

Assessing the Impact of Work Experiences: Special Considerations

Certain of the structured leadership development activities that are described in this handbook have, as part of their fundamental architecture, a process for measuring outcomes. Feedback-intensive programs and skill-based training, for instance, assess current skill levels at the beginning and evaluate change at the end. But it is one of our basic beliefs that leadership skills derive from many sources, informal as well as formal. We know that on-the-job experiences can produce startling insights and trigger profound changes, yet their full value is sometimes not realized because there is no ready way to measure it. The person involved thus misses out on an opportunity to reflect on what was learned, and the organization loses a valuable piece of information that could be put to good use with other employees.

We are speaking here of such important experiences as developmental relationships and developmental assignments. Unless people have the opportunity for some form of assessment, they do not usually know, going in, that the strengths they have are relevant to the experience, or what personal development needs the experience might address.

To get the most benefit from these types of experience, it is extremely valuable to begin with a formal assessment of a person's strengths and development needs, and also to assess the assignment or the relationship partner. Knowing what each has to offer the participant, it is then possible to create the most effective person-assignment or person-person combination. It is even more beneficial, to both the individual and the organization, if the experience begins with defining individual development goals tied to the company's strategic goals.

Then, to assess change in the person over time, use any of the methods described here. Techniques such as journaling and coaching encourage the person to reflect on what is being learned, thereby enhancing development even more.

Assessing the Impact of Leadership Development on Groups

It seems reasonable that improving the effectiveness of individual leaders should have a positive impact on the workgroups they lead—on morale, productivity, innovation, or profitability. However, these group-level outcomes are affected by many things in addition to the quality of leadership, and it is very difficult (if not impossible) to document precisely the relationships between individual development events and organizational outcomes. Nevertheless, it is worth making the effort, for even general tracking yields important information about what is getting in the way of desired group outcomes. Tracking also gives the leader valuable postprogram feedback on how efforts to change are being received and what more has to be done.

Although it is hard to conceive of *groups* as gaining new knowledge or new self-awareness (individuals in groups gain these things), it does make sense to think that individuals gain new perspectives about the group, such as the importance of working as a team, the role of the group in the organization, and how it relates to other groups. New awarenesses of this type can result from having all group members participate in a feedback-intensive leadership or team development program.

There are group skills that can be developed (such as dialogue or organizational learning competencies) and behaviors that groups together can work to change (for instance, how they interact as a group with other groups, the work they take on as a group, their productivity level). Some group skills, such as dialogue, may need to be developed through targeted and specific skills training (see Chapter Four), while others are developable through working in real time as a team.

To document impact at the group or organizational level, conduct focus group interviews with the target group and other groups they work with. An instrument used to assess teamwork might also be used to assess change in this area, though with all the caveats expressed earlier about pre-and-post comparisons. You can use a variety of instruments to assess organizational climate or specific aspects of it. Finally, collect data about the group from other groups within the organization, before and after the development event; look for changes in group behavior and compare that to data on individual impact.

Once you have collected a full range of data concerning both individuals and groups, you can undoubtedly fill in all the blocks in Figure 9.2 to complete a picture of the quantity, quality, and reasons for the impact of a development experience for individuals, groups, and the organization as a whole.

Assessing Impact on the Bottom Line

In for-profit organizations, goals are naturally centered around increased profitability. When senior executives of these organizations send a group of managers to formal development programs, they often expect to see a demonstrated impact on the bottom line. In most cases these expectations are likely to remain unfulfilled, for at least two reasons. First, most organizations take an event approach to leadership development, using only a single strategy. But no single event by itself produces the multifaceted set of changes needed to improve the productivity of large groups of employees.

Second, even if productivity of workgroups were magically improved by making their managers better leaders, too many other factors affect the bottom line. No leadership development program can protect a company against economic downturns, market changes, shifts in the political or regulatory climate, chaos in the money market, natural disasters that damage the supply of raw materials or production facilities, labor stoppages, or the fickle taste of consumers.

Nonetheless, there will always be interest in documenting bottom-line impact. Toward that end, it is especially important to design a study that carefully assesses individual impact in all possible domains, and that captures both changes at the workgroup level (in satisfaction, climate, and productivity) and the reasons for lack of change at that level. This kind of study tracks how individuals are developing and also sheds light on what other factors are influencing the achievement of organizational goals.

A Tool for Organizational Learning

Traditionally, most assessment of development initiatives has taken the "report card" approach: evaluate the program to see how well it is meeting its goals. This approach to evaluation, which is technically known as summative evaluation, is often used to determine whether a program or process should be continued or discontinued. But the knowledge that is gained through a summative evaluation is often applied only to the program in question. Then a decision is made based on the information, and that is the end of it. Whatever is learned from the evaluation is not considered generalizable.

Formative evaluation, in contrast, focuses on finding out how the development event or system can better meet its goals. In a spirit of continuous improvement, it attempts to discover what level of impact is present and how events can be improved to create maximum impact. The central question is "What can we learn and improve?" rather than "How well did it do?"

A large-scale study of impact can have both formative and summative phases. For example, you may conduct a formative study during the pilot phase of a mentoring program and follow that with a summative approach once the program is up and running. Even so, the specific program is still the only focus of attention.

There are ways to go about evaluation research that push the organization toward broader benefits. A series of new approaches variously called "participatory evaluation," "collaborative evaluation," "empowerment evaluation," and "evaluative inquiry" are getting more attention recently because of their added value in promoting learning across the organization (Cousins and Earl, 1992, 1995; Fetterman, 1994, 1996; Preskill and Torres, 1996). These approaches are characterized by collaborative and participative relationships that empower program participants to contribute directly to their own and to others' learning. Through reflection, dialogue, and action planning, participants play a role in collecting evaluation data at the same time they are increasing their own understanding of what they learned.

For an organization to learn, the individuals within it must continuously learn and the collective too must learn (Dixon, 1996). As evaluation, especially formative evaluation, is used regularly, people become used to asking, "What can we learn and how can we improve?" Over time, this mind-set helps produce a learning orientation in the organization as a whole.

Summary and Guidelines for Practitioners

In summary, to do an effective job of addressing the impact of leadership development strategies, it is important to

- Understand the goals that stakeholders in your organization have for the event or program
- Know what can reasonably be expected from the kind of development experience you are evaluating
- Be clear on your goals in assessing the impact of a development experience

If the focus is on the event itself, several key questions should be asked, general questions that can be used to frame other aspects of the impact study design:

- What outcomes did the event or program generate?
- How did the various aspects contribute? (In an assignment, this might be the boss, coworker support, the work itself, etc.)
- How and why did the impact on individual participants vary?

A comprehensive evaluation design should take into account (and provide a way to capture) most of the impact of a program. This allows you to draw more valid and complete conclusions from looking across different pieces of data and capturing unintended outcomes, which are sometimes important. In addition to the previous questions, the following checkpoints and general suggestions are useful in designing a comprehensive impact study:

- Examine development from multiple perspectives, including self, boss, peers, and direct reports.
- Assess multiple domains, including knowledge acquisition, self-awareness, transformational perspective change, skill development, and behavior change.
- Use multiple methods, covering all the domains of impact that might be of interest.
- Assess change over time, because the several kinds of development take place at different points.
- Assess both individual and group-level change, especially if impact on the bottom line is an important outcome.

- Use control groups for comparison, to be sure that development and change you find is attributable to the development experience and not to other organizational events.

One final consideration: remember that if development experiences are linked in a organizationwide system for development, evaluation should be a key part of that system. If that happens, assessment of impact is being used for the most powerful of purposes: to create and maintain an organization focused on learning.

PART THREE

LEADERSHIP DEVELOPMENT: ISSUES

LEADERSHIP DEVELOPMENT ACROSS RACE AND GENDER

Marian N. Ruderman
Martha W. Hughes-James

When the Center for Creative Leadership (CCL) first opened its doors in 1970, most managers attending our programs were white and male. Thus, much of CCL's early work in leadership development was designed for this population. As the demographics of the managerial world changed, so did our client base. White women managers started to come through our doors; so did managers of color, both male and female. We began to wonder whether traditional leadership development methods still worked with heterogeneous populations. A review of the research literature confirmed what common sense suggested: if leadership development practices reflect only the experiences and careers of white men, women and people of color can be disadvantaged (Morrison and Von Glinow, 1990).

We would like to thank Ancella Livers, Kate Panzer, Dana McDonald-Mann, Craig Chappelow, Davida Sharpe, Sharon Rogolsky, Sara King, Carl Bryant, Bill Howland, Ellen Kossek, Kelly Spence, and Martin Davidson for sharing their views on many of the concepts presented in this chapter.

This chapter examines the suitability of using common leadership development strategies for a pool of managers that is growing increasingly more diverse with each passing year. In particular, we use the lenses of race and sex to examine 360-degree feedback, feedback-intensive programs, challenging assignments, developmental relationships, and recognition practices.

History of Leadership Diversity Work

CCL first formally asked if the knowledge base we had developed on white males was appropriate for managers from diverse demographic groups in the mid-1980s. We had conducted a key study on how American executives learn, grow, and change (McCall, Lombardo, and Morrison, 1988). The sample turned out to be virtually all white men because they constituted the vast majority of executives at that time. The study found that executives develop from a series of increasingly challenging transitions, assignments, and experiences; these results highlighted the role of challenge as a key developmental strategy. As this study of male executives was being completed, Ann Morrison, Randy White, and Ellen Van Velsor replicated it with female executives. They had to search extensively to find enough women executives to form the basis of a study. Of the seventy-six executives in their study, seventy-three were white and three were black. Their research culminated in the 1987 book *Breaking the Glass Ceiling*, which demonstrated that the path to the executive suite for these women was both similar to and different from that for white men. They found that although many of the same challenging experiences that develop white men also play a role in the development of women, the women faced additional barriers of prejudice and differential treatment. These barriers act as a glass ceiling above which it is difficult or nearly impossible for women to rise.

This research led to the development of a new type of feedback-intensive program at CCL, a program just for women. We initially developed this program as a means of sharing the glass ceiling research, but when we began running it we learned that it had tremendous value in its own right as a place where women managers could focus on their own development as leaders amid the fellowship of women in similar situations. This was the first time we created a program for a single demographic group (although we had programs for particular occupational groups), and it created another venue for learning about the development of women managers.

With this as the beginning, our efforts to understand the leadership development process expanded to include managers from other demographic groups. In 1988, we began collecting data for the Guidelines on Leadership Diversity (GOLD) project. This study looked at organizational practices for developing leadership among men and women of color—African Americans, Hispanics, Asian Americans—in addition to white women. Findings suggest that the glass ceiling applies not just to women of all races but to nonwhite males as well. Ann Morrison reported this research in *The New Leaders* (1992), which analyzes the corporate practices that are most effective in developing a diverse managerial workforce.

These large-scale studies were complemented by several others, smaller in scope, that dealt with specific issues: a comparison of the developmental experiences of white men and women (Van Velsor and Hughes-James, 1990), the different managerial job experiences of men and women (Ohlott, Ruderman, and McCauley, 1994), a conference on best practices for diversity (Morrison, Ruderman, and Hughes-James, 1993), promotion dynamics for men and women (Ruderman, Ohlott, and Kram, 1995), and the diversity of workteams (Jackson and Ruderman, 1995; Ruderman, Hughes-James, and Jackson, 1996). Collectively, they gave us a deeper understanding of particular aspects of the leadership development process.

Client demand further influenced our agenda. In 1994, concerned that their African American managers weren't getting access to the same opportunities as their white managers, clients asked us to develop a feedback-intensive program for African American managers. In addition to the usual leadership development curriculum, this program deals with some of the issues unique to people from a demographic group that historically has been discriminated against in the United States.

Focus of this Chapter

This chapter highlights CCL's work with regard to development of African American managers and white women managers. In addition to our classroom experience and the published research described above, we also draw on two large-scale studies now in process. One study looks at racial differences in how executives learn, grow, and change; the other focuses on trends in the development of a group of predominantly white women managers.

An important caveat is that most of our knowledge base comes from work with white women and African American men and women who work in large U.S. corporations where white men have traditionally held the authority positions. We do not look at leadership in other sectors, such as education or volunteer organizations, where white women leaders or African American leaders may be more common. Nor do we look at racial differences much beyond a black and white comparison. These limits are based on the type of information we have; our database on other groups is quite small. Additionally, our focus in this chapter is on the United States, where race relations reflect a historical background of slavery and oppression. Other chapters in this handbook deal more closely with cultural and national differences in leadership as well as the demands made of a global manager.

Although in this chapter we look at the shared experiences of white women, black women, and black men in managerial positions, we do not assume that their experiences in organizations are the same (Kossek and Zonia, 1993). Differences among these groups are many and important. Black women face racial barriers in organizations that white women do not (Betters-Reed and Moore, 1995). Black men do not have to deal with sexism at the workplace; they benefit from the privileges associated with being male in American society. Where possible, we discuss the different experiences of these groups. However, the limited data preclude an in-depth discussion of the differential effects of race and sex in leadership development methods.

A final boundary is that both authors of this chapter are American white women. Although we try to bring an objective perspective, our lenses cannot help reflecting our own experiences. To add diversity to our own views, we have incorporated feedback from a diverse group of colleagues: trainers and researchers, men and women, African Americans and whites.

This chapter is organized into three main sections. It starts with a discussion of some of the contextual issues involved in the development of white women and of black men and women. The next section reviews common leadership development practices. The final section summarizes and discusses implications of this line of work.

The Context

Leadership development does not happen in a vacuum. To advance in corporate America, African American men and women and white women must overcome considerable obstacles. In this section, first we look at six of the most pervasive barriers. Then we focus on the challenge of developing a managerial identity in the face of stereotypes and socialization practices that automatically portray managers as being white and male.

Barriers to Advancement

Since the early 1980s, there has been substantial documentation that white women as well as men and women of color face several hurdles in addition to the normal challenges of leadership development. In *The New Leaders* (1992), based on interviews with 196 managers, Morrison described six barriers shared by groups historically underrepresented in management.

Prejudice. Prejudice was the barrier most frequently mentioned. Morrison defines prejudice as "the tendency to view people who are different from some reference group in terms of sex, ethnic background, or racial characteristics such as skin color as being deficient" (1992, p. 345). In other words, prejudice is the assumption that being different from the majority group automatically implies an inability to perform.

Several other studies of career barriers have also found prejudice to be a major obstacle, including the 1995 report of the Department of Labor Federal Glass Ceiling Commission's investigation into forces that have blocked advancement of minorities and women in the private sector. Catalyst, an organization devoted to understanding and monitoring the progress of women in organizations, also found that stereotypic preconceptions were a major obstacle (1996). Every woman in a recent study of eighteen prominent African American and white women in the United States reported having to deal with sexism and/or racism on the job (Richie and others, 1997).

Many of these prejudices are passed on as prevalent stereotypes implying that women and people of color are unsuited for senior management. For example, male managers portray women as deficient in the qualities associated with successful management (Heilman, Block, and Martell, 1995). In general, men and women are characterized differently, with males seen as more competent, active, potent, emotionally stable, independent, and rational than their female counterparts. In addition, when women are portrayed as successful managers, they lose some of the positive aspects of the female stereotype of being good with relationships: they are seen as more hostile than women in general. The stereotypes of African Americans and other people of color are even more negative.

Stereotypes become particularly important when leadership potential is evaluated or staffing assignments are made. Stereotypes can get in the way of making decisions based on merit or ability (Ruderman and Ohlott, 1990). Prejudice has an enormous impact, preventing supervisors and peers from seeing others as they really are.

Poor Career Planning. Poor career planning was also identified as a barrier. Women and people of color get limited exposure to the mix of assignments, experiences, and relationships that would prepare them for senior positions. Typically, men get more of the high-visibility, high-stakes line assignments that lead to advancement (Ohlott, Ruderman, and McCauley, 1994). Even at the executive level, women have less authority than men, as indicated by numbers of direct reports (Lyness and Thompson, 1997). African American managers in large corporations are clustered in staff positions and therefore are not getting access to the line experiences needed for advancement (U.S. Department of Labor, Federal Glass Ceiling Commission [hereafter, "Federal Glass Ceiling Commission"], 1995).

Morrison (1992) notes that poor career planning also results from different experiences with mentors and networks. Among other benefits, using mentors and networks allows exchange of job-related information, support, and advice. But many women and nonwhite managers do not have mentors or anyone else to ask for career support, and this deficiency contributes to poor career planning.

Poor Working Environment. The third barrier is a poor working environment. Essentially, this has to do with the pressures of being on a lonely journey in an organization. At the upper levels of organizations, people of color and white women are greatly outnumbered by white men, many of whom (intentionally or not) treat them differently. They are left out of the information loop. To make matters worse, another consequence of this isolation is that many of those being left out feel they have no one they can discuss career issues with or get advice from. This issue is especially pronounced for black women; they receive substantially less collegial support than white women do (Bell and Nkomo, cited in Federal Glass Ceiling Commission, 1995).

Along with isolation, the lack of role models also contributes to a poor working environment (Morrison, 1992). Blacks and white women who rise above middle management have few role models and mentors.

In contrast, ambitious white male managers have many role models with whom to identify.

Lack of Organizational Savvy. The fourth barrier identified by Morrison is lack of organizational savvy. Getting ahead in organizations today requires a certain level of conformity to the business environment. People of color and white women often fail to advance because they don't know how to play the game. They pay insufficient attention to organizational politics and the agendas of colleagues and bosses. They also miss out on some informal ways people learn the ropes: going out after work, for instance, or socializing at the gym or on the golf course. As one sign of this lack of savvy, many women don't know how to negotiate for titles because they assume that others play fairly and give them the titles they deserve (Morrison, 1992).

Comfort Dealing with One's Own Kind. The fifth barrier is the fact that people tend to find greater comfort in dealing with their own kind. People prefer to be with others who are similar (Byrne, 1971). Thus, white men in the dominant business group may be less comfortable reaching out to dissimilar others and including them in the business elite (Kanter, 1977). Bosses take into account their comfort level with a direct report when making a promotion decision (Ruderman and Ohlott, 1994). People who do not fit the mold are informally excluded and denied access to opportunities because differences in gender, cultural background, and race make others uncomfortable. This phenomenon is often more pronounced in situations where the stakes are high.

Balancing Career and Family. The final barrier has to do with the difficulty in balancing career and family. Even in dual career marriages, women still take most of the responsibility for home and family (Morrison, 1992; Newman, 1993). Careers in senior management often require complete dedication. For many women, the childbearing years are the same ones as the career-building years (the time when organizations traditionally expect managers to prove themselves); elder care responsibilities can come at almost any point in a career. Many corporate policies are still based on the 1950s' assumption that there is someone at home to manage family responsibilities.

To succeed in the corporate world, many women give up the idea of having a family altogether. Generally, women executives are less likely than male executives to be married or have children (Lyness and Thompson, 1997). Extreme devotion to career in combination with lack of a family life may exact a cost for those women who choose this type of lifestyle. They lose out on the emotional and developmental benefits from having a family, and they grow different from their colleagues on yet another dimension.

These six barriers are important for our purposes here because they are outside the normal challenges of development. In their journey to the executive suite, nontraditional managers must deal with these obstacles in addition to developing new skills and perspectives. Furthermore, these obstacles are particularly potent because they are not just a function of simple prejudices. Rather, they are reflections of a larger, complicated setting in the United States, where racial relations are steeped in the historical backdrop of slavery (Nkomo, 1992) and gender relations are embedded in the legacy of old-fashioned patriarchy (McBroom, 1992). These larger societal issues form part of the landscape against which the process of leadership development occurs.

Managerial Identity and Demographic Group Membership

In setting the stage for looking at the leadership development process for white women and people of color, it is important also to consider the impact of race and sex on managerial identity. Developing a view of oneself as a leader is a complicated process, involving multiple stages of growth and development (Hill, 1992). This process becomes more complex if the leader does not fit the stereotype of a leader, faces prejudice, and has no role models or help to point the way.

In addition to the normal task of forming a managerial identity, members of groups historically denied these opportunities must grapple with two additional tasks: managing multiple identities and fitting in.

Managing Multiple Identities. Every manager must struggle with developing a self-view as a leader. African Americans and women must figure out how to do this and still maintain a sense of self that incorporates their racial or sexual identity.

The dilemma of trying to manage multiple identities has been eloquently described by Ella Bell (1990) in her research on the bicultural life experience of black career women. She describes the bicultural world these women live in, a world that requires them to develop careers in the professional world (which tends to be white and male) while making a place for themselves and a personal life in the black world. In addition to learning how to be a professional, they must learn how to deal with the tensions arising from having a place in two communities with sometimes conflicting requirements and expectations. According to Bell, out of necessity these women learn how to be boundary spanners, continuously making transitions from one community to the other.

Managing multiple identities is a key issue for the women (most of whom are white) participating in our study of managerial women. They are very drawn to their identity as achievers and place extreme emphasis on work. Yet at the same time, they long for an identity that includes a sense of self beyond work. Along with their managerial identity, they want to incorporate views of themselves as athletes, artists, and musicians, as mothers, lovers, children, and friends. Many of the women talk of "hidden identities," aspects of themselves they feel they have left behind in their quest to become the ultimate manager. They struggle with shaping a multifaceted identity in a business world that emphasizes the managerial role to the exclusion of others.

Fitting In. A second identity-related tension is figuring out what it takes to fit in to an organization. All managers regardless of race and sex struggle with this issue, and it is never easy: what it takes to fit in varies by organization and department. It is, however, generally easier for white men because corporate managerial expectations are more consistent with how they have been socialized. For managers from other demographic groups, this is more difficult.

For white women, there is the issue of the narrow band: the very limited range of acceptable behavior for women managers (Morrison, White, and Van Velsor, 1987). Executive women are to some extent subject to conflicting expectations from their work role and their gender role. They must act like men, but not so much so that they appear "unfeminine." They must act like women but not appear "too feminine." The difficulty is to fashion a coherent identity that embraces some very disparate qualities. To be perceived as an authority, women managers need to engage in both stereotypically female behaviors such as listening and helping others and stereotypically male traits such as being forceful and results-oriented.

Several of the women attending our leadership development program for women talk about the difficulty of being nurturing and forceful at the same time. Ashley, for example, got feedback that she was "more macho than the guys." After reflection, she admitted that it was true. In an effort to be taken seriously, she had adopted an extreme approach because she had seen other women punished for taking softer, more nurturant approaches. After she got this feedback, Ashley vowed to temper some of the pressure she was putting on her staff. She assumed more confidence in her style as a manager and realized that although it was important to be strong-minded she didn't have to be so tough to get results.

Fitting in is even more difficult for women who refuse to jump through the hoops of the narrow band. They do not want to fit in with the stereotypical managerial model that equates individual accomplishment with effectiveness. They prefer an alternative approach, one that relies on the notion that effectiveness and growth come from empowering others (Fletcher, 1996). This relational approach favors behaviors such as enabling others, nurturing, and listening rather than being tough on subordinates.

The relational approach stands in contrast to the view, characteristic of hierarchical organizations, that effectiveness equates with individual achievements. In these organizations, a relational style is undervalued, making women who engage in these behaviors feel as if they are behaving counter to standard practice. Women who see this as their primary way to be effective have a hard time fitting in to traditional organizations.

Fitting in may be even more complicated for African Americans. They face the task of developing an identity as a leader in a setting where African Americans have historically been relegated to lower-level positions. With few role models and coaches to help, they must work on identifying what behavior is acceptable.

One of the issues African Americans deal with is figuring out just how "black" they can be and still be accepted by whites in the organization (Dickens and Dickens, 1991). Some of the managers we have interviewed report being cautioned that to appear as a leader, they must limit how they express their individuality, their blackness. They have been told to tone down their hairstyle, dress, and emotional expressiveness. For many African Americans, the question is how to fit in with corporate America without losing key aspects of themselves.

In our leadership development program for African Americans, conversations about fitting in often deal with expression of strong emotions. Whites have more license to show emotions in organizations and more leeway in how they do it. In order to fit in, blacks have to pay much more attention to managing the perceptions of others. For example, a white man who disagrees with someone else can afford to raise his voice and even pound the table; he will be seen as strong-minded and passionate. If a black man raises his voice and pounds the table, he is more likely to be seen as an aggressive bully.

In sum, achieving a view of oneself as a leader—always a complex process—is far more complicated for people in groups historically underrepresented in the top level of organizations. They do not fit others' (or sometimes even their own) image of the corporate manager, and they must figure out how to be one in the absence of role models and with limited coaching—all this in the face of sometimes severely conflicting expectations.

Leadership Development Practices

With this discussion of career barriers and group identity as background, we now turn to four key leadership development practices described at length in other chapters of this handbook: 360-degree feedback, feedback-intensive programs, challenging assignments, and developmental relationships. We examine how factors of race and gender introduce complexities to these practices. We then describe one other strategy that is critical with people historically underrepresented in management: recognition.

Formal Assessment: 360-Degree Feedback

In recent years, 360-degree feedback instruments (see Chapter One) have become a popular technique. In these structured processes, bosses, peers, direct reports, and sometimes even clients are asked to anonymously rate the effectiveness of an individual manager. This assessment is then compared to self-ratings and shared with the individual. The comparative data help the manager understand where he or she is with regard to a set of behaviors that are linked to managerial effectiveness.

This kind of assessment is important because it allows managers to see themselves as others do. It is particularly important to white women and black managers because they tend to get less informal feedback than white men do (Morrison, 1992).

As is true of other management development tools, most experience with these 360-degree instruments is drawn from the largest pool of managers and executives available in the United States: white men. The success of these assessments hinges on the credibility and usefulness of the feedback. The career barriers described earlier, however, compromise this credibility and applicability. In particular, if these instruments are used with a diverse population, four questions arise:

1. Is the content useful for this population of managers?
2. Is this instrument valid for populations other than white males?
3. Do the norms vary for different groups?
4. Are the ratings biased?

Appropriateness of Assessment Content. An important consideration in deciding to use a 360-degree feedback instrument is the origin of the questions used on the instrument (Van Velsor, Leslie, and Fleenor, 1997). For the feedback to be credible and useful, the questions need to reflect relevant and appropriate managerial competencies. The managerial competencies on most instruments are based on theories of effectiveness or practitioner experience, or some combination of the two, and this basis has in the past made them acceptable to managers at large. However, to be relevant to a diverse managerial population, the instrument must be based on data or theory that reflects a heterogeneous population.

Basing an instrument on only one segment of the managerial population leads to a limited view of effectiveness and competence; including other groups leads to an expanded definition. For example, what is called contextual fluidity, which is the ability to successfully move from one cultural context to another, is obviously an important skill for African Americans in a bicultural world (Dickens and Dickens, 1991). However, it is also becoming an important capacity for all managers, as increasing global diversity demands people who can competently move from one cultural context to another (Thomas, 1996).

Similarly, in addition to demonstrating many of the individual competencies displayed by men in organizations, women managers are also known for taking a relational approach to professional growth and organizational effectiveness (Fletcher, 1996). Women place great value on enabling others, seeing projects holistically, empowering others, and achieving through others (Fletcher, 1996). These are the types of practice that modern, learning organizations are calling for (Senge, 1990) as well as the very competencies required in developing emotionally competent managers (Goleman, 1995). Ironically, these are also practices that tend to be undervalued in traditional models of effectiveness (Fletcher, 1996). Including women's experiences in the content of an instrument therefore leads to an expanded sense of what is effective.

Another consideration: some areas of content generate feedback that is more useful for members of one particular subgroup than another. In the field of educational psychology, Sedlacek and colleagues have found stronger relationships between noncognitive variables and student success for black students than for white ones. For blacks in predominantly white colleges, certain variables are important predictors with respect to grades and persistence in school: positive self-concept, realistic self-appraisal, understanding of and ability to deal with racism, preference of long-range goals over short-term needs, availability of a strong support person, successful leadership experience, demonstrated community service, and academic familiarity (Sedlacek, 1987; Tracey and Sedlacek, 1984, 1985, 1987). These variables reflect on the ability to navigate as a minority in a college environment. There may be an analogous set of noncognitive variables that predict success in the predominantly white business world; it would be a useful tool for feedback for black managers. Like the students, black managers must have a wide range of skills in order to handle the complex problems associated with racism and minority status. Including a more heterogeneous sample of managers in the models forming the basis of 360-degree feedback instruments would lead to more appropriate content.

Validity. In addition to wanting the content of the instrument to be appropriate for a population, it is important that it also be valid for that group. In other words, scores on an instrument should be related to a measure of effectiveness for the target group. This is, of course, important for any population, but with a diverse population it is vital to understand whether the relationship between the instrument scores and the effectiveness criterion is the same for different groups (Van Velsor, Leslie, and Fleenor, 1997). Does a high score on a particular dimension for group A have the same meaning as for group B? For example, does a high score on a measure of building relationships have the same relationship to a criterion for men as it does for women? This is known as comparative validity. For assessment information to be seen as credible and useful, the scores need to mean the same thing for managers of different races and both genders.

Knowledge about the comparative validity of different multirater feedback instruments is relatively sparse. CCL and other providers of these instruments have done some studies with regard to gender and have found that particular instruments have similar relationships to effectiveness for men and women. We are unaware of published reports of the comparative validity for different ethnic or racial groups. CCL currently has a study in process that looks at the comparative validity of one of our 360-degree feedback instruments, for African Americans and whites.

Differences in Norms. Most multirater instruments report assessment data in comparison to some standard or norm. This helps the people getting feedback to understand how they are doing compared to others, which in turn adds to the power of the feedback. Clearly it is important for an instrument to use a normative group that is appropriate for those being assessed.

Men and women of color and white women may be interested in getting feedback on how they compare to their own identity group and also to managers at large. For example, there are some small differences in the norms for different identity groups on a 360-degree evaluation instrument commonly used by the Center (Fleenor, 1995). On most dimensions, African American managers outperform white managers and women score higher than men, but there are a few dimensions for which this pattern is different. These differential norms should be shared, so that women and people of color can put their feedback in context.

Everyone who uses a 360-degree feedback instrument, no matter its source, should pay attention to the normative database. It is important to understand what population the normative database is drawn from and whether there are different norms for various groups. Training manuals and support materials should include these norms.

Bias in Ratings. For feedback to have the desired effects, the recipient must believe the data are credible, important, and useful (Dalton and Hollenbeck, 1996). Feedback that is seen as accurate and honest can be a catalyst for change; that is, after all, the point.

The expected response when managers receive positive feedback is that they see it as indicating an area of strength. The expected response for negative feedback is that the manager sees it as signaling a need for change. There is, however, the potential for this process to go awry should the recipient believe negative feedback is shaped by prejudice and bias (Cox, 1993). Minority men and women managers face the added complexity of figuring out whether prejudice or discrimination has influenced their feedback. Managers are not able to learn from discrepancies between self-views and the views of others if they believe prejudice is involved. Thus, whenever minority managers are included in the population being assessed, the potential for bias becomes an important consideration.

Whether there are actually differences in the ratings that can be attributed to bias is still an open research question. Very little has been done to look explicitly at rater bias in developmental feedback. Numerous studies have been done on rater bias more generally, but their findings are inconsistent. Chen and DiTomaso (1996) have completed a detailed review of this confusing and oftentimes contradictory literature.

Only one study actually looked at bias in the context of developmental 360-degree feedback. This study, reported in 1997 by Mount, Sytsma, Hazucha, and Holt, examined the question of whether or not raters give higher ratings to managers of their own race. Working with a large sample consisting exclusively of managers, the researchers found that some categories of raters (subordinates, peers, and bosses) do indeed assign higher ratings to managers of their own race. White bosses rate whites higher than they do blacks. White subordinates, however, do not rate whites higher than they do blacks. The findings about ratings from white peers were inconclusive. The patterns were different with black raters. All three categories of black raters (bosses, peers, and subordinates) rate blacks' performance higher than whites' performance, suggesting that black managers favor managers of their own race.

One implication for feedback is that black managers with white raters may want to pay the most attention to what their subordinates say. This supports the use of an assessment method that provides a 360-degree view of a person. It also raises questions about the value of getting feedback from a single source, such as a boss. It may be helpful to black managers to get boss ratings from more than one source, including a black boss or senior manager, if one is available.

There has not been a similar study of assessment-for-development ratings with respect to sex. There have, however, been numerous studies of gender effects on performance ratings in general. One study worth noting is a meta-analysis of the literature on gender and evaluation of leaders by Eagly, Makhijani, and Klonsky (1992). This analysis looked across all the experimental studies of leader evaluations. The strength of these studies is that the characteristics of leaders other than sex are held constant. Thus any differences in evaluation of male and female leaders can be attributed to gender. The downside is that these studies are conducted in laboratories with college students, and not in organizations with experienced adult workers.

Looking across sixty-one laboratory studies, Eagly and colleagues found that people evaluate female leaders slightly more negatively than male leaders with equivalent qualifications. This very small trend was magnified under certain circumstances: if women used an autocratic, nonparticipative leadership style (a style that is stereotypically male and currently out of favor), they were evaluated more negatively; and if the evaluator was male, the evaluation was even lower. This suggests that women get lower ratings from men if they act in a way thought to be typically male, inappropriate, or both.

Although the evidence of bias in 360-degree developmental ratings is scant, the fact that many managers believe prejudice to be alive and well in organizations is well documented (Morrison, 1992, Catalyst, 1996, Federal Glass Ceiling Commission, 1995). The implication of this is that if your organization uses 360-degree feedback instruments with diverse populations, you should be equipped to facilitate discussions of how stereotypes may influence results.

Participants may want to figure out to what extent feedback is based on realistic performance evaluation so they can sort out what to change and what not to change. As facilitator of the process, you should help concerned managers probe and try to understand whether ratings are biased. Prepare to discuss the relationship of behaviors to perceptions and how perceptions can be distorted.

A real challenge, however, is to conduct these discussions in a way that recognizes the reality of prejudice but does not provide an easy excuse for overlooking or ignoring negative feedback. It is also important to point out that the perceptions of coworkers are part of the reality at work, regardless of whether those perceptions are accurate.

Despite these difficulties in applying 360-degree feedback practices to women and African American managers, it is important that these managers get access to such assessment. Especially where differences between people make informal communication difficult, facilitated formal assessment processes can help managers get more of the information they need for their own development and to improve performance on their jobs.

The Feedback-Intensive Program

One way to ensure that white women and African American men and women get opportunities for assessment is through a formal feedback-intensive program (described fully in Chapter Two of this handbook).

African American managers and women managers have the option of attending traditional, heterogeneous programs or programs specially tailored for their identity group, the latter called single-identity programs. CCL offers an African American leadership program and a women's leadership program. Like CCL's traditional mixed-group programs, both of these focus on issues of leadership development; however, they do so in a setting that encourages additional content having to do with identity issues and complexities in the workplace arising from the career barriers discussed earlier. They also help people capitalize on their special cultural and situational life experiences, which are a function of membership in that group.

Although single-identity programs have many advantages, they remain a controversial environment for development (Ohlott and Hughes-James, 1997). The next section looks at the arguments for and against such training. These arguments are summarized in Table 10.1.

TABLE 10.1. ADVANTAGES AND DISADVANTAGES OF ATTENDING A SINGLE-IDENTITY GROUP FEEDBACK-INTENSIVE PROGRAM.

Advantages
Validates experience of being minority manager in a majority organization
Offers safe, supportive environment for sharing experiences, taking risks, practicing skills
Provides opportunity to be with others like oneself, in contrast to the isolation usually experienced; provides source of peers, role models, and chance to rehearse culture
Pays attention to appropriateness of feedback for the identity group: uses feedback-intensive instruments created for the population or provides feedback on traditional instruments with norms for the single-identity group
Helps manager determine what parts of his or her feedback are valid versus what parts may be filtered through prejudicial lenses
Contains specialized content relevant for the identity group

Disadvantages
May highlight perceived differences, producing stigma of deficiency
Training does not take place in the "real world"; generalizability of skills may be affected if not learned in a mixed-race or mixed-gender setting
Participation may suggest managers are receiving favorable treatment or are conspiring against majority-group managers, creating the potential for backlash

Advantages of Single-Identity Feedback-Intensive Programs. Perhaps the biggest advantage of these programs is that they offer the participants a validating experience. They give managers the opportunity to learn, through the sharing that takes place, that what they feel and experience is similar for other women or African American managers, that they are not alone or crazy. The words of one woman manager poignantly express this feeling of normalization:

> This program was just so powerful, because I think I didn't realize how much angst I carried inside myself, that I just didn't have anybody to affirm it or validate it, so I just kind of went forward and carried it. Being there I found myself really emotionally touched, which I wasn't really prepared for. . . . I thought it would be more of a cogni-

tive enrichment, but instead I was just overwhelmed at the emotional release that I had, and I just think it was a validation that my trip had been hard, it wasn't in my head. It was some real tough times.

A second benefit of these programs is that they offer a safe, supportive place to share experiences, doubts, fears, and successes as well as the experiences of racism and/or sexism. Participants work on issues that could not be discussed in a mixed group.

White women and people of color, especially those who are the "firsts" in their organizations, are more likely to have their work and behavior scrutinized for mistakes and be held to higher performance standards (Morrison, 1992; Federal Glass Ceiling Commission, 1995). Given this, they must be cautious with certain behaviors, such as publicly exposing vulnerability. Single-group programs offer people space for taking risks, asking questions, making mistakes, and expressing feelings without fear of being labeled inferior or being ridiculed or reprimanded (Baskerville, 1992; Josefowitz, 1990).

In a program with similar others, managers can practice new skills and "let their guard down" in a safe, supportive environment. Martin, an African American participant, explains: "In a mixed group, I definitely would not have opened up and exposed myself because in the back of my mind I would try to avoid reinforcing negative perceptions generalized about African Americans."

A third benefit of such a program is that it is very nurturing and supportive. Many of these managers, particularly African Americans, are isolated in their organizations. They have no other black managers to learn from, get feedback from, or socialize with. The single-group experience gives them a room full of peers and role models. The comfort-with-your-own-kind factor that contributes to white male managers' hiring other white male managers kicks in for these African American managers. For many, it is the first time in their careers they have been surrounded by African Americans facing similar corporate managerial challenges. For many, it is their first experience, in a work-related setting, of being in the majority.

At a CCL conference, Derald Sue, a noted psychologist specializing in multicultural counseling, explained how important it is for people to have occasions where they cluster with similar others. According to Sue (cited in Morrison, Ruderman, and Hughes-James, 1993, p. 65), clustering provides "cultural nutrients" for members: "All groups, all cultures, have a need to practice and rehearse their culture. Especially with racial and ethnic minorities in the workforce in institutions that are primarily white in orientation, there is a chronic sense of invalidation that occurs."

This opportunity to be with others who are likely to face similar job situations can be extremely reinforcing for people who are relatively isolated in their own organization. But more than support, they also learn some solutions, ideas, and approaches that have worked for others, as they share information about how to manage the workplace and themselves in it.

Another advantage of single-identity intensive-feedback programs has to do with actual feedback of data. These programs can use feedback instruments created just for the population, or customized from traditional instruments. For instance, a special 360-degree feedback instrument was developed for our feedback-intensive program for women; in addition to feedback on traditional leadership skills, areas of special relevance to women in predominantly male workplaces were added. The program for African Americans uses the same 360-degree instrument used in our most popular traditional program, but it includes norms for African Americans. These norms provide validation that African Americans have different experiences in organizations than whites do. We are currently investigating both the criterion validity of the 360-degree instrument used in the program for African American managers and the theoretical and empirical database it is drawn from to ensure the instrument is fully appropriate for African American managers.

Women-only or African American–only programs help the managers figure out what aspects of their feedback are unique to them and what aspects are a function of being in a minority position. This happens through discussion of feedback, presentation of normative data for their group, and peer feedback from other managers in the program. If negative performance feedback is received, these managers must deal with the additional step of ciphering out what's valid in the feedback from what may be filtered through prejudicial lenses. Single-identity programs help with this process if facilitators are attuned to the problem and incorporate content that addresses it.

Another key advantage of single-identity programs is the opportunity to use specialized content in addition to the standard content of understanding strengths and weaknesses as they relate to leadership. Although they use different methodologies, the two CCL single-identity programs address how being in a minority position in an organization affects leadership development; they also cover the barriers to advancement identified earlier and provide a springboard for discussing strategies to manage them.

In addition, the program for African American managers brings in content on the four phases of the development of black managers from Dickens and Dickens (1991): entry, adjusting, planned growth, and success. It also incorporates the concepts of cultural paranoia and protective hesitation, two common coping reactions to a racial climate. These concepts help to explain certain misunderstandings arising between blacks and whites.

Cultural paranoia is a sociological concept describing a coping mechanism that has evolved for dealing with the consequences of racism. It has to do with expectations of mistreatment and the self-preparation one must go through to cope with a potentially racialized situation. Protective hesitation is an individual behavior in which blacks hesitate before interacting with whites, as a way of protecting themselves from inadvertently stimulating biases of whites. Protective hesitation means being cautious in interactions with whites; it can take the form of a black person preplanning or prethinking words and actions before approaching a white person, knowing that how he says something may be held against him.

The program for women has specialized content as well. It includes a section on understanding and recognizing political behavior in organizations, since a lack of organizational savvy is often a barrier to women's advancement (Morrison, 1992; Catalyst, 1996). The women's program also places more value on relationships than many mixed-gender programs do, especially the potential clash between how women value relationships and the likely devaluing of relationships by the corporate culture (Miller, 1986; Van Velsor and Hughes-James, 1990). Finally, the women's program also has content dealing with the difficulty of managing a multiple-role lifestyle, since this is an issue for many women and is often cited as an impediment to women's careers (Morrison, 1992). The program helps women deepen their understanding of what they value and want out of life.

Despite these benefits, single-identity programs remain controversial. There are many reasons why people who belong to these demographic groups may not choose to use them. Most of the literature that describes arguments against single-identity group programs relates to those for women. We believe these questions apply to the program for African Americans as well.

Disadvantages of Single-Identity Feedback-Intensive Programs.

Among the questions raised is the argument that because they highlight perceived differences, single-identity programs prove detrimental in the long run. Heilman (1995) argues that programs designed only for women can inadvertently nourish stereotypic attitudes in men. According to this line of thought, if women have special needs, as the existence of a women-only program attests, they must be "different." These differences, in turn, draw attention to perceptions of deficiency and inferiority (Fondas, 1986; Langrish, 1980). Managers may choose to enroll in programs provided to their majority counterparts because they do not want other people to think they are lacking in any way.

Then there is the "real world" argument. Proponents of this argument (for example, Langrish, 1980) believe that training should mirror the so-called real world, the workplace dominated by male managers. Single-identity group programs create an artificial environment for social interaction since majority managers are absent. The belief is that knowledge, skills, and experiences used in the workplace should be learned in mixed settings, or else the generalizability of certain skills is affected (Fondas, 1986).

The potential for backlash is another reason given to avoid single-identity programs. The feelings of togetherness that are so validating for the single-identity program participants may be threatening to others. Participants in segregated programs may be seen as receiving favorable treatment (Harlan and Weiss, 1980), thus fostering resentment among peers and bosses. There is also the concern that single-identity group programs are designed to degrade whites or males. Some people see participants in single-identity groups together and assume they are conspiring in some way, especially when all the program participants are drawn from the same organization. Managers may avoid participating for fear of being labeled militant (Baskerville, 1992).

Our trainers report that, in fact, very little if any such bashing takes place, no more so than in the mixed-group programs. Participants are highly focused on their own strengths and weaknesses; they do not spend time tearing apart other groups.

Which Is Better? Although we have described several possible reasons for managers choosing not to attend a single-identity program, we believe the advantages far outweigh the disadvantages. The criticisms against these programs were primarily taken from the literature; our classroom experiences indicate the arguments may be concerns for the managers but that the strengths of these programs outweigh the concerns. However, the bottom line of this discussion is that managers must choose for themselves which type of program leaves them more comfortable. (For guidance in this decision, see "Questions to Consider.")

Both single-identity and mixed-identity programs carefully provide feedback and support for growth and development. They both offer expert help in understanding one's strengths and weaknesses. Participants need to decide whether they prefer to take their journey of self-exploration in a standard way that has been used by the majority of executives, or whether they prefer a customized approach in the company of others likely to be experiencing similar career barriers. Both choices are good ones. The important point is that people be given valid feedback in a competent, caring, and relevant way.

Selecting a Mixed-Group or Single-Identity Development Program: Questions to Consider.

Managers must evaluate their own needs and reasons for attending a development program. The following questions may guide the individual as he or she decides which is more appropriate: a traditional mixed-group program or a program designed for a single-identity group.

- Does the manager believe that race (or gender) is affecting his or her career?
- Is the manager more comfortable learning in a mixed group or in a group made up of people similar to himself or herself?
- Does the manager at present need a sense of connection and bonding with others who are like him or her and who may be experiencing similar career issues?
- Does the manager want to try out and practice new skills and behaviors in an environment that mirrors his or her organization or in an environment made up of others similar to himself or herself?
- Has the manager already attended a traditional development program?
- If the person's organization routinely sends its managers to a traditional leadership development program, would attending a single-gender or single-race program make him or her feel left out?

(*Source:* Ohlott and Hughes-James, 1997)

Challenging Assignments

Challenging job assignments—job experiences that push people to do something new or differently—are another key strategy for development. Challenging jobs are important to advancement because they offer the opportunity for learning to handle a variety of leadership tasks and positions (see Chapter Four).

Such jobs promote growth for all managers, men and women, black and white. Through studies conducted at different times, we have found that executives attribute much of their success to challenging experiences (McCall, Lombardo, and Morrison, 1988; Van Velsor and Hughes-James, 1990; Rogolsky and Dalton, 1995). There are, however, some noticeable differences in how challenges occur in various demographic groups. Senior executives of both genders and a variety of ethnicities have their own stories to tell about the kinds of challenge they experienced. Women and people of color don't always have access to the kind of challenging assignments they need for development, and they must navigate additional challenges stemming from racism and sexism that are not experienced by majority men.

A comparison of job experiences found that men have a greater variety of challenging job assignments than women (Van Velsor and Hughes-James, 1990). In particular, men reported greater exposure to start-up situations, fix-it situations, and switches from line to staff jobs, all of which are experiences fruitful for learning. Generally, compared to men at the same level of management, women experience their jobs as less critical and less visible to the organization (Ohlott, Ruderman, and McCauley, 1994). This suggests that although women and men may be promoted to similar organizational levels, men are actually exposed to more significant learning opportunities. This is a subtle form of prejudice in which men and women holding jobs at similar levels appear to get different developmental opportunities.

Additional Challenges. In addition to less experience with challenges critical to development, women experience additional challenges that men do not (Morrison, White, and Van Velsor, 1987; Rogolsky and Dalton, 1995). These extra challenges stem from some of the barriers mentioned earlier: obstacles arising from prejudice, isolation, and the multiple demands made on women. Women pioneers in organizations argue that on top of the day-to-day press of business, dealing with discrimination and harassment is a significant barrier to accomplishment. Women who are the first to hold a position have to struggle to gain acceptance and then must continuously work to convince people they are capable. There is no mention of these types of challenge in the experiences of white male executives (McCall, Lombardo, and Morrison, 1988).

We are currently investigating differences in the experiences of black managers and white managers with a sample of managers from the mid-1990s. The patterns we are finding are similar to those of the comparison of white women to white men. For example, African American managers of both genders experience proportionally fewer key job assignments than the white managers do, and they tend to get fewer of the really critical opportunities. Moreover, like the white women, African American managers of both genders experience challenges that white men do not. They had a similar being-first experience, as the first black manager in their organization's history or the first to obtain a certain position.

Another form of challenge emerging from our preliminary analysis is something we call "race mattered." This category depicts the incidents of prejudice, stereotyping, and discrimination that African Americans have experienced throughout their careers—situations when race mattered. Examples include dealing with other people's perceptions that they got job assignments and promotions because of being African American, and having to confront the boss about racial tension in the relationship after receiving negative performance appraisals. Managers described these race-mattered experiences as leading to lasting change in how they manage. "I learned that to succeed, my management competence would need to be clearly demonstrable to all," one said. Another added, "I learned that I will have to find innovative ways to break down some barriers I face."

As a group, the nonmajority leaders experience other sources of challenge in addition to those key events mentioned here. Many of these stem from the fact that they must do their jobs under different circumstances than what their white male counterparts face (Morrison, 1992). One additional burden carried by many of the managers is to act as a role model or to represent their demographic group. In the name of "diversity," they are sometimes called on to speak about their experiences to the media or others in the organization.

Janice, a white engineering manager, told us that she has been photographed over and over again for recruiting materials on college campuses. African American managers are often sought out to be mentors for others and spokespersons for the black community. Successful women of all races are frequently asked to represent women's issues or mentor large numbers of more junior women. Most find it difficult to say no, yet these opportunities add another set of duties to all their other job obligations. One African American male manager told us, "It feels like I have three jobs—that I have my job in research and development, that I have a job as representative of the company on black stuff, and then I have a job in terms of connecting and aiding the cause of black people in the organization."

A further challenge comes from some of the identity-related issues raised earlier. Many of the new leaders live in two worlds and must balance career demands with outside demands. Women often have additional responsibilities for child care and elder care that men do not. African American managers face the challenge of making and maintaining a place for themselves in the African American community. One of our program participants, an African American woman who was the head of a nonprofit agency and had several advanced degrees, felt it was incumbent on her to act as a role model in the community and thus took on substantial responsibilities working with African American teenagers who were either single mothers or pregnant.

Given all this, it is often true that the level of overall challenge experienced by women and people of color is different from that of a white man in a similar job. Managers who are female or of color may have to do additional work to get the same job done.

Implications. Morrison (1992) cautions that it is easy to misuse challenge in developing women or African American leaders. On the one hand there is the danger of too much challenge. Extreme amounts of challenge, and the stress that comes with it, can make it difficult to learn at all. Some organizations are in such a hurry to get a black or a woman into the executive suite that they try to rush development and give managers key jobs before they are ready. In one company we worked with, a black executive was given a key operating role without ever having had any significant line experience. Although he was very talented and well educated (Stanford MBA), this was an enormous and difficult transition for him.

On the other hand, some organizations err on the side of too little challenge. Fearing that women may fail, executives and managers tend to be more cautious with promoting them (Ruderman, Ohlott, and Kram, 1995). It takes more steps for women than men to advance to the same level of an organization because women tend to get more promotions of smaller scope (Flanders and Anderson, 1973). The danger is that such a cautious approach limits learning. Managers learn from taking on major responsibilities, dealing with risks, and handling novel situations; modest changes in job responsibilities create less opportunity to learn. This situation also creates a catch-22 for further career advancement. The lower the developmental value of an assignment a woman receives, the greater the rationale for bypassing her in future promotions (Auster, 1989).

A second implication of the different challenges experienced by various groups has to do with organizations' need to understand how they use challenges for development. Meaningful job assignments are among the most potent forces for development. Some organizations are better at using challenge for development than others. If they are to develop potential executives from *all* backgrounds, organizations must look at how they use challenge in their setting and assess how developmental assignments are distributed to different groups.

Another means of helping organizations use challenging assignments for development has to do with the support given to those managers who take them on. Morrison (1992) has found that multiple sources of support help managers select which additional challenges to accept, and then help deal with them. Among the many forms of support are collegiality, information, feedback, and stress relief.

Developmental Relationships

Developmental relationships—alliances that enhance a person's learning and development—are a successful strategy for fostering leadership development, but there are certain obstacles and complicating dynamics for women and people of color. Here we focus on the effects of race and gender on two specific types of developmental relationships: informal junior-senior mentoring relationships and informal networks.

Junior-Senior Mentoring Relationships. As important as relationships are in the development equation (see Chapter Five for a comprehensive discussion), women and people of color can find them particularly difficult to obtain. Researchers have found that African Americans develop fewer mentoring relationships than whites (Cox and Nkomo, 1991) and that women are less likely to be mentored than men (Ragins and Cotton, 1991). There are limited opportunities for both these groups to develop mentoring relationships with their counterparts because they simply are not there, especially at senior levels (Morrison, 1992; Federal Glass Ceiling Commission, 1995; Thomas, 1990). African Americans who want to develop relationships with other African Americans are more likely to have to go beyond their immediate department and hierarchical boundaries (Thomas, 1990). Jennifer, a white manager, found that senior white women were reluctant to support her, and bitter because they had been denied access to similar mentors in their own lonely journey up the corporate ladder. In our studies, we have heard of similar stories from other white women and African American managers.

These situations leave minority managers in the very difficult position of relying on white males for developmental relationships, which is often not forthcoming. White men tend to associate with others like themselves (Dickens and Dickens, 1991), thus reducing opportunities to create alliances with members of other groups. Some white men worry that supporting women and people of color may be seen as a threat to their next promotion—or even their job (Kram and Hall, 1996).

Ragins and Cotton (1991) found several perceived barriers to women's obtaining a male mentor: (1) women have less informal access to men, such as through sports or other social outings, (2) women are reluctant to develop a mentoring relationship with a man because others may disapprove of the relationship, (3) women fear that mentors or others may misconstrue it as a sexual advance, and (4) potential male mentors are unwilling to engage in relationships with women. Several participants in our study on the influence of race on managers' development have described white male managers as reluctant to form alliances because they are not willing to take the risk of having a junior minority manager fail. They fear possible repercussions on their own careers as well as the implications for future white women and people of color.

All these undercurrents contribute to lack of mentoring support for white women and people of color. In addition, there are special dynamics in cross-race and cross-gender relationships that affect the nature of the relationships and the forms of support that people receive. For instance, in both cross-race and cross-sex relationships, white women and people of color receive career support (such as sponsorship, advocacy for promotions, feedback, and coaching), but they receive less psychosocial support (the emotional, interpersonal bond) than people in same-race and same-sex relationships (Thomas, 1990). This difference is likely due to the social complexities involved. For instance, people in cross-gender relationships are less likely to engage in socializing behaviors such as joining each other for activities after work (Ragins and McFarlin, 1990); socializing is one means for relationships to develop into friendships, a function of psychosocial support.

At our 1992 conference on workplace diversity, David Thomas described the complexities encountered in cross-race and cross-sex relationships. Examples of these complexities are negative stereotyping of and incorrect assumptions about each other; inhibitions about sexuality and intimacy; discomfort in cross-race relationships in organizations experiencing racial conflict (is the person of color "selling out?"); and pressure from public scrutiny, given the higher visibility of cross-race and cross-sex relationships (Morrison, Ruderman, and Hughes-James, 1993).

Given these complexities, it is understandable that the managers in these relationships keep their emotional distance, forming less intense and less personalized relationships (Thomas, 1989). The implication is that white women and people of color in cross-sex or cross-race relationships are at a disadvantage; they may miss out on the psychosocial component of mentoring, such as developing professional identity, friendship, counseling, confirmation, and acceptance. We already know that white women and people of color face additional challenges when it comes to fitting in and managing multiple identities, from working in an isolated environment and from lack of access to informal and formal assessment. All of these challenges are somewhat alleviated with a strong mentoring relationship. By not receiving support from cross-race and cross-gender relationships, women and African American managers are missing out on a critical role that mentoring relationships could serve for them.

Network Relationships. Networks are another form of developmental relationship, and as with mentoring relationships they are important in the career development process (Ibarra, 1995). They provide a form of support for managers who share similar issues and challenges; provide informal organizational information channels; lead to sources of feedback on abilities, performance, and perceptions of others; and enhance organizational savvy (Morrison, 1992).

Two types of relationships are formed through networks: instrumental and expressive. Dan, a senior manager of a division that was growing, was posting a newly created position. He had been working on a special task force with Kathryn, a manager just beginning her career in the company. He thought the new position would be a good match for Kathryn, so he called her and told her about the job. That evening Kathryn called Robin, her friend and confidante who had joined the company at the same time as she, to share her excitement at Dan's interest in her career, and to ask Robin's help in thinking through the pros and cons of applying for the new position.

Dan's relationship with Kathryn is an example of an instrumental relationship: one that provides job-related, career-enhancing benefits such as access to resources, exchange of information, expertise, advice, political access, and material resources. Kathryn's relationship with Robin is an example of an expressive relationship. Characterized by higher levels of closeness and trust than ties that are only instrumental, expressive relationships provide friendship and social support (Ibarra, 1993).

In some ways, formal networks resemble a formal organizational chart: they consist of work-related relationships such as subordinate-supervisor dyads, workgroups, project teams, and committees. These relationships tend to produce (but are not limited to) mostly instrumental relationships. Informal networks, on the other hand, emerge naturally within the organization. They are usually broader than formal networks because they include relationships that are work-related, social, or both, and because they are more likely to produce expressive relationships in addition to instrumental ones. Another distinction between formal and informal networks is that informal networks are selected by the individual, who thus creates a network as diverse or homogeneous as he or she wants. In this sense, informal networks can be used as a strategy for career advancement because they are determined by the manager. It is this type of network that the research literature has focused on in relation to racial and sexual differences.

The strategic benefits of networks can be substantial. The composition of a person's network can determine her access to resources, power, and ability to implement her agenda (Ibarra, 1993). That is, the higher the organizational status of the people in someone's network, and the further out in the organization the network reaches, the potentially more powerful it is.

For women and people of color, the networks are likely to be heavily white because that is whom they have most contact with. Cross-race and cross-sex relationships, you will remember, are less likely to develop into close friendships and so tend to be no more than instrumental. Also, the networks of women and people of color are also likely to be composed of similar others because that is who they are drawn to for friend-ship (Ibarra, 1995, forthcoming) and for the sense of validation pro-vided by "cultural nutrients" (Sue, cited in Morrison, Ruderman, and Hughes-James, 1993). These are the relationships that yield expressive ties. Yet, because women and people of color are not prevalent in or-ganizations, minority managers have difficulty finding cultural nutrients within their immediate work environment, so they must reach far into the organization to establish network relationships that produce ex-pressive ties (Ibarra, 1993, 1995).

For all these reasons, minority managers tend to have more racially heterogeneous networks with fewer expressive ties, more contacts out-side their immediate groups, and fewer relationships with high-status individuals (Ibarra, 1995). It is clear that white women and people of color have different network opportunities and therefore differing forms of relationships, resulting in additional challenges in obtaining devel-opmental relationships.

Implications. There are numerous actions that white women and peo-ple of color can take to increase their access to relationships for learn-ing. Attending a single-identity training program provides an excellent source of support in a safe environment. It also sets the foundation for networks and developmental relationships outside of one's organization.

Many participants in the Center's programs maintain contact with one another long after the end of the program. For instance, in the women's feedback-intensive program, peer groups are created for the women to use as sounding boards, to provide advice, feedback, and sup-port throughout the program. Many of the women stay in touch with other participants after the program through round-robin letters and calls. The program for African American managers has recently created a Website for its alumni, to serve as an electronic means of connecting with fellow African Americans. The relationships that are formed in these pro-grams often lead to important sources of networking and friendship.

Another avenue for increasing access to developmental relationships with senior managers is an organization's formal mentoring programs.

These programs are sponsored by the company, but the individual manager has to take the initiative to enroll. Individuals must also take the initiative to seek out mentors (minority and majority managers), look for natural learning opportunities in regular work activities, and avoid overrelying on one mentor by developing relationships with several. In our current study of the influence of race on managerial development, one manager described his devastation when his mentor left the company. He realized that he was on his own and that it was critical to set up his own network in order to cultivate multiple relationships.

On the reverse side, becoming a mentor also has its payoffs. Research has shown that managers serving in mentor positions are colearners, too, and the "seniors" also receive important benefits from the relationship (Kram and Hall, 1996; McCauley and Hughes-James, 1994).

Likewise, if organizations offer employee associations or single-identity networks, white women and people of color might gain by joining them. Mary, an African American manager in our study, is cochair of the black employee network recently established at her corporation. She described the variety of roles the network serves for African American managers: "We have subteams responsible for recruitment and retention, community involvement and marketplace imaging, education and awareness, and employee development. We have done many things—like, presented to our senior leadership team, who in turn gave us feedback on how well we are doing. The network also has guest speakers who are successful people of color. We have a mentor program. And if nothing else, I can just call somebody in my office and say 'Hey, I heard this was going on out there; tell me about it.'"

Providing access to others like oneself through such formal mechanisms helps minority managers broaden their informal social network and provides opportunities to create expressive ties as well as instrumental ones. Other sources are found outside the organization, in local or national professional groups and community or volunteer organizations. Both offer access to other white women and people of color, as well as opportunities to help others.

Recognition

The development experiences we have described so far—360-degree feedback, feedback-intensive program, challenging assignments, and developmental relationships—are significant for all managers. When combined into a well-thought-out system, these experiences interact to facilitate the growth of adults in leadership positions. However, studies of the career experiences of women and people of color suggest that a critical piece is missing. The missing strategy is recognition (Morrison, 1992).

Recognition is important because it reinforces managers for their education, training, skills, risk taking, and capabilities. Rewards acknowledge a job well done. This in turn enhances self-esteem and increases commitment to the organization. Furthermore, rewards symbolize worth and value to the organization.

In many organizations there is a reluctance to give people of color and women the same rewards that go to white male executives. The new leaders are not getting the same return on their investment in self as the more traditional managers. They receive fewer rewards and resources than they legitimately deserve.

One type of recognition reflecting a large differential between white men and other managers is compensation. There is a great deal of evidence that white men lead the way in compensation even when women and people of color are comparably qualified. According to the report of the Federal Glass Ceiling Commission, (1995, p. 9) ". . . African American men with professional degrees earn only 79 percent of the amount of their white male counterparts; African American women with professional degrees earn only 60 percent of what white males earn." This same report found that "the ratio of female-to-male earnings in managers' jobs ranged from a low of 50 percent in the banking industry to a high of 85 percent for managers in human services" (p. 13).

Another significant form of reward is promotion, and here too there are differences in how decisions are made. Managers outside the mainstream usually carry the responsibility for a particular job before getting the formal promotion. One organization we worked with was reluctant to reward women with big promotions (Ruderman, Ohlott, and Kram, 1995) and often required them to become "acting manager" or fill "assistant positions" before they were promoted to the actual position. When they asked why, the women were told they were not "ready"— even though men with similar career histories were promoted directly to those slots without first serving in an apprenticeship position. Similar situations happen to black managers (Dickens and Dickens, 1991).

These small promotions create discrepancies in recognition. They make capable, competent managers feel devalued. In the words of one of our African American study participants, "My boss tells me I'm doing extremely well . . . but here I am at this level down here and those people with [fewer direct reports], with less challenge, a narrower scope to their work are at a higher level. And in the salary plane, they are thinking about bringing me to the same level this year. I don't know how to process that in my head without being angry."

Women and men of color often work under a double burden: they believe they work harder than their majority counterparts and receive less recognition. They are dealing with additional challenges, such as being the first and pressures to perform better than white men. This creates a feeling of imbalance that Morrison suggests leads to turnover or ambivalence about advancing in the corporation. Many women (Catalyst, 1996) and African Americans (Dickens and Dickens, 1991) are leaving corporate life because they do not feel the rewards for investing in their career are there. To keep people of color and women with executive potential in the corporation and on track with their development, it is important that organizations reward them fairly and appropriately.

A different problem with rewards is that they can become overused. In an effort to make their diversity efforts highly visible, some corporations give out rewards to people of color and white women before the managers are ready. For example, Linda, a white woman we worked with, had been promoted too fast and was struggling in a job she wasn't prepared for. This led many people—including Linda herself—to question the integrity of the diversity effort. For rewards to be used as force for development, they must be seen as deserved.

One complexity in using rewards for development is that they have the potential to be misused through overapplication or underapplication. Overly positive, unearned rewards are as much of a problem as lack of recognition.

Although recognition as an element for development comes out of Morrison's work on the new leaders, it seems to us that it is an important strategy for development for all potential leaders. Developing executive leadership skills requires an incredible investment of time, energy, and effort. Recognition for handling challenges well, taking risks, learning, and growing is essential and should be there for all.

Implications for Practitioners

To foster development of a diverse group of managers, those responsible for leadership development within an organization need to make some changes. The basic practices of 360-degree feedback, feedback-intensive programs, challenging assignments, and developmental relationships are as important for the development of women and people of color as they are for white men. These experiences promote and sustain development and address the common needs of all employees. They improve everybody's leadership potential.

However, the harsh reality is that women and people of color have less access to these experiences than white males. If they are to develop their full leadership strength and contribute fully to their organizations, this reality must change. Companies must modify their development practices to ensure that they are accessible to all and appropriately applied. One other concern is that these strategies not be the only major forces for development in this population. Recognition of skills, efforts, and abilities plays a key role in the leadership development process and should not be overlooked.

What can human resource professionals do to make sure their development programs fully address the needs of white women and men and women of color? Here are some ideas:

• Increase the opportunities for informal assessment of women and people of color by dealing with their isolation. Encourage development of formal employee associations or networks for particular identity groups. These homogeneous groups help managers share common experiences and concerns. They give managers the opportunity to form developmental relationships with each other. Such relationships provide support as well as opportunities for informal feedback. Since 1991, Raychem Corporation has had a women's network program to address the isolation of women in the company (Federal Glass Ceiling Commission, 1995).

• Encourage women and people of color to take advantage of opportunities for formal developmental assessment. Structured assessment and feedback, such as that offered through 360-degree instruments, can be part of a larger developmental program. Opportunities exist to get this feedback in a single-identity or mixed-identity group. One industry association we work with has arranged for large numbers of its managerial women to participate in feedback-intensive programs. This association sponsors a single-identity program for high-potential women from different organizations in the industry so that women can get support from each other and assessment data at the same time.

• Educate facilitators and trainers in how to provide 360-degree feedback to a diverse population. Make them aware of the norms for different groups. Prepare them to handle discussions about the impact of prejudice on perceptions. Make sure they select feedback tools based on diverse samples and valid for multiple groups.

• Help decision makers understand how to develop and create appropriately challenging assignments, taking into account the extra challenges experienced by African American managers and white women managers. Too little challenge results in little growth; too much challenge overwhelms the learning processes. Decision makers need guidance in matching individual managers with developmental assignments; they may need training in understanding the different sources of challenge and identifying them in assignments. One major American corporation we work with is studying the distribution of assignments among blacks and whites, men and women. It relies heavily on challenging assignments for development and is interested in seeing that all managers get access to key developmental opportunities. In the process of doing this, the company's leaders are improving their skills in identifying and creating challenging assignments.

• Help managers learn from these challenging assignments. Although challenging situations provide opportunities for development, they do not guarantee it. They only provide the data for possible learning. To help people extract learning from the experience, make sure the assignment includes some opportunity for reflection (Seibert, 1996).

• Educate majority managers on how to initiate and develop relationships with people who are different from themselves. Relational competency is a key requirement for successful performance in the organizations of today and the near future (Goleman, 1995; Hall and Associates, 1996). People skilled in relationships with those different from themselves can use these skills broadly in organizations. At Digital Equipment, Barbara Walker used "core groups" to help develop these relational skills (Walker and Hansen, 1992). The groups provided opportunities for discussing and understanding differences. Top-level managers met with blacks and women to openly discuss their thoughts and feelings about racial and gender differences. The groups gave all attendees practice in getting along with each other. This approach allowed people to explore, and sometimes even confront, their stereotypes and assumptions. Other models and methods of teaching relational competencies in diverse organizations are available (Ferdman and Brody, 1996).

• Examine the formal developmental relationships presently offered in your organization: formal mentoring programs, mentoring circles, learning partners, and so forth. Are they genuinely accessible to managers not in the mainstream? These kinds of programs provide learning opportunities and support to everyone involved, but they are especially important for overcoming the extra challenges faced by white women and people of color.

• Review the types and levels of rewards distributed to members of different groups. Specifically, compensation, promotion, and bonus levels need to be reviewed to assess whether or not there are disparities in race or gender. Such disparities undermine the best-laid plans for developing diversity. Softer forms of rewards (invitations to work with senior executives, announcements of achievements, awards) need to be examined as well.

A Systemic Approach to Leadership Development

Modifying opportunities and procedures for assessment, effectively using challenge, shoring up systems of support, and assessing the fairness of formal and informal rewards are important steps to take in developing the leadership abilities of women and people of color; however, these steps should not be considered in isolation from one another. It is important that these elements be considered interdependent parts of a larger system of development. They work in concert with one another; together they are more than the sum of the parts.

Bell Atlantic, for example, has developed a leadership diversity program that weaves these elements together. Their Accelerating Leadership Diversity (ALD) process follows a strategy of combining assessment, mentoring relationships, and a significant leadership development course with highly challenging assignments. Participants in ALD are part of a group whose members provide each other with support. In addition, they are assigned a mentor, assessed through a 360-degree instrument as part of a leadership development program, asked to publicly commit to a personal development plan, exposed to workshops on power and politics, and given assignments with significant responsibilities. The assessment data they receive help them deal with the demands of their jobs. The support they receive from each other and their mentors helps them understand the assessment data and deal with the stretches inherent in developmental assignments. Participation in this program brings with it recognition of being high-potential, which helps to reinforce lessons learned. The integrated nature of this program helps to maximize the developmental power of the different practices.

In considering the interdependencies of strategies of assessment, challenge, support, and recognition, it is important that these strategies be balanced (Morrison, 1992). For example, too much job challenge without recognition and support leads to problems. The extra challenges women and people of color experience can deter even the most ambitious of people unless they are mitigated by support and recognition. Organizations are losing some of their most promising talent because challenges are not counterbalanced with support, recognition, and assessment. A contrasting example: too much support without much challenge or assessment leads to superficial learning. Inappropriate recognition, such as continuously putting minorities in the limelight, can create resentment from peers and overscrutiny of the managers.

Developing leaders need a balance of elements of all four of these forces. This issue of balancing assessment, challenge, support, and recognition is discussed in both of our single-identity group development programs for women and African Americans. Participants discuss the issue so they can figure out how to manage areas where they may be out of balance. This discussion, however, is even more appropriate at the organizational level, looking across groups of employees. Most methods of managing imbalance require organizational solutions as well as individual ones. The modifications discussed earlier offer ways to help balance these four principles in an organization.

Organizational Strategies for Diversity

In addition to examining how these elements of leadership development interact with one another, it is important to consider them in the context of the larger organizational system promoting diversity. To effectively develop diversity, the whole organization needs to be in the picture. Providing African American managers and white women with opportunities for assessment, challenge, support, and recognition is a necessary but insufficient condition. The roles of majority managers need to be considered as well. Organizations that effectively develop diversity use a strategy that encompasses elements of enforcement, education, and exposure (Morrison, 1992).

Enforcement. Enforcement is necessary to ensure that diversity practices are adhered to. If women and people of color are to be developed for leadership positions, senior managers must be held accountable for how they distribute challenging assignments, support their personnel, and reward them. Given the historical tendencies in the United States, these changes are unlikely to happen without enforcement practices. Tying managers' performance ratings, bonuses, or other perks to development of women and people of color is an important tool for facilitating diversity (Catalyst, 1996).

Many companies known for their diversity efforts use techniques of enforcement. Texas Instruments, for example, has an incentive compensation system that rewards managers for demonstrating commitment to diversity (Caudron and Hayes, 1997). Avon Products (the cosmetics company) is another business that holds managers accountable for developing a diverse group of direct reports (White, 1997). The City of San Diego builds accountability for commitment to the diversity initiative into the management evaluation system (White, 1997).

Education. Education on many fronts is essential as well. Managers of training and development often spend considerable time learning about the latest tools and techniques for development, and not enough time learning about their populace. Applying a one-size-fits-all approach to management development does not work.

People charged with developing others, both HR managers and line executives with responsibility for development programs, need to learn how to facilitate the development of white women and African Americans. This includes looking hard at their existing systems to see whether they need to be modified or adjusted. At the same time, people with formal responsibilities for development must realize that women and people of color need to be treated as individuals having diverse career goals, strengths, and weaknesses. The challenge is to view each manager as an individual while at the same time understanding the special issues associated with membership in a particular demographic group. Human resource managers need education as to how to incorporate these special issues into developmental systems.

Exposure. Exposure is the final thread in this strategy for leadership development. Executives and managers, blacks and whites, men and women need opportunities to interact meaningfully with each other. It seems undeniable that all people are most comfortable with others just like themselves, but in modern organizations it is imperative that managers be exposed, in meaningful ways, to those who are different. Working together toward a common goal is one way to bridge differences across identity groups (Brewer, 1995).

Lastly, we point out that truly increasing diversity in an organization depends on more than a strong system of leadership development. To have the best chance at developing a diverse organization, all human resource systems need to be modified so that they are inclusive of all managers. The leadership development practices discussed here are just part of the work. Succession planning, staffing, compensation, benefit policies, etc., need to be modified as well. Although it is outside the scope of this chapter to discuss the steps necessary to make such sweeping changes, several helpful resources exist (Kossek and Lobel, 1996; Morrison, 1992; Jackson, 1992; Cox, 1993).

CHAPTER ELEVEN

CROSS-CULTURAL ISSUES IN LEADERSHIP DEVELOPMENT

Michael H. Hoppe

Two colleagues in the human resource function of a well-known transnational corporation bumped into each other in the coffee room on a Monday morning. One had just returned from conducting a leadership development program in the company's European head-quarters.

"How did it go?"

"It was murder. You know we had people from our offices in Paris, Berlin, Milan, from all over, right? Seven different countries in all. I've never been so frustrated in my life. It was like pulling teeth every single minute."

"What do you mean?"

"Well, we had to justify everything we did. They were always asking us why we wanted them to do this or that. Especially the guys from France. *And* the Germans. Instead of just doing a particular exercise or role-play and sorting things out as they went along, like people tend to do here at home, they insisted that we first give them a rationale for every single activity. Man, am I glad to be home. Give me Americans any day."

Nearly everyone who has ever conducted training programs outside the native country recognizes the feelings expressed in this fictionalized exchange (with the names of nationalities no doubt changed). Frustrations aside, most of them are likely to reflect on the experience and wonder: "Why did they [the French, or the Japanese, or the Mexicans] react this way? What could I have done differently to stimulate the discussion? Should I have lectured more? Why didn't they buy into my definition of leadership? Why did they always seem to challenge my expertise or authority?"

Asked more generally, the questions become: Are the models of leadership and leadership development that are being used applicable in the cultures of the participants? If not, why not? What adjustments should be made so they will work? What changes need to be made in methods, practices, instruments, philosophies? In short, what should be done to successfully transfer leadership development models and practices from one culture to another?

The question is important not just for training organizations or consultants, and not just for megacorporations. Increasingly, U.S. organizations are, in one way or another, incorporating people from other cultures into their ranks, either as direct employees or as international work partners. Whenever any company's standard development practices or off-the-shelf programs or products—built on U.S. cultural assumptions—are used as-is with people from other cultures, resistance of the sort our make-believe friend encountered is bound to happen.

Chapter Overview

Most U.S. leadership development programs and products rest on a set of cultural assumptions about what leadership entails and how development is best achieved. When those programs and products are used with people from other cultures, whose assumptions may be markedly different, the results are often disappointing: puzzled participants, unreliable data, unsatisfactory outcomes.

This chapter hopes to lay the foundation for improving cross-cultural transfer of leadership development practices, first by exploring the cultural assumptions on which they are based and then by examining the practicalities of the transfer.

The chapter is divided into two major sections. The first focuses on how cultural values and beliefs affect the practice of leadership development. It begins by discussing the assumptions underlying leadership development models and practices (using, for purposes of discussion, the model featured in this handbook). It goes on to describe some of the key values and beliefs in U.S. culture and locates this country's values in "cultural space" by comparing them on several cultural dimensions to those held by other countries to which U.S. leadership development products and practices are now being transferred.

The second major section turns its attention specifically to the three key elements of the model presented in this handbook: assessment, challenge, and support. Since the element of assessment poses the greatest challenge cross-culturally, it is accorded the longest discussion. We use the specific technique of 360-degree feedback as an example of the cross-culturally problematic assumptions that underlie U.S. practices. The second section then addresses cross-cultural issues in providing challenge and support for leadership development. Because these two elements are seen as less problematic, their discussions are shorter. The chapter concludes with a summary of general to-do's to guide practitioners involved in cross-cultural work.

Assumptions and Definitions

It is helpful, particularly when dealing with something as complex as cross-cultural transfer of leadership development practices, to establish early on the specific parameters and assumptions of the discussion. In this chapter, the term *cross-cultural* refers to comparisons among societies—in fact, among the mainstreams of societies. However, this is not to deny the existence of multitudes of cultures *within* a society, whether along ethnic, gender, or organizational lines. Implicit in this notion of societal culture is the claim that culture matters. *Culture* is seen as a set of shared values, beliefs, and preferred actions among the members of a society that largely determine, among other things, the boundaries within which leadership development is possible. Once again, this does not diminish the influence of other variables, such as the availability of economic resources or the effects of past or current colonization.

It is assumed that every society is engaged in leadership development of some sort. What the notion means; how it is practiced; or where, when, or through whom it is done may differ significantly across some cultures. Yet the need for leadership and its development is universal. In fact, this contention is extended to the three basic elements of developmental experiences (assessment, challenge, and support).

Finally, we note that because this chapter is part of a handbook about U.S. leadership development experiences and practices, the discussion of cross-cultural issues is pursued from a U.S. vantage point. That is, cultural comparisons are made almost exclusively between the United States and one or more other societies. Generally, the other societies are highly developed economically, for they are the ones in which formal leadership development efforts, similar to the one discussed in this handbook, tend to take place. However, this in no way should be construed to mean that U.S. leadership development practice is to be considered the yardstick for other cultures. Any country, independent of its economic level, can enrich the understanding of leadership and leadership development around the world. By the same token, in-depth discussion of the values and assumptions that shape U.S. leadership development is meant to assist in possible transfer of its practice, *not* to criticize U.S.-based practice. It is in this spirit that the discussion hopes to be of use.

Culture and Leadership Development

Cultural values and beliefs affect the practice of leadership development because they relate directly to the assumptions on which this practice is built.

Culturally Based Assumptions of the Leadership Development Model

"Cultural self-awareness," Stewart and Bennett write, "is not always easy since culture is internalized patterns of thinking and behaving that are believed to be 'natural'—simply the way things are. Awareness of their subjective culture is particularly difficult for [U.S.] Americans since they often interpret cultural factors as characteristics of individual personality. This view of internalized cultural patterns, disregarding their social origins, is a characteristic of [U.S.] American culture. It is not a universal point of view" (1991, p. x).

In many U.S. based models of leadership development, development is seen as lifelong expansion of an individual's capacities to effectively respond in leadership situations. Leadership development is considered development of the whole person, "synonymous with what is often labeled *personal development*" (as was said in the Introduction). In this view, development can occur anywhere and anytime in a person's life, through formal or informal roles and in many kinds of activities, ranging from heading up a strategic task force to facilitating a meeting of peers or being actively involved in the neighborhood's fight of a rezoning ordinance. U.S. practices tend to be geared toward developing in the individual a greater self-awareness, systems thinking, creativity, ability to get along with others, learning to learn, and other capacities called for in leadership situations. They also tend to imply that leadership capacities can be developed by everybody (barring gross mental or psychological dysfunction).

The model presented in this handbook is based on years of research and practice, principally with U.S. managers. It necessarily makes a number of assumptions that may or may not hold when it crosses cultural boundaries:

Culturally Based Assumptions of the Leadership Development Model

Leadership development is development of individuals.

Leadership development is development of the whole person (that is, personal development).

(Almost) everybody can develop leadership capacities.

(Almost) everybody is called on to lead at times.

Leadership can be learned.

It is good to face challenging tasks in life.

Personal advancement is desirable.

Ambiguity and uncertainty are natural.

Being open to change is good.

Leading is learning by doing.

Data and measurement are good.

Practical experience is good.

Improvement and progress are normal.

Taking action is essential.

Objective feedback is good.

In the United States, it would be hard to find a development specialist who would seriously disagree with many of these statements. Most would shrug and say, "Of course, that's obvious." Yet people from other cultures might not consider them obvious at all. What looks, sounds, or seems natural or obvious to any group is the reflection of implicit preferences—that is, values (what people in that culture hold dear or consider important) and beliefs (what they think ought to be). This is why, in thinking about leadership and leadership development, culture matters, because it largely determines the boundaries within which leadership development is understood and practiced.

Although culture facilitates certain practices, it also inhibits others, thereby limiting the behavioral options that its members consider important and relevant. For example, leadership development in the United States tends to emphasize practical experience and deemphasize intellectual and theoretical qualities. In U.S. models of leadership, there tends to be relatively little discussion of the concept of power, and therefore less attention is paid to helping people understand the politics of organizational life. Similarly, U.S. leadership development courses tend to focus on the individual as leader rather than conceptualizing leadership as a function of the group or organization as a whole.

Selected Values and Beliefs in U.S. Culture

Alexis de Tocqueville observed that "[U.S. Americans] are external-izers, doers, and achievers." Two contemporary writers offer comple-mentary notions: "To call an American [of the United States] 'impractical' would be a severe criticism" (Cavanagh, 1984) and "The idea that people can control their own destiny is totally alien to most of the world cultures" (Kohls, 1996). What is it in U.S. culture that ac-counts for its notion of leadership development? What specific values and beliefs bring a focus to certain aspects of leadership and inatten-tion to others?

The patterns of U.S. culture have received a great deal of atten-tion from researchers. Stewart and Bennett (1991) and Kohls (1996) provide authoritative and easily accessible summaries of U.S. cultural patterns, which are distinctive (stand out) from a cross-cultural per-spective. These value patterns, derived originally in the work of such anthropologists as Hall (1966) and Kluckhohn and Strodtbeck (1961), were confirmed by large-scale, empirical, cross-cultural studies during the past two decades (Hofstede, 1980; Hoppe, 1993; Schwartz, 1994). In all of these studies, U.S. mainstream culture is consistently described as being highly individualistic, egalitarian, achievement-driven, com-fortable with change, and action- and data-oriented. (For additional resources on cultural value differences, see the list at the end of this

TABLE 11.1. SELECTED U.S. VALUES.

Individualism	The right to pursue one's own happiness
Equality	Existential equality among members of society
Work	Hard work and achievement as the basis for a good life
Change	Openness to change and self-improvement
Data	Eminence of empirical, observable, measurable facts
Practicality	Preference for inductive and operational thinking
Action	Making progress and taking action as individual duty

chapter.) Table 11.1 offers an overview of those values that are pertinent to this chapter.

A comparison of Table 11.1 (cultural values and beliefs) and the preceding list of cultural assumptions about leadership development makes several relationships immediately apparent. To think of leadership development as individual and personal development neatly fits with the value of individualism. The notion that leadership capacities can be developed by almost everyone clearly reflects the value of equality, and the idea that skills are acquired by doing reflects the orientation to action. The assumption that objective, data-based feedback should be a mainstay of effective leadership development mirrors the U.S. preference for empirical, measurable, and observable data. And the emphasis on change and self-improvement in U.S. culture parallels the importance of growth, development, and lifelong learning that defines the model presented here.

Of course, this is not to say that members of other societies do not hold similar values. Many do. Sweden, for example, is also highly individualistic, egalitarian, and data-oriented. Therefore this model, and many other U.S.-based leadership development practices, is likely to transfer to Swedish society without much difficulty. However, many cultures have more differences from the United States than similarities. Table 11.2 offers a framework, created by Wilson, Hoppe, and Sayles (1996) and slightly revised for this chapter, that shows U.S. values and beliefs in comparison to nine other countries from around the world. The information in this table can be used to locate U.S. values (from Table 11.1) and leadership development assumptions (from the earlier list) in cross-cultural space.

U.S. Values and Beliefs in Cross-Cultural Perspective

Table 11.2 groups ten countries along six bipolar cultural dimensions: *individual-collective, same-different, tough-tender, dynamic-stable, active-reflective, and doing-being.* The countries were chosen with two purposes: to illustrate the range of cultural differences along the dimensions and to represent a

TABLE 11.2. CULTURAL VALUE ORIENTATIONS: A CROSS-CULTURAL COMPARISON.

Individual (individualism)	Same (equality)	Tough (live to work)	Dynamic (change)	Active (data/practice)	Doing (action)
• Leadership development is individual, personal development • Leadership development is individual responsibility	• Everybody can learn to lead • All people are existentially the same • Privileges need to be earned	• Challenging tasks are good • Work and career are central • Competition is good	• Ambiguity and uncertainty are natural • Openness to change is good	• Leading is learning by doing and practice • Data and measurement essential	• Progress and improvement • Taking action is personal duty
USA Australia Sweden France Germany	Sweden Germany Australia USA	Japan Mexico Germany USA Australia	Sweden USA Australia	USA Sweden Australia	USA Germany Australia Sweden France
Japan Iran Arab countries	Japan China Iran	Arab countries China France Iran	China Iran Germany Arab countries	China Germany Iran	Mexico Japan
Mexico China	France Arab countries Mexico	Sweden	Mexico France Japan	Japan Mexico Arab countries France	China Iran Arab countries
• Leadership development is group or organization's responsibility • Leadership development is development of group or organization	• Privileges are granted by birth, name, position • Leaders existentially differ from others • Few are born to lead	• Cooperation is good • Solidarity and good relationships among people are primary • Quality of whole life essential	• Stability and continuity are good • Ambiguity and uncertainty are to be avoided	• Reflection and theory are primary • Leading is learning by intellect	• Living in harmony with universe essential • Accepting place in life as inner duty
(collectivism) Collective	(inequality) Different	(work to live) Tender	(stability) Stable	(observation) Reflective	(acceptance) Being

Note: Country locations on dimensions one through four (from left) are based on Hofstede (1980). Locations on dimensions five and six are based on reading of literature, but more speculative. "Arab countries" are a composite of data from Egypt, Iraq, Kuwait, Lebanon, Libya, Saudi Arabia, and the United Arab Emirates. Most of the data on China are a combination of data from Taiwan and Hong Kong. Groupings of countries within each dimension near the poles, or in the midrange, signal noticeable differences among these groups of countries.

broad range of nations from around the world. Countries that cluster near the poles of a certain dimension share the cultural assumptions that describe the poles; by extension, they differ significantly from the countries near the other pole of that dimension. Countries in the midrange are culturally different from those near either end. For example, the United States, Australia, Sweden, France, and Germany are individualistic societies (with the United States being the most individualistic); China and Mexico are considered collectivist; and Japan, Iran, and the "Arab countries" have moderate degrees of individualism and collectivism relative to either pole of a dimension.

The information in Table 11.2 is referred to throughout the balance of this chapter. It is important to keep in mind, however, that, culturally, there are no *good* or *bad* value orientations. The fact that the United States happens to be located near the "top" of each dimension signals its unique cultural orientation, *not* its superiority (or inferiority, for that matter). (As Grove and Hallowell put it, "'Unique' is a word that applies to the United States. The [U.S.] American mind-set is invigorated by a constellation of values unlike that found in any nation" [1994, p. 24].) Instead, the table merely serves as a graphic illustration of the degree to which countries hold the values and beliefs described by the poles of each dimension and their relative similarity or dissimilarity to U.S. values. From these relationships, it is possible to quickly deduce how easy or difficult it would be to transfer U.S. leadership development models and practices to other countries.

On the six scales, the U.S. places near the *individual, same, tough, dynamic, active,* and *doing* poles. It is not surprising then, that in the United States leadership is viewed as an individual activity that is accessible to (almost) everyone and that is rich in challenge, change, active learning, and self-improvement. It is also not surprising that these notions are mirrored in the implicit and explicit features of the leadership development model presented in this handbook. Conversely, the Arab countries, Mexico, China, and Japan are most culturally different from the United States on these dimensions. In those areas of the world, then, transferability of our model might be most problematic (see "Doesn't Everybody Want a Promotion?!").

Doesn't Everybody Want a Promotion?!

"The human resources manager of a global pharmaceutical company who had been assigned to the Far East discovered to his surprise that his greatest challenge was to persuade the company's Chinese, Malaysian, Taiwanese, and South Korean managers to accept promotions. These managers [from collectivist countries] did not wish to compete with their peers for career rewards or personal gain—nor were they interested in breaking their ties to their communities in order to assume cross-national responsibilities."
(Reported by Wilson, Hoppe, and Sayles, 1996, p. 7.)

Australia, Sweden, and Germany are most similar to the United States; in these countries, the model should transfer rather smoothly. However, Sweden and Germany differ from the United States' cultural profile in some respects. Sweden is located close to the *tender* pole, and Germany is in the midrange of the *dynamic-stable* and *active-reflective* dimensions.

A few brief examples illustrate potential implications of these differences for leadership development; they are drawn largely from Derr's research (1987) on the different ways in which organizations in selected European countries identify and develop their "fast-track" managers.

Tender and Same Values: The Case of Sweden. In Sweden, Derr reports, leadership development opportunities are readily available and largely independent of the person's technical background or functional expertise. However, many Swedish managers find it less than desirable to be singled-out, even as high-potentials. It threatens to limit their time for self and family, and it isolates them from their coworkers by elevating them in status (values describing the *tender* pole). In addition, the increase in authority that tends to accompany higher levels of responsibility is considered a mixed blessing by many Swedish managers, since in a highly egalitarian society such as Sweden (the *same* pole) the managerial prerogative is curtailed by high expectations of participation and consensus building among the employees. In sum, considering the potential damage to personal time, quality of life, and good relationships with their coworkers, the Swedes anticipate few rewards from becoming a manager.

Yet in one way this handbook's model of leadership development is facilitated in societies close to the *tender* pole (Sweden, Denmark, Finland, the Netherlands, and Norway): its definition of leadership development as *personal* development. Seeing development as something that involves the whole person—personality, intellect, competencies, personal aspirations, and family and community life—and not just career is an expression of values (*tender* pole) that are almost countercultural in mainstream U.S. (business) culture. Stewart and Bennett describe them in their combination as an "orientation [that] emerged as a cultural motif in the 1960s and [that] assumes a dominant position in movements with sources in humanistic and transpersonal psychology and in growth theories in education" (1991, p. 71).

Germany: The Importance of Technical and Administrative Competence.

In Germany, leadership development is typically understood as advancement of technical and administrative expertise, an emphasis that is reflected in the apprentice system and admiration for the *Meister*, who has proven his or her technical expertise in the classroom and through years of experience. In fact, the highly technical fields of engineering and microeconomics have been primary gateways to the managerial ranks, and "25 percent of German CEOs have risen through the ranks" of the apprentice system (Hill, 1994, p. 42). Thus, the leadership models and practices that would likely transfer well to Germany are those that recognize the role of technical and administrative competence in leadership capability and that balance action orientations with a theoretical approach.

France: Valuing Authority, Structure, and Theory.

France is an altogether different challenge. It is located near the *different, stable,* and *reflective* poles—opposite the U.S. on those scales. In other words, French culture highly values authority, status, rules, structure, and theory and intellect. It is well known that the main springboard for a French executive's career is a degree from the *polytechniques,* or *grandes écoles.* As Barsoux and Lawrence observe, managers in France tend to feel "that their career had been mapped out for them on the day they completed their education. They could also foresee how their careers would unfold and where their promotional ceiling would be, irrespective of their career aspirations" (1997, p. 6).

In short, development of leaders in France tends to take place within a system of strict performance reviews, succession planning, and career tracking mechanisms. Still, within this system, the individual leader remains the target of leadership development. However, for optimal transfer of U.S.-based models and practices, leadership development would need to deemphasize, at least at first, the personal (holistic) aspect of the model, stress leadership as an expression of authority and status, and appeal to the intellect and theoretical bent among French executives (see "Rule Orientation in European Countries: The Power of Reason").

Rule Orientation in European Countries: The Power of Reason.

French, German, Spanish, and Italian societies are often described as highly rule-bound (Hofstede, 1991). They may be, but with a twist, as the following data by Barsoux and Lawrence (1997) show.

"Basically, I Will Carry Out Instructions from My Superior."

Denmark	57 percent
Great Britain	49 percent
Ireland	45 percent
Holland	39 percent
Spain	29 percent
West Germany	28 percent
France	25 percent
Italy	24 percent

"I Will Only Follow My Superior's Instructions When My Reason Is Convinced."

France	57 percent
West Germany	51 percent
Spain	41 percent
Italy	39 percent
Great Britain	34 percent
Holland	33 percent
Ireland	26 percent
Denmark	21 percent

(*Note*: This may explain why French and German participants in the real-life example at the beginning of the chapter insisted on knowing the rationale behind the activities.)

The other countries in Table 11.2 (China, Iran, Japan, Mexico, and the Arab countries) pose still other sets of challenges. Development in these countries, especially China and Japan, would need to emphasize much more the development of the group, by the group. Even though development of the individual remains desirable, it needs to be put into the context and service of the group. Furthermore, development programs in these cultures must place greater emphasis on hierarchy, seniority, organizational rules and structure, reflection, and acceptance of what life gives.

Assessment, Challenge, and Support in Cross-Cultural Perspective

The model of leadership development presented in this handbook states that the most potent development experiences have three elements: assessment, challenge, and support. Although it is probably true that leaders everywhere can benefit from all three elements, how each element is implemented cross-culturally in any development experience is problematic. Experiences that are seen as acceptable and developmental in one culture often differ significantly from those seen as acceptable and developmental in another.

At this point, we explore these cultural differences in more detail by specifically examining the issues that surround assessment, challenge, and support outside the United States.

The Role of Assessment in Leadership Development

Of the three elements in the model, assessment is the most problematic in its transfer across cultures. To state the matter simply, not all cultures believe that assessing people in a public forum is a good thing. The idea that assessment—formal or informal praise or criticism, delivered in written or verbal form—is a critical part of the process of personal improvement is based on values and beliefs that other cultures may not share with the United States.

At the very core of most U.S. assessment models and practices lies the assumption that quantification and "objective" measurement of human characteristics and competencies are critical elements of effective leadership development. Not all cultures share this assumption, or the resulting fondness for hard data—and therein lies the difficulty. In the sections that follow, we look more closely at this assumption, relating the U.S. beliefs and values that underlie it to the oftentimes different beliefs in other cultures. Although most of the discussion is relevant to assessment in its broadest sense, and to all data-driven assessment techniques, it uses one specific and widely familiar type of assessment instrument, 360-degree feedback, to illustrate the more general points.

The U.S. Preference for Quantification

Americans, in general, find quantification and measurement useful and important. In fact, this preference for so-called objective quantification and measurement is one cultural value that underlies the popularity of instrument-based assessments in the United States.

Cultures that tend toward the *active* pole—the U.S. is one—usually see data and empirical measurement as essential (see Table 11.2). In these cultures, quantitative and empirical data tend to take on an objective reality all of their own; people tend to believe that data can be used to take action (the *active* pole) toward economic progress or self-improvement, which is seen as a good and worthwhile goal (the *doing* pole).

The preference for and openness to empirical data ("facts") and their measurement are not equally shared by all cultures. In France and Germany, for instance, theory is more highly valued. Empirical data may even be looked upon with suspicion, since data don't make the underlying theory or set of assumptions immediately apparent. In cultures that value theory, citing facts in isolation can be seen as indicative of inferior thinking and dismissed as trivial. In these cultures, there may also be less of an inner urge to act on data because people believe that better thinking leads to improvement, rather than more data, as in the common saying that there is nothing as practical as a good theory.

In Japanese and Chinese society, for example, there is greater appreciation for relational, synchronic, and metaphorical thinking that pays less attention to isolated, linear, analytical data and instead emphasizes the broader context of human relationships and events to provide meaning (see Stewart and Bennett, 1991, chapter two). In Hindu religious thought, the meaning of a fact becomes meaningless, since life is seen as an illusion altogether.

In short, objective data, for a variety of reasons, don't carry the same power of conviction in other cultures as in the United States (see "What's in a Number?").

What's in a Number?

The Mississippi is 2,348 miles long. Lou Gehrig had a lifetime batting average of .340. The annual per capita income in Ethiopia is $150. A painting by Picasso sold for $1.5 million.

U.S. culture is fascinated with numbers. Numbers convey something concrete, something comprehensible—or do they? Do they truly capture the

majesty, fury, or serenity of the "Old Man River"? Can they sum up the sheer talent, effort, and determination of Lou Gehrig? Do they truly help understand a mother's struggle in Ethiopia to feed her children, or describe the genius behind Picasso's art? U.S. tourists are known the world over for their questions of "How long did it take to build it?" "How much did it cost?" or "How tall is it?" while visitors from some other cultures may ask questions about history, aesthetics, or politics. The Kpelle of Liberia may even feel threatened by having numbers attached to things. They may "refrain from counting chickens or other domestic animals aloud to avoid some harm befalling them."
(*Source:* Stewart and Bennett, 1991, p. 126.)

What is it in U.S. culture that provokes this preference for data and measurement? It is, in part, an expression of a scientific worldview that stresses linear, objective, quantifiable models of all things—including human behavior. In part, it reflects the American experience of moving west and defining progress in terms of miles traveled, acres cultivated, or towns settled. In part, it may be seen as an equitable way of establishing someone's identity in a society where factors such as social class, tribe, clan, or religion are seldom used to define a person. Cultures with these characteristics are often referred to as having a "low-context" environment.

Low-Context Environment. The practice of providing specific, measurable, direct, and objective feedback in U.S. society, and by extension in leadership development, is described by Simons, Vazquez, and Harris as "[a U.S.] American peculiarity" (1993, p. 127). Its cultural explanation is largely reflected in Tables 11.1 and 11.2. U.S. emphasis on the individual, coupled with the well-documented geographical mobility of its citizens, means that close and lasting information-rich networks among family, friends, neighbors, and colleagues are the exception in the United States, not the rule as in more collective societies such as Japan, Indonesia, or the Mediterranean countries. As a result, U.S. society is typically described as a low-context environment (Hall and Hall, 1990), meaning one lacking "contextual" information (about a person's background, status, or interpersonal relationships within a group). Because this sort of contextual information is not a part of the natural environment, detailed data about personal relationships, work, or personal achievements need to be obtained and exchanged. This high need for "contexting" is seen as one of the cultural roots for the prominence of the data-driven assessments in the model.

"Universalistic" Thinking. A related explanation can be found in the cultural profile produced by the combination of high individualism (the *individual* pole in Table 11.2), belief in the existential equality among people (*same* pole), and emphasis on hard work and career (*tough* pole). This cultural profile calls on U.S. society to find ways to let its members know where they stand. Since heritage, religion, or social class have been deemphasized, and since advancement and career are considered important, then quantitative and objective data on traits, abilities, and competencies become essential as tools. The assumption is that nobody ought to be exempt from this type of assessment, or deprived of its feedback.

The U.S. approach represents a culturally "universalistic" way of thinking that contrasts with a "particularistic" approach in which preferential treatment is seen as natural. For example, in Arab countries, selection decisions and feedback data are influenced by the "data" that *their* cultures consider important (and that are applied to everybody): religion, tribal membership, family ties, or friendships (Ali, 1990; Khadra, 1990). In a nutshell, whether for selection or feedback purposes, in many cultures specific, measurable, objective data are only seen as one set of data, and often *not* the most important one.

Challenges in Transfer of Assessment Instruments

The U.S. preference for quantification is reflected in one of the most popular assessment methodologies in the United States: 360-degree feedback. A 360-degree assessment instrument basically asks many people who know the individual well (superiors, peers, direct reports, family members, customers, or others) to rate his or her performance or psychological characteristics by responding to multiple questionnaire items. The answers of the raters are then aggregated and, together with self-ratings, fed back to the individual for purposes of individual leadership development (see Chapter One of this handbook or Tornow, London, and CCL Associates, 1998, for more in-depth discussion).

What happens, then, when 360-degree assessment instruments and feedback processes developed in the United States are exported to other cultures? Four challenges are encountered in this transfer:

- Acceptance or appeal of 360-degree assessment may be low in other cultures.
- Dimensions of leadership assessed by the instrument may be culturally biased.
- Assumptions about the assessment process may not transfer to other cultures.
- Interpreting the feedback may be problematic.

Cultural Differences in Acceptance of 360-Degree Feedback

HR practitioners may encounter lack of acceptance of 360-degree feedback in other cultures. The resistance may be due to lack of trust among people who would be expected to give each other feedback. For example, members of former communist countries, or people currently living in one-person or one-party dictatorships, may not be as open to soliciting and sharing data about themselves because of historical violations of trust. Take the experiences of members of the former German Democratic Republic (East Germany). After the Berlin Wall came down, more than five million people (out of seventeen million) learned that friends, colleagues, neighbors, and even family members had spied on them and passed their information on to the East German equivalent of the KBG.

Of course, threats to acceptance of feedback data may occur anywhere. A history of mistrust, breach of confidentiality, ambiguity as to use of the data, or confrontational relationships between management and unionized employees may seriously undermine its practice even in this country. However, with a unique cultural profile (as depicted in Table 11.2) coupled with a low-context environment and universalist beliefs, the United States provides the most fertile ground for use of 360-degree feedback. In Stewart and Bennett's words, "when faced with a problem, Americans like to get to its source. This means facing the facts, meeting the problem head on, putting the cards on the table, and getting information 'straight from the horse's mouth'" (1991, p. 96).

U.S. managers prefer to face data head on, regardless of whether they are receiving positive or negative feedback. In fact, in a recent study by Dorfman and others (1997) comparing managers and professionals from the United States, Japan, Mexico, South Korea, and Taiwan, the U.S. sample was the only one that responded positively (meaning in terms of increased organization commitment) to negative feedback, while positive feedback had a positive impact on employees in all five countries. In other words, direct, honest, specific, and measurable feedback for developmental purposes (and performance appraisal) tends to be welcomed in the U.S. workplace—whether it points out strengths or shortcomings (see "Trust?—Whom?").

Trust?—Whom?

Issues of trust and confidence in 360–degree feedback data are not limited to former communist states or dictatorships, to wit: "A number of French managers told our research group that they did not trust feedback from peers as they had been competing with their peers since the first years of school and did not believe that their peers could rise above this competitive mode to provide them with objective information."
(*Source:* Dalton, 1995, p. 5.)

The practice of giving and receiving feedback looks very different in some cultures. For example, in high-context environments, which are also usually collectivist cultures such as China, Japan, and South Korea, feedback is delivered in a much more subtle, indirect, and face-saving way. Employees tend to learn where they stand and where they may need to improve through the numerous daily interactions with their group members. If their superiors want to convey developmental feedback, they may direct it to the group as a whole and let the group convey it to the individual member. If the employee does not pick up on it or fail to change, group members or the superior may provide more direct feedback after work (the practice of *tsuikiai*) when, for instance, "during lengthy drinking bouts much performance feedback is imparted to a Japanese employee" (Filipczak, 1992, p. 24).

In addition, in these and such other countries as Brazil, Mexico, Saudi Arabia, and Turkey, the importance of ongoing leadership development in general and formal, extensive feedback on performance in particular may be balanced (or outweighed?) by the importance of loyalty, seniority, harmony, conformity, diligence, or obedience among organizational members. Their more *collective* and *different* (inequality) cultural orientation (see Table 11.2) tends to make performance secondary to the latter values and, consequently, diminish the need for developmental data, as typically gathered through 360-degree instruments. Where, then, does this leave use of intensive, formal multirater instruments in these cultures?

On the one hand, there is little use for them. They provide data that are either already available through context-rich interactions or that are not seen to be critical. Yet 360-degree feedback may become increasingly important as more organizations from these and similar cultures become active in the global market and (through a combination of information technology, transnational mergers, and organizational change) lose traditional channels for assessing their employees. The heightened competition, or collaboration, may add to the need to gather sound performance data on employees for making informed selection and development decisions. On the other hand, these very dynamics hamper the practice of 360-degree feedback, since organizational members, in particular those in leadership roles, may be more geographically dispersed, frequently change their reference groups (boss, peers, direct reports, or customers), and as a result make input by raters logistically and substantively more difficult.

Cultural Biases in the Content of 360-Degree Instruments

It is no secret that the "practice of psychology within the U.S. is dominated by Western thought, with significant emphases given to white, middle-class, male attitudes, beliefs, worldviews, and values" (Leach, 1997, p.165). What happens when assessment instruments developed by U.S. psychologists, reflecting U.S. models of human behavior, are exported to other cultures? How much is the content of these instruments applicable beyond the original cultural sphere? This is the ever-present issue of *generalizability.*

Everything that has been said so far about cultural differences in values, beliefs, and thinking suggests that U.S. leadership development instruments are reasonably applicable in some countries (for example, other Anglo-Saxon countries or Sweden and its northern neighbors), but questionable in others (China, Japan, or the Arab countries). In the latter cultures, societal expressions, and by extension leadership behaviors, of power (*same-different* dimension), communication (*individual-collective* dimension), change and innovation (*dynamic-stable* dimension), or action (*doing-being* dimension) differ greatly. As a result, what are considered effective leadership behaviors in, for example, Saudi Arabian culture (with its emphasis on respect for authority and position, indirectness in communication with others, tradition, and religion) are unlikely to be found in U.S. instruments (Feghali, 1997).

On the other hand, the issue of generalizability may be somewhat tempered by the effect of *globalization.* The emergence of the global market over the past three decades has created large transnational organizations with similar organizational and managerial functions. Because these organizations face the same challenges no matter where they are located, they seem to require largely the same leadership competencies. A recent survey by Yeung and Ready (1995), for instance, found that executives and managers from ten global companies in eight countries largely agreed on the capabilities that they consider most important for their own leadership development: ability to articulate a tangible vision, values, and strategy; being a catalyst for strategic change; being result-oriented; empowering others to do their best; being a catalyst for cultural change; and exhibiting a strong customer orientation.

Not surprisingly, given the theme of this chapter, Yeung and Ready also found distinct differences in the priorities that countries assign to these and other competencies. For example, the U.S. sample ranked "get results—manage strategy to action" as the most important. In contrast, France, Germany, Japan, Korea, and Spain did not include this capability at all among the five choices that they were allowed to make from a total of forty-five. "Empowering others to be their best" was selected among the top five choices by the executives and managers from Australia, Germany, Japan, Spain, and the United States, but it was missing from the list of the French, Italian, Korean, and British samples. In other words, *the power of culture* persists, despite similarities in the demands of the global market.

Furthermore, even if the global economy should result in emergence of similar leadership competencies across countries and organizations, how these competencies are enacted and interpreted may differ noticeably. This means that how these competencies are expressed in various instruments also differs (see "Same Concepts, Different Meanings?"). For example, "making decisions" is seen as a generic leadership function everywhere. However, its effective practice tends to be defined as "quick and approximate rather than slow and precise" in the United States, "deliberate and precise, rather than quick and approximate" in France, and "consensual and long-term rather than unilateral and short-term" in Japan. Similarly, "showing consideration for employees who have personal difficulties" is considered a universal function of effective leadership, but "a supervisor who talks about a subordinate's personal difficulties to his colleagues when the person was absent was deemed inconsiderate in Britain and the USA, but considerate in Hong Kong and Japan" (Smith and Peterson, 1988, p. 110).

Same Concepts, Different Meanings?

A colleague of mine reported that "[W]hen we validated Benchmark [a multi-rater instrument developed by the Center for Creative Leadership] with French managers in France, we found that an item that measures decisiveness in U.S. managers (the subject is 'quick and approximate rather than slow and precise') indicated a lack of integrity to French managers. We also found real problems with the U.S. concept that senior managers need not be technical experts to manage a group of technical experts, and we found that the way we used the word *delegation* implied laziness or a sloughing off of responsibility to French raters."
(*Source:* Dalton, 1995, p. 5.)

Practical Steps Toward Dealing with the Challenge of Generalizability

A good first step in dealing with the challenges described above would be to ascertain the cultural affinity, or lack thereof, between the United States and a society in which the instruments are to be used. Table 11.2 provides some initial guidance for nine countries. For countries not included there, the widely used cultural clustering by Ronen and Shenkar (1985), shown in Figure 11.1, offers additional assistance. In general, the closer the visual proximity between the United States and another society, the greater the cultural similarity. Therefore, using U.S. instruments in those countries is warranted.

However, close proximity does not preclude noticeable differences between two countries. England, for example, jokingly described as being very similar to the United States but separated from it by the same language, tends to place less emphasis on practicality and business experience (Hill, 1994). Similarly, the earlier examples of career development practices in Sweden and Germany suggest that 360-degree feedback instruments in Sweden may have to emphasize measures such as "balance between work and personal life" and "ability to build consensus" while those in Germany may need to provide extended feedback

FIGURE 11.1. SYNTHESIS OF COUNTRY CLUSTERS.

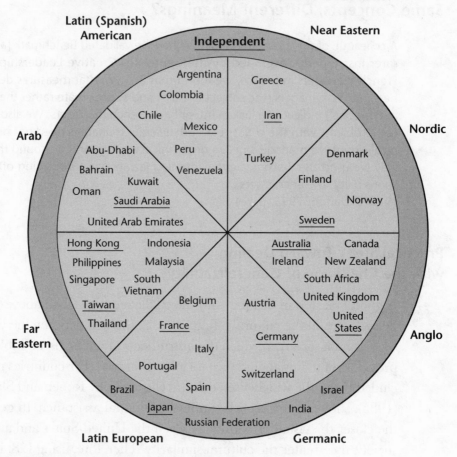

Note: Underlined countries are included in Table 11.2.
Source: Adapted from Ronen and Shenkar (1985), p. 449.

on "technical and administrative experience" and "leading by organizing and structuring."

An alternative approach is to use instruments developed in the culture where the feedback is to take place. Unfortunately, although this
approach would be particularly valuable in countries that significantly
differ from the United States, such as China, Japan, or Saudi Arabia,
that is also where it may be most difficult to implement. For one thing,
there is much less propensity in these societies for measuring people

through instrumentation. For another, the research infrastructure for developing measurements is significantly less extensive. Triandis (1980), for instance, estimates that only 20 percent of all psychologists who ever lived and are currently alive are found outside the United States, and most of those are from Europe.

This is not to imply that no useful non-U.S. instruments are available, but it does suggest that the choice is limited. It also suggests that those delivering the feedback may not be proficient in the terminology of the instrument. Also, unless they are savvy insiders or knowledgeable expatriates, they may be unfamiliar with its implicit cultural meanings.

If specific-country instruments are not available, another strategy is to look for 360-degree instruments that have been cross-culturally validated, that is, questionnaires that have been shown to measure what is considered important across many societies and whose meaning and measurement are reasonably equivalent across these cultures. Unfortunately, there are very few cross-culturally reliable and valid instruments on the market today, and many organizations are using instruments with no known reliability or validity outside of the United States. Even though Leslie and Fleenor document translations of twenty U.S. leadership instruments into more than twenty languages, they conclude that "much is unknown about the international validity and reliability of instruments developed and used in the U.S. and on no instrument so far has cross-cultural validity research done more than scratch the surface." Although there is some promising work being done in this area, "In the meantime, individual results should be interpreted to international managers with much caution" (1998, p. 18).

Even if cross-culturally validated leadership instruments should become more available, a basic challenge remains: the uniqueness of each culture. As Table 11.2 and Figure 11.1 illustrate, societies vary greatly in their cultural makeup. Any 360-degree instrument that attempts to capture this richness of diversity is bound to reduce it to some broad categories that have little to do with daily, hands-on, unique expressions of leadership in these cultures. Furthermore, organizations and the communities in which they operate add layers of complexity that make it important to heed the following advice: "To be effective and effica-cious, leadership capabilities need to be contextualized with each com-pany's unique organizational cultures, histories, technologies, and socially complex interactions. To derive competitive advantage, it is clearly insufficient for corporations to simply benchmark from high-profile, successful companies. They must define, develop, and measure leadership capabilities based on their company-specific needs, chal-lenges, and national cultures" (Yeung and Ready, 1995, p. 538).

Some General Guidelines for Choosing an Instrument

In the face of these problems with the generalizability of assessment in-strument content, a few basic guidelines are helpful in avoiding some of the pitfalls described here:

1. A good way to start is to read appropriate literature. Acquaint your-self with the leadership capabilities that are seen as universally de-sirable (see Brake, 1997; Rhinesmith, 1993; Yeung and Ready, 1995), and begin to prioritize them for the culture in question.
2. Next, as soon as a 360-degree instrument has been selected or is being developed, get help from knowledgeable practitioners and scholars from within the culture. Ask them if the items on the ques-tionnaire adequately capture the behaviors that are seen as effective in that culture.
3. Also ask them to help identify leadership capabilities that are not ad-equately covered, and have questionnaire items developed that mea-sure them.
4. Another way to include areas otherwise neglected is to use an in-strument that provides open space for soliciting additional leader-ship strengths and development needs (and their meanings) directly from respondents. This set of questions helps expand or refine the instrument over time. (See "Ten Questions Toward Acceptability.")
5. Finally, make sure that the instrument reflects standard professional practices for validity and reliability.

Ten Questions Toward Acceptability.

Based on their review of the literature, MacLachlan, Mapundi, Zimba, and Carr (1995, p. 647) suggest the following ten questions to test whether a valid and reliable instrument is acceptable outside its country of origin.

On a scale from 1 to 5,

1. I enjoyed completing the questionnaire.
2. I found the questionnaire interesting to complete.
3. Many questions were difficult to understand.
4. The questions were relevant to my work.
5. All the questions were relevant to the culture.
6. I believe that the results of the questionnaire might help identify training needs.
7. I don't know how the questionnaire can detect relevant personality traits for personnel selection and development.
8. I was put off because the questionnaire was too long.
9. It is acceptable to ask these questions in the workplace.
10. An individual with a high score on these questions would be seen as an excellent manager in our company.

Cultural Assumptions About the Assessment Process

Even if all the difficulties of generalizability of instrument content are overcome, there are some additional cultural assumptions about the assessment process that need to be examined.

First, *who owns the data?* The efficacy of 360-degree feedback in the United States is greatly strengthened by the fact that the individual manager owns the data. Even though the employer typically pays for the assessment, it is up to the individual how to use the data and with whom to share them. Culturally, this practice is largely informed by the individualistic and egalitarian orientation of U.S. society. However, in a more collectivist environment, such as China or Japan, individual managers may consider the data property of the group. For example, contrary to the U.S. practice of discussing the data primarily with a person's own feedback specialist, a colleague of mine reported that a group of Japanese managers felt it more appropriate (more "natural") to process their 360-degree feedback data, from the beginning, with their group members.

In addition, in societies near the *different* (inequality) pole of Table 11.2, such as France, Mexico, and Saudi Arabia, superiors are likely to consider it their duty to know everything about their employees and insist on knowing the data. This tendency is exacerbated in those cultures that see leaders as existentially different (*different* pole) *and also* have a high need for stability, structure, and certainty (*stable* pole), countries such as France, Mexico, and Singapore. In these cultures, organizations as a whole see themselves as the guardian and depository of all data, including those that may have been collected for individual developmental purposes.

This practice raises a second question: *How "good" are the data, when those providing them (including self) know or suspect that their input is known to others?* Research in the U.S. suggests that feedback data tend to be more accurate when raters believe that their input remains anonymous (Leslie, Gryskiewicz, and Dalton, 1998). This, in turn, heightens the recipient's sense of ownership and acceptance of the feedback.

If anonymity cannot be guaranteed (the boss's ratings are typically excepted), multiple scenarios arise. Peers in France may rate each other down, because that is one way of gaining an advantage in their highly hierarchical and competitive environment. Direct reports in China or Japan may inflate their ratings to please their boss. For example, Leslie, Gryskiewicz, and Dalton (1998) relate the story of a Chinese manager whose direct reports had given him perfect scores on all scales of an instrument, but he felt that they had only done so because they did not believe that their answers would remain anonymous. Individual managers (self) in the United States may boost their own ratings, against their better judgment, out of fear that the data may be used against them, either to slow down their career or diminish expected salary increases.

Cultural Sensitivity in Interpreting Results

In interpreting 360-degree feedback results, the participant pays particular attention to the pattern of scores from various sources (self, boss, peer, subordinate) and on how his or her scores compare to other managers who have taken the instrument (norm groups). Cultural differences need to be taken into account as part of this interpretation process.

Interpretation of Rater-Group Comparisons

One of the basic premises of 360-degree assessment is that the gap between self-ratings and those of other raters (superiors, peers, direct reports, etc.) suggests areas for development, especially when the competencies are considered important for success in a given organization. It is hoped that the gap is meaningful, that it is not the result of inaccurate data or systematic response patterns that have little or nothing to do with the person being rated. Unfortunately, as Leslie, Gryskiewicz, and Dalton write, "while the use and production of 360-degree instruments has grown over the years, research interpreting the gap between self and others' ratings has not kept pace. The absence of research on self-and-other differences as they relate to culture is even more stark" (1998, p. 27).

Moreover, it is well established that cultural response patterns among countries commonly show up in these ratings. For example, relatively collectivist cultures such as Greece, Portugal, and Turkey significantly rate everything as more important or agree with it ("yesmanship") than more individualistic societies do (Hofstede, 1980; Hoppe, 1990). Furthermore, there is some evidence that raters in Japan and China tend to avoid the extremes of a response scale, while Hispanics prefer to use them. In the United States, self-ratings tend to be higher than those from supervisors or peers (Fleenor, McCauley, and Brutus, 1996); in

Taiwan they are lower. Thus, "self-other gaps in the feedback may be larger for managers from some countries not because of their raters' inability to rate certain skills or abilities, or performance differences, but because of cultural influences in *rating patterns*" (Leslie, Gryskiewicz, and Dalton, 1998, p. 29).

What can be done? As with any successful cross-cultural intervention, it is essential to know the tendencies of one's own culture as well as those of the recipient country. For information on the tendencies of the other culture, savvy insiders and knowledgeable expatriates are once again critical resources. It is also advisable to educate raters ahead of time about the format and purposes of the instrument, and go over instructions for answering the questionnaire.

Perhaps the most helpful solution is to begin any feedback discussion with an exploration of the various ways the respondents (self and others) may interpret the instrument scales and response format. This allows all (available) parties to gain insights into each other's cultural assumptions regarding possible answer patterns, and it sets the stage for an open and meaningful interpretation of the data. As the global economy makes it more likely that individual leaders receive 360-degree feedback data from people of a different nationality, this practice becomes increasingly important.

Selection of Norms

A remaining challenge concerns the question of which norms to use to gauge a person's standing. For example, more and more work is being done in multicultural organizations and groups. Which culture's norms should apply? In this case, it is the organizational culture that is relevant, and so it may be appropriate to use an organizational norm, instead of a cultural norm.

The challenge is somewhat less ambiguous if the instrument is transferred from the United States to just one other culture at a time. In this case, it is most appropriate to use that culture's instrument norm, if available. However, in a situation where people from just two cultures are expected to work together—individuals from the United States and Japan, for instance—it might make more sense to apply the same norms to both groups. (However, see the discussion of response bias later in this chapter.)

In other words, the question of which norms to use goes beyond the properties of the instrument itself. It raises questions as to the purpose of the assessment—questions that go beyond that of the development of the individual leader.

A Few More Thoughts About Assessment

In addition to the four challenges just described, in general collecting and processing multirater instrument data tends to become complex if it is taken across national boundaries. Physical distances, people's mobility, differences in time zones, or the realities of geographically dispersed teams whose members communicate electronically make data collection cumbersome. Adding to the complexity are language barriers, possibly unsound translation of existing instruments into other languages, unfamiliarity with the practice, and limited financial resources (for more details, see Leslie, Gryskiewicz, and Dalton, 1998).

Although computer technology and education help ameliorate many of these hindrances to wider use of the practice in the future, the fundamental challenge remains: How can 360-degree feedback, with its preference for quantification, measurement, and objective data, be brought in line with the cultural values, beliefs, and practices of other cultures that do not share those preferences? The answer needs to be found case by case, and the responsibility for doing so rests with those who practice it.

Clearly, the practice of assessment using 360-degree instruments poses a host of cross-cultural challenges that require a thoughtful approach to its transfer across boundaries. A similarly thoughtful and responsible approach is needed for the other two elements that make for a successful developmental experience in leadership development: challenge and support.

Challenge and Support in Cross-Cultural Perspective

The leadership development model in this book, a model that is being examined from a cross-cultural viewpoint in this chapter, proposes that the more experiences involve assessment and challenge and support, the more developmental they are. Assessment was discussed in the previous section. Challenge is the component that stretches people beyond their existing levels of thought, skill, and expertise. Challenge can be generated by exposing people to novel, difficult, conflictual, or ill-defined situations. It can also come from exposing them to diverse perspectives, through interaction with others or through exposure to new ideas. The element of challenge causes people to call into question current ways of thinking and acting.

The support elements in a development experience work to maintain self-esteem by letting people know that their current strengths have value. Support elements also provide encouragement to people engaged in new experiences or change processes. Support comes from feedback that affirms the individual's skills and self-worth. Support in the form of encouragement is offered by family; friends; coworkers; or the organization, community, or society as a whole. It expresses itself through interpersonal encouragement, resources, or norms that value personal growth and development.

The Element of Challenge

There is strong evidence that the desire for challenge and variety at work is universal, but cultural differences may affect what people define as challenging and determine how comfortable they are with different kinds of experiences.

Universal Desire for Challenge. There is sound empirical evidence that managers and professionals around the world value variety and challenging tasks, and that they derive a sense of personal accomplishment from them (Hofstede, 1980; Hoppe, 1990). There are equally convincing findings that they consider experience, such as different job assignments or participation in task forces, as the best teacher for dealing with the complex challenges of their role (Yeung and Ready, 1995; Smith and Peterson, 1995). Thus, the emphasis on varied, work-related, development experiences, as promoted throughout this handbook, is likely to transfer well across cultural boundaries. The main questions that remain concern the degree to which these experiences are offered by the organization and differences in the type of experience that people find challenging.

Differences in Tolerance for Uncertainty. On the whole, U.S. values and beliefs encourage Americans to engage in the types of developmental experience described throughout this handbook (challenging assignments, feedback-intensive program, developmental relationships). For example, cross-cultural comparisons consistently find U.S. mainstream culture very open to experiences of change, personal growth, and lifelong mobility (*dynamic* pole in Table 11.2). The entrepreneur as cultural hero, who may fail many times over before he or she succeeds, is one of the most visible manifestations of this observation. In the present leadership discussion, it is captured in Peter Vaill's admonition (1996) that we need to learn the competence of incompetency to succeed in a world of turbulence.

Moreover, societies such as the United States where people are relatively comfortable with uncertainty tend also to be countries where people value learning by doing, since learning by doing (*active-reflective* dimension) implies that the learner cannot know exactly what will happen next.

Cultural norms in Australia, Great Britain, and Sweden support a similarly active approach to learning. However, the same cultural preferences cannot be expected everywhere. For example, managers and professionals from France, Germany, Turkey, or Japan are noticeably more concerned with stability, continuity, and certainty. They tend to show less inclination to get involved in novel, ill-defined, and potentially conflictual situations that push them beyond their comfort zone. As Hofstede (1991) and Hoppe (1990) point out, they find greater comfort in rules, structure, standard procedures, functional expertise, intellectual models, predictability, and job security (see "Preferences and Beliefs in the Workplace: Not Everybody Wants the Same!"). This helps explain, for instance, the greater emphasis on technical and administrative competence in Germany and on theory and intellectual development in France. As a consequence, leadership development in these countries tends to be more planful, functional, incremental, and tied to organizational needs.

Preferences and Beliefs in the Workplace: Not Everybody Wants the Same!

Hoppe (1990) collected data from high-level managers and professionals in nineteen mostly Western European countries, Turkey, and the United States, using Hofstede's work-related values and beliefs questions (1982). Here is a snapshot of some of the results for selected countries and items. (Rankings are by item across countries: 1 = highest agreement with statement, 6 = lowest agreement.)

	US	UK	SWE	GER	FRA	TUR
Variety and adventure at work important	2	1	3	4	5	6
Well-defined job *not* important	1	2	3	4	5	6
Security of employment *not* important	1	4	2	5	3	6
Not best to stay with same employer to get ahead	3	1	2	6	4	5
It's all right for a manager *not* to have all the answers	3	2	1	5	4	6
It's all right to have two bosses	1	4	2	5	3	6

Note: SWE = Sweden, GER = (former West) Germany, FRA = France, TUR = Turkey. Complete versions of items in Hoppe (1990). Respondents came from the private, public, and third sectors.

The Group as Source and Target of Development. Additional cultural dynamics come into play in the more collectivist cultural environments of China, Indonesia, or Japan, where seniority and group loyalty are important values.

Seniority in this sense means that employees know that the purpose of their development "is to create a lasting bond between employees and the company, rather than teach a set of transferable skills. . . . Training is called the 'professional ability development program' and is closely linked to organizational development" (Harris and Moran, 1993, p. 200). That is, developmental opportunities are decoupled from short-term advancements or greater marketability of workers' skills. They are likely to be more incremental, and they are designed to avoid failure, embarrassment, and discomfort.

Emphasis on group loyalty also results in a markedly different approach to development. It becomes a developmental challenge not only to the individual, in his or her role as a group or organizational member, but to the entire group. Elashmawi and Harris (1993) describe an incident in which a German technician attempts to train a group of Japanese, one at a time, in the use of a new machine. The manager of the group approaches him at some point and says "I am sorry, we are a group and expect to be trained together. Please, could you show us, as a group, how to use the machine?" (p. 38). In these societies, learning, growth, and accompanying experiences of stress and uncertainty become embedded in the collective effort.

Need for Adjustment. It is apparent from these examples that what people consider challenging is to varying degrees attributable to cultural patterns. People with different cultural values also have different levels of comfort with challenging experiences. These differences suggest different kinds of approaches and activities, as the model is transferred across countries. The assistance of savvy insiders is invaluable in understanding how to adjust to building developmental challenge into a program, an assignment, or any kind of development experience.

The notion of challenge as an essential element of development must expand to include collective learning, whether it occurs in the service of the individual, the group, or the organization as a whole. This latter task is likely to be the more challenging one, since the focus on the individual is so thoroughly ingrained in U.S. thought and action.

However, a greater emphasis on group learning and goals may buffer the individual from some of the stresses, failures, or disappointments that individual leadership development entails.

The Element of Support

The notion of support encourages people to reach out to a variety of others for feedback, encouragement, and advice, as a balance to the challenges encountered in a developmental experience. Yet here again, culture plays a strong hand, both in the comfort that managers feel with relying on others for support and in the breadth of sources of support available to them.

Although there are many cultures outside the United States where values and beliefs work to support the idea of relying on others for help and advice, among U.S. managers there tends to be low comfort with support. Ironically, the U.S. manager has a variety of potential sources of support, including bosses, peers, direct reports, human resource professionals, family, and friends. In many other cultures, where reliance on support seems more natural, the sources of support are much narrower.

Differences in Level of Comfort with Supportive Relationships. Independence is one of the most deeply cherished ideals in U.S. society (*individual* pole in Table 11.2). Admiration for the self-made man or woman exemplifies this value. In fact, overdependence on a mentor or advocate was considered one of the ten fatal flaws in McCall and Lombardo's study (1983) of executive success and derailment. Even though overdependence as a reason for derailment has disappeared in more recent research (Leslie and Van Velsor, 1996), perhaps on account of today's faster pace of change in organizational alliances and work relationships, being dependent on others is clearly viewed as undesirable in mainstream U.S. culture. ("For many [U.S.] Americans, the search for autonomy, self-actualization, and personal growth has supplanted the mythic desire to save frontier towns single-handedly from outlaw bands. The social norm persists, however, as an avoidance of dependence.

Since [U.S.] Americans can envisage few fates worse than dependence, they stress self-reliance. . . ." [Stewart and Bennett, 1991, p.].) Members of U.S. society also tend to see success as something to be achieved in competition with others (*tough* pole). Together, these cultural orientations create the image of the individual achiever who succeeds through his or her own talents, abilities, and efforts.

Paradoxically, by encouraging people to reach out to others for encouragement and advice, the notion of support in our handbook model requires them to acknowledge to themselves that they cannot or should not do all the work alone. Many U.S. managers resist this idea. Yet there are good examples of fruitful relationships among U.S. managers involved in development experiences. Young and Dixon (1996), for example, document the high-impact role that spouses, friends, superiors, or coworkers played in helping executives take more effective action in their various leadership challenges.

Establishing developmental relationships may be significantly less problematic in other cultures, especially collectivist societies where "dependence on others is desirable, for it strengthens the relationship among people and affirms a broad definition of self" (Stewart and Bennett, 1991, pp. 137–138). For example, managers in China, Mexico, Japan, Indonesia, and Singapore consider it their duty to guide and counsel their employees. Similarly, the workgroup believes itself responsible for helping each member's professional development. The organizational norms tend to support multiple layers of help from others. Moreover, emphasis on cooperation, solidarity, and good working relationships among organizational members in countries near the *tender* pole suggests a generally supportive environment for personal growth and development.

Availability of Sources for Support. From an individual point of view, the opportunities for direct personal support are very limited in some cultures outside the United States, particularly in those cultures where the needs of the group or organization take precedence (*collective* pole in Table 11.2). Moreover, in countries combining collective norms with those of born leadership (*different* pole)—such as Colombia, Indonesia, Mexico, and Singapore—the autocratic leader (as an example, the Mexican *patrón*) may be caring and supportive but, in return, expect complete loyalty and subordination. In those cultures, sources of support can be very narrow, and developmental relationships are likely to be limited to the one between the employee and the superior (see "A Lunchtime Conversation in San Francisco").

A Lunchtime Conversation in San Francisco.

After the conclusion of a conference on international leadership, the following conversation among four participants from Indonesia, Iran, Mexico, and the United States took place over a delicious meal.

U.S. participant: When does your responsibility as a leader end? For, example, let's say that you do everything possible to provide the needed resources and support, including your own time, encouragement, and experience, for your employees to be successful, but they still don't succeed as you think they could or should. Don't you say to yourself at some point, I did what I could, it's their responsibility now, not mine?

Indonesian participant: No! I will always feel responsible, even if I tried everything. I can always do more. That's what I owe them. They trust that I will take care of them, no matter what.

Iranian participant: Same for me; in fact, I would try harder. It's like with my children. If my son, in U.S. terminology, brings home a C from school or fails to get into a good college, I would try everything to better the situation. That's my role as a father.

Mexican participant: I agree. There is no point at which I could just say that I did everything in my power and could absolve myself from my responsibility. I may not only try harder but become downright dictatorial. My employees, and children, owe it to me that they try their absolute best.

Smith and Peterson provide indirect support for this latter expectation. They asked middle managers from twenty-nine countries what sources they accessed to help them make sense of the problems they encountered at work. The answers: superiors, colleagues, direct reports, and specialists, but also the managers' own experience and training, formal rules and procedures, unwritten rules, and widespread beliefs. Particularly relevant within the context of this discussion, they found that managers from more collectivist countries that also hold norms of born leadership (*different* pole) significantly relied more on "formal rules and procedures and their superiors." Conversely, managers from individualistic countries with norms of equality reported "greater reliance on their own experience and training and on subordinates" (1995, p. 19).

The Potential for Enrichment of U.S. Practice. In sum, as with the elements of assessment and challenge, the type and degree of support that individuals can expect for their own leadership development is partly a function of the cultural norms that exist in their society. Therefore, U.S. practices must be adjusted when transferred to other parts of the world. However, unlike the first two elements, establishment of supportive developmental relationships may be culturally more in line with the values and beliefs of other cultures than with that of the United States itself. This feature of the leadership development model may therefore transfer well to some countries, and in addition U.S. practice in this area can be enriched by practices in those cultures, as it increasingly crosses national boundaries.

Conclusions and Some Practical To-Do's

The conclusion is clear: culture matters. Leadership and its development tend to be profoundly steeped in the culture of origin (the leadership model presented in this handbook is no exception). Culturally, there is nothing particularly good or bad about the model, as long as it is used in its own cultural environment. However, as with any other model from any other country, philosophical and practical questions arise whenever it is used outside the United States. The more philosophical questions touch on the dilemma that transfer carries with it the risk of imposing U.S. cultural values and beliefs on the recipient cultures. The more practical questions concern the steps that need to be taken to make the transfer successful. Here are suggested steps for cross-cultural work:

General To-Do's

Know the cultural assumptions, values, and beliefs that inform your models and practices

Learn as much as possible about cultural assumptions, values, and beliefs of the recipient culture

Involve savvy insiders and outside country experts in designing and delivering intervention

As much as possible, use models and instruments developed in the host country

Establish joint ventures with other providers who know the market you are entering

Assist host country recipients in understanding your own culture's assumptions, values, and beliefs

Consider multiple solutions, scenarios, cases, and simulations for greater relevance in the recipient culture

Adjust names, dates, symbols, etc., to those of the host country

Become a participant observer in the new environment

Encourage development of local capacities

Use Table 11.2 and Figure 11.1 in this text for an initial check of cultural affinity between the host and U.S. cultures

Access resources listed at the end of the chapter as needed

Assessment

Keep in mind the U.S. preference for objective, direct, measurable feedback

Identify cross-culturally validated scales and adjust or add according to local needs

Discuss instrument scales, answer format, operationalization of items, and so on, with the recipient

Use an instrument in the local language if available and if you are confident in the quality of translation

Use appropriate norms depending on the culture of the recipients and purpose of the assessment

Check for any history of or threats to confidentiality, anonymity, and acceptance of data

Become aware of local practices of feedback, for example, whether it is based on low-context or high-context environment

Be clear on who owns the data, for reasons of confidentiality and practice of feedback

Check for possible cultural response patterns and discuss them with recipients before the feedback session

Be aware of limited research data on the meaning of gaps between and among rater groups

Prepare for greater complexity of data collection and delivery

Challenge

Keep in mind differences in the degree and type of challenge across countries, depending on the location on the *dynamic-stable* and *active-reflective* dimensions

Check the role and responsibility of the individual, group, and organization as a whole in providing challenge

Be aware of the targets for challenge (individual, group, or both)

Support

Recognize possible ambivalence in U.S. culture around use of support (*individual-collective* and *tough-tender* dimensions)

Keep in mind differences in degree and sources of support across countries, depending on the location on the *individual-collective* and *same-different* dimensions

Overall, there are no shortcuts in successful transfer of leadership development models and practices. The main reason is fundamental:

leadership development touches on the deepest layers of human existence—its values, beliefs, hopes, and fears. By definition, these are personal, communal, and cultural in nature. Although they are in many ways very similar across cultures, they are also different. As a result, the challenge of cross-cultural leadership development calls for a deep understanding of both the similarities and the differences, and in the process an openness to learning by everyone involved. In the words of Oliver Wendell Holmes, Jr., "[an individual's] mind, stretched by a new idea, can never go back to its original dimensions."

Resources for In-Depth Understanding of Cultural Differences and Practical Guidance

The 1980s and 1990s generated a wealth of empirical data on greater understanding of differences and similarities among cultures. The following resources are offered for their practicality and easy access.

Elashmawi, F., and Harris, P. R. *Multicultural Management: New Skills for Global Success.* Houston: Gulf, 1993.

Hall, E. T., and Hall, M. R. *Understanding Cultural Differences: Germans, French, and Americans.* Yarmouth, Maine: Intercultural Press, 1989.

Harris, P. R., and Moran, R. T. *Managing Cultural Differences: High-Performance Strategies for a New World of Business* (3rd ed.). Houston: Gulf, 1993.

Hill, R. *EuroManagers and Martians: The Business Culture of Europe's Trading Nations.* Brussels, Belgium: Europublications, Europublic SA/NV, 1994.

Hofstede, G. *Cultures and Organizations: Software of the Mind.* New York: McGraw-Hill, 1991.

Kohls, L. R. *Survival Kit for Overseas Living: For Americans Planning to Live and Work Abroad.* Yarmouth, Maine: Intercultural Press, 1996.

Moran, R. T., Harris, P. R., and Stripp, W. G. *Developing the Global Organization: Strategies for Human Resource Professionals.* Houston: Gulf, 1993.

Stewart, E. C., and Bennett, M. J. *American Cultural Patterns: A Cross-Cultural Perspective.* Yarmouth, Maine: Intercultural Press, 1991.

Wilson, M., Hoppe, W. H., and Sayles, L. R. *Managing Across Cultures: A Learning Framework.* Greensboro, N.C.: Center for Creative Leadership, 1996.

CHAPTER TWELVE

DEVELOPING LEADERS FOR GLOBAL ROLES

Maxine A. Dalton

The theme weaving all the chapters of this book together is the proposition that a person who is willing and able to learn can develop leadership skills through a process that includes assessment, a variety of challenging experiences, and support. Within the United States, this process is put into operation through the leadership development strategies described in Chapters One through Six of this book. This U.S.-based model is firmly grounded in some cultural assumptions: that adults can learn; that individuals can and should take responsibility for their own destiny; that performance rather than age, family connections, or education is the key to advancement; and that career success is central to identity.

Chapter Eleven discusses what happens when the tools and practices of leadership development "made in the USA" are thoughtlessly exported to other cultures where widely differing assumptions prevail. For example, attempting to teach Japanese managers how to manage Japanese subordinates within Japan using U.S. methods and models may be silly at best, and irresponsible at worst.

However, in today's global economy, there is a population of people for whom the do's and don'ts of leadership development practices are not so clear. These are the people who are, or will be, managers and leaders with global responsibilities working in international organizations. It is to them that this chapter is addressed.

To summarize, Chapter Eleven addresses the transfer of U.S.-based leadership development practices to other cultures. This chapter looks at issues of developing individuals whose roles require them to manage and lead across a number of cultures simultaneously.

A few words about context: this chapter describes roles and responsibilities of senior managers, for it is only at senior levels that the scope of responsibility (managing across multiple countries) becomes truly global. For the purpose of this chapter, cross-cultural work at the individual-contributor level is framed as one of the experiences that prepare people for senior global roles. Also, because my experience is primarily with leaders and managers working within for-profit organizations, the discussion and the examples come from that realm.

This is one of the more theoretical and speculative chapters in this book. Leadership development—the theory, the practice, and the research—has most often been a U.S. phenomenon. Although some researchers are starting to examine the "within culture" implications, grappling with the development of people for roles that span multiple cultures is relatively new—as, indeed, is the role itself.

The Context: What Is a Global Organization?

William Greider (1997) has written a lucid, intelligent book describing the nature of global work and its consequences. He defines a global organization as one in which the elements of production are dispersed across many nations. The strategy of the global organization is to produce in low-wage markets (but where the technical competence required for production exists) and to sell in high-wage markets. Global organizations thrive on predictable currency values, stable and favorable political and legal frameworks, advantageous tax structures, a skilled but compliant labor force, shared overhead, and an existing management and marketing network. However, because these desired conditions are neither stable nor predictable—subject to shifts in demand, price, currency values, politics, and so forth—global organizations must build redundancy into their systems to protect against surpluses and be able to deploy elements of production to other sites when necessary.

For example, a global organization whose product is sports apparel might source the fabric in China, design the clothing in the United States, manufacture it in Bangladesh, and sell it through a chain of stores located in the United States, Canada, Europe, Singapore, and Japan. All these activities are planned, managed, coordinated, and led from a central office that could be located anywhere in the world; no activity is so permanently rooted that it cannot be shifted to another locale. If the political climate becomes too unstable in China, sourcing can be moved to Mexico; if labor costs become too expensive in Bangladesh, manufacturing can be relocated to Alabama. Because time-to-market is of critical importance in the sports apparel industry and customers can be lost during the transition, the company may have two factories, one in Bangladesh and one in Alabama, each operating at half capacity, so that in the event of instability one can be shut down and the other can take up the slack without missing a beat.

Multiply this example for every product the company has—shorts, golf shirts, bathing suits, baseball caps, sweatsuits—each with the potential for a shared or different process of sourcing, manufacturing, distributing, and selling, and you see the global organization. Its leadership functions are carried out by people recruited from all over the world for their knowledge, skills, and abilities, not their nationalities.

To implement this strategy, organizations have adopted a variety of structures. Much of the current debate on globalization is about what *global* really means and how an organization should be structured to do business globally. Some authors describe a continuum of structure from multinational to global as if global were a more desirable state. A particularly helpful discussion of structure comes from Bartlett and Ghoshal

(1989), who argue that structure must be determined by the task and that organizations doing business globally most likely encompass multiple structures. In other words, some activities of the organization may be organized geographically, some by function, and some by product line. Bartlett and Ghoshal call an organization that incorporates all of these structures a *transnational organization*.

In the sports apparel example, let us say that sales are organized by geography to capitalize on knowledge of the local customer, human resources are organized by function in each region to establish equitable and consistent policies and procedures within a particular legal or political framework, and manufacturing is organized by product line worldwide to capture economies of scale. Those who work within these structure therefore have a variety of responsibilities, bounded by geography, function, product, or any combination of the three.

What Is the Work of Managers and Leaders Who Have Global Responsibilities?

When can we say that a person's work responsibilities are global in scope? One definition draws a distinction between *global* and *international*. An executive with global responsibilities "operates from an understanding of the worldwide business environment, while the traditional international or expatriate manager focuses on a single foreign country and on managing relationships between headquarters and that country" (Adler and Bartholomew, 1992, p. 53). An executive with domestic responsibilities, by contrast, focuses on the issues of the business within a single country: that person's own country. These definitions suggests that only when a person reaches a certain level of accountability—responsibilities for operations across more than two countries—is the work truly global.

In a synthesis of the literature on global organizations and global work, Janet de Merode (1997) has characterized the role demands of global work:

- Cross-cultural: motivates multicultural teams; conducts cross-cultural negotiations; discerns and manages cultural influences on business practice, marketing and sales; selects and evaluates staff in different cultural settings
- Communications: manages information across multiple time zones; integrates local and global information for multisite decision making; internally, inspires information sharing and exchange among actors who do not see or know each other; externally, represents corporate interests at multiple levels of interaction in public and private sectors; operates effectively in a foreign language, even if through translation
- Relationships: seeks and maintains relationships leading to alliances, mergers, acquisitions, joint ventures, and licensing arrangements, being able to analyze and choose the best format for collaboration; applies knowledge of public regulatory framework in multiple countries; facilitates corporate engagement in multiple local settings
- Marketing: leads sharp client focus in disparate markets to find growth segments, develop niche strategies, etc.; creates innovative corporate culture to constantly customize products for clients and markets where information is still new and different from one's own experience; taps local market knowledge and uses it to underpin overall corporate strategy
- Business practice: performs wage, technology, and foreign-exchange arbitrage and leverage in multiple markets simultaneously; carries out negotiations with multiple risk factors and unknowns; negotiates effectively in different business environments, even with jet lag and through translation

At first glance, these role demands appear to be the same as for any senior executive in any corporation. Certainly, domestic leaders must motivate, negotiate, select and evaluate staff, manage information, integrate information, and make decisions. But I believe that the infinite variety of factors to be attended to in global work renders it both quantitatively and qualitatively different.

In a domestic role, even if the workgroup is extremely heterogeneous and scattered across several time zones, everyone is still working within the same dominant culture, the same legal and political structure, and so on. In the global role, location determines dominance of cultural style, laws, and politics; the global manager is responsible for multiples of each of these variables. Because of cultural differences, profound moral and ethical contradictions are imbedded in this role, having to do with human freedom, cultural and environmental disruption, and the built-in conflict between national interests and the desires of the investors and stockholders who are, in fact, the owners of the global corporation (Greider, 1997).

For example, is a major oil company responsible to any degree for the hanging of three environmental activists in Africa who protested the loss of the country's natural resources to a foreign power? Is it wrong to put twenty-five-dollar-per-hour workers in Youngstown, Ohio, out of work and move production to Bangladesh where workers earn seven dollars a day (a good local wage)? Is a gift of cash intended to establish goodwill in China to be construed as bribery, or a broker's fee? And what of the inherent conflict between national interest and corporate interest? Is it not the conventional wisdom that foreign nationals cannot be trusted to work in their own countries because the best interests of the company may be in conflict with the best interests of the country?

Global leaders do their work across boundaries of time, space, country, and culture. In the next section, we address the capacities they need, or need to develop, to meet these role demands.

Capacities Needed by Global Leaders

Both popular and academic writers have struggled to describe the skill set of the manager in a global role. This is a difficult literature to summarize since some authors are writing about managers who work in global organizations, or managers working within the competitive global environment, but not necessarily about managers who have global responsibilities within their jobs. Discussions of global work sometimes cross over into the expatriate literature, which is often focused on preparing individuals and their families to live and work in another country. The literature cited here is meant to provide a look at the state of the art in discussing the capacities of the effective global manager, but it is certainly not intended as an exhaustive review.

David Weeks (1992), working for the Conference Board, described the successful global manager as someone who has knowledge of the business, a high degree of tolerance and flexibility, and the ability to work with people. Rosabeth Moss Kanter (1995) describes global corporate leaders as being cosmopolitans, those who can integrate and cross-fertilize knowledge; moving capital, ideas, people where they are needed, creating multiple points of input and output, generating new routes of communication, and managing dispersed centers of expertise, influence, and production. Bartlett and Ghoshal (1989) describe effective global managers as people able to hold the matrix of a multistructured entity in their mind, reorganizing form to follow function as the business demand might dictate. Wills and Barham (1994) attempt to describe the international manager (someone managing across a number of countries and cultures simultaneously) more holistically as a person who exists "being-in-the-world." They define the elements of this inextricably linked whole as cognitive complexity, psychological maturity, and emotional energy.

Even this cursory review begs the question of whether the skills and capacities necessary to be effective in a global role are truly different from those needed in a domestic role. Kanter's description seems closest to capturing something unique about the complexity of global work. She describes an individual with the ability to learn from and leverage the heterogeneity and chaos of the worldwide marketplace. It is one thing to adapt to cultural differences and another to actually leverage those differences to competitive advantage. In a similar vein, Adler and Bartholomew (1992) describe the skills of the transnational manager as the ability to use cross-cultural interaction not just on foreign assignments but on a daily basis, to enrich knowledge and create a culturally dynamic organization.

These various descriptions capture the flavor of the debate. Drawing from the work of these authors and others, and particularly from the integrative work of de Merode, the hypothesis of this chapter is that global roles present unique demands. To meet these demands leaders must possess

- A high level of cognitive complexity. The constant change imbedded in the role of global manager demands the ability to gather and make sense of huge amounts of contradictory information from multiple locations—information about markets, currencies, regulatory changes, and labor conditions—and to make reasoned and timely decisions.
- Excellent interpersonal skills. The recognition that different customs, values, and expectations of management's role exist in different cultures challenges managers to exhibit excellent interpersonal skill as the glue that holds things together while they figure out the appropriate behavior in a given country and situation. An attitude of deep-seated courtesy and respect often buys forgiveness for behavior based on cultural misunderstanding.
- The ability to learn from experience. Managers working within several cultures continuously receive information about business and about people. But that information is useless unless they are open to accepting it and willing to act on it—that is, open to learn from experience.
- Advanced moral reasoning. An appreciation that ethical dilemmas are imbedded within the valued practice of cultural tolerance demands advanced moral reasoning.

All of these skills can be developed using the practices described in this book, but the simultaneous cross-cultural nature of the work puts a different spin on how one goes about the learning.

Again, to differentiate this chapter from Chapter Eleven, keep in mind the target population. Individuals assuming global responsibilities may be chosen from anyplace in the world regardless of where headquarters are located. The board of directors may comprise people from many countries. Members of management teams could come from anywhere in the world; in fact, each might be from a different country, and some of them might also be expatriates.

For this population, it is not sufficient to say that we have to develop them within the context of their own cultural expectations. For them, the only cultural expectation can be: Where am I today? Who is sitting across the table from me today? And how can I be most effective in this context? The prototypical manager with global responsibilities may in any given month spend two weeks traveling among three sites in the United States, move on for a week in Singapore, and end up with a week at headquarters in the United Kingdom. How is a person to be developed for this level of complexity?

Integrating Job Assignments, Feedback, and Relationships

The most powerful tool for developing the capacities and skills needed in global work is a job assignment thoughtfully integrated with feedback and supportive relationships.

Learning by doing—learning because it needs to be done—would seem to be a universal tenet of adult development. However, all too often learning from a job assignment is a fortunate accident, comprehended only in hindsight. Instead, the use of assignments for development should be framed as purposeful opportunism (Seibert, Hall, and Kram, 1995). This requires knowing the kinds of assignments likely to be available, what these assignments are likely to develop, and who might benefit from a given assignment.

Unfortunately, it is impossible to direct a business so as to present a neat and tidy menu of job assignments ready for someone's development on demand. Rather, employees must be made ready to recognize and take advantage of an assignment, a potential developmental opportunity, when it occurs. They must understand that the assignment alone is not sufficient to leverage the learning. Critical to the learning are a clear developmental goal (clarified through assessment); a strategy for receiving ongoing feedback as new behaviors are attempted; and the relational support provided by coaches, role models, and a variety of others as described in Chapter Five.

To organize a company's developmental processes around the dynamic of purposeful opportunism, a pool of potential global managers must be identified, people with the desire and potential for global work. Those targeted for this pool must have clear developmental goals arrived at through some culturally appropriate process of assessment (see Chapter Eleven). That is, to take advantage of opportunities as they appear, candidates must understand their strengths and weaknesses and know the kinds of experiences that they are looking for.

Human resource development professionals or line managers must understand how assignments drive development. They must know, in general, the types of assignment likely to be available, and they must be charged with disseminating this information throughout the organization. For their part, individuals and their bosses must be ready to take advantage of work assignments as they come along. They must also be prepared to learn from the assignment by being taught how to solicit and use feedback and how to identify role models and coaches as support for learning within the assignment.

Thus, all parties to a person's development for a global job—the company's human resource professionals, the individuals themselves, and their managers—have a role to play in that development. To be most effective, the development process must contain the three core elements of assessment, challenge, and support.

This discussion is to some extent a reiteration of principles put forth in other chapters, but I repeat it here because what follows is a list of assignments that teach the skills required of global work. Such a list suggests a linear sequence, but things never work out so smoothly in real life. Real development in real organizations is messy. Developing leaders for global work is like developing leaders for any other work: it functions best when the developmental task and the work task are meshed.

This dynamic process is poignantly illustrated in the life story of one man who is now a senior executive in his company with international responsibilities. When asked about the experiences—personal and work related–that prepared him for his present job, he told the following story.

As a child, he visited several foreign countries, for his family liked to travel. As a college student he spent several summer vacations hitch-hiking through the United Kingdom and Europe with his brother. Upon graduation he joined a company with production facilities around the world. After some early success as a research and development engineer, he was assigned (because of his technical expertise) to headquarters as staff assistant to the vice president of operations for Asia. This vice president was an experienced international manager with the ability to get along with people wherever he found himself. The assistant traveled throughout Asia with his boss and had the opportunity to observe how skillfully he worked with people.

His next assignment was as a production manager. Then he learned through the grapevine about a new project team being formed to develop a quality-control process that could be used in manufacturing plants in Bangladesh, Alabama, Wales, and Malaysia. The team would be made up of people from all four participating countries. Because he had traveled in both the United Kingdom and Asia, he volunteered for the team.

Here the organization, in the person of a human resource staff member, made a developmental intervention. The young manager was told that in addition to the team goal—coming up with a quality-control process that could be successfully installed at all sites—he would also be expected to achieve an individual goal: learning how to be a more effective member of a cross-cultural team. So this young manager was assessed on such skills as active listening, acting with integrity, bringing out the best in others on the team, and demonstrating appreciation of cultural differences. He was asked to set developmental goals based on this assessment before joining the team and was encouraged to share his developmental goals with the other team members. After the assignment he was debriefed on the dilemmas of the task, what he learned, how he learned it, and how the organization could use what he learned in forming cross-cultural project teams in the future. It was a positive experience for him, so he continued to look for international opportunities.

Today this manager attributes his success to the fortunate happenstance of love for travel, experience outside the country, a good role model with international experience, and an HR professional who showed him how to leverage the learning from his experiences.

With this example in mind, let us turn to the critical question. What processes, what rough sequence of experiences, might reasonably be expected to develop the skills hypothesized as essential for global work: the skills of cognitive complexity, interpersonal acumen, moral reasoning, and the ability to learn from experience?

Identification and Assessment Processes

Identifying the developmental challenges in the work that needs to be done takes time and attention. But sometimes it is necessary to fill a slot quickly. To take full advantage of developmental opportunities as they emerge, line managers and human resource professionals must know who the potential global managers are.

Early Identification, Exposure, and Work Previews. Those in the organization who are responsible for the global development career track must be on the lookout for people eligible for and interested in a career path leading to global responsibilities. A possible first step in the process is to identify people early in their careers who show a liking for travel, novelty, and international work; who speak other languages; and whose life experience includes time spent living in foreign locations.

Some people do not like to travel. Some people would never be willing to go on an international assignment. Some people demonstrate that they cannot or will not grapple with diversity within their own countries. Some people have life and work goals in conflict with the time demands inherent in global work. Then there are those who have good potential, but they are simply unsure whether they would like to try an international assignment. Look for opportunities to let them host foreign guests, be exposed to cultural differences including within-country cultures, and in general broaden their horizons.

Feedback-Intensive Program and Process. The point has been made that people need clear developmental goals to identify opportunity as it presents itself. For U.S. managers, a feedback-intensive program in which strengths and weaknesses are identified can be a powerful way to gain clarity on development goals. A goal-setting process should be carried out as soon as an individual is identified as someone interested in a global career track, and again before each major assignment. Goal accomplishment should also be debriefed following an assignment. How this feedback and goal setting occur, however, needs to be culturally determined (see Chapter Eleven). A feedback-intensive program, as described in Chapter Two, may not be culturally appropriate for a given individual within a particular country.

A Variety of Challenging Assignments

In any organization, there are a variety of assignments representing the work that needs to be done. These assignments differ in length, intensity, and scope. Each of these assignments can provide the ready learner with the opportunity to master a different set of skills.

Business Trips and Long-Distance Multicountry Projects. Business travel and multicountry assignments afford exposure to cultural differences within a business context: people, money, laws, customs, language. Through these experiences, people develop the ability to listen, put others at ease, communicate orally and in writing across language barriers (perhaps through translators), and recognize that others make sense of events differently from one's preferred viewpoint. Experiencing, not just knowing, that differences in perspectives exist is an early step toward developing "global" skills.

Working as a Member of a Cross-Cultural Team. Serving as a member of a cross-cultural team gives people the chance to experience the simultaneous and multiple cross-cultural influences characteristic of senior-level global work. More often than not, the team is geographically dispersed, so that the physical cues associated with words are absent. People learn to interpret meaning across time, distance, and culture, and they learn to trust.

An Expatriate Assignment. As in the previous assignment, people have the chance to learn what they do not know, practice perspective taking, and increase self-awareness and interpersonal skill. They also have the chance to start noting the ethical dilemmas that are often imbedded in culturally driven business practices, and they begin to appreciate what it is like to accomplish tasks within a different cultural context.

An Expatriate Assignment with Managerial Responsibilities. A managerial assignment provides the opportunity for a boundary-spanning role: explaining headquarters to the host country and the host country to headquarters. Depending on level and location, this assignment also provides the manager with an important external role: working to understand the framework of laws and politics within a country and learning to negotiate within that frame. In this framework, the ethical dilemmas may become more profound.

A Repatriate Assignment. Here is an opportunity for people to teach others what they have learned. The repatriate experience can be harvested to inform business strategy as well as administrative policies that support expatriate selection, preparation, and deployment. Ironically, in many U.S. companies repatriates are at best ignored and at worst derailed because of their absence. Interviewers (Dalton and Wilson, 1996) asked sixteen senior-level repatriates in a Fortune 100 company, "How has the organization used what you learned during your expatriate assignment?" The unanimous answer was, "It has not." One interviewee commented, "You are the first person to even ask, and I have been back for two years." Another commented, "No one even asked to see my slides."

It is troubling that companies scramble to be globally competitive yet are so careless about developing the people they need. The biggest impediment to developing individuals for global work is poor treatment of expatriates. Unless this changes, talented people will not take the assignments, and in the long run the organization will not thrive as a global entity.

Managing a Major Multicountry Project. This type of assignment brings the experience of working in multiple cultures and across distance. Learning opportunities include creating and maintaining virtual teams, managing individuals that one doesn't see very often, using the teams to leverage cultural differences in service to innovation, and using the situation to develop the team members.

Assignments with Regional Responsibilities. This type of assignment involves working across more than one culture, as in the Americas, the Pacific Rim, the Middle East, or Europe. Since the assignment is probably within a functional area such as sales, human resources, or finance, the influence of laws, foreign currency, and local custom becomes especially salient.

Global Responsibility for a Product. Lastly, the true global assignment—managing across many cultures—calls on all of the skills previously acquired and pushes for development of cognitive complexity. Unlike project management, this assignment calls for long-term management of a product or process throughout the business cycle. This is the level of responsibility described earlier by both Greider and Kanter, where strategic decisions that affect the life and future of the organization are made. The person chosen for this type of assignment is undoubtedly a senior executive with significant experience under his or her belt. I believe that success in this role is largely dependent on the variety and intensity of experiences in the executive's career history.

Supportive Relationships. Threaded throughout their career assignments, managers who aspire to global work should have role models and mentors who themselves have successful global careers and can provide advice, support, and feedback. Young managers who are interested in global work and have been identified as having high potential in this area ideally are given the opportunity to work within the sphere of these successful global executives at several points in their careers.

Tying All Three Elements Together

The list of assignments presented earlier in the chapter suggests a chronology built on an ever-increasing scope of responsibility, from early previews and exposure to things international, through short trips and expatriate assignments, to global responsibilities for projects and products. Whatever the sequence of assignments that fall to an individual, each should in some way build on the previous assignment but in other ways be qualitatively different from it.

CCL is developing technologies for assessing the developmental challenges that exist in a job and the skills that an assignment can teach (see, for example, McCauley, Ruderman, Ohlott, and Morrow, 1994). These technologies need to be explored as possible tools for better confirming and expanding what the assignments discussed here teach. In a study of expatriates, Dalton and Wilson (1996) identified more than forty-three lessons that expatriates said they had learned on an expatriate assignment. These lessons clustered under the general headings of interpersonal skills, cultural knowledge, cognitive skills, personal skills, business knowledge, and management skills. The following quotes illustrate the kind of learning that occurred:

> One has to learn to listen with one's body besides paying attention with one's ears when you listen to others. You discover what is of value to them. In order to persuade others, you have to uncover their worldview and frame.

I learned a whole other perspective and way of doing things. I learned to listen, to reevaluate the value of a collaborative style. But it was hard. It is hard to trust people who are so different. . . . You have to establish the relationship and see if the trust is there.

I learned to observe, adopt, reject. I had to ask, What is valuable for me without losing my personality and values, approaches, beliefs? All of this was a challenge, all by itself.

Finally, when international assignments are interspersed with domestic assignments, the learning from one should be reinforced and harvested during the other. For example, organizations can create opportunities for those returning from international assignments to orient potential expatriates, take part in planning discussions about a product launch in another country, or sit in on human resource discussions about developing policies or training programs for implementation in other countries.

So far, development of individuals for global roles seems to track with the development strategies offered in the previous chapters: judicious use of assignments, feedback, and relationships directed toward a strategic developmental goal. What will probably be different in using these strategies to acquire global skills is the process of the learning itself.

The Ability and Willingness to Learn Across Cultures

For global work, ability and willingness to learn is both a part of a process (represented by the model described in the introductory chapter) and an outcome—a set of skills, a meta-competency. It is, in fact, an outcome for all kinds of work, but it is particularly important to the dynamic nature of global work.

What is meant by the term *learning skills*? How might they be different for people involved in global work? Baird, Briscoe, and Tuden (1996) urge that aspiring global managers be taught the skills of action learning and self-reflection; they label these learning skills as awareness, flexibility, and adaptability. Spreitzer, McCall, and Mahoney (1997) have developed a more elaborate scheme for labeling and assessing the learning skills required of aspiring international executives.

Building on work begun at the Center for Creative Leadership in the mid-1980s, Gretchen Spreitzer, Morgan McCall, and Joan Mahoney extended the idea that critical management and leadership skills are learned from experience (McCall, Lombardo, and Morrison, 1988; McCauley, Ruderman, Ohlott, and Morrow, 1994) and addressed themselves to those behaviors that facilitate learning from the experience. They particularly targeted international managers ("an executive who is in a job with some international scope, whether as an expatriate or in a job dealing with international issues more generally").

Spreitzer and colleagues identified fourteen behavior sets that they believe discriminate individuals able to learn from and be effective in international experiences. They divide these into two groups: (1) learning-oriented behaviors, and (2) end-state competencies (see "Learning-Oriented Behaviors and Competencies Important in International Roles"). Young managers who, early in their careers, exhibit the learning-oriented behaviors are those most likely to achieve the end-state competencies and subsequent effectiveness. The competencies, in turn, are a group of behaviors, skills, and attributes found in established and effective managers who have had rich and varied managerial careers.

Learning-Oriented Behaviors and Competencies Important in International Roles.

Behaviors

Uses feedback

Seeks feedback

Cross-culturally adventurous

Seeks opportunities to learn

Is open to criticism

Is flexible

Competencies

Is sensitive to cultural differences

Acts with integrity

Is committed to success

Has broad business knowledge

Brings out the best in people

Is insightful

Has the courage to take a stand

Takes risks

(*Source:* Spreitzer, McCall, and Mahoney, 1997; used with permission.)

Spreitzer and colleagues found in particular that people who were perceived to be cross-culturally adventurous, who seek opportunities to learn, and who are insightful and open to criticism are most likely to be described as effective in an international role.

Using the work of Spreitzer, McCall, and Mahoney as a foundation, developmental assessment for global roles can be based on behaviors identified as important to learning from experience. If people are able to take this assessment feedback and use it to improve their ability to learn from experience, in theory they are better able to take advantage of the variety of challenges that prepare them for senior-level global roles. Being assessed on learning behaviors rather than on end-state competencies or personality traits is a different way of applying assessment technology.

But how an individual learns is determined by his or her cultural frame. This may be the crux of what is different about developing skills to be an effective global manager. Learning from experience is a universal human phenomenon. Having support for the learning and receiving ongoing feedback about behaviors that approximate goal attainment are probably also critical to the learning, regardless of culture.

But how these learning behaviors—engaging in a challenging experience, seeking and using feedback, soliciting relational support—are played out is culturally determined. These learning behaviors are different in various cultures, even though they have the same meaning and purpose.

Thus managers who are going to work globally must first understand how to learn within their own culture. But as they work in other parts of the world, they must learn how learning is supported in that culture. For example, a U.S. manager may seek and use feedback by "pursuing feedback even when others are reluctant to give it"—an item that shows the ability to learn, from the Spreitzer, McCall, and Mahoney perspective. However, as evidence of the ability to learn, this behavior may be peculiarly American. If this same U.S. manager is in Japan on assignment, she may seek feedback directly and risk offending people. Or she may think she is not getting feedback when in fact she is not recognizing it. Instead of the feedback coming directly to her, it may be transmitted through her boss to a peer, to another peer, and finally delivered to her over a drink at a bar after work.

Another example of how learning behaviors lead to unintended results is the construct of "seeking opportunities to learn." Although in many Western cultures failure to seek and engage in an opportunity might be interpreted as lack of ambition or initiative, in other cultures aggressive pursuit of opportunity could be interpreted as lack of modesty, or violation of group norms around the interaction of opportunity, age, and tenure.

For an illustration, let us imagine a project team made up of store managers from Tokyo, London, New York City, Singapore, and Montreal. Their task is to create a better system for getting customer feedback to the designers in Florida in a more timely manner. The task has two parts: (1) create the system and (2) build a standing committee that can come together quickly to solve common retailing problems. To be able to come together and work quickly, the members of the standing committee have to learn to respect and trust one another, share information, and provide feedback both face-to-face and long distance. But how is that feedback to be given and received? Should the representative from New York tell the representative from Japan in the public meeting that he does not feel that his ideas are being heard (giving feedback)? Should the Japanese member take the New York representative out drinking and, after several drinks, tell him that he talks too much in meetings (giving feedback)? For this team to move forward, each member has to learn how to learn within the cultural expectations of all the other members of the team.

To summarize, as people move into global roles, they need to understand how the processes of learning are carried out within a given culture so that they know how to engage in opportunity, and how to solicit and recognize support and feedback. In other words, the behaviors that represent the learning process are culturally distinct. To develop leaders for global roles means to help them understand

- How learning from experience occurs (a general principle)
- How the principle is put into operation within their own culture (a specific tactic)
- How it is operationalized in each of the cultures in which they work (learning how to learn globally)

The Development of Moral Reasoning

The other skill set that seems qualitatively different in thinking about developing individuals for global responsibilities is development of moral reasoning. People who are working globally are expected to tolerate and adapt to cultural differences. For global executives, this means multiple cultural differences. Every time the phone rings, the person on the other end may be from another culture with a unique problem to be solved. Inevitably, there is a point on the spectrum of tolerance and adaptation where the other culture presents a practice that becomes morally or ethically questionable from the perspective of the global manager.

In fact, the most difficult developmental task faced by someone in a global assignment may be dealing with the moral and ethical dilemmas inherent in cross-cultural work. It is here that the rational economic model used earlier in this chapter—produce in low-wage countries, sell in high-wage countries, maximize value for the stockholder—comes face-to-face with the human condition in a world of finite natural resources. It is in this domain that the skill (or lack of skill) of global leaders has the greatest impact on our collective future.

The globalization of business is changing the world, and the global executives who run these businesses are the unelected, unappointed, and often invisible instruments of this change. "They were in China, or Malaysia, or Eastern Europe to cope with the new global realities on behalf of their own firms. They would survive or fail as individuals based on whether their companies survived and flourished; not on what happened to the prosperity of their own country" (Greider, 1997, p.217)—or, I would add, that of the host country.

Some believe that this globalization of interests will save the world, and some believe it will exacerbate its agonies. These are complex and difficult issues. A key part of developing individuals for global roles is to build in and underscore opportunities to grapple with complex ethical issues. These are every bit as important as learning to read balance sheets, speak a foreign language, or introduce a new product into a new market—perhaps more so.

Organizations need to develop their own formal standards of ethical business conduct, but individuals need to have practice and support in grappling with moral ambiguity: "In a global business environment, values in tension are the rule rather than the exception" (Donaldson, 1996, p. 62). This is not tension over which fork to use (if indeed forks are used at all). These are tensions concerning basic human rights or sacred traditions, as defined within the context of economic and cultural perspective. Greider (1997) describes how a high-tech company taught young Moslem women to open their own bank accounts so that they could keep their paychecks and not have to turn them over to their fathers. This act could be viewed as positive by those who value independence for women, or negative by those concerned with maintaining traditional family roles and values.

To begin to develop their moral reasoning, people need to be provided with challenging assignments that have consequences, and these consequences need to be visible and public. It is not sufficient to describe a successful international assignment as one in which the individual meets the company's goals and does not get into any legal or political trouble. Owning, discussing, and resolving moral and ethical dilemmas across cultural frames and economic realities is perhaps the most critical developmental opportunity for the global leader to have.

Thinking back to the list of assignments that might teach the skills needed for global work, I have added three others specifically designed to address the skill of complex moral reasoning:

1. An excellent developmental experience is to serve on a cross-cultural task force to design an organization's ethical code of business.
2. Another is to take that code to sites around the world and explain it, receive feedback on it, and rework it based on the feedback. Of course, in some countries, giving feedback to a representative from headquarters is considered impolite or unpolitic, so the task of getting input becomes part of the challenge.
3. A third opportunity is serving as a member of a worldwide ethical business council where thorny issues are discussed and resolved.

Again, grappling with the ethical and moral dilemmas of global work may be the most critical developmental need of any global executive. It is not about damage control or staying out of trouble. It is about development as a human being and as a member of a responsible organization.

Summary

Increasingly, organizations are doing business internationally and individuals are needed to staff critical international roles. Once again, practice has outpaced research. Organizations face serious practical questions that have not been answered empirically:

- How do we develop individuals for global roles?
- What are the skills and capacities that an individual must have to do global work?
- Are these skills and capacities really different than the skills of an effective domestic manager?

The basic model of this book is appropriate for global work as well as domestic work, but some aspects of it require a special focus. In particular, the nature of developmental job assignments is different, and there is a need to understand more about which assignments are most likely to provide the best opportunities to learn needed skills. This is all the more critical because we believe that developmental assignments are the best avenue for international learning. The core skill—the ability to learn—also takes on a different coloration, for those doing global work need to learn how to learn in a variety of cultures. Finally, special attention needs to be paid to the ethical and moral issues inherent in working cross-culturally.

CHAPTER THIRTEEN

APPROACHING THE FUTURE
OF LEADERSHIP DEVELOPMENT

Wilfred H. Drath

Were I to guess what readers are thinking here at the end of this book, it might be something like, "How are we going to prepare the leaders of the future?" Or perhaps, "Where are the leaders of the future going to come from?" Whether you are a human resource manager, a corporate executive, a nonprofit volunteer, a civic leader, or just a concerned citizen, if you are reading this book, then you have probably noticed worry about the future of leadership crossing your mind more than once.

Two contradictory themes in modern life bring this worry to the fore. Although the world seems to be smaller, and its people brought together by communications and transportation advances, they seem at

I am deeply grateful to the following people, who have been a sustaining source of challenge and support: Robert Burnside, Cedric Crocker, Michael Hoppe, Winn Legerton, Cindy McCauley, Russ Moxley, Chuck Palus, Joan Tavares, Ellen Van Velsor, and Martin Wilcox. I also wish to express my debt and appreciation to Robert Kegan and Kenneth Gergen, whose ideas have been central to the development of the concepts presented here.

the same time more fractured and divided, less cohesive. It appears that as we humans come into closer contact, we are simultaneously retreating from one another into enclaves of special interest, whether formed by race, gender, nationality, religion, profession, or economic status. As we struggle with becoming more inclusive, we are continuously tempted to become more exclusive.

This causes thoughtful people to worry about leadership in the future. Since leadership is supposed to be about getting people to work together toward common goals, the spectacle of such diversity of special interests and the force with which people are asserting their particular points of view throw the prospects for effective leadership into doubt. People ask, "How can we in this organization (or community, or nation) find a leader who can articulate a vision that brings together all of our various agendas, values, needs, and differing perspectives?" It is a poignant question because the insistent, implied answer is: "We can't. Such a leader no longer exists."

Yet, along with this sense of pessimism, a new note of optimism is also arising. It is being sounded by people who sense that perhaps *a* leader is not the answer, that leadership is larger than the actions of a single person. Although it is a young idea, its meaning far from clear, many people in organizations and communities are beginning to think of leadership as a distributed process shared by many ordinary people instead of the expression of a single extraordinary person.

It is to this new spirit of leadership that this chapter is addressed. The preceding chapters offer wisdom and expertise on developing individuals as leaders; this is something we will in all likelihood always need. This chapter, however, tries to envision a future in which a significantly larger number of people in organizations and communities will want to, and be required to, participate in leadership. What will leadership development look like in such a future? How can we begin to make a transition from developing individuals as leaders toward developing whole groups of people as participants in leadership processes?

The Evolving Idea of Leadership

Developing leaders has been a concern since antiquity. From ancient Egypt there is evidence that preparing the pharaohs for leadership was a matter of importance to which great thought and analysis were devoted. In *The Republic,* Plato describes leaders as men of "gold" to distinguish them from artisans and workers, men of "bronze" who are obviously not intended to lead. Aristotle was responsible for the development of Alexander the Great, the future leader of an empire. But this age-old approach is one of developing leaders—people assumed by birth to be leaders—which is different from the idea of developing *leadership.*

More recent ideas hold that learned abilities and circumstances make the main difference in leadership: the sergeant who is thrust into leading the squad in time of war; the office boy who works hard and becomes president of the company; the visionary who nurtures an idea into a giant enterprise; the quiet juror who steps forward in a time of indecision and takes charge of deliberations. These are all examples of people *becoming* leaders, of the quality of leadership emerging in a person in a certain context. This is usually what we have in mind when we think about developing leadership today: developing the general human capacity of most people to act as leaders when needed. This is quite different from the old idea of training and developing someone presumed to be born as a leader.

This change in approach to leadership development has come about because of changes in the idea of leadership itself. Had this book been written fifty or one hundred years ago, its focus would have been on nurturing and educating preconceived leaders, preparing people of "obvious" leadership potential to discharge their duty. As assumptions that leadership was purely inborn were replaced by ideas of leadership as something that a person could learn to do, something that could emerge if circumstances required it, the approach to leadership development changed from one of nurturing innate ability in a select few toward one of teaching people in general how to become leaders. This book rests on that foundation: how to develop the leadership ability of any reasonably intelligent, mature person.

In other words, the ideas of leadership itself and of leadership development have changed in tandem. When thinking about how to develop leadership, it matters a great deal what leadership is assumed to be. Which brings us to the subject of this chapter. How might the idea of leadership be changing again, and how might these changes affect the practice of leadership development in the coming years?

Changes in leadership are not only about how leadership is defined but also about how people practice leadership, that is, what people in workgroups, teams, and organizations actually do. What people actually do depends a lot on what they think; ideas and definitions provide frameworks for action. Changes in leadership thus reflect changes both in action and in thinking about action.

Leadership might seem to be something that hasn't changed much down through the centuries. As becomes clear in this chapter, I believe the practice of leadership has changed a great deal. What hasn't changed is the need for leadership. People have always appeared to need some force within their various groups, communities, tribes, and organizations to help them create direction, avoid disorder, and respond to changes in their surroundings. Humans survive on this planet by pulling together, and leadership is a name we give to whatever it is that gets us going in a common direction. The goals of creating direction and responding to external changes remain as much alive today as ever before. But what does seem to change constantly throughout history is the means by which humans try to create this leadership force.

In the ancient world, the idea of leadership seems to have been that of domination, ruling over followers; there were kings and there were subjects. Kings led, subjects followed, as by natural law. This idea of leadership prevailed for thousands of years. But by the time of the American Revolution a distinctly different idea of leadership began to surface, one in line with a more enlightened approach that included the rise of democracy. This is an idea of leadership as social influence, where a leader sees the need to respect and understand followers and tries to motivate them through rational and emotional appeals. This has been termed *transactional* leadership (Bass, 1985.)

In the twentieth century, the evolution of a modern idea of leadership reflected an understanding of humanity as having inner psychological motives as well as outer, social concerns. The modern idea of leadership is one of creating in people an inner commitment to social goals, of transforming a person's self-interest into a larger social concern. This has been called *transformational* leadership (Bass, 1985) and represents a sophisticated and well-researched understanding of leadership.

In each of these changes in the idea and practice of leadership, there seems to have been a consistent tendency to increase the equality between the leader and followers. From the ancient idea that the leader was the absolute ruler, to the idea that the leader's job was to influence people to do what the leader saw as needing to be done, to the idea that leaders and followers must share an inner sense of commitment to a larger purpose, the gap between the power and role of the leader and that of the follower has narrowed.

There are some indications today that the idea and practice of leadership are undergoing yet another change. Although the new form is not yet clear by any means, the change in leadership this time may involve erasing altogether the distinction between leaders and followers. In the not-too-distant future, leadership may be understood as a process that plays out in reciprocal actions. By this I mean that people who work together, in whatever roles of authority and power they may have, will be thought of as reciprocating partners in determining what makes sense, how to adapt to change, what is a useful direction—the guiding vision, that is, formerly provided by an individual leader.

Table 13.1 summarizes this picture of leadership as an evolving set of ideas.

As the idea of leadership evolves, nothing useful is left behind. This means, for example, that the "ancient" idea of leadership (dominance) is still alive and well today, but only to the extent that it still serves useful

TABLE 13.1. EVOLVING MODELS OF LEADERSHIP.

	Ancient	Traditional	Modern	Future
Idea of leadership	Domination	Influence	Common goals	Reciprocal relations
Action of leadership	Commanding followers	Motivating followers	Creating inner commitment	Mutual meaning making
Focus of leadership development	Power of the leader	Interpersonal skills of the leader	Self-knowledge of the leader	Interactions of the group

purposes. Instead of thinking that each idea of leadership ceases to exist as it is replaced by the next one, it is more helpful to think of every new idea as containing the previous ideas and building something new on them, using the older ideas as a base.

Newer ideas in general tend to come along because of some limitation in an older idea, some way that the older idea has outlived its usefulness. In the case of leadership, for example, the idea of domination, as many a would-be tyrant has discovered, is limited in its power to truly motivate people. Followers often merely comply to avoid punishment, and the quality of their work suffers greatly as a result. To address this limitation, the idea of influence is developed. It builds on dominance, keeping what is useful (such as the leader as a focal point of decision making to avoid confusion and conflict) but trying to overcome its limitations, using positive motivation to gain a better quality of effort.

In the same way, the modern idea of leadership—creating inner commitment to common goals—addresses the limitations in the idea of influence. Influence is limited by the leader's capacity to create true motivation through appealing to external needs and rewards alone. The notion of common goals adds the idea that motivation is strengthened if people work toward a common goal that includes their own goals; internal, intrinsic motivation is called into play. The role of the leader becomes that of managing a process of fashioning and articulating common goals and gaining commitment to them. The idea of influence is not thrown out, because the leader often uses influence (appeals to reason and feelings) in the process, but influence is put in service of a larger idea. The idea of influence is thus augmented and its limitations addressed.

The idea of leadership, then, is a complex and layered construction that has built up over the course of history. This layered meaning makes it complex and hard to define, but it also makes it a versatile, useful tool that can be employed in a variety of forms.

In time, those forms wear out; old solutions become problems themselves as the world changes. If we wish to think about how leadership might be changing now and in the near future, we need to ask in what way modern leadership—the idea of gaining internal commitment to common goals—might be outliving its usefulness. As we learn more about the diversity of ideas among people who are increasingly entrenched in special interests, the limitations of modern leadership may be found in the very idea of common goals.

As the world becomes more connected through global transportation and communication and a greater diversity of cultures and points of view are being brought to bear as people work together, common goals are becoming increasingly difficult to fashion and articulate from a single, unified point of view. But more than difficulty is involved. Perhaps it is less useful and effective to define goals from a unified, common perspective.

For example, how could a goal of "developing our city" be expressed effectively from a single point of view? Many people may consider that a desirable goal, but it is open to a host of interpretations depending on whether the goal is espoused by a conservationist, a business owner, a land developer, an hourly wage earner, a homeless person, or a young professional just starting out. Each of these people has a view of what developing our city means that is legitimate in its own right but may be different from, and even not comparable to, other views. The views of the land developer and the conservationist, let us say, differ, but along the same axis: they disagree about values while agreeing on the basic terms of the debate. The view of the homeless person, on the other hand, seems unrelated to this debate, as in comparing apples and oranges. How can this point of view be integrated into leadership on the issue?

As the idea of leadership has evolved to include wider diversity of voice (especially with the modern idea of creating inner commitment), it has also created the potential for confusion as voices don't seem to be speaking the same language. This often results in much more than heated arguments at local government meetings and a polarizing of sides; it also results in a sense of not even being in the same community, and it can breed paralysis. If people turn to the leader (the mayor, a representative, a local business leader) and expect this person to create visions of the future that somehow take all the points of view into account, they are usually disappointed and decry the lack of good leadership.

If the views of individuals who see the world in significantly different ways are to be transformed from self-interest to a concern for a larger social good, as the modern idea calls for, then the larger social good must be conceived in highly differentiated, not highly unified, terms. It is just this kind of situation I have in mind when I suggest that limitations in the idea of common goals may be calling forth a new way to think about leadership.

In a world (or a city) operating with multiple ways of understanding the world, common goals need to be expressed in multiple forms of thought and value, multiple forms of meaning. The individual leader is not well equipped to do this. Any model of leadership in which a person is understood to be the leader and others are understood as followers may not be adequate to the complex demands of a such a world. What seems to be needed is a form of leadership that actually engages differences and sustains them in creative and useful ways rather than seeking their resolution through conflict, suppression, or compromise.

Is there evidence in the practice of leadership that such an approach is actually being called for? In the following section, I offer some examples of organizational practice that seem to do so. These are examples of people in organizations acting as if they think about and understand leadership in a new light.

Why Change Is Needed:
Current Trends in Organizations

Some companies are organizing around teams and making teams responsible for their own work without management supervision. In such a situation, each team is accountable to all the other teams with which it is interdependently linked. This creates a kind of marketplace accountability in which the work of each team is appraised for its quality and timeliness by the other teams with which the team has connections. The meaning of such a system starts with satisfying the needs of the customer, both internal and external. Each person, and each team, and all the interlinked teams that make up the organization participate in this leadership.

There is often literally no one "making decisions" from a "higher level" in order to control the work of the teams. In many cases, the various teams are coordinating by something very close to mutual adjustment. In the past, mutual adjustment as a method for gaining coordination and shared direction has been limited to relatively small groups of tightly integrated people. The idea of expanding mutual adjustment to include larger organizational units is fostering a significantly different idea of leadership.

In a related vein, many organizations are trying to break down the strict barriers, the silos, that have separated and defined different functions. Boundaries do not go away, but our ideas about the nature of boundaries can change. In most organizations, functional boundaries are the product of coordination from above, from a level of more abstraction—the classic bureaucratic hierarchy. As organizations try to create a context in which functions can work together more closely, coordination from the top seems to be giving way to coordination from the side—from workgroup to workgroup instead of from manager to manager. This makes the leadership task significantly more complex and requires an approach to leadership that embraces the differences within and among groups. A model of leadership that acknowledges and accommodates the need for direction and meaning *between* functions seems to be called for.

Increasing diversity in organizations also suggests the need for a new model of leadership. If organizations are going to embrace differing cultures, they need to be able to embrace differing values, philosophies, attitudes, ideas, and feelings all at once, seeing differing values and perspectives as mutually sustaining. Older approaches to leadership depending on the idea that a leader can generate a vision to guide, motivate, or gain the commitment of others are unlikely to serve this need very well simply because the vision of a leader—even if it is informed by the ideas of followers—is of necessity the vision of a single culture and a single worldview, because it is expressed from a single point of view. Vision in diverse organizations needs to be multifaceted, and meaning in diverse organizations needs to be reciprocal, forged in continuous interaction. An idea of leadership as shared process may be a step in this direction.

The need to make organizations more directly responsive to customers is leading to the practice of granting increased nonroutine decision-making authority to operational people. This move also seems to call for a new model of leadership. Making people more directly responsible for their work and the outcomes of their work puts the identity and reputation of the organization into the hands of many, rather than of a strategic few at the top. As operational employees take responsibility for making decisions in direct communication with customers, depending less on following a script and more on their own judgment, the enacted strategy of the organization unfolds in the day-to-day actions of a multitude of people. If the strategy of the organization is to be effective, people at all levels and doing all kinds of work need to be participants in the evolution of that strategy. Again, an approach to leadership as a shared process is being called forth.

Finally, the whole set of ideas implicit in what is being called the learning organization may depend upon a new idea of leadership. Fundamentally, the difference between the learning organization and the traditional organization lies in the concept of open and closed systems.

The traditional organization was conceived as a more or less closed system, with a goal of stability in the face of environmental change. The learning organization is being conceived (and we are still far from understanding what this means in everyday terms) as an open system that evolves continuously as it interacts with its environment. Although the traditional organization was well served by a model of leadership that emphasized a single, controlling vision created by a leader who had a highly abstracted view of the enterprise—the leader created the leadership that kept the organization stable—the learning organization needs a model of leadership that points toward continuous adaptive change.

This suggests that somehow we have to figure out how to achieve flexible navigation that adjusts to changes as they happen, not in annual or other time-specific cycles. It's an image of a ship on which the sailors are calling out to one another what they are doing and what they have learned about the sea in which they are sailing. Instead of regarding a sea captain as the leader, the entire ship-sailor system is seen as leadership. If companies are to steer by this kind of large-scale mutual adjustment, an approach to leadership is needed that enables direction to emerge from the reciprocity of interrelated work.

In addition to these changes happening in organizations, a number of writers on leadership are also beginning to reflect new ideas of leadership. The idea of transformational leadership (Bass, 1985), mentioned above as the idea underlying modern leadership, points to the reciprocity of commitment and interpretation between leaders and followers. Joseph Rost (1991) discusses leadership as a process shared equally between leader and followers. I have collaborated in trying to understand leadership as meaning-making (Drath and Palus, 1994). Ronald Heifetz (1994) describes leadership as the process of making adaptations that require people to examine and redefine their basic assumptions. He points out that existing ideas of leadership are too often confused with ideas about authority and hence tied to the person of the authority figure, who is seldom in a position to ring in the kind of adaptive changes leadership requires. Writing about the need to change ideas of leadership in the schools, Lambert and her associates (1995) define leadership in terms of "reciprocal processes" between leaders and followers. Karl Weick (1995) emphasizes the importance of sense-making processes in creating organizational action: processes involving the interconnections of work and people's mutual interpretations of events. Thus, in recent years the theory of leadership has been building toward a new view in tandem with the practice of leadership.

The final step in trying to understand how these changes in the idea of leadership affect the practice of leadership development is to try to describe in more detail just what such leadership might look like. How is it different from the traditional idea of influence and the modern idea of shared commitment?

Leadership as Shared Meaning Making

The idea of leadership that seems to be emerging calls for rethinking the source of leadership. It will no longer be thought of as something initiated by the leader (or by followers) but understood to begin in *the reciprocal connections of people working together.* This is a significant change from even the most current ideas of leadership, which are still rooted in the idea that leadership is a product of individual initiative and action. Even in the modern idea, it is still usually presumed that the leader initiates the shared process.

The idea that leadership is initiated by interactions of people instead of by people as individuals goes well beyond the idea that leadership is a personal trait. It also goes beyond the idea that anyone can be a leader. It even goes beyond the idea that leadership can and should be shared between leader and followers.

This new idea says that leadership begins and ends in the interrelations of people working together. It is not that the process is most effective when it is shared by a leader with followers; sharing is where the process comes from. It doesn't come from leaders and it doesn't come from followers; it doesn't come from any one person alone. It comes instead from what goes on between people, from people making reciprocal meaning (promises, commitments, interpretations, agreements) when they work together. This is leadership as shared meaning making.

The concept can be hard to understand. What exactly do I mean by "shared meaning making?" Without getting too entangled in philosophy, I suggest that it refers to joint or reciprocal interpretation of experience, especially experiences that are readily open to multiple interpretations. To use the old analogy of the blind men and the elephant, I mean the synthesis of all the partial observations. This is more than a summary of the various views—the size of the leg, the length of the trunk, the feel of the tail. It means that all those who hold the various observations from differing points of reference arrive at an agreed-upon view of the whole animal. Shared meaning making, then, refers to the reciprocal social processes by which a group of people agree on how to understand some phenomenon and what value to place on it. I hope this becomes clearer as the chapter progresses.

An Example

What might this idea of leadership look like? Could it include the older ideas of leadership by dominance, influence, and shared commitment? If it is true that leadership sometimes needs to come from a strong, directive person, how can leadership as shared meaning making account for this? The answer is by thinking of a strong, directive leader's effectiveness as a result not just of the leader's competence but of how the whole group makes sense of (arrives at an agreement on how to understand and value) its work.

For example, take a group of apprentices in the workshop of a master mechanic. The apprentices do not know what the master knows; they need the master for guidance, need to be told how to do something in order to do it correctly. Theirs is a reciprocal relationship in which the master teaches in exchange for labor in the workshop. In light of that agreed-upon meaning, apprentices consider strong direction from the master only natural; they take it for granted.

This quality of taken-for-granted reality is a hallmark of meaning that has been made and agreed to. If strong directive leadership seems natural and people take it for granted that it simply makes good common sense, then the group, in its reciprocal relations, can be said to create its own leadership process.

But what happens as the apprentices learn more and gain more experience of their own? Perhaps they work on newly designed machines like nothing the master has ever seen before; they gain experiences the master has never had. At this point, the relationship of the apprentices to the master changes. The old reciprocity no longer makes good sense: the apprentices no longer exchange their work (now expert in its own right) for learning from the master. A new reciprocity evolves in which the former apprentices teach the master about the new machines while the master continues to provide them with a shop and customers.

This new reciprocity brings into being a new process of leadership, a new way of making meaning of their work. It is not so much the master who needs to change a directive leadership style as it is a change in the whole system of making sense together. As I explore later, this need of a whole system to evolve a new leadership process is the idea of leadership development that may operate in the future.

For now, this rather simplified example helps illustrate how leadership as shared meaning making includes the older ideas of leadership as dominance, influence, and shared commitment. It is an idea of leadership that looks at people who are called leaders and followers not as creators of the leadership process, but as *outcomes* of the process. People make the process go when they work together and also try to understand what is important or valuable about working together, and how to go forward together—in short, when they make meaning of their work together. On the other hand, when they fail to make meaning of their work together, they fail to create leadership between them.

New Possibilities

This idea, while including the useful aspects of preceding ideas of leadership, creates new possibilities for leadership and tries to overcome the limitations of the modern idea of common goals as discussed earlier. To get a better sense of the possibilities this new idea of leadership opens up, we need to engage in a little imagination, a thought experiment.

Imagine that you live in a world where leadership has never been conceived of as coming from a person called a leader. Imagine you have always lived in a world where leadership was simply presumed to come out of the reciprocal relationships between people working together. Let's say you live in this imaginary world (which is just like our world except for the change in assumptions about leadership) and you are a member of a company that has been having trouble deciding how to respond to some recent changes in the market for your products.

People in the company have a variety of interpretations of the "problem." Some people are certain it's a manufacturing issue, and they point to a lot of evidence to support their position. Others are equally certain that the problem lies in better customer education and a new marketing strategy. They too have surveys and impressive evidence to support their point of view. Still others insist that there is a very real threat from new competitors, and they have facts and figures to back this up. There are even some people who don't see a problem at all; they point to similar periods in the past where the company has been successful by essentially staying the course.

It is a very complex situation with no easy answer. In a world where leadership is assumed to be shared meaning making, how is this situation addressed?

First of all, there is no blaming the current leader or leadership group for getting the company into the mess. No one says, "If they [meaning top management] would only listen to me. . . ." People understand without needing to say so that it is the company's ways of talking, working, and thinking together that has put it where it is. If a shared sense of how to go forward together is lacking, people need to look not to leaders but to interrelationships.

So the first area for inquiry is the differences of viewpoint on the cause and nature of the problem. The first leadership action is to ask: why do we see this differently? How have our various experiences created these differing interpretations? The goal is not to discover which interpretation is "right," because in this imaginary world people assume that no interpretation is right in and of itself. Interpretations are all simply ways of making sense of what's happening. The goal is to find the interpretation that is most useful in helping the company choose appropriate actions, decisions, directions, and so forth. This is done by inquiring into what assumptions, values, feelings—in short, what meaning—lies beneath the various perspectives being offered. The search for leadership is engaged by looking at what is going on between people.

In its best case, if this leadership process is effective, it leads to dynamic decisions and actions that create a period of long-term vitality for the company. In the worst case, if the leadership process fails, it could lead to paralysis, a deadlock of irresolute perspectives and values. This is a fact of life in this imaginary world, just as there are certain facts of life about effective and ineffective leadership in our real world. This is not a utopian vision of leadership; rather it is a version of leadership that can be either effective or ineffective depending on the sensitivity, skill, and experience with which it is engaged.

So is everyone somehow equal in this imaginary world? Probably not. People vary in their desire for power, authority, responsibility, and being held accountable; they also vary in their experience, learning, and maturity. There may be people—teachers, advisors, mentors, elders—who have a powerful effect on the meanings that get made yet are not seen as making leadership itself happen. They are understood as participants in the process like anyone else. They may even be entrusted with certain power and authority that serves the meaning making of the whole, though they are not seen as causing meaning making or as initiating leadership. There may be others who are less experienced, less willing to take authority, less knowledgeable, but they are not seen as the object of leadership. Even though their role may be to carry out plans, they themselves make sense of these plans in their interrelationships, and thus they are responsible for the whole, not just their job.

The effectiveness of leadership, then, is determined by the vitality of the process itself, that is, by the vitality of the interactions between the people involved and by the extent to which people are willing to take responsibility for those interactions, for nurturing and improving them. People with less experience and authority improve the leadership process as much as people with great experience and more authority. Improving the whole process of leadership is, in fact, how people think of leadership development.

This little imaginary excursion is intended to do nothing more than evoke the possibility that an idea of leadership as a process of shared meaning making is at least conceivable, and to suggest that such an idea of leadership has profound implications for the practice of leadership development.

Implications for the Future of Leadership Development

If this is an idea of leadership whose time is coming, what implications are there for the practice of leadership development? What will leadership development mean? What will it include? How will it be carried out?

Definitive answers to these questions are not in view, because the idea of leadership I am describing has so far been used only very tentatively. What is needed now are ideas of how to move from leadership development as it is practiced today toward the future—a transitional way to work with people who think of themselves as leaders in the traditional sense while opening up the possibility that in the not-too-distant future these very same people will begin to see themselves in a significantly different light.

Transitional Ideas

Three changes in approaching leadership development are useful in making this transition.

Develop the Individual's Ability to Take Part. Moving the source of leadership beyond the leader and into the reciprocal relations of people working together means seeing the leader as a participant in a process, as an incomplete, interdependent part rather than a more or less autonomous initiator, motivator, and evaluator.

Leadership development, then, will eventually move away from developing those personal characteristics that prepare people to act in an autonomous, take-charge mode. It will move away from being about how to develop people who can stand alone and make the tough call (take responsibility alone) and move toward developing the capacity of people to maintain themselves as responsible, active agents within a context of interdependence (take responsibility individually *and* with others). The curriculum will slowly evolve toward being more about taking part than taking charge, more about interdependence than independence.

The design of such a curriculum needs to take into account people's relative readiness to embrace interdependence, and provide supports for the challenge of stretching beyond existing concepts of authority and leadership (Palus and Drath, 1995). In other words, the idea of interdependence cannot be developed before a person develops the capacity for independence. Much of the development I am describing presupposes that people who develop the capacity for fully taking independent responsibility are the population for such developmental work. Robert Kegan (1994) addresses this concern with putting people "in over their heads."

A related curricular change is that of developing what is considered the "leader" type of person. As the idea of leadership itself gradually changes, the idea that some people are "natural" leaders is called increasingly into question. As people gain more experience in making decisions, solving problems, and setting direction in an interdependent mode, leadership development activities geared toward bringing out the natural-leader qualities of certain leaderlike people are sure to become increasingly irrelevant. As people work more interdependently and begin to take responsibility individually and together, rather than "delegating responsibility up" to a leader, they are invited to conclude that leadership is effective or ineffective more in relation to their collective ability to interrelate and less to characteristics of any one of them.

Develop People in Context. Leadership development professionals will thus be invited to see individuals in context. Relationships are of more central concern, not just thinking more about how people enter into and conduct themselves in relationships (interpersonal skills) but significantly shifting the focus of concern from individuals to the interrelationship of individuals. In other words, to see individuals in context, to usefully take account of the interrelatedness of people so as to view leadership as a reciprocal meaning making process, it is useful to shift the way the individual is viewed (Gergen, 1994). Instead of thinking that my relationship with you is conflicted because I am argumentative and you are rigid in your thinking (our characteristics and qualities are "causing the relationship" to be what it is,) we are invited to see in addition how our interrelatedness brings my argumentativeness and your rigidity into being (our interaction makes us who we are).

This view of relationships as the ground of personal qualities and behavior in turn opens the way to understanding how something like leadership—direction giving, value creating, inspirational—can arise not "in" an individual but in the joint action, the reciprocal relatedness, of individuals.

As I said before, new ideas about leadership suggest that leadership development is less and less about enhancing generalizable abilities of individuals. The leadership development curriculum will move toward being about taking part, not taking charge. With a shift in viewpoint toward the interrelational nature of the individual, the leadership development professional is invited to think more about leadership development as the enhancement of interrelating in specific contexts.

A useful idea in this regard is the notion of heedful interrelating (Weick, 1995) or, following ideas of Ellen Langer (1989), mindful interrelating. The idea here is that people often interrelate on a kind of autopilot, mindlessly or without heeding the effect of their interrelating. As leadership becomes more an idea of shared meaning making, leadership development activities need to pay attention to the quality of interrelating, its possible forms, how people can effectively participate in these various forms, and so forth. In other words, the quality of leadership is seen to be related to the vitality of interrelating; to develop leadership, we are being called on to develop the process of interrelating toward skilled, mindful, heedful forms. Recent interest in dialogue in organizations as an approach to organizational learning (Dixon, 1996) is complementary to this focus.

To emphasize, this is not just interpersonal training warmed over as leadership development. Interpersonal skills training, while quite likely to remain useful in a new leadership development context, tends to make the assumption that interpersonal skill is an individual capacity exercised in a social setting. This assumption diverts attention from the reciprocal way that interrelating creates roles or parts to play, and thus the way that relatedness creates people to fill those roles and parts. It is this whole activity of reciprocating relationships that might be addressed in a revised leadership development curriculum. In a later section, I describe one attempt to work with a group of people on increasing their heedful interrelating as a way of developing their capacity to participate in a process of leadership.

Develop the Leadership Capacity of Work Groups. With this new idea of leadership, the focus of leadership development activity shifts away from the individual and toward the interdependent work group. In the future, leadership development will be aimed at improvements in the quality of interrelating among people engaged in interdependent work.

This brings leadership development into the domain of what we have come to think of as team development (team building) or even organization development, yet with a distinct difference. Older ideas of leadership see organizations and teams as objects of leadership activity; the individual leader *acts on* a team, workgroup, or organization. The team, workgroup, or organization is an entity outside of, and in some ways distinct from, the leader.

The new idea of leadership invites a different conception of the team and the organization: not as an entity outside the individual that the individual "joins," but rather the sum total of all interactions. It is less a "thing" that individuals can join and upon which they can act than it is a constantly evolving and changing pattern of interrelationships that individuals create and that creates them.

But when we change the view of the organization from that of a "thing" to that of a vital pattern of reciprocal relations, what about the leaders? How can they participate in the organization as if they are a part of it and not separate from it, above it, acting on it (Sayles, 1993)? The traditional view assumes that leadership is a process that rank-and-file workers can be allowed to enter into by the dispensation of leaders (who "own" the process). The emerging view sees leadership as an all-embracing process that people occupying traditional leadership roles—and thus limited by traditional expectations (their own and others')—need to work extra hard to get in on.

The leadership development profession is therefore being called on to find ways to work in the context of these patterns of reciprocal relations. What we have thought of as team building and organization development is being called on to expand toward leadership development, while what we have thought of as leadership development is being called toward the realm of group development. Perhaps these two domains of developmental work—the individual and the organizational, individual learning and organizational learning—are bound to meet somewhere in the middle in service of a new concept of leadership.

Integrating Team and Organization Development with Leadership Development

I am often asked to explain the difference between what I am saying and existing ideas about team development and organization development. It seems to some people that I am reinventing the wheel, saying that leadership development is team building. "We already understand a lot about team building," I am told, "so why do we need all these new ideas?" It's a good question, and one that leads into a discussion of how team and organization development may be headed for integration with leadership development.

Organization development (OD) is in the first place highly congenial with the idea of leadership that I suggest is emerging; in fact, OD has probably played a major role in this emergence. By looking at the organization as a system and by working at the system level, OD practitioners have continuously focused people in organizations on the issues of reciprocal relations to which I have so often referred. In some respects, much of what I am saying is old news to many OD professionals.

Yet currently OD tends to view leadership as one of the subsystems in the organization. In line with existing ideas of leadership, the role of influence or commitment to shared goals is seen as but one component of the total organizational system. If, on the other hand, leadership is viewed as the meaning-making process shared throughout the organization, then OD moves much closer to leadership development because developing the organization means developing the reciprocal relations that make up the organization. What I am suggesting is that whereas in the past we have kept leadership development activity and organization development activity somewhat in separate boxes, in the future we may see these activities become more integrated.

In many, if not most, organizations, the management development function and the organization development function are not just separate organizational structures; they also represent differing cultures and ways of viewing the world. The management development culture tends to view the world from the individual point of view, taking as its focus the developmental needs of the individual manager. OD, on the other hand, sees the world from the systems perspective, looking at teams and whole organizational systems. The view of leadership and leadership development I am suggesting here leads to an integration of the cultures of personal and organizational development.

Some of the specific areas in which leadership and organization development might be integrated include, but are not limited to, (1) paying attention to the meaning-making and sense-making processes that individuals use as reciprocal partners with others, that is, becoming heedful about interrelating; (2) identifying and making use of differing values, perspectives, and cultural truths that exist within and among individuals as well as within and among workgroups; and (3) inquiring into assumptions and openly reflecting on the differing interpretations of policies, strategies, and decisions brought about by differences in world-view at the individual, group, and intergroup levels.

Team Development as Leadership Development: Case Study

To illustrate some of the issues involved in trying to think about this kind of integration between leadership development and team development, I offer the following informal case study based on work two colleagues and I have done with the marketing team of a medium-sized pharmaceutical company.

People who need to coordinate their work create patterns of coherent ideas (Weick, 1995.) Using the language I propose in this chapter, this pattern of coherent ideas might be called a "made meaning." In the marketing group of the pharmaceutical company, one such pattern of coherent ideas, or made meaning, has been labeled "product marketing." This is an approach to marketing the company's products that involves matching each product with those customers (doctors and other health professionals) who need that particular product. Using this approach, products get marketed by matching product A with classes of buyers of product A; by trying to increase the number of such matches, sales increase. The underlying coherence involves trying to understand which health professionals need product A and under what circumstances.

The concept of product marketing has long been in use in the marketing group and is in this sense the traditional approach. Through this long use, and because the company has sold its products to health professionals using this approach, product marketing has also taken on a certain status as being demonstrably effective. There are examples of success in using the approach. Also, because people have been engaged in the practice of product marketing for some time, they have learned its particular pattern of coherence and language well, and this facilitates creation of many useful reciprocal interactions among people engaged in the practice. In short, from a meaning-making perspective, product marketing can be seen as a powerful and effective leadership process that makes sense of people's mutual work and gives them a feeling of carrying on meaningful activity together.

What can happen in such a setting that disturbs the coherence of the product-marketing process of meaning making? One answer is that a different perspective (that is, a different coherent pattern of working together) may arise, one that in some senses critiques and challenges the traditional product-marketing approach. If this happens, calling into question the current patterns of reciprocal relations that constitute leadership creates the potential for leadership development.

This is just what has happened in the marketing group. The existing coherent meaning of product marketing has been challenged by a different approach that revolves around identifying buyers not by their needs but by their location. Instead of trying to find out which kinds of health professionals need product A, this geographical marketing approach makes sense of the work of marketing by trying to find out what mix of products all the professionals in a certain area need. Geographical marketing directly and indirectly challenges the perceived "truth" of the effectiveness of product marketing in this particular marketing group at this particular moment in its history. This moment helps show how team development can become integrated with the idea of leadership development.

(As a side note, this moment holds another lesson as well. This new geographic approach is being introduced by several people in the marketing area, including the vice president. Introducing a challenge to an existing way of making sense tends to position people as "innovators" or "people with new and different ideas." Ironically, in the company where the vice president formerly worked, this geographical approach was the traditional approach, and she interacted with others there not as an innovator but as a traditional practitioner. This serves as a reminder to see people in context and to remember that their personal attributes—innovative, traditional—can be thought of as constituents of social interaction.)

If one coherent pattern of interaction (product marketing) comes under critique and challenge from another coherent pattern of interaction (geographical marketing), several things may happen within the community of the marketing group. The outcomes in this case can be described in terms of five processes:

1. For perhaps the first time, people engaged in the practice of product marketing feel called upon to explain, defend, and provide rationale for their coherent pattern of interaction.

2. The taken-for-granted reality that product marketing is "how we work around here" has been cast in a relative light with respect to another possible coherent pattern. The taken-for-granted stance people adopted in the past toward product marketing will never be the same again; something has changed and will never unchange. This is one feature of development: a change in perspective that relativizes earlier perspectives (Kegan, 1994.)

3. Two approaches are created where there was just one. More than that, each approach creates its own pattern of reciprocal relations that make sense of marketing from its own standpoint, and this creates two differing meaning-making communities. Each group understands its own approach as making sense (because it literally makes sense of the work they have been doing) while at the same time seeing the other approach as not making so much sense. Where before there was one predominant meaning-making process (in other words, one leadership process,) there are now two meaning-making processes (two processes of leadership) happening at the same time. These are therefore two possible "directions," two possible ways of creating order and responding to the environment, each of which makes sense to some but not to everyone.

4. This results in each side's conceiving the "other" side as something problematic, a problem to be solved. From the product marketing viewpoint, it is "How do we assert our continued effectiveness in the face of this new approach?" From the geographical side, it is "How do we establish our approach with some people holding on to the traditional ways?"

5. The vice president, taking a position somewhat aligned with the geographical approach but also trying to see beyond the conflict, has asked us to help in "integrating" the two approaches.

Notice her role in this. Her desire for integration is, in traditional terms, a "leadership" act that can be attributed to her good sense and ability to rise above departmental politics and seek common ground. The attempts of this analysis to understand the leadership process in that department in different terms do not, of course, change the terms in which it is actually being understood at the moment. The vice president as an individual is constantly being called on to "be the leader," to take away from the group as a whole the responsibility for dealing with the challenging conflict of the two approaches. She has sensed that this is not the best way for her to behave and has called us in to try to get the whole department involved in working through the issue. She is caught between paradigms of leadership, doing the best she can to meet traditional expectations while exploring new and as-yet only dimly understood ideas of leadership.

My colleagues and I are just at the beginning of trying to understand how we might enter into such a context in ways that facilitate leadership development as the development of meaning-making processes. Briefly, here is how we have tried to interact with the marketing group, to become temporary collaborators and participants in their leadership process.

One focus we have taken is to highlight the two patterns of coherence as each being equally defensible and equally challengeable. Our thought is that if we can participate in creating geographical marketing as a legitimate approach, and thus remove somewhat the ascribed "newness" which may also imply "untested and risky," while at the same time helping the product-marketing community express its coherence appreciatively (that is, without "defending" it), then the process of constituting each other as "the competition" might be reversed and people may soon come to appreciate the other side.

We approached this task by dividing the department into the product and geography subgroups and having them write on index cards any statements or phrases that they spoke or heard applied to either their own or the other subgroup in the preceding few months. This generated large stacks of cards at each subgroup table. Then we had them sort these cards, still working as subgroups at separate tables, into three categories: (1) statements or phrases that are "obviously true"; (2) statements that are controversial—some people think they are true, but other people in the group disagree; and (3) statements that are considered undiscussable—a person might think it but would not say it out loud.

Then we simply asked each group to have someone read the cards aloud, starting with the "obvious" pile, then moving on to the "controversial" pile, and ending with the "unexpressed" pile. In each case the groups were allowed complete control over which cards they read and which they kept to themselves. Most of the cards were read, including some in the last category that expressed highly critical viewpoints toward the other group.

At the end of the exercise, people in the marketing group overall expressed a feeling of being helped in their work together. Perhaps this is because the exercise (and other work we have done with them) has helped to reconstitute all the people in the marketing group by subtly but powerfully re-relating them to their own subgroup as well as to the "other." The possibility of a more united marketing group is thus created. We hope that if they reexamine their own commitments to their ways of sense making in terms of another framework for sense making, they are aided in their own effort to make sense of doing two kinds of marketing at once. If we are successful, what has been seen as competing approaches can move toward integration. The hypothesis I entertain here is that such reexaminations and creation of more inclusive patterns of reciprocal relations develop the leadership process because they increase the means for making sense of diverse work.

From this example, it is clear that the meaning of *leadership development* depends on what we take leadership and development to be. From a point of view that sees leadership as a shared meaning-making process, leadership development becomes development of reciprocal relations toward a greater integration of difference. So leadership development is not, as it is in the individual case, development of people we take to be leaders; rather, it is development of the process of shared meaning making. It is a multipersonal rather than personal phenomenon.

In the case of the marketing group, from this point of view leadership development has everything to do with the challenge offered to the traditional made meaning (called product marketing) by a newly proposed way of making meaning (called geographical marketing). Leadership development can be understood as the process of enlarging the capacity of the marketing group to make communal sense of its mutual work by taking on and taking in geographical marketing, while the new kids on the block take on and take in the traditional approach.

To say this another way, if the group relinquishes thinking of product marketing and geographical marketing as competing approaches and instead thinks of marketing as including two different aspects of the whole, we can construe this as an increase in the capacity of the group to understand and deal with novel demands and to adapt to change. The purpose of leadership development, in this view, becomes something like increasing the capacity of workgroups to handle new conditions, meet unexpected challenges to current made meanings, and make adaptive change an ongoing aspect of their worklife.

This line of reasoning suggests that the vice president's stated wish to "integrate product and geographical marketing" is really a wish to develop the leadership of the marketing group. This creates the possibility that work done toward "organization development" and "team development" can be usefully reframed and re-recognized as leadership development work: developing the leadership capacity of people doing work in mutual interaction.

The interesting thing about framing the vice president's wish as a wish for leadership development is that in working with the group on the challenge of taking on and taking in a new pattern of coherence, we may also be increasing the vice president's capacity to make useful decisions and influence others toward mutually beneficial outcomes—in short, her capacity to demonstrate some of the qualities associated with effective influence and commitment-building leadership. This way of looking in two directions at once—toward both new ideas of leadership and traditional ideas—is needed as we work with organizations in transition.

Conclusion

In this chapter I have framed a view of the future of leadership development in terms of changes in the idea of leadership itself. As the very idea of leadership changes, so does the approach to leadership development.

Up to now, leadership has always been thought of in terms of the leader. Even as the role of the follower becomes more important and more nearly equal to that of the leader, the assumption that leadership is the product of individual minds acting on one another remains. Yet there are indications that in the heat of practice, on the firing line in organizations, where the complexity of an increasingly interconnected world must be negotiated in practical ways every day, the effectiveness of this assumption is being challenged. The creation of common direction, of a mutual sense of meaning and value—the desired outcome of leadership—is increasingly understood as effectively happening in interactions between people, especially when people differ significantly in their worldviews and cultures. A sense of leadership as shared meaning making is emerging.

This changes the whole context in which leadership development professionals work. A reexamination of some basic assumptions guiding the philosophy and practice of leadership development is being called forth. Leadership development as a profession is being asked to play a vital role both in bringing forth a new idea of leadership and in supporting the new idea as it emerges. Some current practices, especially those seeking to combine leadership development with ongoing work and those seeking to create a framework for practicing leadership development more systemically in organizations, are already pointing the way toward promising new directions.

Finally, approaches to individual leadership development and approaches to team and organization development are being called to integrate. From the individual leadership development perspective, this means thinking about the person in context, doing leadership development on the job in conjunction with ongoing work, and working with whole teams instead of just the managers of teams. From an OD perspective, integration means thinking of the development of teams and organizations in ways that frame trust, surfacing of feelings, making use of group resources, open communications, and effective interaction as elements of leadership; that is, seeing leadership not just as a subsystem but as a process that constitutes the system and its subsystems.

The view of leadership and leadership development I am proposing here cuts in two directions at once. On the one hand, it diminishes the role ascribed to individuals as leaders, relativizing their impact in terms of a larger social process. In this sense, this view of leadership is sympathetic with the perspective that sees leadership as being not very important in the overall function and effectiveness of a complex organization; the full complexity of the organization as a system and its highly differentiated relationship to the outside world are far beyond the power of those people called leaders to significantly effect.

On the other hand, the view of leadership I propose augments and elaborates leadership beyond an interpersonal influence process and places it at the heart of the processes by which people come to understand and attach meaning to shared work. In this sense, leadership is understood as being much more important than before because not only does it involve creating shared goals and motivating people to work toward them but it also constitutes the very ground that makes goals (or even a lack of goals) meaningful.

AFTERWORD

Russ S. Moxley
Ellen Van Velsor
Cynthia D. McCauley

In this handbook, we present much of what we at the Center have learned about how people become better leaders. We ask, and answer, important questions about leadership development, and we hope that we have done so in a way that is useful to you.

But as we said in the beginning, we realize that this handbook captures a view on development of leadership capacity at a particular point in time. Forces both external and internal to organizations are driving changes in how companies organize themselves to get work done, in where work is done, and how those employees doing the work understand the meaning of careers. External forces include, for example, globalization and rapid development of technology. Internal forces include downsizing and restructuring and the changing demographics of the workforce.

These same forces are bringing new questions about leadership and leadership development whose answers broaden and expand our perspective. Here is a sampling of the questions we are now asking:

  • *Are the capacities needed to be an effective leader universal, or are they specific to a particular country and culture?*

The marketplace trend seems clear. More and more, companies are looking beyond their domestic borders for new markets. Changes in technology (including information technology) and transportation make it possible for products to be made and sold anywhere, and the growth of developing nations makes it attractive to do so.

Fred Steingraber, chief executive at A. T. Kearney, suggests that there are four primary reasons that global trade has exploded in the last twenty-five years:

1. There is excess capacity in companies around the world. When this is combined with lower tariffs and fewer regulations, companies have new reasons and new opportunities to market globally.
2. Technology is facilitating globalization and is itself a rich source of new products and services.
3. There is an increasing shift in economic power from the developed nations to the developing nations. According to Steinbrager, in the next twenty-five years, nine of the fifteen largest economies will be in what are now emerging markets.
4. There is a convergence of customer needs. According to research done at A. T. Kearney, there is a declining preference for local products and a growing preference for global ones.

We know that globalization is bringing together diverse people. But what do these diverse people have in common? What differences do they have? What conception of leadership will they bring?

Answers to these questions broaden our understanding of the capacities needed to effectively perform in leadership roles, and they add to our understanding of how these capacities can be developed. In Chapters Eleven and Twelve, Michael Hoppe and Maxine Dalton shared the state of our present knowledge. But this is a relatively new area of research and practice for us, and we know that right now we—and, in fact, others working in this area—have more questions than answers.

- *Given the realities of the new employment contract, what's the motivation for organizations to continue to invest in leadership development?*

In this handbook, we suggest that leadership development is an ongoing process that happens over time, involving a variety of development experiences, embedded in a particular organization, with considerable investment by the organization. The realities of what it takes for people to develop the leadership capacities they need seem to fit well with the old employment contract. Implicit in this contract was the guarantee of lifetime employment, which meant that organizations knew they could get a good return on their investment in the development of individuals.

Today, people are likely to change employers, if not careers, several times during their working lives. "The career of the 21st century . . . will be driven by the person, not the organization, and will be reinvented by the person from time to time, as the environment and the person change" (Hall, 1996, p. 8). Under this circumstance, it is harder for organizations to realize a return on their investment in leadership development. If, for example, an organization invests in high-potential people in their first seven years by providing several stretching assignments, a development coach, and a feedback-intensive program, it could easily find at the end of those seven years, just when the investment is beginning to bear fruit, that the people are moving on to new organizations, either on their own initiative or because they were downsized out of this one.

Will organizations continue to invest in long-term leadership development if careers are driven by individuals? Or will a new context for development emerge, a context in which several organizations join together in an alliance to share responsibility for leadership development? Or, under the new employment contract, will individuals assume more responsibility for planning and initiating the development experiences they need, just as they have assumed more responsibility for their careers?

A related question is, "How will downsizing affect our understanding of leadership?" Peter Drucker recently suggested that one consequence of downsizing and the related new employment contract is that now all workers are volunteers. Another way to think of this is to see workers as individual entrepreneurs, more loyal to their job and their profession than they are to the organization. With this change, paternalistic practices of leadership appear as outmoded as the old employment contract. The question then becomes: How can leadership be effectively practiced in this new environment? What new skills and knowledge are needed by those in leadership roles?

• *Can leadership development be accelerated?*

More and more, speed has become a desirable quality in organizational life. How fast can organizations get a new product to market? How fast can they respond to a customer's needs? Can they spot and react to an emerging trend faster than a competitor does? It is no surprise, then, that another question is, Can they develop leaders faster? It is not just impatience that drives this question. Organizations are growing and are in constant need of people who can lead new operations. Also, as organizations move to flatter structures, leadership is dispersed and is needed from more people.

Throughout this handbook, we stress that leadership development takes time. To optimally learn from a job assignment, for example, it is estimated that a person needs to be in the job two or three years to experience the consequences of decisions made and actions taken and to dig beneath the glaring problems to encounter the subtle ones. A longer time frame must also be taken on seemingly short-term events such as formal 360-degree feedback: changing a set of behaviors based on this feedback takes practice and ongoing feedback over a concentrated period of time.

So we take a cautious stance toward the notion that the leadership development process can be "fast-forwarded." But our caution does not minimize the importance of some fundamental questions: What can be done to enhance the leadership development process? How can we better integrate development into the work of the organization so that leaders can learn on the fly? What new development experiences can we create and use to help individuals, teams, and organizations speed up the process of learning?

> • *How will rapid advancements in information and communication technology affect leadership? Can leadership capacity be developed in a virtual world?*

The rapid advances in information and communication technology—which allows people to more easily generate, organize, and access information—have real implications for both the capacities that leaders need and the design of developmental experiences.

New technology has the potential to affect the distribution of power and the development of relationships in organizations. A number of propositions have been made about these factors and their implications for leadership. We mention two of the more salient ones: (1) greater access to information across the organization has a leveling effect (those in formal leadership roles are no longer the main conduit through which information flows), and (2) the sheer volume of accessible information strains a person's ability to make sense of the information (making sense of all these data and their implications for the organization is an increasingly complex leadership task).

Although many of the traditional capacities of leaders (self-awareness, working in social systems, creativity) continue to be relevant, technology is undeniably changing our understanding of leadership. Advances in technology have already profoundly affected how information is shared, not to mention the sheer volume of information. This is certain to continue, and even accelerate. Understanding this new base of information undoubtedly calls for new knowledge, skills, and abilities, and in turn influences our understanding of what leadership development needs to be.

For example, consider developing the capacity to work in social systems. Because of technology, we now need to include in that concept the ability to work with geographically dispersed teams and to work in systems where information flow is not based on hierarchy or formal roles.

What other changes are in store? In what other ways does advancement of technology expand current understanding and practice of leadership? Some wonder if we can develop leadership capacity in a virtual world. Many of the authors in Part One point to some of the possibilities: collecting and processing 360-degree feedback online, using distance learning techniques in skill-based training, accessing coaching and learning networks online, and using knowledge systems to collect and share information online.

Applying technology to the leadership development process has the promise of making some developmental experiences more widely available and more directly accessible on demand. This is significant because timeliness and relevance are two important characteristics of an effective development experience, and both are potential advantages of online applications; people can learn what they need when they need it.

Still, questions remain: Which leadership capacities can effectively be learned from online applications? How can online applications be integrated with other development experiences? What is the right balance of high-tech and high touch?

• *Will leadership development and team development become synonymous?*

One very real change in our model of leadership is being driven by self-managed workteams. They are flatter, nonhierarchical, trust-based modes of organizing. In any self-organizing system, the concept of leadership is redefined: leadership is understood as a shared activity that happens within the team. In Chapter Thirteen, Wilfred Drath begins exploring these ideas.

This movement to self-managing teams has generated its own set of questions. What does it mean to think about team development as leadership development? How do we provide assessment, challenge, and support for teams? What does it mean to talk about the strengths and development needs of teams? What new knowledge and skills do teams need if they are to function effectively in their leadership role? And does this new definition of leadership migrate to other parts of organizations?

• *How will the changing demographics of the workforce affect our view of leadership and our practice of leadership development?*

Workforce 2000, and other studies like it, have clearly shown that the demographics of the workforce are changing, and changing dramatically. Women and other minorities will soon be the majority of workers. They bring with them different values, different hopes and expectations, different expectations about leadership. The changing demographics put a new demand on those in leadership roles to pay attention to a greater diversity of perspectives and to help find common ground between and among them.

As we noted in Chapter Ten, thus far the Center's research and practice have focused primarily on white men, and to a lesser extent on white women and African American women and men. We do not have much data or experience with groups other than these.

We believe that changing demographics introduce different practices of leadership. We have some evidence that this is true for women. As reported in Chapter Ten, women are known to take a "relational approach to professional growth and organizational effectiveness," and they place great value on "enabling others, seeing projects holistically, mutual empowerment, and achieving mutual goals." But the question of how groups other than women affect the practice of leadership remains to be fully explored.

We also are asking how changing demographics change the practice of leadership development. Already we have learned that the development experiences found to be important for white men—360-degree feedback programs, feedback-intensive programs, assignments, developmental relationships—were also important for white women and African Americans, but they had to be modified to make sure they were accessible and appropriately applied. We do not yet know how ideas and practice of leadership development are affected as other groups are included.

At CCL we work hard to turn ideas into action and action into ideas. This means we try to ask the right questions in our research, make sure that what we learn in our research expands our understanding of leadership and affects our practice of leadership development, and then make sure that what we learn in our practice affects the research questions we ask. In one way or another, the beginning point for our learning is asking the right questions. Although this is the end of the *Handbook of Leadership Development,* the questions we have posed are the beginning of new learning for us.

ABOUT THE CENTER FOR CREATIVE LEADERSHIP

The Center for Creative Leadership is an international, nonprofit, educational institution whose mission is to advance the understanding, practice, and development of leadership for the benefit of society worldwide. Founded in Greensboro, North Carolina, in 1970 by the Smith Richardson Foundation, the Center is today one of the largest institutions in the world focusing on leadership. In addition to our locations in Greensboro; Colorado Springs, Colorado; San Diego, California; and Brussels, Belgium, we have an office in New York City and maintain relationships with more than twenty-eight network associates and other partners in the United States and abroad.

We conduct research, produce publications, and provide a variety of educational programs and products to leaders and organizations in the public, corporate, educational, and nonprofit sectors. Each year through our programs, we reach more than twenty-seven thousand leaders and several thousand organizations worldwide. The Center also serves as a clearinghouse for ideas on leadership and creativity. We regularly convene conferences and colloquia by scholars and practitioners, and our staff members are frequent presenters at conferences around the world.

We derive our funding primarily from tuition, sales of products and publications, royalties, and fees for service. The Center seeks grants and donations from corporations, foundations, and individuals in support of its educational mission.

For more information on the Center and its work, call Client Services at (336) 545–2810, send an e-mail to info@leaders.ccl.org, or visit our World Wide Web home page at http://www.ccl.org

Products, Programs, and Publications

The Center offers a variety of assessment tools, simulations, publications, and programs that help individuals, teams, and organizations learn about themselves.

Assessment Tools and Simulations

Benchmarks® is a comprehensive 360-degree leadership tool for middle- to upper-level managers. Assessing strengths and development needs, it provides indications of promotability to future leadership positions (as well as the potential of derailment), a strategy for change that links development needs with specific suggestions that the manager can use to effect change, and valid, reliable, comparative data that individuals can use to compare themselves to other managers in similar positions.

Skillscope® is a straightforward, effective, 360-degree feedback tool that assesses managerial strengths and development needs. It creates a channel through which managers and supervisors can get feedback from peers, direct reports, superiors, and bosses.

Prospector™ is designed to measure an individual's ability to learn and take advantage of growth experiences that will facilitate his or her development as a leader. It was developed primarily under a grant from the International Consortium for Executive Development Research (ICEDR). Additional support was received from the Center for Effective Organizations (CEO), the International Business Education and Research program (IBEAR), and the Leadership Institute at the University of Southern California School of Business. Research for Prospector was conducted by Morgan McCall, Gretchen Spreitzer, and Joan Mahoney, faculty members at the University of Southern California School of Business.

EdgeWork® is a unique and powerful business simulation that allows workgroups to address difficult issues of real-life work (for instance, transition, conflict, and ambiguity) in a safe, monitored environment. It aims to provide in-house human resource professionals and consultants with a high-quality, flexible training tool that can be the springboard for group learning and development.

Looking Glass, Inc.® (LGI) is a simulation that provides participants with the opportunity to actively learn the lessons that are critical to being effective managers. Designed to fit into a variety of managerial training and development designs, it can be used as an assessment tool to help managers understand their strengths and development needs; a training tool to assist managers in learning particular skills such as problem solving, agenda setting, and networking; an organizational diagnostic tool to enable managers from the same organization to identify company norms and culture, and, during debriefs, to consider the impact of these norms on their own behavior; and a team-building tool to provide intact teams with the opportunity to look at team dynamics and to choose and work on actionable goals.

Programs

Leadership Development Program helps middle-level to upper-level managers and executives enhance their leadership skills in a variety of organizational settings, improve their ability to develop employees, and promote excellence in all aspects of their lives.

Leadership Development for Human Resource Professionals helps participants become more effective and productive and, as leaders, assist others in achieving these goals.

Tools for Developing Successful Executives helps human resource executives, line managers, and career development professionals learn and apply some of CCL's best research-based, executive-development practices and tools.

Benchmarks® Certification Workshop prepares human resource managers, career development professionals, and consultants to use Benchmarks. Benchmarks certification is also available as an optional addition to the Tools for Developing Successful Executives program.

The Women's Leadership Program helps women executives examine a wide range of issues affecting their roles and advancement in organizations, develop a deeper understanding of the forces that influence their lives and careers, and shape strategies for their development as individuals, professionals, and leaders.

Foundations of Leadership helps managers with three to five years' experience whose roles increasingly include a leadership component requiring an ability to set and communicate a clear direction, motivate, provide coaching and feedback, and assist others in their organizations to succeed.

The African American Leadership Program provides middle-level to senior-level African American managers with an open and candid environment in which to consider the forces influencing their professional performance and career advancement.

Leadership at the Peak gives top executives the opportunity, in a small but powerful group of peers, to evaluate themselves as leaders, gain new insights on topics that are important to them and their organizations, and focus on the challenges of leadership. (Participants must apply for admission to this program.)

Publications

Feedback to Managers (third edition) presents an in-depth evaluation of twenty-five of the leading 360-degree-feedback instruments. For each instrument, such issues as target audience, reliability and validity, types of feedback display, scoring process, and cost are considered.

Formal Mentoring Programs in Organizations: An Annotated Bibliography offers an introduction to the practical and academic literature on programs that facilitate the developmental relationship between junior and senior managers.

Helping Leaders Take Effective Action: A Program Evaluation gauges the success of such action-oriented developmental activities as keeping a learning journal, working with a change partner, and taking part in artistic activities.

Making Common Sense: Leadership as Meaning-Making in a Community of Practice suggests an alternative to the widespread notion of leadership as a process of social influence.

How to Design an Effective System for Developing Managers and Executives describes a six-step approach, developed in CCL's Tools for Developing Successful Executives program, for carrying out a leadership development initiative.

CENTER FOR CREATIVE LEADERSHIP

LEADERSHIP.
LEARNING.
LIFE.

GREENSBORO
BRUSSELS
COLORADO SPRINGS
SAN DIEGO

REFERENCES

Adler, N. J., & Bartholomew, S. (1992). Managing globally competent people. *Academy of Management Executive, 6*(3), 52–65.

Alden, J., & Kirkhorn, J. (1996). Case studies. In R. L. Craig (ed.), *The ASTD training and development handbook.* (4th ed.). New York: McGraw-Hill.

Aldwin, C. M. (1994). *Stress, coping, and development.* New York: Guilford Press.

Ali, A. J. (1990). Management theory in a transitional society: The Arab's experience. *International Studies of Management & Organization, 20*(3), 7–35.

Anderson, T. (1993). *Den of lions.* New York: Ballantine.

Argyris, C. (1991). Teaching smart people how to learn. *Harvard Business Review, 69*(3), 99–109.

Ashford, S. J. (1986). The role of feedback seeking in individual adaptation: A resource perspective. *Academy of Management Journal, 29*(3), 465–487.

Atwater, L., Rousch, P., & Fischtal, A. (1995). The influence of upward feedback on self and follower ratings of leadership. *Personnel Psychology, 48,* 35–59.

Auster, E. (1989). Task characteristics as a bridge between macro- and micro-level research on salary inequality between men and women. *Academy of Management Review, 14*(2), 173–193.

Baird, L., Briscoe, J., & Tuden, L. (1996). Globalizing management to meet the challenges of global business. Presentation to the Executive Development Roundtable, Boston University School of Management.

Baldwin, T. T., & Padgett, M. Y. (1993). Management development: A review and commentary. In C. L. Cooper & I. T. Robertson (eds.), *International review of industrial and organizational psychology (vol. 8)*. Chichester, England: Wiley.

Bandura, A. (1986). *Social foundations of thought and action: A social cognitive theory.* Upper Saddle River, N.J.: Prentice-Hall.

Barclay, D. (1992). Commitment from the top makes it work. *IEEE Spectrum, 29*(6), 24–27.

Barrick, M. R., & Mount, M. K. (1991). The big five personality dimensions and job performance: A meta-analysis. *Personnel Psychology, 44*(1) 1–26.

Barsoux, J. L., & Lawrence, L. P. (1997). *French management.* London, England: Cassel.

Bartlett, C., & Ghoshal, S. (1989). *Managing across borders: the transnational solution.* Boston: Harvard Business School Press.

Bartlett, C., & Ghoshal, S. (1997). The myth of the generic manager: New personal competencies for new management roles. *California Management Review, 40*(1), 92–93.

Baskerville, D. M. (1992). Are career seminars for black managers worth it? *Black Enterprise, 23*(5), 122–129.

Bass, B. M. (1985). *Leadership and performance beyond expectations.* New York: Free Press.

Bedian, A. G., & Armenakis, A. A. (1989). Promise and prospects: The case of the alpha, beta, gamma change typology. *Group and Organizational Studies, 14,* 155–160.

Bell, E. L. (1990). The bicultural life experiences of career-oriented black women. *Journal of Organizational Behavior, 11*(6), 459–477.

Betters-Reed, B. L., & Moore, L. L. (1995). Shifting the management development paradigm for women. *Journal of Management Development, 14*(2), 24–38.

Brake, T. (1997). *The global leader: Critical factors for creating the world class organization.* Burr Ridge, Ill.: Irwin.

Brett, J. M. (1984). Job transitions and personal role development. In K. M. Rowland & G. R. Ferris (eds.), *Research in personnel and human resources management.* Greenwich, Conn.: JAI Press.

Brewer, M. B. (1995). Managing diversity: The role of social identities. In S. E. Jackson & M. N. Ruderman (eds.), *Diversity in work teams: Research paradigms for a changing workplace.* Washington, D.C.: American Psychological Association.

Brockner, J. (1988). *Self-esteem at work: research, theory, and practice.* San Francisco: New Lexington Press.

Broderick, R. (1983). How Honeywell teaches its managers to manage. *Training 20*(1), 18–23.

Bunker, K., & Webb, A. (1992). *Learning how to learn from experience: Impact of stress and coping.* Greensboro, N.C.: Center for Creative Leadership.

Burgoyne, J. G., & Hodgson, V. E. (1983). Natural learning and managerial action: A phenomenological study in the field setting. *Journal of Management Studies, 20*(3), 387–399.

Burke, M. J., & Day, R. R. (1986). A cumulative study of the effectiveness of managerial training. *Journal of Applied Psychology, 71*(2), 232–245.

Byrne, D. (1971). *The attraction paradigm.* New York: Academic Press.

Campbell, D. P., & Nilsen, D. (1993). Self-observer rating discrepancies: Once an overrater, always an overrater? *Human Resource Management, 32*(2, 3) 265–281.

Catalyst. (1996). *Women in corporate leadership: Progress and prospects.* New York: Catalyst.

Caudron, S., & Hayes, C. (1997). Are diversity programs benefiting African Americans? *Black Enterprise, 27*(7), 121–132.

Cavanagh, G. F. (1984). *American business values* (2nd ed.). Paramus, N.J.: Prentice-Hall.

Center for Creative Leadership. (1998). *Reflections.* Greensboro, N.C.: Center for Creative Leadership.

Chen, C. C., & DiTomaso, N. (1996). Performance appraisal and demographic diversity: Issues regarding appraisals, appraisers, and appraising. In E. E. Kossek & S. A. Lobel (eds.), *Managing diversity: Human resource strategies for transforming the workplace.* Cambridge, Mass.: Blackwell.

Chiaramonte, P., & Higgins, A. (1993). Coaching for high performance. *Business Quarterly, 58*(1), 81–87.

Clark, K. C., & Clark, M. B. (1994). *Choosing to lead.* (2nd edition). Greensboro, N.C.: Center for Creative Leadership.

Clark, L. A., & Lyness, K. S. (1991). Succession planning as a strategic activity at Citicorp. In L. W. Foster (ed.), *Advances in applied business strategy (vol. 2).* Greenwich, Conn.: JAI Press.

Cobb, J., & Gibbs, J. (1990). A new, competency-based, on-the-job programme for developing professional excellence in engineering. *Journal of Management Development, 9*(3), 60–72.

Collins, L. M., & Horn, J. L. (1991). *Best methods for the analysis of change: Recent advances, unanswered questions, future directions.* Washington, D.C.: American Psychological Association.

Conger, J. A. (1992). *Learning to lead: The art of transforming managers into leaders.* San Francisco: Jossey-Bass.

Conger, J. A., & Kanungo, J. A. (1988). *Charismatic leadership: The elusive factor in organizational effectiveness.* San Francisco: Jossey-Bass.

Covey, S. R. (1991). *Principle-centered leadership.* New York: Simon & Schuster.

Cousins, J. B., & Earl, L. M. (1992). The case for participatory evaluation. *Educational Evaluation and Policy Analysis, 14*(4), 397–418.

Cousins, J. B., & Earl, L. M. (eds.). (1995). *Participatory evaluation in education: Studies in evaluation use and organizational learning.* London: Falmer Press.

Cox, T. H., Jr. (1993). *Cultural diversity in organizations: Theory, research & practice.* San Francisco: Berrett-Koehler.

Cox, T. H., Jr., & Nkomo, S. M. (1991). A race and gender-group analysis of the early career experience of MBAs. *Work and Occupations, 18*(4), 431–446.

Curtis, L. B., & Russell, E. A. (1993). A study of succession planning programs in Fortune 500 firms. Paper presented at the annual meeting of the Society for Industrial and Organizational Psychology, April 29–May 2, San Francisco.

Dalton, M. (1995). Going international with assessment for development. *Issues & Observations, 15*(2), 5–6.

Dalton, M. A., & Hollenbeck, G. P. (1996). *How to design an effective system for developing managers and executives.* Greensboro, N.C.: Center for Creative Leadership.

Dalton, M. A., & Hollenbeck, G. P. (1997). *Best practices in 360-degree feedback processes.* Presentation, Tools for Developing Successful Executives, Center for Creative Leadership, Greensboro, N.C. (November 1997).

Dalton, M., & Wilson, M. (1996). Antecedent conditions of expatriate effectiveness. A paper presented at the American Psychological Association, August, Toronto, Canada.

Davies, J., & Easterby-Smith, M. (1984). Learning and developing from managerial work experiences. *Journal of Management Studies, 21*(2), 169–183.

Dechant, K. (1990). Knowing how to learn: The "neglected" management ability. *Journal of Management Development, 9*(4), 40–49.

Dechant, K. (1994). Making the most of job assignments: An exercise in planning for learning. *Journal of Management Education, 18*(2), 198–211.

de Merode, J. (1997). An annotated review prepared for the Global Leadership Development Research Project. Greensboro, N.C.: Center for Creative Leadership.

Derr, C. B. (1987). Managing high potentials in Europe. *European Management Journal, 5*(2), 72–80.

Dickens, F., Jr., & Dickens, J. B. (1991). *The black manager: Making it in the corporate world.* (Rev. ed.). New York: AMACOM.

Dixon, N. M. (1990). The relationship between trainee responses on participant reaction forms and posttest scores. *Human Resource Development Quarterly, 1*(2), 129–137.

Dixon, N. M. (1996). *Perspectives on dialogue: Making talk developmental for individuals and organizations.* Greensboro, N.C.: Center for Creative Leadership.

Donaldson, T. (1996). Values in tension: Ethics away from home. *Harvard Business Review, 74*(5), 48–62.

Dorfman, P. W., Howell, J. P., Hibino, S., Lee, J. K., Tate, U., & Bautista, A. (1997). Leadership in Western and Asian countries: Commonalities and differences in effective leadership processes across cultures. *Leadership Quarterly, 8*(3), 233–274.

Douglas, C. A. (1997). *Formal mentoring programs in organizations: An annotated bibliography.* Greensboro, N.C.: Center for Creative Leadership.

Douglas, C. A., & McCauley, C. D. (1997). A survey on the use of formal developmental relationships in organizations. *Issues & Observations, 17*(1/2), 6.

Douglas, C. A., & Schoorman, F. D. (1987). The role of mentoring in career and psychosocial development. Unpublished master's thesis.

Drath, W. H., & Palus, C. J. (1994). *Making common sense: Leadership as meaning-making in a community of practice.* Greensboro, N.C.: Center for Creative Leadership.

Dunnette, M. (1993). My hammer or your hammer? *Human Resource Management, 32*(2, 3), 373–384.

Eagly, A. H., Makhijani, M. G., & Klonsky, B. G. (1992). Gender and the evaluation of leaders: A meta-analysis. *Psychological Bulletin, 111*(1), 3–22.

Elashmawi, F., & Harris, P. R. (1993). *Multicultural management: New skills for global success.* Houston: Gulf.

Evered, R. D., & Selman, J. C. (1989). "Coaching" and the art of management. *Organizational Dynamics, 18*(2), 16–32.

Feghali, E. (1997). Arab cultural communication patterns. *International Journal of Intercultural Relations, 21*(3), 345–378.

Ferdman, B. M., & Brody, S. E. (1996). Models of diversity training. In D. Landis & R. S. Bhagat (eds.), *Handbook of intercultural training* (2nd ed.). Thousand Oaks, Calif.: Sage.

Fetterman, D. (1994). Empowerment evaluation. *Evaluation Practice, 15*(1), 1–15.

Fetterman, D. (1996). *Empowerment evaluation: Knowledge and tools for self-assessment and accountability.* Thousand Oaks, Calif.: Sage.

Filipczak, B. (1992). Working for the Japanese. *Training, 29*(12), 23–29.

Flanders, D. P., & Anderson, P. E. (1973). Sex discrimination in employment: Theory and practice. *Industrial and Labor Relations Review, 26*(3), 938–955.

Fleenor, J. W. (1995). Race differences in Benchmarks ratings. Unpublished manuscript, Center for Creative Leadership, Greensboro, N.C.

Fleenor, J. W., McCauley, C. D., & Brutus, S. (1996). Self-other rating agreement and leader effectiveness. *Leadership Quarterly, 4,* 487–506.

Fletcher, J. K. (1996). *Relational theory in the workplace.* (Technical report no. 77). Wellesley, Mass.: Stone Center, Wellesley College.

Fondas, N. (1986). Single-sex vs. mixed-sex training. *Journal of European Industrial Training, 10*(7), 28–33.

Friedman, S. D. (1986). Succession systems in large corporations: Characteristics and correlates of performance. *Human Resource Management, 25*(2), 191–213.

Gabarro, J. (1987). *The dynamics of taking charge.* Boston: Harvard Business School Press.

Gardner, H. (1993). *Frames of mind: The theory of multiple intelligences.* New York: Basic Books.

Geber, B. (1992). From manager into coach. *Training, 29*(2), 25–31.

Gergen, K. J. (1994). *Realities and relationships.* Cambridge, Mass.: Harvard University Press.

Goldstein, I. L. (1993). *Training in organizations.* (3rd ed.). Pacific Grove, Calif.: Brooks/Cole.

Goldstein, A. P., & Sorcher, M. (1974). *Changing supervisor behavior.* New York: Pergamon Press.

Goleman, D. (1995). *Emotional intelligence.* New York: Bantam.

Golembiewski, R. T. (1989) The alpha, beta, gamma change typology: Perspectives on acceptance as well as resistance. *Group and Organization Studies, 14,* 150–154.

Graham, S., Wedman, J. F., & Garvin-Kester, B. (1993). Manager coaching skills: Development and application. *Performance Improvement Quarterly, 6*(1), 2–13.

Greider, W. (1997). *One world, ready or not: The manic logic of global capitalism.* New York: Simon & Schuster.

Grove, C., & Hallowell, W. (1994). *Final report of the DIAD Project.* Brooklyn: Cornelius Grove & Associates.

Hall, D. T. (1996). Protean careers of the 21st century. *Academy of Management Executive, 10*(4), 8–16.

Hall, D. T., & Associates. (1996). *The career is dead—long live the career: A relational approach to careers.* San Francisco: Jossey-Bass.

Hall, E. T. (1966). *The hidden dimension.* New York: Doubleday.

Hall, E. T., & Hall, M. R. (1990). *Understanding cultural differences: Germans, French, and Americans.* Yarmouth, Maine: Intercultural Press.

Hargrove, R. (1995). *Masterful coaching.* San Francisco: Pfeiffer.

Harlan, A., & Weiss, C. (1980). *Moving up: Women in managerial careers: Third progress report.* Wellesley, Mass.: Wellesley Center for Research on Women.

Harris, M., & Schaubroeck, J. (1988). A meta-analysis of self-supervisor, self-peer, and peer-supervisor ratings. *Personnel Psychology, 41*(1), 43–61.

Harris, P. R., & Moran, R. T. (1993). *Managing cultural differences: High-performance strategies for a new world of business* (3rd ed.). Houston: Gulf.

Hazucha, J. F., Hezlett, S. A., & Schneider, R. J. (1993). The impact of 360-degree feedback on management skills development. *Human Resource Management, 32*(2, 3), 325–351.

Heifetz, R. A. (1994). *Leadership without easy answers.* Cambridge, Mass.: Harvard University Press.

Heilman, M. E. (1995). Sex stereotypes and their effects in the workplace: What we know and what we don't know. In N. J. Struthers (ed.), Gender in the workplace. (Special issue). *Journal of Social Behavior and Personality, 10*(6), 3–26.

Heilman, M. E., Block, C. J., & Martell, R. F. (1995). Sex stereotypes: Do they influence perceptions of managers? In N. J. Struthers (ed.), Gender in the workplace. (Special issue). *Journal of Social Behavior and Personality, 10*(6), 237–252.

Hendricks, W., and Associates (1996). *Coaching, mentoring, and managing.* Franklin Lakes, N.J.: Career Press.

Henry, B., Moffit, T. E., Caspi, A., Langley, J., & Silva, P. A. (1994). On the remembrance of things past: A longitudinal evaluation of the retrospective method. *Psychological Assessment, 6*(2), 92–101.

Hill, L. A. (1992). *Becoming a manager: Mastery of a new identity.* Boston: Harvard Business School Press.

Hill, R. (1994). *Euromanagers and Martians: The business culture of Europe's trading nations.* Brussels, Belgium: Europublications, Europublic SA/NV.

Hofstede, G. (1980). *Culture's consequences: International differences in work-related values.* Thousand Oaks, Calif.: Sage.

Hofstede, G. (1982). *Values Survey Module (VSM) and scoring guide.* Delft, Netherlands: Institute for Research on Intercultural Cooperation.

Hofstede, G. (1991). *Cultures and organizations: Software of the mind.* London, England: McGraw-Hill.

Hollenbeck, G. P., & McCall, M. W., Jr. (forthcoming). Leadership development: Contemporary practice. In A. K. Kraut & A. K. Korman (eds.), *Changing concepts and practices for human resources management: Contributions from industrial/organizational psychology.* New Directions in Industrial Psychology. San Francisco: Jossey-Bass.

Hoogstraten, J. (1982). The retrospective pretest in an educational training context. *Journal of Experimental Education, 50*(4), 200–204.

Hoppe, M. H. (1990). A comparative study of country elite: International differences in work-related values and learning and their implications for management training and development. Unpublished doctoral dissertation, University of North Carolina at Chapel Hill.

Hoppe, M. H. (1993). The effects of national culture on the theory and practice of managing R&D professionals abroad. *Research and Development Management, 23*(4), 313–325.

House, R. S. (1996). Classroom instruction. In R. L. Craig (ed.), *The ASTD training and development handbook.* (4th ed.). New York: McGraw-Hill.

Howard, G. S. (1993). I think I can! I think I can! Reconsidering the place for practice methodologies in psychological research. *Professional Psychology Research and Practice, 24*(3), 237–244.

Ibarra, H. (1993). Personal networks of women and minorities in management: A conceptual framework. *Academy of Management Review, 18*(1), 56–87.

Ibarra, H. (1995). Race, opportunity, and diversity of social circles in managerial networks. *Academy of Management Journal, 38*(3), 673–703.

Ibarra, H. (forthcoming). Paving an alternate route: Gender differences in managerial networks. *Social Psychology Quarterly.*

Institute for Research on Learning. (1993). *Reflections on workplace learning.* Palo Alto, Calif.: Institute for Research on Learning.

Jackson, S. E. (1992). Stepping into the future: Guidelines for action. In S. E. Jackson & Associates (eds.), *Diversity in the workplace: Human resources initiatives.* New York: Guilford Press.

Jackson, S. E., & Ruderman, M. N. (eds.). (1995). *Diversity in work teams: Research paradigms for a changing workplace.* Washington, D.C.: American Psychological Association.

Johnson, D. W., & Johnson, R. T. (1989). *Cooperation and competition: Theory and research.* Edina, Minn.: Interaction.

Josefowitz, N. (1990). Teaching management skills to women: Why women learn management skills better in all-female groups. *San Diego Woman* (Apr.), 12–14.

Kanter, R. M. (1977). *Men and women of the organization.* New York: Basic Books.

Kanter, R. M. (1995). World class: Thriving locally in the global economy. New York: Simon & Schuster.

Kaplan, R., Drath, W., & Kofodimos, J. (1985). *High hurdles: The challenge of executive self-development.* Greensboro, N.C.: Center for Creative Leadership.

Kaye, B., & Jacobson, B. (1995). Mentoring: A group guide. *Training and Development, 49*(4), 22–27.

Kaye, B., & Jacobson, B. (1997). Rebooting your mentoring program: Accelerating the learning process. Paper presented at the Tools for Developing Executives Users' Conference, Center for Creative Leadership, April, Greensboro, N.C.

Kegan, R. (1994). *In over our heads.* Cambridge, Mass.: Harvard University Press.

Kelleher, D., Finestone, P., & Lowy, A. (1986). Managerial learning: First notes from an unstudied frontier. *Group and Organization Studies, 11*(3), 169–202.

Kernis, M. H., Cornell, D. P., Chien-Ru, S., Berry, A., & Harlow, T. (1993). There's more to self-esteem than whether it's high or low: The importance of stability. *Journal of Personality and Social Psychology, 65*(6), 1190–1204.

Khadra, B. (1990). The prophetic-caliphal model of leadership: An empirical study. *International Studies of Management & Organization, 20*(3), 37–51.

Kinlaw, D. C. (1993). *Coaching for commitment: Managerial strategies for obtaining superior performance.* San Francisco: Pfeiffer.

Kizilos, P. (1990). Take my mentor, please! *Training, 27*(4), 49–55.

Kluckhohn, F. R., & Strodtbeck, F. L. (1961). *Variations in value orientations.* Westport, Conn.: Greenwood Press.

Kluger, A. N. (1997). Feedback-expectation discrepancy, arousal and locus of cognition. In M. Erez, U. Kleinbeck, & H. Thierry (eds.), *Work motivation in the context of a globalizing economy.* Hillsdale, N.J.: Lawrence Erlbaum.

Kluger, A. N., & DeNisi, A. (1996). The effects of feedback interventions on performance: A historical review, a meta-analysis, and a preliminary feedback intervention theory. *Psychological Bulletin, 119*, 254–284.

Kofodimos, J. (1989). *Why executives lose their balance.* Greensboro, N.C.: Center for Creative Leadership.

Kohls, L. R. (1996). *Survival kit for overseas living: For Americans planning to live and work abroad.* Yarmouth, Maine: Intercultural Press.

Kossek, E. E., & Lobel, S. (1996). *Managing diversity: Human resource strategies for transforming the workplace.* Cambridge, Mass.: Blackwell.

Kossek, E. E., & Zonia, S. C. (1993). Assessing diversity climate: A field study of reactions to employer efforts to promote diversity. *Journal of Organizational Behavior, 14*(1), 61–81.

Kotter, J. P. (1982). *The general managers.* New York: Free Press.

Kouzes, J. H., & Posner, B. Z. (1987). *The leadership challenge: How to get extraordinary things done in organizations.* San Francisco: Jossey-Bass.

Kram, K. E. (1985). *Mentoring at work.* Glenville, Ill.: Scott, Foresman.

Kram, K. E., & Bragar, M. C. (1992). Development through mentoring: A strategic approach. In D. Montross and C. Shinkman (eds.), *Career development: Theory and practice.* Chicago: Thomas.

Kram, K. E., & Hall, D. T. (1989). Mentoring as an antidote to stress during corporate trauma. *Human Resource Management, 28*(4), 493–510.

Kram, K. E., & Hall, D. T. (1996). Mentoring in a context of diversity and turbulence. In E. E. Kossek and S. A. Lobel (eds.), *Managing diversity: Human resource strategies for transforming the workplace.* Cambridge, Mass.: Blackwell.

Kram, K. E., & Isabella, L. A. (1985). Mentoring alternatives: The role of peer relationships in career development. *Academy of Management Journal, 28*(1), 110–132.

Lambert, L. (1995). *The constructivist leader.* New York: Teachers College Press.

Langer, E. J. (1989). *Mindfulness.* Reading, Mass.: Addison-Wesley.

Langrish, S. (1980). Single sex management training—A personal view. *Women and Training News, 1*(Winter), 3–4.

Leach, M. M. (1997). Training global psychologists: An introduction. *International Journal of Intercultural Relations, 21*(2),161–174.

Lee, R., Guthrie, V., & Young, D. (1995). The lessons of life at work: continuous personal development. *Career Planning and Adult Development Journal, 11*(3), 31–35.

Lepsinger, R., & Lucia, A. D. (1997). *The art and science of 360° feedback.* San Francisco: Pfeiffer.

Leslie, J. B., & Fleenor, J. W. (1998). *Feedback to managers.* (3rd ed.). Greensboro, N.C.: Center for Creative Leadership.

Leslie, J. B., Gryskiewicz, N., & Dalton, M. (1998). Cultural influences on the 360-degree feedback process. In W. W. Tornow and M. London (eds.), *Maximizing the value of 360-degree feedback: A process for successful individual and organizational development.* San Francisco: Jossey-Bass.

Leslie, J. B., & Van Velsor, E. (1996). *A look at derailment today: Europe and the United States.* Greensboro, N.C.: Center for Creative Leadership.

Levinson, D. J. (1978). *The seasons of a man's life.* New York: Knopf.

Lombardo, M. M., & Eichinger, R. W. (1989). *Eighty-eight assignments for development in place: Enhancing the development challenge of existing jobs.* Greensboro, N.C.: Center for Creative Leadership.

London, M. (1995). Can multisource feedback change self-evaluations, skill development, and performance? Theory-based actions and directions for research. *Personnel Psychology, 48*(4), 803–840.

London, M., & Beatty, R. W. (1993). 360-degree feedback as a competitive advantage. *Human Resource Management, 32*(2, 3), 357–372.

Lyness, K. S., & Thompson, D. E. (1997). Above the glass ceiling? A comparison of matched samples of female and male executives. *Journal of Applied Psychology, 82*(3), 359–379.

MacLachlan, M., Mapundi, J., Zimba, C. G., & Carr, S. C. (1995). The acceptability of Western psychometric instruments in a non-Western society. *Journal of Social Psychology, 135*(5), 645–648.

Martineau, J. (1998). Assessing change using 360-degree feedback. In W. W. Tornow and M. London (eds.), *Maximizing the value of 360-degree feedback: A process for successful individual and organizational development.* San Francisco: Jossey-Bass.

McBroom, P. A. (1992). *The third sex: The new professional woman.* New York: Paragon House.

McCall, M. W. (1997). *High flyers: Developing the next generation of leaders.* Boston: Harvard Business School Press.

McCall, M. W., & Lombardo, M. M. (1983). *Off the track: Why and how successful executives get derailed.* Greensboro, N.C.: Center for Creative Leadership.

McCall, M. W., Lombardo, M. M., & Morrison, A. M. (1988). *The lessons of experience: How successful executives develop on the job.* Lexington, Mass.: Lexington Books.

McCarthy, B., & Keene, C. (1996). *About learning.* Barrington, Ill.: Excel.

McCauley, C. D., & Brutus, S. (1998). *Management development through job experiences: An annotated bibliography.* Greensboro, N.C.: Center for Creative Leadership.

McCauley, C. D., & Hughes-James, M. W. (1994). *An evaluation of the outcomes of a leadership development program.* Greensboro, N.C.: Center for Creative Leadership.

McCauley, C. D., Lombardo, M. M., & Usher, C. (1989). Diagnosing management development needs: An instrument based on how managers develop. *Journal of Management, 15*(3), 389–403.

McCauley, C. D., Ruderman, M. N., Ohlott, P. J., & Morrow, J. E. (1994). Assessing the developmental components of managerial jobs. *Journal of Applied Psychology, 79*(4), 544–560.

McCauley, C. D., & Young, D. P. (1993). Creating developmental relationships: roles and strategies. *Human Resource Management Review, 3*(3), 219–230.

McCrae, R. R., & Costa, P. T., Jr. (1985). Openness to experience. In R. Hagan and W. H. Jones (eds.), *Perspectives in personality, vol. 1.* Greenwich, Conn.: JAI Press.

McCrae, R. R., & Costa, P. T., Jr. (1987). Validation of the five-factor model across instruments and observers. *Journal of Personality & Social Psychology, 52,* 81–90.

Miller, J. B. (1986). *Toward a new psychology of women.* Boston: Beacon Press.

Millsap, R. E., & Hartog, S. B. (1988). Alpha, beta, and gamma change in evaluation research: A structural equation approach. *Journal of Applied Psychology, 73,* 574–584.

Mink, O. G. (1993). *Developing high-performance people: The art of coaching.* Reading, Mass.: Addison-Wesley.

Moran, R. T., Harris, P. R., & Stripp, W. G. (1993). *Developing the global organization: Strategies for human resource professionals.* Houston: Gulf.

Morrison, A. M. (1992). *The new leaders: Guidelines on leadership diversity in America.* San Francisco: Jossey-Bass.

Morrison, A. M., Ruderman, M. N., & Hughes-James, M. W. (1993). *Making diversity happen: Controversies and solutions.* Greensboro, N.C.: Center for Creative Leadership.

Morrison, A. M., & Von Glinow, M. A. (1990). Women and minorities in management. (Special issue). *American Psychologist, 45*(2), 200–208.

Morrison, A. M., White, R. P., & Van Velsor, E. (1987). *Breaking the glass ceiling: Can women reach the top of America's largest corporations?* Reading, Mass.: Addison-Wesley. (Revised edition 1992)

Mount, M. K., Sytsma, M. R., Hazucha, J. F., & Holt, K. E. (1997). Rater-ratee race effects in developmental performance ratings of managers. *Personnel Psychology, 50,* 51–69.

Moxley, R. S., & McCauley, C. D. (1996). Developmental 360: How feedback can make managers more effective. *Career Development International, 1*(3), 15–19.

Murray, M., & Owen, M. A. (1991). *Beyond the myths and magic of mentoring: How to facilitate an effective mentoring program.* San Francisco: Jossey-Bass.

NCR Corporation. (1992). *Developing NCR engineers.* Dayton, Ohio: NCR.

Nadler, L., & Nadler, Z. (1994). *Designing training programs: The critical events model* (2nd ed.). Houston: Gulf.

Newman, M. A. (1993). Career advancement: Does gender make a difference? *American Review of Public Administration, 23*(4), 361–384.

Nicholson, N., & West, M. (1988). *Managerial job change: Men and women in transition.* Cambridge, England: Cambridge University Press.

Nkomo, S. M. (1992). The emperor has no clothes: Rewriting "race in organizations." *Academy of Management Review, 17*(3), 487–513.

Noe, R. A. (1991). Mentoring relationships for employee development. In J. W. Jones, B. D. Steffy, & D. W. Bray (eds.), *Applying psychology in business: The handbook for managers and human resource professionals.* Lexington, Mass.: Heath.

Noer, D. N. (1993). *Healing the wounds.* San Francisco: Jossey-Bass.

Northcraft, G. B., Griffith, T. L., & Shalley, C. E. (1992). Building top management muscle in a slow growth environment. *Academy of Management Executive, 6*(1), 32–40.

Ohlott, P. J., & Hughes-James, M. W. (1997). Single-gender and single-race leadership development programs: Concerns and benefits. *Leadership in Action, 17*(4), 8–12.

Ohlott, P. J., McCauley, C. D., & Ruderman, M. N. (1993). *Developmental Challenge Profile: learning from job experiences: Manual and trainers guide.* Greensboro, N.C.: Center for Creative Leadership.

Ohlott, P. J., Ruderman, M. N., & McCauley, C. D. (1994). Gender differences in managers' developmental job experiences. *Academy of Management Journal, 37*(1), 46–67.

O'Reilly, B. (1994). 360 feedback can change your life. *Fortune, 130*(8), 93–100.

Orth, C. D., Wildinson, H. E., & Benfari, R. C. (1987). The manager's role as coach and mentor. *Organizational Dynamics, 15*(4), 66–74.

Palus, C. J., & Drath, W. H. (1995). *Evolving leaders: A model for promoting leadership development in programs.* Greensboro, N.C.: Center for Creative Leadership.

Palus, C. J., & Rogolsky, S. R. (1996). *Development of, and development within, a global, feedback-intensive organization.* Unpublished manuscript, Center for Creative Leadership.

Peters, H. (1996). Peer coaching for executives. *Training & Development, 50*(3), 39–41.

Peterson, D., and Hicks, M. D. (1996). *Leader as coach.* Minneapolis: Personnel Decisions.

Preskill, H., & Torres, R. T. (1996). From evaluation to evaluative inquiry for organizational learning. Paper presented at the American Evaluation Association annual conference, November, Atlanta, Georgia.

Ragins, B. R., & Cotton, J. L. (1991). Easier said than done: Gender differences in perceived barriers to gaining a mentor. *Academy of Management Journal, 34*(4), 939–951.

Ragins, B. R., & McFarlin, D. B. (1990). Perceptions of mentor roles in cross-gender mentoring relationships. *Journal of Vocational Behavior, 37,* 321–339.

Rhinesmith, S. H. (1993). *A manager's guide to globalization: Six keys to success in a changing world.* Alexandria, Va.: Business One Irwin.

Richie, B. S., Fassinger, R. E., Linn, S. G., Johnson, J., Prosser, J., & Robinson, S. (1997). Persistence, connection, and passion: A qualitative study of the career development of highly achieving African American–black and white women. *Journal of Counseling Psychology, 44*(2), 133–148.

Rogolsky, S., & Dalton, M. A. (1995). Is that still true: Women recall career shaping events. Unpublished manuscript, Center for Creative Leadership, Greensboro, N.C.

Ronen, S., & Shenkar, O. (1985). Clustering countries on attitudinal dimensions: A review and synthesis. *Academy of Management Review, 10,* 435–454.

Rost, J. C. (1991). *Leadership for the twenty-first century.* New York: Praeger.

Rouillier, J. Z., & Goldstein, I. L. (1990). Determinants of the climate for transfer of training. Paper presented at the meeting of the Society of Industrial and Organizational Psychology, St. Louis.

Ruderman, M. N., Hughes-James, M., & Jackson, S. E. (eds.). (1996). *Selected research on work team diversity.* Washington, D.C.: American Psychological Association.

Ruderman, M. N., McCauley, C. D., Ohlott, P. J., & McCall, M. W., Jr. (1993). *Developmental Challenge Profile: Learning from job experiences.* Greensboro, N.C.: Center for Creative Leadership.

Ruderman, M. N., & Ohlott, P. J. (1990). *Traps and pitfalls in the judgment of executive potential.* Greensboro, N.C.: Center for Creative Leadership.

Ruderman, M. N., & Ohlott, P. J. (1994). *The realities of management promotion.* Greensboro, N.C.: Center for Creative Leadership.

Ruderman, M. N., Ohlott, P. J., & Kram, K. E. (1995). Promotion decisions as a diversity practice. *Journal of Management Development, 14*(2), 6–23.

Ruderman, M. N., Ohlott, P. J., & McCauley, C. D. (1996). Developing from job experiences: The role of self-esteem and self-efficacy. Paper presented at the meeting of the Society for Industrial and Organizational Psychology, April, San Diego.

Sayles, L. R. (1993). *The working leader.* New York: Free Press.

Schwartz, S. H. (1994). Beyond individualism/collectivism: New cultural dimensions of values. In U. Kim and others (eds.), *Individualism and collectivism: Theory, methods, and applications.* Thousand Oaks, Calif.: Sage.

Sedlacek, W. E. (1987). Black students on white campuses: 20 years of research. *Journal of College Student Personnel, 28*(6), 484–495.

Seibert, K. W. (1996). Experience is the best teacher, if you can learn from it: Real-time reflection and development. In D. T. Hall & Associates (eds.), *The career is dead—long live the career: A relational approach to careers.* San Francisco: Jossey-Bass.

Seibert, K. W., Hall, D. T., & Kram, K. E. (1995). Strengthening the weak link in strategic executive development: Integrating individual development and global business strategy. *Human Resource Management, 34*(4), 549–567.

Senge, P. (1990). *The fifth discipline.* New York: Doubleday.

Sherman, S. (1995). How tomorrow's best leaders are learning their stuff. *Fortune* (Nov. 27), 90–102.

Simons, G. F., Vazquez, C., & Harris, P. R. (1993). *Transcultural leadership: Empowering the diverse workforce.* Houston: Gulf.

Smith, P. B., & Peterson, M. F. (1988). *Leadership, organizations, and culture: An event management model.* London, England: Sage.

Smith, P. B., & Peterson, M. F. (1995). Beyond value comparisons: Sources used to give meaning to management work events in twenty-nine countries. Paper presented at Academy of Management annual meeting, Aug. 6–9, Vancouver, B.C.

Smither, J. W., London, M., Vasilopoulos, N., Reilly, R. R., Millsap, R. E., & Salvemini, N. (1995). An examination of the effects of an upward feedback program over time. *Personnel Psychology, 48*(1), 1–34.

Spreitzer, G. M., McCall, M. W., & Mahoney, J. (1995). Ability to learn from experience and the early identification of international executive potential. Paper presented at the National Academy of Management meeting, Aug. 6–9, Vancouver, B.C.

Spreitzer, G. M., McCall, M. W., & Mahoney, J. D. (1997). Early identification of international executive potential. *Journal of Applied Psychology, 82*(1), 6–29.

Steingraber, F. G. (1996). The new business realities of the twenty-first century. *Business Horizons,* Nov.–Dec., 2–5.

Stewart, E. C., & Bennett, M. J.(1991). *American cultural patterns: A cross-cultural perspective.* Yarmouth, Maine: Intercultural Press.

Sutter, S. (1994). Making management development an organizational reality. Society for Industrial and Organizational Psychology Workshop, Apr. 7, Nashville, Tenn.

Tennis, C. N. (1989). Responses to the alpha, beta, gamma change typology. *Group and Organization Studies, 14,* 134–149.

Terborg, J. R., Howard, G. S., & Maxwell, S. E. (1980). Evaluating planned organizational change: A method for assessing alpha, beta, and gamma change. *Academy of Management Review, 5,* 109–121.

Thiagarajan, S. (1996). Instructional games, simulations, and role-plays. In R. L. Craig (ed.), *The ASTD training and development handbook.* (4th ed.). New York: McGraw-Hill.

Thomas, D. A. (1989). Mentoring and irrationality: The role of racial taboos. *Human Resource Management, 28*(2), 279–290.

Thomas, D. A. (1990). The impact of race on managers' experiences of developmental relationships (mentoring and sponsorship): An intra-organizational study. *Journal of Organizational Behavior, 11,* 479–492.

Thomas, K. M. (1996). Psychological privilege and ethnocentrism as barriers to cross-cultural adjustment and effective intercultural interactions. *Leadership Quarterly, 7*(2), 215–228.

Tornow, W. W., and London, M. (eds.). (1998). *Maximizing the value of 360-degree feedback: A process for successful individual and organizational development.* San Francisco: Jossey-Bass.

Tracey, T. J., & Sedlacek, W. E. (1984). Noncognitive variables in predicting academic success by race. *Measurement and Evaluation in Guidance, 16,* 172–178.

Tracey, T. J., & Sedlacek, W. E. (1985). The relationship of noncognitive variables to academic success: A longitudinal comparison by race. *Journal of College Student Personnel, 26,* 405–410.

Tracey, T. J., & Sedlacek, W. E. (1987). Prediction of college graduation using noncognitive variables by race. *Measurement and Evaluation in Counseling and Development, 19,* 177–184.

Triandis, H. C. (1980). Introduction to handbook of cross-cultural psychology. In H. C. Triandis and W. W. Lambert (eds.), *Handbook of cross-cultural psychology.* Boston: Allyn & Bacon.

U.S. Department of Labor, Federal Glass Ceiling Commission. (1995). *Good for business: Making full use of the nation's human capital.* Washington, D.C.: U.S. Government Printing Office.

Vaill, P. B. (1996). *Learning as a way of being: Strategies for survival in a world of permanent white water.* San Francisco: Jossey-Bass.

Valerio, A. M. (1990). A study of the developmental experiences of managers. In K. E. Clark & M. B. Clark (eds.), *Measures of leadership.* West Orange, N.J.: Leadership Library of America.

Van Maanen, J., & Schein, E. H. (1979). Toward a theory of organizational socialization. In B. M. Staw (ed.), *Research in organizational behavior (vol. 1).* Greenwich, Conn.: JAI Press.

Van Velsor, E., & Hughes-James, M. W. (1990). *Gender differences in the development of managers: How women managers learn from experience.* Greensboro, N.C.: Center for Creative Leadership.

Van Velsor, E., Leslie, J. B., & Fleenor, J. W. (1997). *Choosing 360: A guide to evaluating multirater feedback instruments for management development.* Greensboro, N.C.: Center for Creative Leadership.

Van Velsor, E., & Musselwhite, W. C. (1986). The timing of training, learning, and transfer. *Training and Development Journal, 40*(8), 58–59.

Van Velsor, E., Ruderman, M. N., & Phillips, D. (1989). The lessons of Looking Glass: Management simulations and the real world of action. *Leadership and Organization Development Journal, 10*(6), 27–31.

Van Velsor, E., Ruderman, M. N., & Phillips, D. (1992). The impact of feedback on self-assessment and performance in three domains of management behavior. Paper presented at the annual meeting of the Society for Industrial and Organizational Psychology, April, St. Louis.

Van Velsor, E., & Wall, S. (1992). How to choose a feedback instrument. *Training, 29*(3), 47–52.

Waldroop, J., and Butler, T. (1996). The executive as coach. *Harvard Business Review, 74*(6), 111–119.

Walker, B. A., & Hansen, W. C. (1992). Valuing differences at Digital Equipment Corporation. In S. Jackson & Associates (eds.), *Diversity in the workplace: Human resource initiatives.* New York: Guilford Press.

Weeks, D. A. (1992). *Recruiting and selecting international managers.* (Report no. 998). New York: Conference Board.

Weick, K. E. (1995). *Sense-making in organizations.* Thousand Oaks, Calif.: Sage.

White, R. P. (1992). Job as classroom: Using assignments to leverage development. In D. H. Montross & C. J. Shinkman (eds.), *Career development: Theory and practice.* Springfield, Ill.: Thomey.

White, M. B. (1997). Changing course: New diversity initiatives at Avon, AT&T and TVA. *The diversity factor, 5*(2), 29–46.

Wick, C. W. (1989). How people develop: An in-depth look. *HR Report, 6*(7), 1–3.

Wills, S., & Barham, K. (1994). Being an international manager. *European Management Journal, 12*(1), 49–58.

Wilson, M., Hoppe, W. H., & Sayles, L. R. (1996). *Managing across cultures: A learning framework.* Greensboro, N.C.: Center for Creative Leadership.

Witherspoon, R., & White, R. P. (1997). *Four essential ways that coaching can help executives.* Greensboro, N.C.: Center for Creative Leadership.

Yeung, A. K., & Ready, D. A. (1995). Developing leadership capabilities of global corporations: A comparative study in eight nations. *Human Resource Management, 34*(4), 529–547.

Young, D., & Dixon, N. (1996). *Helping leaders take effective action: A program evaluation.* Greensboro, N.C.: Center for Creative Leadership.

Yukl, G. A. (1989). *Leadership in organizations* (2nd ed.). Englewood Cliffs, N.J.: Prentice-Hall.

Zemke, R. (1985). The Honeywell studies: How managers learn to manage. *Training 22*(8), 46–51.

Zey, M. G. (1991). *The mentor connection.* New Brunswick, N.J.: Transaction.

NAME INDEX

A

Adler, N. J., 382, 385
Alden, J., 114
Aldwin, C. M., 161
Alexander the Great, 405
Ali, A. J., 353
Anderson, P. E., 320
Anderson, T., 29–31, 36, 38
Argyris, C., 246
Aristotle, 405
Armenakis, A. A., 275
Ashford, S. J., 248
Atwater, L., 32
Auster, E., 320

B

Baird, L., 395–396
Baldwin, T. T., 155
Bandura, A., 16, 115, 160
Barclay, D., 177
Barham, K., 385
Barrick, M. R., 249
Barsoux, J. L., 348–349
Bartholomew, S., 382, 385

Bartlett, C., 63, 381–382, 385
Baskerville, D. M., 311, 315
Bass, B. M., 407, 413
Beatty, R. W., 37
Bedian, A. G., 275
Bell, E. L., 297, 300
Benfari, R. C., 193
Bennett, M. J., 340, 342, 347,
    351–352, 355, 373, 378
Betters-Reed, B. L., 294
Block, C. J., 296
Bragar, M. C., 183, 184, 189
Brake, T., 362
Brett, J. M., 134
Brewer, M. B., 335
Briscoe, J., 395–396
Brockner, J., 248
Broderick, R., 128
Brody, S. E., 331
Brutus, S., 53–54, 158, 365
Bunker, K., 121, 227, 242,
    252
Burgoyne, J. G., 139–140
Burke, M. J., 116
Butler, T., 174, 175, 193
Byrne, D., 298

C

Campbell, D. P., 53
Carr, S. C., 363
Catalyst, 296, 308, 314, 328, 334
Caudron, S., 334
Cavanagh, G. F., 342
CCL Associates, 31, 256, 354
Chappelow, C. T., 29
Chen, C. C., 307
Chiaramonte, P., 193
Clark, K. S., 129, 149, 154
Cobb, J., 149, 175
Collins, L. M., 278
Conger, J. A., 107, 109, 258
Costa, P. T., Jr., 249
Cotton, J. L., 321, 322
Cousins, J. B., 286
Cox, T. H., Jr., 307, 321, 335
Curtis, L. B., 153

D

Dalton, M. A., 42, 59, 306, 317,
    355, 359, 364, 365, 366, 367,
    379, 392–393, 394–395, 434

Davies, J., 134
Day, R. R., 116
De Merode, J., 386
Dechant, K., 149
DeNisi, A., 280
Derr, C. B., 346–347
Dickens, F., Jr., 302, 304, 313, 321, 328
Dickens, J. B., 302, 304, 313, 321, 328
DiTomaso, N., 307
Dixon, N. M., 99–101, 249, 256, 274, 278, 373, 422
Donaldson, T., 400
Dorfman, P. W., 355
Dorn, R. C., 66
Douglas, C. A., 160, 178, 184, 187
Drath, W. H., 35, 413, 420, 438
Drucker, P., 435
Dunnette, M., 53

E

Eagly, A. H., 308
Earl, L. M., 286
Easterby-Smith, M., 134
Eichinger, R. W., 142–143, 155, 260
Elashmawi, F., 371, 378
Eliot, T. S., 2
Evered, R. D., 193

F

Federal Glass Ceiling Commission, 296, 297, 308, 311, 321, 327, 330
Feghali, E., 357
Ferdman, B. M., 331
Fetterman, D., 286
Filipczak, B., 356
Finestone, P., 137
Fischtal, A., 32
Flanders, D. P., 320
Fleenor, J. W., 43, 53–54, 76, 256, 304, 305, 306, 361, 365
Fletcher, J. K., 301, 304
Fondas, N., 314, 315
Fortune, 37
Friedman, S. D., 148

G

Gabarro, J., 157
Gardner, H., 246
Garvin-Kester, B., 175
Geber, B., 193
Gergen, K. J., 421
Ghoshal, S., 63, 381–382, 385
Gibbs, J., 149, 175
Goldstein, A. P., 116
Goldstein, I. L., 120, 124–125
Goleman, D., 304, 331
Golembiewski, R. T., 275
Graham, S., 175
Greider, W., 380, 384, 393, 400
Griffith, T. L., 149, 152
Grove, C., 345
Gryskiewicz, N., 364, 365, 366, 367
Guthrie, V. A., 66, 242, 260

H

Haifetz, R. A., 413
Hall, D. T., 149, 152, 172, 321, 326, 331, 387, 435
Hall, E. T., 342, 352, 378
Hall, M. R., 352, 378
Hallowell, W., 345
Hansen, W. C., 331
Harlan, A., 315
Harris, M., 53
Harris, P. R., 352, 369, 371, 378
Hartog, S. B., 275
Hayes, C., 334
Hazucha, J. F., 32, 57, 307
Heifetz, R., 13
Heilman, M. E., 296, 314
Hendricks, W., 193
Henry, B., 278
Hezlett, S. A., 32, 57
Hicks, M. D., 174, 193
Higgins, A., 193
Hill, L. A., 12
Hill, R., 299, 347, 359, 378
Hodgson, V. E., 139–140
Hofstede, G., 342, 348, 365, 369, 370, 378
Hollenbeck, G. P., 42, 59, 154, 306
Holmes, O. W., Jr., 378

Holt, K. E., 307
Hoppe, M. H., 336, 342, 343, 346, 365, 369, 370, 378, 434
Horn, J. L., 278
House, R. S., 114
Howard, G. S., 275, 278
Hughes-James, M. W., 177, 263, 291, 293, 309, 312, 314, 315–316, 317, 323, 325, 326

I

Ibarra, H., 323, 324, 325
Institute for Research on Learning, 161
Isabella, L. A., 184

J

Jackson, S. E., 293, 335
Jacobsen, D., 29–30
Jacobson, B., 186
Johnson, D. W., 161
Johnson, R. T., 161
Josefowitz, N., 311

K

Kanter, R. M., 298, 385, 393
Kanungo, J. A., 109
Kaplan, R., 35
Kaye, B., 186
Keene, C., 73
Kegan, R., 420, 427
Kelleher, D., 137
Kelly-Radford, L., 66
Kernis, M. H., 248
Khadra, B., 353
Kinlaw, D. C., 193
Kirkhorn, J., 114
Kizilos, P., 183
Klonsky, B. G., 308
Kluckhohn, F. R., 342
Kluger, A. N., 280
Kofodimos, J., 35
Kohls, L. R., 342, 378
Kossek, E. E., 294, 335
Kotter, J. P., 140
Kram, K. E., 149, 152, 168, 172, 183, 184, 189, 293, 320, 321, 326, 328, 387

L

Lambert, L., 414
Langer, E. J., 421
Langrish, S., 314
Lawrence, L. P., 348–349
Leach, M. M., 357
Lee, R., 260
Lepsinger, R., 31
Leslie, J. B., 43, 76, 256, 304, 305,
    361, 364, 365, 366, 367, 372
Levinson, D. J., 168
Lobel, S., 335
Lombardo, M. M., 12, 17, 53,
    55, 128, 131, 134, 140,
    141, 142–143, 155, 165,
    169, 196–197, 198, 209,
    259, 260, 263, 292, 317,
    318, 372, 396
London, M., 31, 37, 42, 256,
    354
Lowy, A., 137
Lucia, A. D., 31
Lyness, K. S., 129, 149, 154, 297,
    299

M

MacLachlan, M., 363
Mahoney, J. D., 396–397, 398
Makhjijani, M. G., 308
Mapundi, J., 363
Martell, R. F., 296
Martineau, J., 277
Maxwell, S. E., 275
McBroom, P. A., 299
McCall, M. W., 12, 17, 53, 55, 63,
    128, 131, 140, 141, 144, 154,
    165, 169, 196–197, 198, 209,
    259, 263, 292, 317, 318, 372,
    394, 396–397, 398
McCarthy, B., 73
McCauley, C. D., 1, 36, 53–54, 131,
    134, 141, 144, 158, 160, 178,
    184, 257, 293, 297, 317, 326,
    365, 396, 433
McCrae, R. R., 249
McDonald-Mann, D. G., 106
McFarlin, D. B., 322
Merode, J. de, 382–383
Miller, J. B., 314

Millsap, R. E., 275
Mink, O. G., 193
Moore, L. L., 294
Moran, R. T., 371, 378
Morrison, A. M., 12, 17, 55,
    128, 131, 140, 141, 165, 177,
    196–197, 198, 209, 259, 263,
    291, 292, 293, 295–299, 301,
    303, 308, 311, 312, 314, 317,
    318, 319, 320, 321, 323, 325,
    327, 328, 329, 333, 334, 335,
    396
Morrow, J. E., 131, 394
Mount, M. K., 249, 307
Moxley, R. S., 1, 36, 194, 217, 433
Murray, M., 183
Musselwhite, W. C., 71, 258

N

Nadler, L., 107
Nadler, Z., 107
Newman, M. A., 298
Nicholson, N., 131, 134
Nilsen, D., 53
Nkomo, S. M., 297, 299, 321
Noe, R. A., 183
Noer, D. N., 205
Northcraft, G. B., 149, 152

O

Ohlott, P. J., 127, 131, 144, 147,
    257, 263, 293, 296, 297, 298,
    309, 315–316, 317, 320, 328,
    394, 396
O'Reilly, B., 37
Orth, C. D., 193
Owen, M. A., 183

P

Padgett, M. Y., 155
Palus, C. J., 176, 413, 420
Peters, H., 184
Peterson, D., 174, 193
Peterson, M. F., 358, 369, 375
Phillips, D., 98, 256, 266
Plato, 405
Preskill, H., 286

R

Ragins, B. R., 321, 322
Ready, D. A., 357, 358, 362, 369
Rhinesmith, S. H., 362
Richie, B. S., 296
Rogolsky, S. R., 176, 317
Ronen, S., 359
Rost, J. C., 413
Rouillier, J. Z., 120
Rousch, P., 32
Ruderman, M. N., 98, 131, 144,
    147, 177, 256, 257, 263, 266,
    291, 293, 296, 297, 298, 312,
    317, 320, 323, 325, 328, 394,
    396
Russell, E. A., 153

S

Sayles, L. R., 343, 346, 378, 423
Schaubroeck, J., 53
Schein, E. H., 160
Schneider, R. J., 32, 57
Schoorman, 184
Schwartz, S. H., 342
Sedlacek, W. E., 305
Seibert, K. W., 149, 152, 331, 387
Selman, J. C., 193
Senge, P., 304
Shalley, C. E., 149, 152
Shenkar, O., 359
Sherman, S., 129
Simons, G. F., 352
Smith, P. B., 358, 369, 375
Smither, J. W., 32
Sorcher, M., 116
Spreitzer, G. M., 396–397, 398
Steingraber, F. G., 434
Stewart, E. C., 340, 342, 347,
    351–352, 355, 373, 378
Stodtbeck, F. L., 342
Stripp, W. G., 378
Sue, D., 312, 325
Sutter, S., 142–143, 155
Sytsma, M. R., 307

T

Tennis, C. N., 275
Terborg, J. R., 275

Thiagarajan, S., 113, 115
Thomas, D. A., 304, 321, 322
Thompson, D. E., 297, 299
Tocqueville, A. de, 342
Tornow, W. W., 31, 256, 354
Torres, R. T., 286
Tracey, T. J., 305
Triandis, H. C., 361
Tuden, L., 395–396

U

U.S. Department of Labor Federal
    Glass Ceiling Commission, 296,
    297, 308, 311, 321, 327, 330
Usher, C., 134, 141

V

Vaill, P. B., 369
Valerio, A. M., 131, 143

Van Maanen, J., 160
Van Velsor, E., 1, 17, 43, 44, 71,
    98, 128, 242, 256, 258, 263,
    266, 292, 293, 301, 304, 305,
    314, 317, 372, 433
Vazquez, C., 352

W

Waldroop, J., 174, 175, 193
Walker, B. A., 331
Wall, S., 44
Watson, T., 198
Webb, A., 121, 227, 242, 252
Wedman, J. F., 175
Weeks, D. A., 382–383
Weick, K. E., 414, 421, 425
Weiss, C., 315
West, M., 131, 134
White, M. B., 334

White, R. P., 17, 128, 143, 180,
    185, 292, 301, 317
Wick, C. W., 128, 137
Wildinson, H. E., 193
Wills, S., 385
Wilson, M., 343, 346, 378,
    392–393, 394–395
Wilson, P. O., 217
Witherspoon, R., 180, 185

Y

Yeung, A. K., 357, 358, 362, 369
Young, D. P., 99–101, 184, 249,
    256, 260, 278, 373

Z

Zemke, R., 128
Zey, M. G., 161
Zimba, C. G., 363
Zonia, S. C., 294

SUBJECT INDEX

A

Ability to learn from experience, 242–261; achievement needs and, 249; across cultures, 386, 395–399; anxiety management and, 250–251; assessment and feedback for enhancing, 255–256; beliefs about learning and, 250; characteristics of, 243–244; conscientiousness and, 249; difficulties of, 244–245; enhancement of, 22–23, 251–261; for global leadership development, 386, 395–399; individual differences in, 245–254; intelligence and, 246–247; locus of control and, 250; openness to experience and, 249; practitioner guidelines for enhancing, 260–261; self-efficacy and, 247–248; self-esteem and, 247–248; support for, 245, 256–257; timing and, 257–259. *See also* Developmental experiences; Learning

ability; Learning skills and strategies
About Learning (McCarthy and Keene), 73
Accessing-others learning tactic, 251, 253–254
Accountability, for diversity programs, 334
Accountant role, 162, 165, 170
Achievement needs, and ability to learn, 249
Achievement orientation, cultural differences in, 342
Acting experiences, in feedback-intensive programs, 87
Action cultural orientation. *See* Doing-being cultural dimension
Action domain of learning, 107–108
Action learning tactics, 95, 251, 252–253; for global leadership development, 396
Action planning: in feedback-intensive programs, 75, 100; follow-up to, 278, 280; for individual development, 146; in systemic

leadership development case study, 235
Active-reflective cultural dimension, 342, 343–345; and attitudes towards assessment, 350–351; and attitudes towards challenge, 369–370; and attitudes towards promotion, 347–348
Administration, 360-degree feedback for, 41–42
African American men, 294; barriers to advancement of, 295–299; developmental experiences and, 303–329; salaries of, versus white men, 327. *See also* Nontraditional managers
African American women, 294; barriers to advancement of, 295–299; developmental experiences and, 303–329; multiple identities of, 300; salaries of, versus white men, 327. *See also* Nontraditional managers; Women
African Americans: assessment content for, 304–305, 313;

469

African Americans *(continued)*
assessment instrument validity
for, 305–306; barriers to advancement of, 295–299; bias
in ratings of, 306–309; developmental relationships for,
321–326; differential norms
and, 306; feedback-intensive
programs for, 293–294, 309–
315; fitting in of, 302; job assignments for, 316–320; leadership development for, 291–335,
438–439; managerial and
African American identities
of, 299–302, 319; practitioner
guidelines for meeting the needs
of, 329–332; prejudice and, 296;
recognition and rewards for,
327–329; 360-degree feedback
for, 303–309. *See also* Nontraditional managers
Agenda setting, 140–141
Alumni groups, of feedback-
intensive programs, 102
American Revolution, 406–407
Anglo country cluster, 360
Anonymity: cross-cultural differences and, 364; in feedback-
intensive programs, 85; in
360-degree feedback, 46–47,
61, 62, 364
Anxiety of learning, 245, 250–251
Apprentice system, in Germany,
347
Arab countries: attitudes towards assessment in, 356; cluster of, 360;
cultural values of, 344; leadership development in, 349; particularistic orientation in, 353
Art and Science of 360° Feedback, The
(Lepsinger and Lucia), 31
Asian Americans, 293
Assessment, 9–11; for administration versus development, 41–42;
cross-cultural perspectives on,
349–367, 376–377; in developmental experience, 6, 22, 222–
223; in developmental relationships, 162–164; for enhancing
ability to learn, 255–256; in
feedback-intensive programs,
67, 76–85, 105; follow-up,

275–277; functions of, 9–11, 23;
for global leadership development, 396–399; in hardship,
211; of impact of developmental experiences, 262–288; in job
assignments, 130; motivational
role of, 9, 10–11; resource role
of, 9, 11; in skill-based training,
118–119; sources of, 10; in 360-
degree feedback, 37; of training
needs, 124–126; types of, 10.
See also Feedback-intensive programs; Formal assessment; Informal assessment; Leadership
development impact assessment;
Self-assessment; 360-degree
feedback
Assignment brokers, 162, 164–165,
170
Association for Managers of Innovation (AMI), 177–178
A.T. Kearney, 434
Australia, 344, 346, 360, 369
Authenticity, of feedback-intensive
program staff, 91
Automated data collection, in
360-degree feedback, 64–65
Avon Products, 334

B

Backlash, and single-identity feedback programs, 315
Balance, learning of, 207
Behavioral assessment, in feedback-
intensive programs, 82–84
Behavioral change: in feedback-
intensive programs, 100–101;
impact domain of, 268; and
360-degree feedback, 40, 62
Behavioral role-modeling: in skill-
based training, 113, 115–116,
117; skills learned in, 117. *See
also* Role models
Being cultural orientation. *See*
Doing-being cultural dimension
Beliefs: about learning, 250; in leadership development, 239. *See
also* Cultural values and beliefs
Bell Atlantic Accelerating Leadership Diversity (ALD) program,
332–333

Benchmark (360-degree instrument), 359
Best practices, in 360-degree feed-
back, 59–60
Bias in ratings: across race and
gender, 306–309; response shift,
277; verbatim, 47
Book solution, 78
Boss-participant 360-degree feed-
back meetings, 57–58
Bottom line: assessing leadership
development impact on, 271,
284–285; tension between, and
development, 245
Boundaryless organizations,
411–412
Breaking the Glass Ceiling (Morrison,
White, and Van Velsor), 292
Business context, leadership devel-
opment embedded in, 225–227
Business startup, 135–136
Business trips, 391

C

Career planning: poor, for women
and African American man-
agers, 297, 317; using 360-de-
gree feedback to encourage, 41
Career setbacks: as hardships,
197, 200–201, 212–213; lessons
learned from, 197, 201; sense
of loss from, 200–201; support
for, 201; types of, 200. *See also*
Hardships
Career transition, feedback-
intensive programs for, 71
Case study method: for skill-based
training, 113, 114–115; skills
learned in, 117
Catalyst, 296
Center for Creative Leadership
(CCL): evaluation research
and development of, 262–263;
feedback-intensive program
research and development of,
66, 97–101; job assignment research of, 128, 140–142; leadership development view of,
1–25; leadership diversity research and development of,
291–294, 306, 309; learning

from hardships research of, 196–197; skill-based training research and development of, 106; 360-degree feedback research and development of, 31, 42, 59–60

Challenge, 11–15; African Americans and, 316–320, 330–331; cross-cultural perspectives on, 368–372, 377; in developmental experience, 6, 22, 222–223; in developmental relationships, 162; in feedback-intensive programs, 67, 85–88, 105; functions of, 11, 14; in hardship, 13, 212; of hardships, 196; in job assignments, 130, 131–139, 155–156; motivational role of, 9, 14; resource role of, 9, 14–15; in skill-based training, 119–120; sources of, 12–13; in 360-degree feedback, 37–38; uncertainty tolerance and, 369–370; universal desire for, 368–369; variety of, 14–15; women and, 316–320, 330–331

Challenging assignments. *See* Job assignments

Change: creating, as developmental challenge, 132, 133, 135–136; in ideas about leadership, 405–410; individual orientations to, 250; individuals' capacity for, 5; methods of assessing, 272–282; in models of leadership, 410–419; through feedback-intensive programs, 97–101; in United States culture, 342. *See also* Dynamic-stable cultural dimension; Evaluation; Organizational change; Outcomes; Perspective change

Checklist for learning, 150, 151

Cheerleaders, 162, 166–167, 170

China: attitudes towards assessment in, 351, 355–356, 363, 364, 365; cultural values of, 344; developmental relationships in, 373; group loyalty in, 370; leadership development in, 349

Choosing 360: A Guide to Evaluating Multi-Rater Instruments for Man-

agement Development (Van Velsor, Leslie, and Fleenor), 43

Citicorp, 129, 149

Classroom-based assessment. *See* Feedback-intensive programs

Climate surveys, 269, 284

Coaches/coaching: cross-level, 176; for developmental job assignments, 150, 152; executive, 182, 184–185; for feedback-intensive program follow-up, 102; in feedback-intensive programs, 96; group, 182, 185–186; guidelines for, 182; peer, 182, 184; resources for, 176; skill-based training linked with, 122; skill-development for, 175–176; for 360-degree feedback, 57–58; types of, 182. *See also* Developmental relationships

Coaching groups, 176, 234, 235

Cognitive complexity, 386

Cohorts, 162, 167, 170

Collaborative evaluation, 286

Collective dimension. *See* Individual-collective dimension

Comfort in dealing with one's own kind, 298

Comfort zones, leaving. *See* Challenge

Communication technology, 437–438

Comparison groups, 272, 288

Comparison points, 162, 163–164, 170

Compassion, hardships and, 206

Compensation differentials, for women and African Americans, 327

Competencies. *See* Ability to learn from experience; Leadership capacities; Social skills

Complexity, 220–221, 240

Conceptual-oriented learners, 95

Confidentiality: in developmental relationships, 188; in feedback-intensive programs, 85; in 360-degree feedback, 46–47, 61, 62

Conflict, as source of challenge, 13

Conscientiousness, and ability to learn, 249

Consequences, 120

Contextual challenges, 138–139, 155–156

Contextual fluidity, 304

Continuous improvement, 286

Control, locus of, 250

Control, loss of: coping with, 206; in hardships, 200, 202–203

Control groups, 272, 288

Council of Jewish Federations (CJF), 190–192

Counselor role, 162, 166, 168

Creative thinking, 111; development of, 20, 109; skills associated with, 110

Critical evaluation, 109, 111–112; skills associated with, 110

Cross-cultural, defined, 337–338

Cross-cultural differences: in acceptance of 360-degree feedback, 354–356; in assessment, 349–367; in assessment content, 357–363; in assessment process, 363–364; in attitudes towards promotion, 346–348; in challenge, 368–372; in contextual orientation, 352–353; and generalizability of 360-degree feedback instruments, 357–363; in learning, 397–399; in locus of control, 250; resources for in-depth understanding of, 378; in support, 372–375; and synthesis of country clusters, 359–360; in uncertainty tolerance, 369–370; in values and beliefs, 343–345. *See also* Cultural values and beliefs

Cross-cultural leadership development: assessment issues in, 349–367, 376–377; attitudes towards promotion and, 346–348; challenge issues in, 368–372, 377; cultural values and beliefs and, 342–345; culturally based assumptions about leadership development and, 340–341; practical guidelines for, 375–378; support issues in, 372–375, 377. *See also* Global leaders

Cross-cultural teams, 392

Cross-functional teamwork, developmental challenge of, 138. *See also* Team development

Cultural assumptions: about assessment process, 363–364; about leadership development, 337–338

Cultural nutrients, 325

Cultural paranoia, 313

Cultural values and beliefs: cross-cultural comparison of, 343–345; dimensions of, 343; in United States culture, 342–343, 344. *See also* Cross-cultural differences; Cross-cultural leadership development

Culture, defined, 338

Customer responsiveness, 412

D

Dance, in feedback-intensive programs, 87

Data orientation. *See* Active-reflective cultural dimension

Debriefing, facilitated, in feedback-intensive programs, 81–82, 102

"Delta Products" case study, 235–237

Den of Lions (Anderson), 29–30

Development planning: based on 360-degree feedback, 54–56; developmental relationships linked with, 177; in feedback-intensive programs, 75; job assignments for, 146–147

Developmental assignments. *See* Job assignments

Developmental audits, 143

Developmental experiences, 6–7, 160–193; for African Americans, 303–329; of assessment, 6, 9–11, 22; of challenge, 6, 9, 11–15, 22; creating rich, 21–22; developmental relationships for, 160–193; elements of, 8–17, 22, 222; enhancing the ability to learn from, 242–261; evaluation of, 262–288; feedback-intensive programs for, 66–105; for global leadership development, 387–395; hardships as, 194–

213; job assignments for, 127–159; learning from, 22–23; linking, with elements, 222–223; linking, with other organizational processes, 222, 225–230, 230–239; linking together, 23–24, 222, 223–225, 231–239, 257; skill-based training for, 106–126; small, day-to-day, 259–260; of support, 6, 9, 15–17, 22; 360-degree feedback for, 29–65; timing of, 257–259; versus training, 218–219, 224–225; types of, 21–22; for women, 303–329. *See also* Ability to learn from experience

Developmental relationships, 161–168; for African Americans, 297–298, 321–326, 331–332; assessing developmental needs for, 169–171, 172; assessment in, 162–164; with bosses versus peers, 169; challenge in, 162; cross-cultural perspectives on, 373–375; designated, 178; encouraging employees to seek out, 176–178; enhancement of formal, 186–189; enhancement of natural, 174–176; evaluation of, 188, 189, 271, 282–283; factors in, 168; formal, 178–183, 331–332; for global leadership development, 388, 394; individual strategies for, 168–172; informal, 174–176, 192; lateral, subordinate, and external, 172; linking, with other development strategies, 189–192; managerial responsibility for, 174–176; multiple, 167–169; networks for, 177–178; organizational strategies for, 173–193; participant choice and involvement in, 187, 189; questions for clarifying, 187, 188; questions for exploring potential, 170–171; role of, in leadership development process, 161–168, 192; roles played by others in, 161–168; roles played by others in, selecting, 169–171; selection and matching procedures for, 189;

short-term, 172; support in, 162, 166–167; for support in learning, 256–257; in systemic leadership development, 232, 234, 235, 236–237; during transitions, 172; types of formal, 181–186; for women, 180, 321–326, 331–332. *See also* Coaches/coaching; Mentors/mentoring

Dialogue partners, 162, 164, 170

Difference cultural dimension. *See* Same-different cultural dimension

Digital Equipment, 331

Disappointments, 13. *See also* Hardships

Disk-based assessment systems, 65

Diversity: education in, 334–335; encountering, in feedback-intensive programs, 88, 95, 98–99; enforcing practices of, 334; exposure to, 335; leadership development and, 291–335, 438–439; and leadership of the future, 403–404, 410, 411–412; organizational strategies for, 333–335; systemic approach to, 332–333. *See also* African American men; African American women; African Americans; Cross-cultural differences; Nontraditional managers; People of color; White women; Women

Doing-being cultural dimension, 243, 343–345; and attitudes towards assessment, 350–351

Domains of impact, 264–268

Downsizing: being responsible for, 205; developmental assignments while, 155–156; as hardship, 197, 204–205; and leadership, 435–436; lessons learned from, 197, 205; losses associated with, 204–205; support during, 204–205. *See also* Organizational change

Dramatic movement, in feedback-intensive programs, 87

Dynamic-stable cultural dimension, 343–345; and attitudes towards challenge, 369–370; and attitudes towards assessment, 364; and attitudes towards promotion, 347–348

E

Earth II exercise, 77–78
Egalitarianism, 342, 343
E-mail, for data collection, 64–65
Employee dialogues, 234–235
Employee empowerment, 41. *See also* Empowerment of others
Employees, problem. *See* Problem employees
Employment contract, new: impact of, on leadership development, 434–436; shared responsibility and, 221
Empowerment evaluation, 286
Empowerment of others, 109, 112; skills associated with, 110. *See also* Employee empowerment
End-of-event evaluations, 273–274
End-state assessments, 63–64
Equality cultural dimension. *See* Same-different cultural dimension
Ethics, of global business, 399–401
Evaluation: of bottom-line outcomes, 284–285; of change over time, 271, 287; control groups for, 272, 287; of developmental experiences, 262–288; of developmental relationships, 188, 189, 282–283; domains of impact and, 264–268; end-of-event, 273–274; formative, 264, 285–286; goals of, 263–264; of group outcomes, 268–269, 283–284; of individual and group-level change, 271–272, 287; individual outcomes and, 264–268; of job assignments, 282–283; large-scale, 264, 285–286, 287–288; methods of, 272–283; methods of, compared, 273; of multiple domains, 270, 287; with multiple methods, 270–271, 287; from multiple perspectives, 269–270, 287; of organizational outcomes, 268–269, 283–284;

practitioner guidelines for, 286–288; principles of, 269–272; summative, 264, 285–286; as tool for organizational learning, 285–286. *See also* Outcomes
Evaluative inquiry, 286
Executive temperament, 141
Expatriate assignments, 392, 394–395
Experience. *See* Ability to learn from experience; Developmental experiences

F

Facilitated debrief, 81–82
Facilitators, of one-on-one feedback sessions: in feedback-intensive programs, 96; in 360-degree feedback, 50–52, 62. *See also* Staff
Failures. *See* Hardships; Mistakes and failures
Family responsibilities, as barriers to advancement of women, 298–299
Far Eastern country cluster, 360
Feedback, 29–31; cultural differences in acceptance of, 354–356; cultural sensitivity in interpreting, 365–367; for enhancing the ability to learn, 255–256, 261; formal versus informal, 33, 35; skill-based training linked with, 122. *See also* Assessment; Feedback-intensive programs; 360-degree feedback
Feedback interpreters, 162, 164, 170
Feedback provider role, 162–163, 170
Feedback sessions, 360-degree feedback: group, 48–49; one-on-one, 50–52
Feedback-intensive programs (FIPs), 66–105; action planning in, 75, 100; activities and design of, 73–75; for African Americans, 293–294, 309–315; assessment element in, 22, 67, 105; assessment instruments for, 82–83; assessment methodologies of,

76–85; assessment of skills and behaviors in, 82–84; Center for Creative Leadership research and development of, 3, 97–101; challenge in, 22, 67, 85–88, 105; classroom content in, 85–86; conceptual framework of, 85–86; confidentiality and anonymity in, 85; defined, 68; defining features of, 68–70; developmental relationships linked with, 190–191; diversity of participants and perspectives in, 88, 95, 98–99; enhancement techniques for, 94–97; for enhancing the ability to learn, 255–256, 261; first day of, 73–74; for global leadership development, 391; goal setting in, 75, 99–100; guidelines for selecting, using, and designing, 104–105; indications for using, 71; knowledge acquisition impact of, 98, 265; last day of, 75; leadership abilities developed in, 109; leadership models and, 85–86; learning community in, 90–94; length of, 101; mixed-group versus single-identity, 315–316; modules of, 74; next-to-last day of, 75; ongoing versus single event, 101–102; open-enrollment versus organization-specific, 103–104; outcomes of, 97–104; participant characteristics and, 88, 94–97; postprogram activities for, 75, 101–102; preprogram activities for, 72–73; program design issues of, 101–102; rating reliability and validity in, 76; rationales for, 71; reflection and consolidation in, 96–97; sample design for, 73; schedule for, 73–75; self-awareness impact of, 69–70, 98, 266; single-identity, 309–316, 325; versus skill-based training, 70, 107, 108; skill-based training linked with, 122; staff behaviors in, 90–94; staff techniques for, 94–97; structured experiences in, 77–82;

Feedback-intensive programs *(continued)*
structured feedback from fellow participants in, 83–84; support in, 22, 67, 75, 89–97, 105; in system leadership development, 235; versus 360-degree feedback, 69–70; 360-degree feedback in, 82–83; unfamiliar activities in, 86–88; for women, 292–293, 309–315; workings of, 72–75
Feeling-oriented learning tactics, 251, 254
Feelings, bruised, in 360-degree feedback, 62
Fitting in, of women and African Americans, 300–302
Flexibility, learning of, 207
Follow-up questionnaires, 273, 275–277
Follow-up to goal setting and action planning, 273, 278, 280
Formal assessment of others, 10. *See also* Assessment; Feedback-intensive programs; 360-degree feedback
Formal feedback, 34, 35; enhancing the success of, 56–65. *See also* Assessment; Feedback-intensive programs; 360-degree feedback
Formative evaluation, 264, 285–286
Fortune, 37
France, 360; attitudes towards assessment in, 351, 355, 364; attitudes towards promotion in, 347–348; cultural values of, 344; leadership development in, 347–348, 359; learning preferences in, 369–370; rule orientation in, 348, 349
Functional boundaries, 411

G

Gender, and leadership development, 291–335. *See also* African American women; Women
General Electric (GE), 129
Generalizability, of assessment instruments across cultures: dealing with, 359–363; and globalization, 357–358

Germanic country cluster, 360
Germany, 360; attitudes towards assessment in, 351; attitudes towards promotion in, 347; cultural values of, 344; leadership development in, 347; learning preferences in, 369–370; rule orientation in, 348, 349; 360-degree feedback instruments for, 359–360
Glass ceiling, 292–293, 295–299
Global leaders, 379–402; capacities needed by, 384–387; developmental relationships for, 388, 394; feedback-intensive programs for, 391; job assignments for, 387–395, 401; leadership development for, 387–395; learning skills for, 386, 395–399; moral reasoning development for, 386, 399–401; role demands of, 382–384; work of, 382–384
Global organizations: characteristics of, 380–381; ethical dilemmas of, 399–401; structures of, 381–382
Global responsibility for a product, 393
"Global Shipping Inc." case study, 233–235
Globalization, 433–434; ethical issues of, 399–401; and generalizability of 360-degree feedback instruments, 357–358
Goal attainment, through feedback-intensive programs, 99–100
Goal letters, 75
Goal setting: based on 360-degree feedback, 55; in feedback-intensive programs, 75, 99–100; follow-up to, 273, 278, 280
Goal-setting reports, in feedback-intensive programs, 102
Goals, difficult, as challenge, 12–13
Grandes écoles, 348
Great Britain: leadership development in, 359; learning preferences in, 369
Greyhound Financial Corporation, 150, 152
Group coaching, 182, 185–186

Group discussions, leaderless, 77–78
Group feedback sessions: in feedback-intensive programs, 97; 360-degree feedback, 48–49
Group loyalty, cultural differences in, 370–371
Group observation exercises, 80–81
Group outcomes, 268–269; assessment of, 283–284; assessment of individual and, 271–272
Groups, 360-degree feedback for assessing, 39–40
Guidelines on Leadership Diversity (GOLD) project, 293

H

Hardships, 194–213; assessment in, 211; challenge in, 13, 196, 212; developmental relationships for support during, 168, 201; HR managers role in, 209–210; individual responses to, 208–209; lessons learned from, 197–205, 206–207; line managers role in, 210–211; linking, to other developmental experiences, 210, 212–213; loss in, 196–197; maximizing learning from, 207–211; versus other developmental experiences, 195–197; support for, 201, 204–205, 212; types of, 197–205; using, for development, 207–211. *See also* Career setbacks; Downsizing; Mistakes and failures; Personal trauma; Problem employees
Helping pairs, in feedback-intensive programs, 102
Hierarchy, 411
High-context cultures, 355–356
High-performing learners, in systemic leadership development case study, 236–237
High-potential development: developmental relationships for, 173–174, 179–180; feedback-intensive programs for, 71; job assignments for, 148–149
Hindu religious thought, 351
Hispanics, 293
History of leadership, 405–409

Hollow Squares exercise, 80–81

Hong Kong, 360

Human resource (HR) managers: diversity education for, 333–334; and global leadership development, 388, 389, 390; strategies of, for helping employees experiencing hardship, 209–211. *See also* Reward systems

Human resource (HR) systems: for increasing diversity, 335; integration of, with leadership development, 228–230

Humility, 199

I

IBM, 198

Ideal outcomes, goals as, 100

Impact domains, 264–268

Impact evaluation. *See* Evaluation; Outcomes

Importance ratings, 52–53

In-basket simulations, 78

In-depth interviewing, 271, 273, 280–282; sample format for, 281

Individual outcomes, domains of, 264–268

Individual-collective dimension, 342, 343–345; and acceptance of feedback, 355–356; and attitudes towards support, 372–375; and contextual orientation, 352–353; and group loyalty, 370–371; and ownership of assessment data, 363–364; and 360-degree feedback ratings, 365–366; and universalistic thinking, 353

Inertia, 240, 242, 244

Informal assessment of others, 10. *See also* Assessment

Informal feedback, 33, 35. *See also* Assessment; Informal assessment of others

Information technology, 437–438

Instruments, 360-degree feedback, 42–45; for African Americans, 312; for assessing ability to learn, 64; content of, cultural

biases in, 357–358; content of, for women and African Americans, 304–305, 313–314; content of, generalizability of, across cultures, 357–363; country-specific, 360–361; cross-cultural issues in, 353–363; differences in norms and, 306; follow-up, 275–277; purpose of, 43; rater anonymity in, 46–47, 61, 62; rationale for, 42–43; selection guidelines for, 43–44, 60–61, 362–363; selection of, cross-culturally, 359–363; standardized versus customized, 44–45; validity of, for women and African Americans, 305–306; for women, 312; written comments in, 46–47. *See also* 360-degree feedback

Instruments, used in feedback-intensive programs, 72–73, 81–82

Intelligence: and ability to learn, 246–247; types of, 246–247

Interaction, and leadership as shared meaning making, 416–431. *See also* Social skills

Interdependence, development of, 419–420

Internet-based assessment systems, 65

Interpersonal intelligence, 246–247

Interpersonal relationships, learning from mistakes in, 199. *See also* Developmental relationships; Social skills

Interrelating: development of, 421–422; heedful, 421–422

Interviewing, in-depth, 271, 273, 280–282; sample format for, 281

Intranet-based assessment systems, 65

Intrapersonal intelligence, 246–247

IQ, 16

Iran, 360; cultural values of, 344; leadership development in, 349

Isolation of minorities, strategies for, 330. *See also* African Americans; Women

J

Japan, 360; attitudes towards assessment in, 351, 355–356, 363–364, 365; cultural values of, 344; developmental relationships in, 373; group loyalty in, 370–371; leadership development in, 349; learning preferences in, 369–370

Job assignments, 55, 127–159; for African Americans, 316–320, 330–331; assessment in, 22, 130; bosses' support for, 152; Center for Creative Leadership research on, 128, 140–142; challenge in, 22, 130, 131–139, 155–156; checklist for learning from, 150, 151; creating change as, 132, 133, 135–136; defined, 129; developmental value of, 130; examples of, by type of challenge, 133; examples of organizations with systems of, 129, 143; follow-up to, 152; for global leadership development, 387–395, 401; high level of responsibility in, 132, 133, 136–137; impact evaluation of, 282–283; important lessons in, 140–141; issues in, 153–157; jobs too important for, 156, 227–228; learning from, 139–142; lecture in, 133; length of, 156–157; leveraging, for development purposes, 142–153; linking, to competency outcomes, 142–144; maximizing learning from, 149–153, 158; nonauthority relationships in, 132, 133, 137–138; obstacles in, 132, 133, 138–139, 155–156; preparing people for, 150; research studies of, 128; resources for, 142–143, 144–145; selecting candidates for, 154, 227–228, 390–391; skill-based training linked with, 122; support in, 22, 130–131, 150, 152; systematic use of, 128–129, 142–153, 157–158; in systemic leadership development process,

Job assignments *(continued)*
231–232; task-related challenges
in, 135–139, 155–156; tracking, over time, 153; transitions
in, 131, 132, 133, 134–135,
155–156; types of global,
391–394, 401; using development as criterion for giving,
146–149; for women, 316–320,
330–331
Job rotation, 128, 157–158
Jobs, existing: development potential in, 56, 144–145, 155–156;
obstacles as developmental
opportunities in, 138–139,
155–156. *See also* Job assignments; On-the-job learning
Journaling: evaluation use of, 282;
in feedback-intensive programs,
96–97

K

Knowledge acquisition: in feedback-
intensive programs, 98, 265; impact domain of, 265–266
Knowledge domain of learning,
107–108

L

Language, and 360-degree feedback
instruments, 367
Latin European country cluster,
360
Leaderless group discussions, 77–78
Leadership: ancient idea of, 405,
407–408; evolving models of,
410–419, 420; future idea of,
407, 408, 413–414; history and
evolution of, 405–410; impact
of downsizing on, 435–436;
impact of technology on,
437–438; modern idea of, 407,
408–409; new possibilities of,
416–419; as shared meaning
making, 414–419; traditional
idea of, 406–407, 408
Leadership capacities, 17–21,
109–112; cross-cultural differences in, 357–358, 433–434;
for global leadership, 384–387,

433–434; learned in job assignments, 140–141; skills associated with, 110–112; technology
and, 437
Leadership development: accelerated, 436; across gender, 291–
335; across race, 291–335; capacities learned with, 17–21;
Center for Creative Leadership
view of, 1–25; complexity of,
220–221; cross-cultural issues
in, 336–378, 433–434; cultural
assumptions about, 340–345;
customizable, 240–241; defined,
4; developmental relationships
and, 161–168, 189–192; embedding, in organizational context, 225–230; enhancement of,
21–24; evaluation of, 262–288;
expectations of, 268–269; future
of, 403, 419–432, 433–439; for
global roles, 379–402, 433–434;
of individuals in context, 421–
422, 426; integration of, into
daily work, 219–220; job assignments and, 128, 130; leadership
models and, 405–419; multidimensional, 240–241; on-
demand, 240–241; perspective
shifts in, 217–221; as process,
25, 217–218; selecting candidates for, 227–228, 235, 236;
shared responsibility for, 221,
228, 237; skills-based training
role in, 118; strategies of, 21–24,
55–56; systemic links in, 222–
230; systemic versus events-
based approach to, 23–24,
224–225, 332–333; systems
approach to, 217–241; team
development integrated with,
422–431, 432, 438; 360-degree
feedback role in, 37–38; for
work groups, 422–423. *See
also* Cross-cultural leadership
development
Leadership development impact assessment, of feedback-intensive
programs, 97–101
Leadership development model,
5–8, 24–25; assumptions of,
4–5, 25; cross-cultural differ-

ences and, 343–378; culturally
based assumptions of, 340–341
Leadership development process, 6,
7–8; ability to learn from experience and, 242–261; equation
for, 223–224; systems approach
to, 217–241
Leadership development systems:
case examples of, 230–239;
challenge of implementing,
239–241; defined, 222; moving
toward, 238–239; systemic links
in, 222–230
Leadership Education Project,
Kennedy School of Govern-
ment, Harvard University, 13
Leadership models: evolution and
future of, 405–419, 433–434;
in feedback-intensive programs,
85–86
Leadership roles and processes, 4–5
Leadership styles, gender bias and,
308
Learners: active versus not active,
242–243; blocked, 252; high-
performing, 236–237
Learning ability, 7–8; assessing,
63–64; basic capacity for, 5;
development of, 20; variables
in, 7. *See also* Ability to learn
from experience
Learning community, 90–94
Learning domains, 107–108
Learning forums, 237
Learning groups, 186, 236–237
Learning leaders, 236
Learning managers, 236
Learning organization, 412–413
Learning partners: in feedback-
intensive programs, 102; for
women and people of color,
331–332
Learning skills and strategies,
251–260; for global work, 386,
395–399. *See also* Ability to learn
from experience
Learning styles and tactics: of accessing others, 251, 253–254;
action-oriented, 95, 251, 252–
253; and feedback-intensive
program methodologies, 95–96;
feeling-oriented, 251–252;

needed by global leaders, 395–397; preferred patterns of, 252; thinking-oriented, 251, 253–254. *See also* Ability to learn from experience

Lecture, 113–114; and job assignments, 133; skills learned in, 117; traditional versus interactive, 114

"Lessons from 'RSA' Leadership Development System," 232

Lessons of Experience (McCall, Lombardo, and Morrison), 142, 196–197, 259

Line managers: strategies of, for helping employees experiencing hardship, 210–211; transition of, to staff roles, 134–135

Locus of control, 250; cultural differences in, 250

Loss, 13; in career setbacks, 200–201; in hardships, 196; of professional identity, 201, 204–205; responses to, 196–197; of sense of control, 200, 202–203, 206. *See also* Hardships

Low-context cultures, 352–353

"Lunchtime Conversation in San Francisco," 374

M

Manager and the Sage story, 1–3

Managerial identity, race and gender identities and, 299–302, 319

Managers, role of, in leadership development system implementation, 240

"Mandel Fellow," 190–192

Maximizing the Value of 360-Degree Feedback (Tornow and London), 31

Meaning making. *See* Shared meaning making

Mentors/mentoring, 168, 178, 180, 182; for African Americans, 297–298, 321–326; cross-sex and cross-race, 321–323; formal, for women and people of color, 325–326, 331–332; guidelines for, 182; informal

junior-senior, 321; one-on-one, 182, 183; types of, 182; for women, 297–298, 321–326. *See also* Developmental relationships

Mexico, 360; attitudes towards assessment in, 356; cultural values of, 344; developmental relationships in, 373; leadership development in, 349

Mistake systems, 199, 212, 228

Mistakes and failures, 13; acknowledging, 199–200; conditions for learning from, 198–199; as hardships, 197, 198–200; lessons learned from, 197, 199–200

Mobil Oil, 175–176

Moral reasoning development, 386, 399–401

Motivation to learn: factors in, 20; role of assessment in, 9, 10–11; role of challenge in, 9, 14; role of support in, 9, 16

Movement exercises, in feedback-intensive programs, 87

Multicountry assignments, 391, 393

Multirater feedback. *See* 360-degree feedback

Myers-Briggs Type Indicator (MBTI), 82

N

National Semiconductor, 184

Natural managerial learning, 140

NCR Corporation, 143

Near Eastern country cluster, 360

Negative role models, 165

Negotiation skills, behavioral role-modeling of, 116

Network-based assessment systems, 65

Networks, 177–178; for African Americans, 323–325, 326, 330; expressive relationships in, 323–324, 325; formal versus informal, 323–324; instrumental relationships in, 323–324; for women, 323–325, 326, 330

New experiences: challenge in, 12, 86–88; in feedback-intensive programs, 86–88; learning from, 22–23

New Leaders, The (Morrison), 293, 295–299

Nonauthority relationships, 132, 133, 136–137

Nonjudgmentalism, 91–92, 93

Nonprescriptive stance, 92–93

Nontraditional managers: barriers to advancement of, 295–299; developmental relationships for, 180; leadership development for, 291–335; monitoring developmental track records of, 153; networks for, 177. *See also* African American men; African American women; African Americans; White women; Women

Nordic country cluster, 360

Normative data, 37

Norms: culture and, 366–367; gender and, 306; race and, 306

NYNEX, 143

O

Obstacles, as developmental challenge, 132, 133, 138–139, 155–156

One-on-one feedback sessions, 360-degree feedback, 50–52

One-on-one mentoring. *See* Mentoring

One-on-one relationships, for learning support, 256–257. *See also* Developmental relationships

On-the-job learning: evaluation of, 282–283; skill-based training versus, 112–113. *See also* Job assignments; Jobs, existing

Open communication, using 360-degree feedback to encourage, 40–41

Openness to experience, 249

Organization development (OD), 233; in case study, 425–431; integrating leadership development with, 423–431

Organizational analysis, 124–125

Organizational change: career setbacks during, 201; developmental relationships during, 181; impact of, on long-term leadership development, 434–436. *See also* Downsizing

Organizational context, 24; leadership development embedded in, 225–230, 230–241; leadership diversity in, 333–335

Organizational learning, 285–288, 412–413, 422

Organizational levels: coaching in different, 176; 360-degree feedback in different, 58

Organizational norms, as source of support, 16

Organizational outcomes, 268–269; assessment of, 283–284; assessment of individual and, 271–272

Organizational savvy, lack of, for women and African Americans, 298, 314

Organizational support: for developmental job assignments, 150, 152; for developmental relationships, 187; for leadership development, 239–240; for transfer of training, 120–122. *See also* Support

Organizational systems, integration of, with leadership development, 228–230

Organizational values, 360-degree feedback for supporting, 40–41

Organizations: creating developmental relationships in, 173–193; current trends in, 411–414; 360-degree feedback in, purposes of, 39–41

Outcomes: assessment of, general principles for, 269–272; assessment of, methods for, 272–282; in behavior-change domain, 268; domains of, 264–268; of feedback-intensive programs, 97–104; group and organizational, 268–269; individual, 264–268; in knowledge acquisition domain, 265–266; of leadership development, 264–269; in perspective-change domain, 266–267; in self-awareness domain, 266; in skill development domain, 267–268; of 360-

degree feedback, 32. *See also* Evaluation

Outdoor exercises, 88

Overconfidence, 248

P

Participants, in feedback-intensive programs: integrating situations of, into activities, 94; learning styles of, 95–96; sharing of perspectives of, 88, 95

Participatory evaluation, 286

Particularistic orientation, 353

Peer coaching, 182, 184

Peer groups, for feedback-intensive postprogram support, 75

Peer interviews, 83–84

Peer observations, 83–84

People of color: developmental relationships for, 180; leadership development for, 291–335. *See also* African American men; African American women; African Americans

Performance appraisal systems, integration of, with leadership development, 228–230

Performance ratings, gender bias in, 308

Person analysis, 124

Personal development: in feedback-intensive programs, 69–70; in leadership development model, 340, 347

Personal trauma: as hardship, 197, 202–203; lessons learned from, 197, 202–203; and timing of learning, 258. *See also* Hardships

Personality, 16; and ability to learn, 246–251

Personality instruments, 82

Perspective change: in feedback-intensive programs, 98–99; impact domain of, 266–267

Polytechniques, 348

Post-then assessment, 271, 273, 278, 279; sample rater form for, 279

Preferences, self-assessment of, 82

"Preferences and Beliefs in the Workplace: Not Everybody Wants the Same!", 370

Prejudice, 296; and job assignments, 317, 318; in 360-degree feedback ratings, 306–309

Problem employees: as hardships, 197, 203–204, 213; lessons learned from, 197, 203–204; types of, 203

Process. *See* Leadership development process

Professional identity, loss of, 201, 204–205

Promotion: cross-cultural comparison of, 346–348; differentials in, for women and African Americans, 327–328

Q

Quantification, United States cultural preference for, 350–353

Questionnaires, follow-up, 273, 275–277

R

Race, and leadership development, 291–335. *See also* African American men; African American women; African Americans

Race-mattered experiences, 318

Racism, 296. *See also* African American men; African American women; African Americans

Rater perspectives, multiple, 269–270

Raters, 360-degree feedback, 34, 37, 46–47; anonymity for, 46–47, 61, 62, 364; cross-cultural issues of, 363–365; in follow-up reassessment, 276, 277; preparation of, 47; selection of, 46; self-, 38, 53–54. *See also* Bias in ratings

Rating patterns, cultural, 365–366

Rating reliability and validity: across cultures, 357–365; across race and gender, 305–306; in feedback-intensive programs, 76. *See also* Bias in ratings

Raychem Corporation, 330

Reading, 56

Reassessment, 275–277

Reciprocal relations, in new way of leadership, 414–432, 423

Recognition, for women and African Americans, 327–329

Reflection: in feedback-intensive programs, 96–97; in job assignments, 152, 331

Reflective cultural orientation. *See* Active-reflective cultural dimension

Reinforcers, 162, 166–167, 170

Relational approach of women, 301–302, 304, 439

Relational competency, 331. *See also* Social skills

Relationships, developmental. *See* Developmental relationships

Reorganization. *See* Downsizing; Organizational change

Repatriate assignments, 392–393

Republic, The (Plato), 405

Respect for participants, in feedback-intensive programs, 91–92

Response shift bias, 277

Responsibility: high levels of, in job assignments, 132, 133, 136–137; personal, for learning, 249; shared, for leadership development, 221, 228, 237

"Retail Stores of America" (RSA) case study, 230–232

Retrospective posttest, 277, 278

Reward systems: for demonstrating commitment to diversity, 334; supportive of leadership development, 228, 229; for women and African Americans, 327–329

Risk taking: in learning, 244, 245; self-esteem and, 247–248; in single-identity feedback programs, 311

Role models, 162, 165, 170; lack of, for women and African Americans, 297–298; women and African Americans singled out to be, 318–319. *See also* Behavioral role-modeling

Role-play: for skill-based training, 113, 115, 117; skills learned in, 117. *See also* Behavioral role-modeling

"Rule Orientation in European Countries: The Power of Reason," 346–347

S

Same-different cultural dimension, 343; and attitudes towards assessment, 356, 364; and attitudes towards promotion, 346–348; and developmental relationships, 373–375; and universalistic thinking, 353

Saudi Arabia, 360

Self-assessment, 10; for career setback, 213; of preferences, in feedback-intensive programs, 82. *See also* Assessment

Self-awareness: development of, 18, 109; development of, in job assignments, 141; feedback-intensive programs and, 69–70, 98, 266; hardships and, 206; impact domain of, 266; and intrapersonal intelligence, 247; post-then rating scale of, 279; 360-feedback and, 31, 69

Self-confidence: development of, 18–19, 109; post-then rating scale of, 279

Self-disclosure, of feedback-intensive program staff, 91, 93–94

Self-efficacy, 16; and ability to learn, 247–248, 256; loss of, in career setbacks, 200–201

Self-esteem: and ability to learn, 247–248, 256, 261; stability of, 248; and supportive bosses, 257; too high, 248; too low, 248

Self-rater agreement/discrepancy, 38, 53–54; cross-cultural differences and, 365–366

Self-reflection, 396

Self-reported learnings, 273, 274–275

Senior executives: development needs of, 180; developmental relationships for, 180–181; executive coaching for, 182, 184–185

Sensitivity, hardships and, 206

Sexism, 296. *See also* African American women; Women

Shared meaning making, 414–419, 424–425, 431–432; in case study, 425–431

Simulations: facilitated debriefing of, 81–82; in feedback-intensive programs, 78–79, 81–82, 86–87; in skill-based training, 113, 116

Single-identity feedback programs, 309–316, 330; advantages of, 310–314; disadvantages of, 310, 314–315; network relationships formed in, 325; selecting, versus mixed-group programs, 315–316

Situational cues, 120

Skill development, impact domain of, 267–268

Skill-based training, 56, 106–126; assessment in, 118–119; behavioral role-modeling in, 113, 115–116, 117; for career setback, 213; case examples of, 108–109, 118–119, 121–122; case study method in, 113, 114–115, 117; challenge in, 119–120; content relevance of, 123–124, 125; defined, 107; domains of learning in, 107–108; effective environment for, 108; enhancement of, 123–126; feedback-intensive programs versus, 70, 107, 108; leadership capacities taught in, 109–112; lecture method in, 113–114, 117; linking, to other developmental experiences, 122; methods of, 113–117; methods of, matched to skills learned, 117; needs assessment for, 124–126; on-the-job learning versus, 112–113; role of, in leadership development, 118; role-play in, 113, 115, 117; simulations in, 113, 116; skills taught in, 110–112; skills taught in, matched to training methods, 117; support in, 120–122; timeliness of, 123; transfer of, to organizational environment, 120–122

Skills assessment, 267–268; in feedback-intensive programs, 82–84; of group skills, 284

Smile sheets, 273–274

Social learning theory, 115–116, 160

Social skills, 110–111; behavioral role-modeling for, 116, 117; development of, 19, 109; for global leaders, 386; job assignments for, 140; for leaders of the future, 419–422; for relating to people who are different from oneself, 331; role-play for, 115, 117; skill-based training for, 109, 110, 115, 116, 117; types of, 110

Socialization, 160, 179

Sounding boards, 162, 163, 170

Speed, 436

Stable cultural dimension. *See* Dynamic-stable cultural dimension

Staff, of feedback-intensive programs: enhancement techniques for, 94–97; facilitative behaviors of, 90–94

Stereotypes, gender and race, 296; and single-identity feedback programs, 314

Strategy, business, leadership development embedded in, 225–227, 230–231, 234

Structured experiences: assessment of skills and behaviors in, 82; challenge in, 86–88; facilitating learning from, 79–82

Structured experiences/exercises, 77–79

Structured feedback, 83–84

Succession planning, developmental approach to, 147–148

Summative evaluation, 264, 285–286

Support, 15–17; cross-cultural perspectives on, 372–375, 377; in developmental experience, 6, 22, 222–223; in developmental relationships, 162, 166–167; in feedback-intensive programs, 22, 67, 75, 89–97, 105; functions of, 15; for global leadership development, 388, 394; for hardships, 201, 204–205, 212; in job assignments, 130–131,

150, 152; in job assignments for women and African Americans, 320; for learning, 245, 256–257; motivational role of, 9, 16; resource role of, 9, 16–17; in single-identity feedback programs, 311–312; in skill-based training, 120–122; sources of, 16; in 360-degree feedback, 38

Supportive environment, 89, 120

Survey fatigue, 60–62

Survey instruments, for assessing developmental aspects of jobs, 144–145. *See also* Instruments, 360-degree feedback

Sustaining metaphor, 88

Sweden, 360; attitudes in, towards promotion, 346–347; cultural values of, 343, 344; leadership development in, 346–347; learning preferences in, 369; 360-degree feedback instruments and, 359

Systemic links, 222–230

Systemic thinking: development of, 19, 109, 110, 111–112; skills associated with, 110

Systems approach: to leadership development, 23–24, 217–241; to leadership diversity programs, 332–333; to organizations, 412–413, 424–425

T

Taiwan, 360, 366

Target population, 227–228

Targeted exercises, 79

Task analysis, 124

Team development, 422–423; case study of, 425–431; integrating, with leadership development, 423–431, 432, 438

Team organization, 411

Technology, and leadership, 437–438

Telephone industry deregulation, 40

Telephone systems, for data collection, 64

"Ten Questions Toward Acceptability," 362, 363

Tender cultural orientation. *See* Tough-tender cultural dimension

Texas Instruments, 334

Thinking-oriented learning tactics, 251, 253–254

3M, 149, 152

360-degree feedback, 29–65; administrative versus developmental use of, 41–42; for African Americans, 303–309, 330; for assessment of ability to learn, 63–64, 255–256; for assessment of group strengths and development needs, 39–40; for assessment of individual managers and leaders, 39; best practices in, 59–60; boss's support for, 57–58; challenge in, 37–38; cross-cultural issues in, 353–367; cross-culturally validated, 361; data collection in, 45–47, 64–65; data confidentiality in, 47, 61, 62; deadlines in, 62; defined, 31–32; development plan based on, 54–56; enhancing the success of, 56–65; feedback delivery in, 48–54; feedback report from, sample, 34; feedback survey for, sample, 33; in feedback-intensive programs, 82–83; feedback-intensive programs versus, 69–70; follow-up, 275–277; future of, 62–65; implementation of, 42–56; importance ratings in, 52–53; instruments for, 42–45, 60–61, 353–363; knowledge acquisition impact of, 265; logistics of, 61–62; as ongoing process versus event, 24, 56; organizational uses of, 39–41; ownership of data of, 363–364; pitfalls in, 60–62; preparation for participants in, 47; purposes and uses of, 31–42; raters for, 34, 37, 46–47; rationale for formal feedback and, 32, 35; rationale for multiple views in, 36–37; role of, in leadership development process, 37–38; sequence and timing of, 58–59; support in, 38; for supporting organizational values, 40–41; in systemic leadership development, 231, 232; for women, 303–309, 330; workings of, 32, 33, 34. *See also* Instruments, 360-degree feedback

Timing: of developmental experiences, 257–259; of 360-degree feedback, 59

Top Ten Reasons for Rejecting Your 360-Degree Feedback, 49

Tough-tender cultural dimension, 343–345; and attitudes towards promotion, 346–347; and attitudes towards support, 373

Training, 56

Training: leadership development versus, 218–219, 224–225; transfer of, 120–122. *See also* Skill-based training

Training methods, 113–117; interaction levels of, 113; matched by skills learned, 117; selection of, 117. *See also* Skill-based training

Training needs assessment, 124–126

Training proficiency, openness to experience and, 249

Transactional leadership, 406–407

Transformational leadership, 406–407, 413–414

Transitional ideas about, 416–423

Transitions, job, 131, 132, 133, 134–135, 155–156; developmental relationships for, 172; as time to learn, 258

Transnational organizations, 382. *See also* Global leaders; Global organizations

Trauma. *See* Personal trauma

Trust, and cross-cultural acceptance of feedback, 354–356

Turkey, 369–370

Turnaround assignments, 135–136

U

Uncertainty tolerance, cultural differences in, 369–370

Unfamiliar activities. *See* New experiences

Unfreezing process, 256

United States, 360; acceptance of feedback in, 355; cultural preference of, for quantification, 350–353; cultural values and beliefs of, 342–343, 344, 345; culturally based assumptions about leadership development in, 340–341; low comfort with support in, 372–373; openness to challenge in, 369

Universalistic thinking, 353

V

Validation: in minority networks, 325; in single-identity feedback programs, 310–311

Validity, of assessment instruments, 305–306, 361. *See also* Instruments, 360-degree feedback

Valued behaviors, using 360-degree feedback to develop, 40

Values: commitment to leadership development, 239; learning, in job assignments, 141. *See also* Cultural values and beliefs

Verbatim bias, 47

Videotaping, in feedback-intensive programs, 81

Visions, goals as, 100

W

White men, as mentors for women and African Americans, 321–323

White women: leadership development for, 291–335, 438–439; poor working environment and, 297–298. *See also* African American women; Women

Women: assessment content for, 304–305, 313–314; assessment instrument validity for, 305–306; barriers to advancement of, 295–299; bias in ratings of, 306–309; Center for Creative Leadership program for, 292–293; developmental experiences and, 303–329; developmental relationships for, 180, 297–298, 321–326; differential norms and, 306; family-career tensions of, 298–299; feedback-intensive programs for, 309–315; fitting in of, 301–302; job assignments for, 316–320; leadership development for, 291–335, 438–439; managerial identity and, 299–302; monitoring developmental track records of, 153; networks for, 177; practitioner guidelines for meeting the needs of, 329–332; prejudice and, 296; recognition and rewards for, 327–329; relational approach of, 301–302, 304, 439; salaries of, versus men, 327; 360-degree feedback for, 303–309. *See also* African American women; Nontraditional managers; White women

Work ethics. *See* Tough-tender cultural dimension

Work groups, leadership development for, 422–423. *See also* Team development

Workforce demographics, 438–439. *See also* Diversity

Workforce 2000, 438

Working environment, for women and African Americans, 297–298